Women, Power, and Politics

Women, Power, and Politics:

The Fight for Gender Equality in the United States

LORI COX HAN
Chapman University

CAROLINE HELDMAN
Occidental College

New York   Oxford

OXFORD UNIVERSITY PRESS

Oxford University Press is a department of the University of Oxford.
It furthers the University's objective of excellence in research, scholarship,
and education by publishing worldwide. Oxford is a registered trademark
of Oxford University Press in the UK and certain other countries.

Published in the United States of America by Oxford University Press
198 Madison Avenue, New York, NY 10016, United States of America.

For titles covered by Section 112 of the US Higher Education
Opportunity Act, please visit www.oup.com/us/he for the
latest information about pricing and alternate formats.

Library of Congress Cataloging-in-Publication Data
Names: Han, Lori Cox, 1966- author. | Heldman, Caroline, 1972- author.
Title: Women, power, and politics : the fight for gender equality in
    the United States / Lori Cox Han, Chapman University, Caroline Heldman,
    Occidental College.
Description: First Edition. | New York : Oxford University Press, [2017] |
Includes bibliographical references and index.
Identifiers: LCCN 2017009764 | ISBN 9780190620240 (pbk.)
Subjects: LCSH: Women's rights—United States—History. | Feminism—United
States—History. | Women—Political activity—United States. | Political
    leadership—United States.
Classification: LCC HQ1236.5.U6 H346 2017 | DDC 320.082/0973—dc23
LC record available at https://lccn.loc.gov/2017009764

For our students,
past, present, and future

BRIEF TABLE OF CONTENTS

TABLE OF CONTENTS

PREFACE

The evolution of this book on gender and politics has spanned many years, and the final result brings together the respective areas of scholarship and teaching expertise we have each developed since graduate school. This is not the first time we have collaborated on a book about women and politics. Our edited volume, *Rethinking Madam President: Are We Ready for a Woman in the White House?* (Boulder, CO: Lynne Rienner, 2007), stemmed from our mutual interest in analyzing when the United States would elect its first woman president. That same year, the earliest version of this work was published as Lori Cox Han's *Women and American Politics: The Challenge of Political Leadership* (New York: McGraw–Hill, 2007; followed by the second edition, *Women and U.S. Politics: The Spectrum of Leadership*, Boulder, CO: Lynne Rienner, 2010). Our training and research interests in electoral politics, the presidency, political history, gender and leadership, intersectional feminist theory, media and popular culture, and public policy make this a unique textbook.

The political landscape has changed immeasurably in the past decade as we have seen a woman serve as Speaker of the House, two more women join the Supreme Court, more women elected and appointed to all levels of government, and women running for president (Hillary Clinton in 2008 and 2016, Michele Bachmann in 2012, and Carly Fiorina in 2016) and vice president (Sarah Palin in 2008). The public policy agenda has also changed dramatically regarding issues of gender equality and justice, exemplified by such issues as the renewed battle regarding reproductive rights, health-care reform, and the nationwide Campus Anti-Rape Movement, to name just a few. These topics, combined with the Democratic Party's selection of Clinton as their presidential nominee in 2016, shows the progress that has been made, but also the work that remains to ensure that all participants in the political process are treated equally and fairly, regardless of gender.

As women continue to gain more prominence as active participants in the American political and electoral process as voters, candidates, and officeholders, it becomes even more important to understand how gender shapes political power and the distribution of resources within our society. There are many areas of research in a variety of disciplines focusing on women, gender, and feminism, and many of them intersect with a discussion of women in American politics. Our goal in writing this book is to present these topics in an interesting, lively, and timely way through an analysis of contemporary political gender-related issues. We hope to have provided just enough of a historical context to get students interested in the evolution of women in American political life and enough theory and analysis to inspire them to seek more information and knowledge about gender justice today. The study of women and U.S. politics, as well as the role gender plays in the broader political context, has emerged as a powerful voice within the discipline of political science in the past few decades. As such, we hope that readers find this text a useful addition to the ongoing dialogue and that instructors find it a useful pedagogical tool for their courses on women/gender and politics.

We have many people to thank for their contributions to this book. First, we are grateful for the guidance of our editor at Oxford University Press, Jennifer Carpenter, who provided much encouragement and enthusiasm along the way. Matthew Rohal also provided invaluable help throughout the editorial process. We are indebted to the many reviewers who provided helpful feedback on individual chapters as well as the manuscript as a whole. Their expertise, time, and commitment to making this textbook as useful as possible for their classes is truly appreciated.

Lori Cox Han thanks Brianna Pressey, an outstanding political science major and research assistant, for all her hard work in gathering the latest research available on women and politics. Patrick Fuery, the dean of Wilkinson College at Chapman University, also deserves thanks for providing funding for this project, as well as Taryn Stroop, who oversees student funding opportunities through Chapman's Building Undergraduate Research Networks program. Finally, Tom Han, Taylor NyBlom, and Davis Han deserve special thanks for their unconditional love, support, and patience, from beginning to end, with this book project.

Caroline Heldman thanks the students in her spring 2016 Gender and Politics class at Occidental College for their thoughtful feedback on an earlier version of this textbook. Special thanks go to Occidental College students Rosa Pleasant, Micol Garinkol, Dana Lough, Gabriella Mueller, and Micaela Stevens for their work on fact checking and their excellent content suggestions. She also thanks Sue Carroll, Cynthia Daniels, Jane Junn, Linda Zerilli, and Drucilla Cornell for their life-changing courses on gender and politics at Rutgers University. Last, she thanks Ian Breckenridge-Jackson for his selfless support during the writing process.

Finally, the many students over the years who have taken Dr. Han's and Dr. Heldman's respective women/gender and politics courses at Chapman University, Austin College, Occidental College, Rutgers University, Fairfield University, and Whittier College deserve thanks for their contributions to our knowledge and perspectives on this important topic.

CHAPTER 1

Introduction:
Women, Power, and Politics

In recent years, one of the most talked about questions regarding American politics was simple: "When will the United States elect its first woman president?" There is no simple explanation for why, despite nearly all the polls, pundits, and political experts saying otherwise, Democratic nominee Hillary Clinton lost the 2016 presidential election to Republican nominee Donald J. Trump. A Hillary Clinton presidency would have been historic. Just eight years after Barack Obama's election in 2008, her election would have marked two presidencies in a row to shatter the long-held tradition of only white men occupying the Oval Office. The symbolism of Clinton's inauguration as the first women president would have resonated worldwide as a mark of the progress that American women have achieved in all walks of life, particularly as the United States edges closer to the 100-year anniversary of women's suffrage. The headline "America Elects Madam President" was not meant to be in 2016, however.

 1st female president is so important because

Clinton's political journey, from first lady to U.S. senator to secretary of state to the first woman nominated by a major political party for president, is a specific case study that fits within a larger, yet simple, question that has also garnered significant attention for decades: "What if women ran the world?"[1] Similarly, if one were to imagine that every position of political leadership in the United States, whether elected or appointed, was suddenly held by a woman—not only the president, but also all of the cabinet positions and her close advisors, all of the leadership positions within the Congress (including the Speaker of the House and the Senate majority leader), and all nine members of the U.S. Supreme Court, along with every state governor, every leadership position in each of the 50 state legislatures, and every mayoral position in every city across the country—would the U.S. governing and political processes, as well as the public policy agenda, suddenly change or, more important, would they improve by becoming more efficient and effective?

This thought experiment demonstrates a useful point. Imaging a political world dominated by women highlights the fact that the U.S. political world has historically been and currently is dominated by men. American women, who have only had the right to vote since 1920, are still struggling to reach parity with their male counterparts in political leadership positions, let alone dominate the political system. In theory, democratically elected political bodies should look something like the larger society that they represent. This provides legitimacy to political institutions, particularly with regard to women, who make up slightly more than half of the population of the United States. Thinking about such an extreme shift in the political landscape is instructive, since it was not that many years ago that men held every political leadership position in Washington, DC.

With that in mind, this book explores the relationship and intersection of gender, power, and politics in the United States. Gender is commonly defined as the behavioral, cultural, or psychological traits typically associated with one sex. Within political science, power is broadly defined as the ability to influence others to get what you want, while politics is defined as "who gets what, when, and how"[2] and represents the process of determining how power and resources are redistributed throughout society. Based on those definitions, we explore several major questions pertaining to gender, power, and politics in the United States. For example, how do Americans view women as political leaders, and does this impact their chance of success within the political arena? And in a political age so driven by the influence of the news media, do negative stereotypes about women as political officeholders and powerbrokers harm their career opportunities in the public sector? Does gender affect how citizens engage in politics? Does gender influence the policies and practices of political leaders? These questions are crucial when

The Women's March on Washington, January 21, 2017.
Approximately half a million people gathered to protest the election of Donald Trump. They were joined by 2.6 million people in women's marches across the globe on that day.
SOURCE: Brian Allen, Voice of America

studying the role of women in American politics, since not only do women have the right as citizens to political participation, but also full participation by women (not only as voters but also as officeholders) has an important impact on the political process and on the outcome of important public policy debates.

WOMEN IN POLITICAL POWER:
A HISTORICAL PERSPECTIVE

According to political scientist Barbara Kellerman, while few women have held formal positions of power throughout world history, that is "not tantamount to saying they did not exercise power or exert influence."[3] Similarly, progress has been made in the past half century in terms of women's opportunities for leadership, but only when including both "informal" and "formal" positions of influence within government, business, nonprofits, and religious organizations, with more women at the bottom as opposed to the top of most organizational hierarchies.[4] The traditional view of American politics suggests that those with political power are those who hold specific leadership positions within government. From that vantage point, how have American women fared?

Within the executive branch, no woman has yet to be elected president or vice president, and only three women have ever served as secretary of state (Madeleine Albright, Condoleezza Rice, and Hillary Clinton) and two as attorney general (Janet Reno and Loretta Lynch). These two cabinet positions, along with secretary of defense and secretary of the treasury, are considered the most prominent cabinet positions among the now 15 cabinet-level departments in the executive branch. And three of the last four presidents made these appointments—with Albright and Reno serving in Bill Clinton's administration, Rice in George W. Bush's administration, and Clinton and Lynch in Barack Obama's administration—which means that this trend is fairly recent. The early cabinet appointments of Frances Perkins by Franklin Roosevelt in 1933 (as secretary of labor) and Oveta Culp Hobby by Dwight Eisenhower in 1953 (as secretary of health, education, and welfare, which is now split between the Department of Health and Human Services and Department of Education) are considered political anomalies; the next woman to be appointed to a cabinet position was not until 1975, when Gerald Ford selected Carla Anderson Hills as secretary of housing and urban development. In total, 40 women have held 45 cabinet or cabinet-level positions since 1933 (the latter category includes the positions of United Nations ambassador, national security advisor, special/U.S. trade representative, director of the Office of Management and Budget, chair of the Council of Economic Advisers, administrator of the Environmental Protection Agency, administrator of the Small Business Administration, and director of the Office of Personnel Management).

Special advisors within the White House are often considered even more powerful and influential than cabinet appointments. No woman has ever served as a chief of staff, and only two women have served as a presidential press secretary (Dee Dee Myers served as Clinton's press secretary from 1993 to 1994, and Dana Perino served as George W. Bush's press secretary from 2007 to 2009) and one as the national security advisor (Condoleezza Rice served in this role during George W. Bush's first term, from 2001 to 2005). Karen Hughes, who held the joint title of director of communications and counselor to the president for George W. Bush from 2001 until her resignation in 2003, is considered one of the most influential women to ever serve in an advisory capacity to a president within the Oval Office. Similarly, Valerie Jarrett held the position of senior advisor and assistant to the president for public engagement and intergovernmental affairs throughout the entire Obama administration.

In the judicia ~~l branch, only four women have served on the U.S. Supreme~~ Court (Sandra Day O'C ~~onnor, nominated~~ ... Bader Ginsberg, nominated by Bi ~~ll~~ ... gan, nomi- nated by Barack ... branch, no woman had ever ... A) ascent in 2003 to Democr ... osi went on to become Spea ... l, when she returned to min ... remains the only woman to ... e level, only 37 women have ... on as gover- nor of Connecti ... ed to the top state executive ... nd in office (due to either h ...

[handwritten annotation over text:] Since women have in a small but rapid way have been in high power leadership roles it gives a false narrative that women are equally represented

Since the ... a" Ferguson (D-TX), both e ... ucceed their husbands, and since Frances Perkins made history ... man cabinet member in Washington, women have made tremendous progress, at least statistically, in gaining access to elective or appointed office at most levels of government. Yet reaching a level of parity that is representative of the population at large, in which women voters slightly outnumber male voters, is still many decades away. And, due to recent gains for women in elected positions, public perceptions seem to indicate that most Americans believe women are receiving equal treatment with regard to leadership opportunities in both the public and private sector. As of 2017, 21 women serve in the Senate and 83 in the House of Representatives. In addition, 76 women hold statewide executive positions, 1,832 women serve as state legislators, and 20 women serve as mayors of the 100 largest U.S. cities.

As impressive as those numbers may be, however, the percentages tell a different story. Of the 535 seats in the U.S. Congress, women hold only 19.4 percent. In statewide executive positions, such as governors, lieutenant governors, and attorney generals, only 24 percent are held by women (and only five of 50 governors are women). A total of 24.8 percent of state legislators are women, and those 20 large-city mayors represent only 20 percent of the 100 largest cities in the nation (topping the list is Mayor Ivy R. Taylor of San Antonio, Texas, which ranks as the seventh largest city in the nation, followed by Mayor Betsy Price of Fort Worth, Texas, which ranks 16th). No woman has ever served as mayor of any of the three largest cities in the United States—New York, Los Angeles, and Chicago.

While women have made tremendous progress in gaining access to positions of political leadership in recent years, they are still "underrepresented at the top and overrepresented at the bottom" in American government at all levels.[5] According to political scientist Susan C. Bourque, public perceptions of women as active participants in the political process have broadened, yet various factors of American life continue to restrict political leadership opportunities for women. These factors include sexual division of labor (women are still predominantly responsible for child care and household chores); work structures and sex-role expectations (lack of "flex time" and other career advancement opportunities for women with family responsibilities); ambivalence about women exercising power; and perpetual issues such as how the media can portray women leaders in a negative light.[6]

STUDYING WOMEN AND POLITICS

Many students ask, why study women and politics, as well as a related question, what is the difference between women and politics and women's studies? Women's studies as an academic discipline grew out of the women's movement in the late 1960s. What began as informal groups of students and professors interested in studying gender and asking questions about how women (as opposed to the generic term "man") fit into the political and social order. Since then and throughout the 1970s and 1980s, the existence of women's and/or gender studies programs has increased dramatically at the college and university level, as has the number of women and politics courses being taught within political science departments across the country. The two areas of study are intricately linked through the development of feminist theories, as well as the methodologies (how we study issues) and core themes of studying women as women (the gendered meanings of social institutions, experiences, events, and ideas). Women's studies courses and programs of study are interdisciplinary, which means that ideas and methodologies come from a variety of disciplines (like political science, history, economics, psychology, philosophy, or communication, to name a few) and are brought together in an attempt to better understand the experiences of women in many facets of life.[7]

The study of women and politics also grew out of the women's movement along with the development of women's studies courses and programs. Prior to the late 1960s, as the feminist movement grew within colleges and universities, only a handful of books or studies had ever been conducted about women as political actors. The study of women and politics grew rapidly throughout the 1970s and 1980s, as did the subfield of women and politics within the American Political Science Association. Women and politics as a field of study is more specific than women's studies, focusing solely on women as political participants, officeholders, and policymakers and how public policy at all levels of governing impacts women. All political scientists, not just those who call themselves women and politics scholars, have benefited from this expansion of disciplinary boundaries by raising questions about what political scientists study and how they study it. By considering "woman" a category of study, "feminist political scientists have been able to call into question some of the central assumptions and frameworks of the discipline."[8] However, while the discipline of political science "now has gender on its agenda," much research remains to be done to better understand the role of race, class, party affiliation, and ideology in shaping how women politicians impact the policymaking process, as well as the role of the media in shaping perceptions of women leaders and how that may limit their political opportunities.[9] This book takes an intersectional approach to studying politics, meaning that it looks beyond gender to factors such as race, income, and sexuality that combine with gender to produce inequalities. This intersectional approach makes this textbook unique in political science.

CONCLUSION

As women continue to gain more prominence as active participants in the American political and electoral process as voters, candidates, and officeholders, it becomes even more important to understand how gender shapes political power and the distribution of resources within our society. In this book, we consider and examine the fight for gender equality through traditional topics found within a women and politics course, and our analysis is firmly grounded within the traditions of women and politics as it has evolved within political science. The book is organized to introduce the historical and theoretical foundations of the women's movement and feminism in the United States, followed by chapters that consider political behavior and representation, institutions and governing, and public policies. In addition, each chapter also features an end-of-chapter summary, study/discussion questions, case studies, resources, and profiles of women in power, all designed to encourage discussion and critical thinking about the topic of gender, power, and politics.

To begin, Chapter 2 will provide a historical analysis of the women's movement in America and its leaders, including the various phases of the women's movement and its generational differences (for example, the fight for suffrage culminating in 1920, followed by the drive for an equal rights amendment to the U.S. Constitution that began in 1923 and continuing until the amendment's close defeat in 1982). In Chapter 3, we introduce readers to the many faces of feminism. The 10 primary types of feminism are described in the first section of this chapter: liberal, radical, Marxist, socialist, psychoanalytic, eco-, postmodern, transnational, intersectional, and third wave. Most of these types of feminism were popularized during the second wave of the feminist movement in the 1960s and 1970s, but some (postmodern and third wave) emerged more recently in response to second wave feminisms. We also explore the political backlash against feminism.

In Chapter 4, we analyze the role that mass media and popular culture play in shaping our society. We focus on entertainment media and its influence on society through film, music, television, radio, video games, books, and online content. We analyze why pop culture matters for politics and power and present evidence that new communication technologies increase the influence of mass media. We also examine the representations of women, men, and gender-nonconforming individuals in pop culture with an emphasis on harmful and damaging misrepresentations. Last, we examine how women's leadership is presented in pop culture and why it matters for perceptions of female leadership in the real world.

Chapter 5 explores the ways in which political participation is gendered and why it matters. Men, women, and gender-nonconforming individuals have different pathways to politics, and they engage in politics in different ways. We look at the different ways in which girls and boys are socialized into politics that lead to differences in political interest, confidence in one's ability to participate in politics, political ambition, and political participation. Early life experiences and political socialization account for gender gaps in partisanship and voting behavior later in life.

Chapter 6 looks at women as political candidates, including the unique challenges that women have faced in running for office at all levels of government. Breaking into the system and becoming political leaders is not an easy task for women candidates, and we will consider the progress that women have made in state and national elections in recent decades.

We then turn to governing institutions. Chapter 7 considers women within Congress and state legislatures, followed by women within the executive branch at the federal level and holding executive positions at the state and local levels in Chapter 8 and women within the federal and state judicial branches in Chapter 9. We consider the offices to which women have been elected and/or appointed and whether that has made a difference in the areas of leadership, governance, and policymaking. We also look at whether women political leaders have effectively raised public awareness of women's policy issues and/or developed workable solutions and whether women governors or legislators govern differently from their male counterparts or even differently from each other.

In Chapter 10, we focus on the economic rights of women and the continuing fight for equity within the workplace and in pursuing an education. We pay particular attention to issues such as the wage gap, gender segregation in job markets, paid family leave, sexual harassment in educational settings and the workplace, the lack of women in corporate leadership positions, gender gaps in higher education, and the history and current status of Title IX. Finally, in Chapters 11 and 12, we examine both the history and current status of the individual rights of women in the policy areas of reproductive rights, sexual violence, and domestic violence. We pay particular attention to recent developments in all areas, including the emergence of reproductive rights and contraception as a political issue in presidential elections, changes in abortion laws at the state level, and the current national campaign against sexual assaults on university campuses.

CHAPTER SUMMARY

- We pose the question, what if all political positions in the United States were held by women? What, if anything, would change about the public policy agenda?
- Women have held informal positions of power with society for much longer than they have held formal elected/appointed positions.

- Historically, women have held few appointed positions within the cabinet or as White House advisors. Only four women have served on the U.S. Supreme Court, and only one woman—Democrat Nancy Pelosi—has held a top leadership position within Congress. At the state level, only 37 women have served as governor.
- Various factors continue to restrict political leadership opportunities for women, including the sexual division of labor, work structures and sex-role expectations, ambivalence about women exercising power, and negative media portrayals of women leaders.
- Women's studies as an academic discipline grew out of the women's movement in the late 1960s. Since then, the existence of women's and/or gender studies programs has increased dramatically at the college and university level.
- The study of women and politics grew rapidly throughout the 1970s and 1980s, as did the subfield of women and politics within the American Political Science Association.
- Women and politics is more specific than women's studies, focusing solely on women as political participants, officeholders, and policymakers and relevant public policies.

STUDY/DISCUSSION QUESTIONS

- What role did the women's movement have on the academic study of women and gender, particularly within the field of political science?
- How has the women and politics subfield within political science shaped our understanding of the category "woman?"

CASE STUDIES

1. **Why are there so few women in politics?**
   Women constitute more than 50 percent of the population in the United States, and while they have made great strides in political leadership in recent decades, they are still numerically underrepresented. What social or political factors do you think account for women's historic and current lack of presence in U.S. political leadership? In other words, what factors account for men's overrepresentation in American politics?

2. **Why is the United States behind when it comes to female heads of state?**
   To date, more than 60 countries have elected or appointed a female head of state. What aspects of American politics explain why the United States has lagged so far behind in this category? Is the office of the presidency uniquely gendered in the United States?

3. **Are men and women different political animals?**
   In this chapter, we asked you to imagine a political world dominated by women. What would that world look like? What policies and practices would

be different if women suddenly held 80 percent of the seats in Congress, 70 percent of seats in state legislatures, and most of federal cabinet positions, governorships, mayoral seats, and city council positions? What policies or practices might be different, if any? In other words, do you think men and women differ when it comes to politics?

RESOURCES

- The **Center for American Women and Politics**, part of the Eagleton Institute of Politics at Rutgers, State University of New Jersey, is a leading scholarly source of research and data about women's participation in American politics. http://cawp.rutgers.edu
- The **Women and Politics Institute** is part of the American University School of Public Affairs. Its mission is to close the gender gap in political leadership through research and practical training. http://www.american.edu/spa/wpi/
- The **Women and Politics Research Section** of the American Political Science Association brings scholars together who study this topic for collaboration on research. http://www.apsanet.org/section16

CHAPTER 2

The Women's Rights Movement in the United States

In 1920, women secured the right to vote with ratification of the Nineteenth Amendment to the U.S. Constitution. While this was a major victory that finally gave women a voice within the electoral process, women's rights activists at the time were far from finished. Alice Paul, a leader of the suffrage movement, turned her attention to a second addition to the Constitution—an equal rights amendment (ERA). First introduced in Congress in 1923, Paul dedicated her life to securing passage of the ERA. The proposed amendment did not gain approval by Congress (to then be sent to the states for consideration) until 1972, when Paul was 87 years old. When she died five years later, 35 of the necessary 38 states had approved the ERA, although it failed to gain support from three remaining states by the deadline set in 1982.

For many, the story of the fight to pass the ERA is a lesson in American history, a key storyline throughout the women's rights movement during the twentieth century with little relevance in today's political environment. But for others, the fight is far from over as several women's interest groups continue to work for passage of the ERA. Since the early 1970s, and certainly since ratification of the Nineteenth Amendment, tremendous progress has been made in securing equal rights—both politically and legally—for women. Some groups, such as the ERA Coalition, believe that amending the Constitution is still necessary, as their mission statement explains: "The ERA is an important statement of principle. The Constitution embodies the nation's core values. Equality between women and men is a fundamental human right that should be guaranteed in the Constitution."[1]

In an era where it is commonplace to hear activists speak of various other causes, equality for women is often thought of as something that already exists or that should be left to the history books. And while the women's rights movement may not make headlines as regularly as it did back in the 1960s and 1970s, the topic of equal rights for women does occasionally grab the media spotlight. The 2015 Academy Awards is one such example. While accepting her Oscar for Best Supporting Actress for the movie "Boyhood," Patricia Arquette highlighted the fact that the Constitution lacks an ERA and that equal pay for equal work has yet to be achieved: "To every woman who gave birth to every taxpayer and citizen of this nation, we have fought for everybody else's equal rights. It's our time to have wage equality once and for all and equal rights for women in the United States of America." Many in the audience cheered Arquette's comments—most notably Meryl Streep and Jennifer Lopez—because lower pay for women in Hollywood had been receiving media attention. However, on Twitter, a backlash ensued from many African Americans and other minorities who believed their own struggles for equality were being ignored by Arquette's focus on women. Backstage, Arquette elaborated on the issue and did not back down: "Equal means equal. And the truth is, the older women get, the less money they make. . . . And it's inexcusable that we go around the world and we talk about equal rights for women in other countries and we don't [here]. . . . The truth is, even though we sort of feel like we have equal rights in America, right under the surface, there are huge issues that are applied that really do affect women. It's time for all the women in America and all the men that love women, and all the gay people, and all the people of color that we've all fought for to fight for us now."[2]

While a simple definition of the women's rights movement in the United States may not exist, as it has included a variety of perspectives as well as diverse participants from its start in the nineteenth century, the fight for political and legal equality has always been the basis of the movement. American history celebrates many prominent women's rights activists; perhaps one of the best known is Susan B. Anthony, a leader of the early women's rights movement and fight for suffrage. Anthony cofounded a weekly newspaper, *The Revolution*, in 1868, which had a motto that transcends each era of the women's rights movement: "The true republic: men, their rights, and nothing more; women, their rights, and nothing less." Since Anthony's time, many political victories have been achieved, but the women's rights movement has also experienced its share of setbacks. It is especially important to note that not all American women have been a part of the women's rights movement or have agreed with the various policy changes that the movement has sought regarding a woman's public role. In general, the women's rights movement has sought the breakdown of what is known as the public versus private sphere, which had been the traditional way of life for men and women since the earliest days of the American colonies—the home was a woman's domain, while public matters, including government and politics, were the sole responsibility of men. As a result, women had no public voice, and the laws that governed them in most cases did not consider them equal citizens.

From the start, those who affiliated themselves with the women's rights movement sought more equality and fairness for women, as well as an end to the patriarchal treatment of women in all aspects of their lives. While many historical moments have shaped the women's rights movement, as well as different policy outcomes that have been sought by the movement's various leaders, some common interests have survived the test of time. According to political scientist Anne N. Costain, "Throughout their long history, women's movements, whether labeled suffrage, temperance, women's liberation, or antislavery, are linked in their consistent cry for democratic inclusion—politically, economically, educationally, and in the professions."[3]

This chapter is not meant to analyze every aspect of the history of the women's rights movement in America, but it will highlight the broadly defined phases or "waves" of the women's rights movement. The first wave is generally considered the fight for women's suffrage, beginning in 1848 at the Seneca Falls Convention and culminating with passage of the Nineteenth Amendment to the U.S. Constitution granting women the right to vote in 1920. The second wave of the women's rights movement emerged in the politically turbulent decade of the 1960s and coincided in part with the civil rights movement, with major attention focused on breaking down the legal barriers to sexual equality and, toward the end of this period, on the failed passage of the ERA to the Constitution. However, the second wave is known for a narrow view of women's rights purported by mostly middle- to upper-class white women (although some recent scholarship has begun to challenge that claim).[4] This period is followed by the third wave of the women's rights movement, which began in the late 1980s and focused on increased political participation by women as well as a more inclusive notion of women's rights to include racial, ethnic, and gender minorities. The chapter concludes with a discussion about the current state of the women's rights movement in the United States and whether a fourth wave has begun.

THE FIRST WAVE: SUFFRAGE

Women have struggled with the issue of the public versus private sphere throughout our nation's history; that is, that men controlled the public sphere, while women were relegated to the household and childrearing chores in the private/domestic sphere. Despite all the talk of liberty and that "all men were created equal" during the American revolutionary period, women in the American colonies were confined to domestic duties and had few legal rights. Women during this period could not vote or hold public office, few had any kind of formal education, and divorce was difficult to obtain. In several colonies, married women could not own property and had no legal rights over their children.

However, the emerging revolutionary ferment in the 1770s offered some women new opportunities through what has been labeled "republican motherhood." Women who were educated became responsible for promoting civic virtue and the ideals of a republican (representative) government to children. In addition, numerous women began to aid the war effort and help the American armies in their fight against the British by raising money, plowing fields, making ammunitions, cooking and sewing, caring for the soldiers, spying, and sparking political conversations at the dinner table.[5] While most women remained in the private sphere during this era, a few outspoken women began to demand equal treatment during and after the war. As early as 1776, Abigail Adams, the future first lady and wife of John Adams, wrote to her husband with her now-famous demand for equality:

> I long to hear that you have declared an independency—and by the way in the new Code of Laws which I suppose it will be necessary for you to make I desire you would Remember the Ladies, and be more generous and favourable to them than your ancestors. Do not put such unlimited power into the hands of the Husbands. Remember all Men would be tyrants if they could. If perticular care and attention is not paid to the Ladies we are determined to foment a Rebelion, and will not hold ourselves bound by any Laws in which we have no voice, or Representation.[6]

Unfortunately, Adams and the other eventual framers of the constitution were not to be persuaded, and the legal status of women did not improve after the American Revolution or with the ratification of the U.S. Constitution in 1789 or the Bill of Rights in 1791. The rights of women were not addressed in the documents, and "by today's standards, it is impossible to deny that the original Constitution was a racist and sexist document or that the Framers wrote it in a way that benefited them."[7] As America moved into the nineteenth century and as the nation began to experience rapid industrialization and urbanization that moved the economy away from its agrarian roots, the "cult of domesticity" (a prominent nineteenth-century value system among upper and middle classes in the United States and Great Britain that emphasized femininity and a woman's role within the home) took a stronger cultural hold on women. The home became a safe haven from the cruel world outside, and it was the responsibility of women to civilize their husbands and children. It also became an accepted social norm that "men and women were designed by God and nature to inhabit 'separate spheres.'"[8] Legal and political rights for women remained much as they had been in the colonial era, with no right to vote and little or no control over property or custody of children.

Seneca Falls and the Fight for Suffrage

The formal women's rights movement began in 1848 at the Seneca Falls Convention, convened by Lucretia Mott and Elizabeth Cady Stanton. Most women who attended had been active in the abolitionist movement for years, even decades. The idea for the convention had been born following the 1840 World Anti-Slavery Convention in London, where female delegates, including Mott and Stanton, had not been allowed to participate and were even forced to sit behind a partition so as not to be seen publicly. Prior to the Seneca Falls Convention, Stanton wrote her famous "Declaration of Sentiments and Resolutions" in 1848, a bold document declaring the rights of women modeled after the Declaration of Independence. Stanton's "Declaration" demanded economic and property rights and denounced many things, including slavery, discrimination in education, exploitation of women in the workforce, the patriarchal family, and divorce and child custody laws; it also denounced organized religion as "perpetuating women's oppression." While suffrage would become the major issue of the latter stages of the first wave of the women's rights movement, that was not the initial case in the claims that came out of Seneca Falls:

> Popular belief has it that the nineteenth-century movement focused solely on suffrage, but that became true only in the movement's later, diluted form. At Seneca Falls, the demand for suffrage was almost an afterthought, a last-minute item Stanton tacked on to the list—the only resolution not unanimously supported. In fact, at its inception, this movement was radical and multi-issued. It named male power over women "absolute tyranny."[9]

Yet, securing the right to vote did emerge as the major issue for the movement, since early activists like Stanton and Anthony, and later activists like Paul, believed suffrage to be the most effective way to gain access to the political system and change the unjust way that women were viewed in the eyes of the law. Thus, a 72-year struggle ensued to earn the right for women to vote. After Seneca Falls, women's rights conventions were held in various cities as the movement began to grow. At one such convention in Akron, Ohio, in 1851, Sojourner Truth, a former slave, abolitionist, and women's rights activist, delivered her famous "Ain't I a Woman?" oratory:

> That man over there says that women need to be helped into carriages, and lifted over ditches, and to have the best place everywhere. Nobody ever helps me into carriages, or over mud-puddles, or gives me any best place! And ain't I a woman? Look at me! Look at my arm! I have ploughed and planted, and gathered into barns, and no man could head me! And ain't I a woman? I could work as much and eat as much as a man—when I could get it—and bear the lash as well! And ain't I a woman? I have borne thirteen children, and seen most all sold off to slavery, and when I cried out with my mother's grief, none but Jesus heard me! And ain't I a woman?[10]

Many of the early leaders of the first wave had gained leadership and organizational skills as activists in the abolitionist movement, so for this and future generations of suffragists, the strategy to achieve what at the time seemed like a radical change to the Constitution went beyond conventions to also include protests, marches, lectures, writings, and various forms of civil disobedience. By 1860, several movement leaders had emerged, recruitment of younger women had begun, and "women's demands had been articulated, many essentials of a feminist ideology had been developed," and a cohesive structure for the suffrage movement had been formed.[11]

From the start, Stanton and Anthony remained prominent leaders within the suffrage movement. Both had been active in the American Equal Rights Association, which had been formed in 1866 to fight for universal suffrage. However, the organization disbanded in 1869 due to internal conflicts involving the political priorities of the group (whether woman's suffrage should be a higher priority than black male suffrage). In May 1869, Stanton and Anthony formed the National Woman Suffrage Association (which would eventually become the League of Women Voters in the 1920s and is still in existence today). Led by

Anthony, the National Woman Suffrage Association preferred fighting for a constitutional amendment to give women the right to vote nationally. A second group, the American Woman Suffrage Association, was formed in November 1869 by Lucy Stone and Henry Blackwell to fight for suffrage on a state-by-state basis. Anthony had gained national attention for the cause of adding a constitutional amendment to give women the vote, as well as much needed support, when she was arrested and tried for voting in the 1872 presidential election. The amendment, first introduced in Congress in 1878, was presented to 40 consecutive sessions of Congress before it finally passed as a proposed amendment in 1919.[12]

Along the way, the suffrage movement faced fierce opposition from a variety of antisuffrage groups. Big business (particularly the liquor industry), the Catholic Church, and political machine bosses feared that women voters would support political reform. Women led many of the temperance efforts of the late nineteenth and early twentieth centuries in an attempt to ban the sale of alcohol. Other organizations, like the National Consumer's League, formed in 1899, and the National Women's Trade Union League, formed in 1903, worked to change labor conditions in various industries. Many southern states also opposed women's suffrage because they did not want African American women to gain access to voting rights or argued that suffrage was a states-rights issue, rather than a federal one.[13] As in the suffrage movement, women also emerged as strong leaders in the antisuffrage movement. The women leaders in both movements tended to be among the social elite—educated, with access to money, and having important social contacts. But many women did not support the breakdown of the public-versus-private sphere dichotomy, fearing that women would lose their power and influence within the domestic sphere and among social networks if they were forced to become participants in public life. As a result, it is important to remember that women's suffrage, or later political efforts within the women's rights movement, did not universally represent all women, as we will discuss later in this chapter.

Between 1878 and 1920, when the Nineteenth Amendment was ratified, activists for women's voting rights relied on a variety of strategies to gain support for the proposed amendment. Legal strategies were used in an attempt to invalidate male-only voting laws, while others sought to pass suffrage laws at the state level. Some women fighting for the cause could not be deterred, enduring hunger strikes, staging rallies or vote-ins, or even being jailed for publicly campaigning for the amendment. The movement became revitalized with an influx of younger women joining the fight by 1910 due to immigration, urbanization, and an expanding female labor force, considered a "time of unprecedented activism and organizing by women workers."[14] The suffrage cause also won a state referendum in Washington in 1910 granting women the right to vote. California would follow in 1911, and by 1912, a total of nine western states had passed legislation giving women the right to vote. (As a territory, Wyoming had granted women full suffrage in 1869 and retained the law when it became a state in 1890. The other six western states included Colorado, Utah, Idaho, Arizona, Kansas, and Oregon).

Another major turning point came in 1916 when a coalition of suffrage organizations, temperance groups, women's social welfare organizations, and reform-minded politicians pooled their efforts and resources to wage a fiercer public battle. The political tide began to turn in the suffragists' favor in 1917, when New York adopted women's suffrage legislation. Then, in 1918, President Woodrow Wilson also changed his position and backed the constitutional amendment. On May 21, 1919, the House of Representatives passed the proposed amendment, followed by the Senate two weeks later. Tennessee became the 36th state to ratify the amendment on August 18, 1920, which gave the amendment the necessary three-fourths support from the states (it was officially certified by Secretary of State Bainbridge Colby eight days later, on August 26, 1920). Few of the early supporters for women's suffrage, including Anthony and Stanton, lived to see the final political victory in 1920.

PROFILE IN POWER

Elizabeth Cady Stanton and Susan B. Anthony

When discussing the early women's rights movement in America, perhaps no two women were as influential as Elizabeth Cady Stanton and Susan B. Anthony. And, due to the lasting partnership that the two developed in pursuing women's rights and women's suffrage, one's contribution to the cause cannot be discussed without also considering the contributions of the other. Each had unique leadership strengths that seemed to perfectly compliment the other's; "Stanton was the leading voice and philosopher of the women's rights and suffrage movements while Anthony was the powerhouse who commandeered the legions of women who struggled to win the ballot for American women."[15] Stanton and Anthony also exemplify what political scientist Bruce Miroff calls "dissenting leadership," a model of leadership for a group that was "denied the fundamental rights of citizenship and was excluded from participation in public life."[16]

Stanton (1815–1902) is known as the "founding mother of feminism" and is remembered as the "boldest and most brilliant leader of the feminist movement in nineteenth-century America."[17] The wife of prominent abolitionist Henry Stanton and a mother of seven, Stanton was 32 years old when she helped to convene the Seneca Falls Convention in 1848. A graduate of Troy Female Seminary, she refused to be merely what she called a "household drudge," and when she and Henry married, the word "obey" was omitted from the ceremony. They honeymooned in London while attending the World Anti-Slavery Convention in 1840. After Stanton's call for a woman's right to vote at Seneca Falls, she was opposed by her fellow organizer Lucretia Mott, as well as Mott's husband, both of whom thought the idea was too radical. Soon after, in 1850, Stanton met and developed a lifelong friendship and partnership with Susan B. Anthony, who joined in Stanton's cause for women's rights and women's suffrage. In 1866, Stanton ran for the House of Representatives, the first woman to ever do so, when she realized that while New York prohibited women from voting, the law did not prohibit them from running for or holding public office. Her election bid was unsuccessful.

Prior to her years as an activist force within the women's rights movement, Anthony (1820–1906) had become a teacher at the age of 17. After teaching for 15 years, she became active in the temperance movement, considered one of the first expressions of American feminism by dealing with the abuses of women and children who suffered from alcoholic husbands. As a woman, however, Anthony was not allowed to speak at public rallies. As a result, she helped to found the Woman's State Temperance Society of New York, one of the first women's associations of its kind. After meeting Stanton in 1850, she soon joined the women's rights movement and dedicated her life to achieving suffrage for women. Unlike Stanton, Anthony never married and did not have the burden of raising children. As a result, she focused her attention on organization within the movement and was more often the one who traveled, lectured, and canvassed nationwide for suffrage. Anthony was arrested for attempting to vote on more than one occasion beginning in 1872, but remained committed to her endless campaign for a constitutional amendment allowing women the right to vote. In 1900, Anthony persuaded the University of Rochester to admit women, and she remained an active lecturer and activist for the cause of suffrage until her death.

Together, Stanton and Anthony formed the Women's Loyal National League in 1863 in New York City to demand the end of slavery. In 1868, they founded the Workingwoman's Association that sought to improve working conditions for women and also started a weekly newspaper aptly named the *Revolution*, which demanded, among other things, equal pay for women. The following year, they founded the National Woman Suffrage Association after they both sought a more radical solution than had been proposed by the American Equal Rights Association. Stanton served as president of the organization for 21 years, although she differed with Anthony regarding the need for suffrage to be the single issue dominating the woman's rights movement. Stanton, "known for her searching intellect, wide-ranging views, and radical positions," is remembered as the "preeminent women's-rights theorist of nineteenth-century America."[18] Anthony, who became the first woman to have her image appear on any form of U.S. currency with the debut of the Susan B. Anthony dollar in 1979, is remembered as the woman most identified with women's suffrage and passage of the Nineteenth Amendment.[19] Together, their early brand of political leadership shaped the lives of millions of American women.

Postsuffrage and the ERA

In the immediate postsuffrage era, several women's rights activists, including Carrie Chapman Catt and Alice Paul, sought to capitalize on the momentum of finally receiving the vote and began to lobby Congress for an ERA to the Constitution. Catt, a leader of the suffrage movement, had served as president of the National American Woman Suffrage Association, which was formed in 1890 when the

National Woman Suffrage Association and the American Woman Suffrage Association merged, from 1900 to 1904, and again from 1915 until ratification of the Nineteenth Amendment in 1920. Catt founded the League of Women Voters that same year. Paul had been instrumental in pushing the suffrage cause to victory as head of the National American Woman Suffrage Association's Congressional Committee, but left that organization in 1913 to form the Congressional Union for Woman Suffrage (which became the National Women's Party in 1917). In 1923, Paul drafted the ERA and the National Women's Party presented it to Congress. Beginning that same year, Congress annually considered various versions of an ERA, yet never passed a constitutional amendment for the states to consider. To amend the U.S. Constitution, a two-thirds vote is necessary in both the House of Representatives and the Senate to propose the amendment for consideration by the states. For ratification, three-fourths of the states must approve the amendment. Finally, in 1972, after intense lobbying by groups such as the National Organization for Women (NOW) and Business and Professional Woman, Congress passed the proposed ERA. The contents of the proposed amendment were brief and to the point:

> Section 1. Equality of rights under the law shall not be denied or abridged by the United States or by any State on account of sex.
>
> Section 2. The Congress shall have the power to enforce, by appropriate legislation, the provisions of this article.
>
> Section 3. The Amendment shall take effect two years after the date of ratification.

By 1973, 22 states had ratified the amendment, but by the initial deadline of 1978, only 35 states had signed on for ratification. Despite an extended deadline to 1982, momentum for passage faltered under intense opposition from religious groups such as the National Council of Catholic Women and the Mormon Church, as well as political groups opposed to the ERA, such as the Eagle Forum led by Phyllis Schlafly. Many observers have noted that the ERA "divided rather than united women politically and culturally."[20] Not only were women divided over whether to support the amendment, but also various opinions existed as to whether the amendment would make a difference in terms of legal rights for women. Some argued that the amendment was merely symbolic, while others feared that passage would do away with various legal protections for women in the workplace, as well as those involving child support and exemption from military registration.

After the initial excitement of the proposed constitutional amendment, public support and political enthusiasm waned in the years leading up the deadline set for 1982. While passage of the amendment would have been a political victory for the women's rights movement, many of the gender-based classifications that ERA supporters hoped to outlaw had already been changed through Supreme Court rulings, legislation in Congress, or presidential executive orders.

According to political scientist Jane J. Mansbridge, the defeat of the amendment was not surprising: "The puzzle is not why the ERA died but why it came so close to passing. . . . The irony in all this is that the ERA would have had much less substantive effect than either proponents or opponents claimed."[21] Yet, the ERA remained a prominent rallying call for the leaders of the second wave of the women's rights movement.

THE SECOND WAVE: POLITICAL AND LEGAL EQUALITY

While the fight for the ERA played an important role in the modern women's rights movement, several other issues began to take center stage for American women throughout the 1960s as the movement entered its second wave. With similarities to the civil rights movement throughout the decade, the mainstream women's rights movement turned its attention to ending the cult of domesticity that had been the ideal during the 1950s. Women had made great progress during the 1940s in the workforce during World War II, when millions of American men served in the military, leaving a variety of jobs open for women. However, many of the women who had experienced professional success and were seen as patriots by helping the American economy during the war were displaced from their jobs when the soldiers returned home. The start of the postwar baby boom era in the late 1940s, coupled with the new trend of suburbanization across the nation, left the lives of most American women once again dominated by responsibilities in the private sphere. According to historian Dorothy Sue Cobble, the iconic image of Rosie the Riveter from World War II suggests both triumph and loss: "Many know that Rosie's wartime day in the sun—enjoying her boost in income, admired for her skill, and basking in societal approval—would not last. At the war's end, it is thought, Rosie the Riveter morphed into Rose the Stay-at-Home Mom, surrounded by her children in a suburban dream home, cheerfully wielding a vacuum cleaner, not a rivet gun."[22]

Women's Rights in the 1960s

The publication of Betty Friedan's book, *The Feminine Mystique*, became one of the most important events for the women's rights movement in the early 1960s. A 1942 graduate of Smith College, Friedan had spent ten years as a suburban New York wife and mother doing occasional freelance writing when she circulated a questionnaire among her Smith classmates in 1957 to determine their satisfaction with their lives. When she discovered that they were resoundingly not satisfied with their life experiences as wives and mothers, and with her undergraduate training in psychology, Friedan embarked on a much more intensive analysis that resulted in *The Feminist Mystique*'s publication in 1963. The book immediately struck a chord with millions of American women who shared Friedan's view that many women were trapped in the supposed domestic bliss of hearth and home and that women had no real identity, simply living vicariously through their husbands and children. The book became an immediate, yet controversial, best-seller. Known for discussing "the problem that has no name," Friedan showed that

> virtually every powerful cultural institution—magazines, television, advice books, schools, and religious leaders—prescribed a middle-class ideal for women: they were to be wives and mothers, nothing more, nothing less. . . . Suburbs gave a new, geographic twist to the old split between private and public, family and work, personal and political. The work suburban women actually did, inventing new forms of creative motherhood and elaborating networks of volunteer institutions, was not seen as, well, *real* work.[23]

The response that Friedan received from thousands of letters written by women from various social backgrounds, telling the author that the book had changed their lives, convinced her that a new chapter in the women's rights movement had been born. And although she had not originally sought such a position, Friedan became the leader of this new wave of the movement. Taking this new leadership role seriously, she began touring the country to talk about practical solutions to some of the problems that women, particularly in the workforce, were facing, such as a lack of affordable day care and flexible work schedules and maternity leaves to accommodate family needs. Inspired by the civil rights movement, Friedan declared the need for a "women's NAACP." In October 1966, with about 40 other activists, she cofounded NOW, a civil rights group dedicated to achieving equality for women in American society. As NOW's first president, a role she held until 1970, Friedan lobbied for an end to sex-classified employment notices, for greater representation of women in political office, for child-care centers for working mothers, and for legalized abortion and other political reforms. The founders of NOW sought a "dramatic restructuring of American gender relations" to bring equality to women politically, socially, and economically through "protests, lawsuits, lobbying and media campaigns."[24] In 1969, she became a founding member of the National Abortion Rights Action League, and in 1971 she also became a founding member of the National Women's Political Caucus. Throughout the 1970s and early 1980s, Friedan also worked as an outspoken proponent for passage of the ERA.[25]

Membership in NOW and other women's organizations grew rapidly during the early 1970s as the women's rights movement capitalized on the political momentum first begun a decade earlier. President John F. Kennedy had formed the Commission on the Status of Women in 1961 in response to concerns about women's equality, and based on the commission's various studies at both the national and state level that showed pay inequity based on sex, Congress passed the Equal Pay Act in 1963. Other political victories for sexual equality came within the decade with Congress's passage of Title IX of the Educational Amendments Act of 1972, which required equal opportunity for women in all aspects of education, including admissions, financial aid, and funding for women's athletic programs. Congress had also finally passed the ERA that same year. And in 1973, the

Supreme Court, in *Roe v. Wade*, struck down state laws banning abortion in the first three months of pregnancy. Advocates for women's rights saw the decision as a major victory since reproductive rights and the ability of women to control their own bodies were at the forefront of their political agenda.

PROFILE IN POWER

Gloria Steinem

Known as a feminist leader, journalist, best-selling author, and social activist, Gloria Steinem has been one of the most enduring forces within the women's rights movement since the 1960s. She is now in her 80s, and there are not many parts of Steinem's life that have not become part of the public dialogue about feminism and the women's rights movement. Her celebrity status, as well as her desire to

SOURCE: Gage Skidmore

remain unconventional, has kept her in the news for decades; from the early days of the modern women's rights movement, the fact that she was physically attractive seemed to defy the media's stereotype of what it meant to be a feminist. Early in her career as a freelance journalist, she infiltrated the Playboy Club as an undercover "bunny" to write an expose about how women employees were sexually harassed and discriminated against in the New York club. She went public with the fact that she had had an abortion during the 1950s while she was in college, a time when the procedure was still illegal in the United States. She had a four-year relationship with Mort Zuckerman, the conservative publisher of *U.S. News and World Report*, and once had to deny a relationship with former secretary of state Henry Kissinger after they were photographed together in public. In 2000, she made headlines again when, at the age of 66, she married for the first time (an institution she had long railed against as destroying a woman's identity and as an "arrangement for one and a half people").

In terms of her political accomplishments, Steinem was among the leaders of the women's rights movement in the late 1960s and early 1970s in the campaign for reproductive rights, equal pay and equal representation, and an end to domestic violence. She helped to found the National Women's Political Caucus in 1971, as well as the groundbreaking *Ms. Magazine* and the Ms. Foundation for Women in 1972. She is also a founding member of the Coalition of Labor Union Women, and her books *Outrageous Acts and Everyday Rebellions* (1983) and *Revolution from Within: A Book of Self-Esteem* (1992) were bestsellers. When *Ms. Magazine* first appeared as a one-time insert in *New York Magazine* in December 1971, no one gave a magazine dedicated to women's rights and feminist views a chance for survival against the traditional women's magazines that gave "advice about saving marriages, raising babies, or using the right cosmetics." But the 300,000 test copies sold out nationwide in only eight days, generating 26,000 subscription orders. According to the *Ms.* web page, "few realized it would become the landmark institution in both women's rights and American journalism that it is today. . . . [and it] was the first national magazine to make feminist voices audible, feminist journalism tenable, and a feminist worldview available to the public."[26] The magazine's success and ability to survive for four decades is even more impressive given the fact that it has remained free of advertising for most of its existence. Steinem has been involved with the magazine, either as an editor or as a writer, for all but a few years of its publication.

Steinem is also known for her compelling, and sometimes controversial, quotes about how women have been treated in American society. Among the most notable include her comments, "If the shoe doesn't fit, must we change the foot?" and "A woman without a man is like a fish without a bicycle" (the latter phrase was first coined by Australian author Irina Dunn, but is often attributed to Steinem as well). Steinem continues to speak out about feminist issues and causes and acknowledges the many changes the women's rights movement has undergone in the past five decades. While women of her generation rebelled against the pressures to marry, have children, take their husband's name, and be the picture of "femininity," Steinem now acknowledges that many women in the twenty-first century embrace the traditional notion of being a wife and mother, but that women now have the choice to lead their life devoted to family, a career, or both. In a January 2005 interview, she stated that while being a wife and mother are no longer "social imperatives" like they were several decades ago, the women's movement is no way diminished and is still necessary: "It's like saying, 'We're living in a post-democracy.' It's ridiculous. We've hardly begun. The good news is that American feminism used to be three crazy women in New York: now a third of the country self-identify as feminists, and 60 percent if you go by the dictionary definition."[27] The debate over feminism and the women's rights movement lives on.

Backlash in the 1970s and 1980s

Not all American women were on board with this new wave of the women's rights movement, and not all believed in the causes supported by Friedan and other prominent feminists, such as Gloria Steinem (the founder *of Ms. Magazine*), Susan Brownmiller (an early organizer of this phase of the women's rights movement and best-selling feminist author), and Flo Kennedy (an attorney and civil rights/women's rights activist who was also the first black woman to graduate from Columbia Law School). Despite the changing workforce in America, where a two-income family became the norm throughout the 1970s and 1980s, many working women did not consider themselves feminists. The victory for pro-choice feminists in legalizing abortion galvanized the pro-life movement at the national level, and organizations opposed to passage of the ERA also gained national prominence. Under the leadership of Phyllis Schlafly, the Eagle Forum, founded in 1972, fought to stop passage of the ERA and to protect what their members believed to be traditional family values and the traditional role of women in society, which they believed was being harmed by feminists. Another group, Concerned Women for America, also became a prominent antifeminist and anti-ERA group. Founded in 1979 by Beverly LaHaye, the wife of fundamentalist Baptist minister and Moral Majority cofounder Tim LaHaye, the mission of

Concerned Women for America was to promote biblical values in all areas of public policy. Both organizations are still in existence. The formation of these groups in response to those supporting the women's rights agenda shows the diversity of viewpoints, even by the 1970s, about women's role in society. As historian Ruth Rosen points out, "Insecure in their separate worlds, women privately sniped at each other: housewives blasted activists as unpatriotic; working women derided housewives as spoiled and lazy; and housewives accused working women of neglecting their children."[28]

Divisions even emerged within the women's rights movement, as more moderate feminists (who tended to represent the view of middle- to upper-class white women) clashed with more radical feminists (who wanted to broaden the movement beyond the pursuit of legal equality to bring about more radical change for women within all aspects of society). Even in the late 1960s, a potential rift within the women's rights movement began to emerge as the women who founded NOW brought together women in labor unions and other professional women who wanted equal employment opportunities, while younger women who had been active in the civil rights and anti-Vietnam movements formed what was known as the "women's liberation" movement. The latter wanted "a more holistic transformation of the society, one that would do away with male dominance in every sphere—in private as well as public—and would challenge all the older gender patterns."[29] In addition, a variety of "feminisms" emerged throughout the 1970s and beyond, as discussed in Chapter 3. By the 1980s, the women's rights movement had succeeded with many legislative and legal changes in granting equality to women, even with the failure of the ERA. Yet the debate over the role of women in American society continued into the 1990s and beyond as a younger generation of feminists weighed in with their views of where the women's rights movement had been and where it should go in the future.

THE THIRD WAVE: REDEFINING THE MOVEMENT

By 1990, many political observers believed that feminism (the fight for political, legal, and social equality for women) in America was dead. But according to women's studies scholar Astrid Henry, the publication of two key books in 1991—*Backlash: The Undeclared War on American Women* by Susan Faludi and *The Beauty Myth: How Images of Beauty Are Used against Women* by Naomi Wolf, began to challenge the idea that the women's rights movement was over. Both Faludi and Wolf represented a "new generation of popular feminist writing" that helped to reinvigorate interest in the women's rights movement.[30] Faludi wrote about how the gains, both political and legal, made by women during the 1970s had been followed by a backlash during the 1980s, a decade in which a conservative Republican—President Ronald Reagan—dominated the political environment. Wolf pointed out some of the key differences in the women's rights movement generations, since those who had fought the battles in the heyday of the second wave did not necessarily represent the same attitudes and beliefs of younger feminists.

Other events during this time also contributed to the renewed public interest in women's issues, including the Supreme Court confirmation hearing of Clarence Thomas in the fall of 1991 (during which he was accused of sexual harassment), as well as the increased number of women running for public office in 1992. Images of strong women were also suddenly prominent in Hollywood, with the release of the movie *Thelma & Louise* in 1991 (about two women fighting back against male violence, which grossed more than $45 million) and the popularity of two top-rated sitcoms starring women—ABC's *Roseanne* (named for the star of the show, Roseanne Barr, who portrayed a strong-willed mother in a working-class family in a small midwestern town) and CBS's *Murphy Brown* (starring Candice Bergen as a single and successful 40-something political reporter of a television network news show set in Washington, DC).[31]

What is now referred to as the third wave of the women's rights movement got its start in the political and social environment of the early 1990s. Unlike the second wave, which largely focused on equality and the inclusion of women in traditionally male-dominated areas, the third wave (known to some as postfeminism) continued to challenge and expand common definitions of gender and sexuality. The third wave, dominated by generation X (the post–baby boomer generation born after 1964), sought to move beyond the political battles—equal access to work, education, and athletics—that the older generation of feminists had fought. This wave of the women's rights movement began to reflect the unique view of women's issues and feminism in the generation of women who came of age mostly in the 1980s, where feminism had already been a part of the world in which they grew up. Third wave feminists began moving beyond the monolithic, white, middle-class views of earlier feminism to embrace a more multicultural view that included women of all races, ethnicity, and socioeconomic backgrounds. Not only did a more global view of women's issues emerge, but also a common theme was found in labeling the third wave a pro-woman movement that stressed personal empowerment, as opposed to the stereotype of anti-man that became part of the image of feminists during the late 1980s and early 1990s.[32] The difference between the two generations, according to Henry, remains a crucial part of the identity for third wave feminists: "This refused identification, or disidentification, is frequently with or against second-wave feminism. . . . for many younger feminists, it is only by refusing to identify themselves with earlier versions of feminism—and frequently with older feminists—that they are able to create a feminism of their own."[33]

Stealth Feminists

The third wave also became synonymous with the term "stealth feminist" due to the media's backlash of painting the women's rights movement as a negative association. Until the early 1990s, the media kept talking about the end of feminism, yet younger generations of women began reshaping the movement with various articles and books about the third wave agenda.[34] According to Debra Michaels,

> beyond endless accounts of young women from so-called Generations X, Y, and Z renouncing feminism with the oft-repeated, "I'm not a feminist, *but* . . . ," lay

another reality: countless thirty-something women not only embracing the label but defining our lives as torchbearers for feminism. In our careers, relationships, childraising strategies (or decisions *not* to have children)—in all our choices—"Stealth Feminists" have been quietly, invisibly, and sometimes even subconsciously continuing the work of the Women's Movement.[35]

Prominent third wave authors included Jennifer Baumgardner and Amy Richards, who pointed out that many women of their generation were taking women's rights and feminism for granted, which caused one of the biggest challenges for the movement: "For anyone born after the early 1960s, the presence of feminism in our lives is taken for granted. For our generation, feminism is like fluoride. We scarcely notice that we have it—it's simply in the water."[36] Baumgardner also argues that third wave feminism became "portable" and lost the "idea of a shared political priority list" as it became more inclusive:

> It inherited critiques of sexist dominant culture (having grown up in a feminist-influenced civilization) and embraced and created pop culture that supported women, from Queen Latifah to bell hooks to Riot Grrrl. Girlie feminists created magazines and fashion statements (and complicated the idea of what a feminist might look like). Sex positivity undermined the notion that porn and sex work were inherently demeaning, and revealed a glimpse of the range of potential sexual expression.[37]

Another prominent voice within the third wave was award-winning author Rebecca Walker, who cofounded Third Wave Foundation, a nonprofit organization dedicated to working with young women and transgender youths ages 15 to 30 to become active citizens and leaders in pursuit of social justice. Walker was considered a "superstar" among third wave feminists, and her first book—an edited volume in 1995 titled *To Be Real: Telling the Truth and Changing the Face of Feminism*—helped to solidify the emerging view of younger feminists as more inclusive of different perspectives and life experiences than the women's rights movement from the 1960s and 1970s. Walker, however, has strong family ties to the second wave of feminism; her mother is feminist author and activist Alice Walker, who won the Pulitzer Prize for the novel *The Color Purple* in 1983, and her godmother is Gloria Steinem. Walker's own personal and life experiences, as well as her decision to write about many facets of her life in her books, represented the intersections of race, ethnicity, and gender that became so prominent in third wave feminism. In her 2001 book, *Black, White, and Jewish: Autobiography of a Shifting Self,* she wrote about growing up with a black mother and a Jewish father, as well as her sexual relationships with both men and women. But as there is no monolithic definition of feminism, Walker's life and views as a feminist have continued to evolve. Her 2007 book *Baby Love: Choosing Motherhood after a Lifetime of Ambivalence,* challenged the view some held of Walker as a radical feminist. Other prominent third wave feminists, such as Baumgardner, view Walker's evolving beliefs on topics such as pregnancy and motherhood as a "contribution to the Third Wave sensibility, not a betrayal of it."[38]

Walker continues to promote a message of the need for acceptance and inclusion within feminism and feminist causes. She has received backlash against her own feminist views from other feminists due to her insistence "on the necessity of inter-generational power sharing within feminist institutions, the full integration of men into organizations working for gender parity, and the necessity of finding commonality with women who don't hold progressive views. In response, I've been attacked, undermined, and politically abused by some of the very women I sought to serve." Walker also recalled a talk she gave to the National Women's Studies Association a few years prior in which she urged members "to be more open, more tolerant, and more inclusive of women and men who do not share a progressive agenda." Her remarks were perceived as both controversial and inappropriate.[39]

Politically, the third wave of the women's rights movement focused on candidate recruitment, campaign resources, democratic inclusion of women, more public roles for women, and finding a new voice for feminism through grass-roots political activism. The agenda also included acknowledging the issues associated with economically disadvantaged as well as racial, ethnic, and gender minorities. There was a strong link to the Democratic Party, particularly during President Bill Clinton's administration (1993–2001) as "softer" women's issues came to the forefront during the economic prosperity of the 1990s, including education, family, jobs, and health care. At the start of the 1990s, national security took a back seat in the national debate with the end of the Cold War. Following the terrorist attacks on September 11, 2001, the national debate again changed, with national security issues eclipsing domestic issues. This, along with a trend supporting conservative Republican victories in Congress (in 1994) and the White House (in 2000), made the pursuit of the third wave agenda on the national level more challenging for feminist leaders.[40] However, many of those domestic policy issues reemerged on the national agenda—including health care, job creation, an increase to the minimum wage, and environmental issues—after the Democratic Party won control of both houses of Congress in 2006 and President Barack Obama's election in 2008.

Conservative Women Activists
Concurrent with the third wave has been the growing political power of conservative women's groups and activists opposed to the feminist agenda. As early as the 1970s, conservative Christian women "created a vibrant and lasting political movement" by channeling their energy and emotions from rebelling against feminism.[41] With a conservative Republican majority in Congress from 1995 to 2007 and a conservative Republican president in the White House from 2001 to 2009, groups such as Concerned Women for America and the Independent Women's Forum became key players in policy debates by "articulating alternative bases for understanding women's political interests." While both groups promote various conservative viewpoints and policies, Concerned Women for America maintains its Christian-based philosophy to promote social conservative causes,

while the Independent Women's Forum (which was first formed in 1992 by women who had organized in 1991 to support the Supreme Court nomination of Clarence Thomas) consists of professional women with an economic conservative viewpoint toward public policies. According to political scientist Ronnee Schreiber, these two groups now play a significant role in the public dialogue and offer a legitimate competing view of women's issues: "As women's political power has increased, so too has a contest among national organizations fighting to represent women's interests in the policymaking process. Although feminists have long dominated the political landscape in terms of numbers and visibility, they are increasingly being challenged by other national organizations—those that are antifeminist and also claim to represent women's interests. These conservative women's groups present a substantial threat to the feminist movement."[42]

#FEMINISM: A FOURTH WAVE?

As the women's rights movement entered the twenty-first century, priorities again shifted and talk began about whether a "fourth wave" had begun. The mind-set developed during the 1990s among third wave feminists merged into more activist practices, focusing "less on generational conflict and more on how to address the political and social inequalities that remained." As millennials began to come of age (those following generation X, born after 1982), and after 9/11, the movement "became even more global, connecting feminists around the world with the Internet technologies that emerged during this period, like blogs and social networks." Among the many issues that remain part of the contemporary women's rights movement, violence against women, sexuality, media representation, work–life balance, and growing economic disparities still dominate as priorities.[43] However, some generational conflict remains among older and younger feminists, particularly over the use of the "wave" terminology and whether it is too simplistic or even useful. As Ednie Kaeh Garrison argues, "waves" should not be bound by particular age cohorts, and the third wave does not belong only to those from generation X: "I believe the question of who counts as the third wave is much more complicated and layered; there are important differences between historical specificity and generational specificity. . . . When we automatically assume 'third' refers to a specific generation, we actually erase the significant presence and contributions of many overlapping and multiple cohorts who count as feminists, and more particularly, of those who can count as third wave feminists."[44]

This generational debate has also garnered media attention, often portrayed as a "catfight" as opposed to a "political movement," which often frames the women's rights movement as feminists fighting with each other as opposed to moving forward on important issues.[45] Baumgardner states that the fourth wave began in 2008 and that "it exists because it says it exists." The millennial view of the women's rights movement has been shaped by the backlash against feminism during the 1980s, Take Our Daughters to Work Day initiatives, and emerging technologies and social media. The fourth wave can be seen in the many blogs,

Twitter campaigns, and online sites such as Feministing and Jezebel. Baumgardner also argues that the fourth wave is a real social and political movement, like those that came before it: "I see the cultural transformation that my generation harvested from the Second Wave's ideas and revolution was the social movement of our day. Likewise, the Fourth Wave's deployment of social media has once again transformed politics and feminism. . . . I believe the Fourth Wave matters, because I remember how sure I was that my generation mattered."[46]

Evidence exists that feminism has entered a new era, marked by a measurable increase in online activism around issues affecting women. Social commentators have dubbed the resurgence of feminist activism that started in the early 2010s the fourth wave of feminism (which is technically the third wave of heightened feminist activity in the United States), or #Feminism. Blogs such as Feministing, Ms. Blog, Racialicious, and Jezebel have given feminists a prominent voice in national conversations. Also, the invention of popular social media platforms starting in the mid-2000s (Facebook in 2004, Twitter in 2006, Tumblr in 2007, and Instagram in 2010) allows feminist ideas to spread more quickly with a wider reach than in the past. Fourth wave activism is more effective than previous activism. Feminists use online petitions, boycotts, and hashtag campaigns to put pressure on corporations, other societal institutions, and individuals to improve media inclusion, media representations, and the treatment of women, LGBTQ individuals, people of color, and others. Feminists can now "swarm" a company online that has done something overtly sexist to demand change. For example, Chip Wilson, the founder of Lululemon, resigned from the company just weeks after stating that "some women's bodies just don't actually work" for wearing the company's yoga pants. His resignation was inspired by three different online petitions calling for women to boycott the high-end athletic apparel brand and a media shaming campaign using the hashtag campaign #TooFatForYogaPants. This call-out culture for corporations forces businesses to be less sexist, racist, etc., in marketing campaigns and public statements. Feminists today use consumer activism at higher rates and with more effectiveness than past activists.

CONCLUSION

The current debate about a fourth wave, or even the "wave" terminology, highlights the fact that there is no simple or single description of the women's rights movement, nor is there one simple definition of the word "feminism" (we discuss the latter in detail in Chapter 3). First used by American women fighting for suffrage at the turn of the twentieth century, the term feminism was more broadly used by the women's rights movement in the 1970s in an attempt to bridge the many ideological and policy issues that divided women activists at the time. According to historian Sara M. Evans, the deep differences among feminists cause some to "regularly challenge others' credentials as feminists. . . . yet the energy of the storm that drives them all comes from their shared challenge to deeply rooted inequalities based on gender."[47] To borrow a broad definition of feminism from political scientist Barbara Arneil, it is the

> recognition that, virtually across time and place, men and women are unequal in the power they have, either in society or over their own lives, and the corollary belief that men and women should be equal; the belief that knowledge has been written about, by and for men and the corollary belief that all schools of knowledge must be re-examined and understood to reveal the extent to which they ignore or distort gender.[48]

The study of both the women's rights movement and feminism also allows for a better understanding of various types of power and how it influences women's lives, as most women's rights advocates agree that men's power and women's lack of power cause the differences between what men and women experience in society. Yet, feminists "disagree on the extent, causes, and impact of these differences on the means and strategies for changing and improving the situation of women."[49]

The story of the women's rights movement in the United States is a diverse and complex history of how women have banded together and also clashed with each other in an attempt to define their preferred place in American society. The public versus private sphere that served to define a woman's role has long served as the catalyst for numerous generations of women fighting for political and legal equality. No one movement, cause, or theory can encapsulate the needs of all women, yet significant progress has been made since the nineteenth century in bringing about political and legal reforms with regard to women's equality. Prominent women leaders such as Elizabeth Cady Stanton, Susan B. Anthony, Carrie Chapman Catt, Betty Friedan, Gloria Steinem, Rebecca Walker, and countless others dedicated much of their lives to fighting for the right for women to enter the public realm at various points in our nation's history. While many barriers for women entering public life have been torn down, many challenges lie ahead for women political leaders today. As we will discuss in the following chapters, women in today's political environment still face many obstacles in terms of entering the political arena, yet the legacy of the modern women's rights movement has provided many more opportunities for women in the public sphere today than for any prior generation.

CHAPTER SUMMARY

- Throughout American history, men controlled the public sphere, while women were relegated to the household and childrearing chores in the private/domestic sphere.
- Although few in number, some outspoken women began to demand equality as citizens as early as the Revolutionary War. However, the rights of women were not addressed in the U.S. Constitution in 1789 or the Bill of Rights in 1791.
- The formal women's rights movement began in 1848 at the Seneca Falls Convention, convened by Lucretia Mott and Elizabeth Cady Stanton, who demanded equality for women through a "Declaration of Sentiments and Resolutions."

- Suffrage emerged as the major issue of the first wave of the women's rights movement. Early leaders of the suffrage movement had gained leadership and organizational skills as activists in the abolitionist movement.
- The Nineteenth Amendment giving women the right to vote was first introduced in Congress in 1878 and was presented to 40 consecutive sessions of Congress before it finally passed as a proposed amendment in 1919. Three-fourths of the necessary states ratified the amendment by 1920.
- In the immediate postsuffrage era, several women's rights activists sought to capitalize on the momentum and began to lobby Congress for an equal rights amendment to the Constitution. First introduced in 1923, the ERA was not sent to the states until 1972, and it failed to reach the needed three-fourths of state ratification before the amendment's 1982 deadline.
- The second wave of the women's rights movement began in the 1960s, as activists sought to do away with the "cult of domesticity" that had dominated the lives of American women. Publication of Betty Friedan's book, *The Feminine Mystique*, was a major event for the women's rights movement in the early 1960s.
- In 1966, Friedan cofounded the National Organization for Women, a civil rights group dedicated to achieving equality for women in American society.
- Congress passed the Equal Pay Act in 1963, as well as Title IX of the Educational Amendments Act of 1972, which required equal opportunity for women in all aspects of education including admissions, financial aid, and funding for women's athletic programs.
- In 1973, the Supreme Court, in *Roe v. Wade*, struck down state laws banning abortion in the first three months of pregnancy.
- Groups opposed to women's equality emerged during the early 1970s. The victory for pro-choice feminists in legalizing abortion galvanized the pro-life movement at the national level. Anti-ERA groups such as the Eagle Forum, led by Phyllis Schlafly, also gained national prominence.
- By the 1970s, divisions emerged within the women's rights movement, as more moderate feminists seeking legal equality clashed with more radical feminists who wanted more dramatic change for women within all aspects of society.
- The third wave began in the early 1990s with a renewed public interest in women's issues and an increase in the number of women running for public office. The third wave (known to some as postfeminism) continued to challenge and expand common definitions of gender and sexuality and embraced a more global, multicultural view of feminism and women's rights.
- The third wave also became synonymous with the term stealth feminist due to the media's backlash of painting the women's rights movement as a negative association.
- Politically, the third wave of the women's rights movement focused on candidate recruitment, campaign resources, democratic inclusion of women, more public roles for women, and finding a new voice for feminism through grass-roots political activism.

- Concurrent with the third wave has also been the growing political power of conservative women's groups and activists opposed to the feminist agenda.
- Debate continues about whether a fourth wave of the women's rights movement exists. Violence against women, sexuality, media representation, work–life balance, and growing economic disparities dominate the contemporary women's rights movement.

STUDY/DISCUSSION QUESTIONS

- Why was the first wave of the women's rights movement so closely tied to both the temperance and abolitionist movements during the nineteenth century?
- Discuss the impact that Elizabeth Cady Stanton and Susan B. Anthony's leadership had on the early women's rights movement.
- Why did it take nearly 75 years after the Seneca Falls Convention for women to earn the right to vote in the United States?
- What is meant by the public/private sphere split, and why did feminists view this as oppressive to women?
- How does the third wave differ from the second wave of the women's rights movement?
- Have millennials created a fourth wave of the women's rights movement?

CASE STUDIES

1. **Which wave would you ride?**
   Different waves of the feminist movement have fought different battles and achieved different outcomes. During the first wave of the women's rights movement, activists battled for the right to vote and won. Feminist activists during the second wave opened educational and economic doors for women through the passage of public policy and court cases and established women's place in educational institutions, the workplace, and the halls of government. Third wave feminists pushed for greater inclusion in the women's rights movement and turned their focus to issues beyond gender equality. Fourth wave feminists are using social media to make feminist ideas and ideals mainstream. If you had a time machine, which wave would you prefer to be a part of and why? Which feminist policies or tactics appeal to you the most?

2. **Is conflict in the women's rights movement a good thing?**
   As noted throughout this chapter, conflict has existed throughout the different waves of the feminist movement. During the first wave, older feminists initially decried the more forceful and sometimes violent tactics of younger feminists seeking to gain the vote for women. The second wave was rife with disagreement between "mainstream" and more radical feminists. The third wave was a critical response to the second wave that pitted younger feminists against those who fought for the rights they were able to take for granted.

There is currently a feminist debate around whether we are experiencing a fourth wave. In what ways is this conflict detrimental to the advancement of gender justice, and in what ways does this conflict benefit the struggle?

3. **Is the wave metaphor divisive?**
Some scholars argue that using the wave metaphor to describe feminist activism is inaccurate since feminist activity has been a constant in U.S. political life since the mid-nineteenth century. Others argue that the wave metaphor is unnecessarily divisive, while others argue that it is misleading because it presents feminist activism as being more united in ideology than it is. The wave metaphor was first introduced during the second wave to remind people that women had struggled for gender justice before, that activism in the 1960s and 1970s was simply an extension of a long tradition of activism. Do you think the wave metaphor has outlived its usefulness in describing the struggle for gender justice in the United States? Why or why not?

RESOURCES

- The **National Women's History Project** is dedicated to promoting knowledge about the many contributions by women throughout U.S. history.
http://www.nwhp.org
- The **National Susan B. Anthony Museum & House** collects artifacts and research materials directly related to Anthony's lifelong dedication to women's suffrage and equality.
http://www.susanbanthonyhouse.org
- The **Feminist Majority Foundation** works to promote public policies focused on women's equality, reproductive health, and nonviolence.
http://www.feminist.org
- The **ERA Coalition** is dedicated to amending the U.S. Constitution to include an equal rights amendment.
http://www.eracoalition.org
- Founded in 1966, the **National Organization for Women** is the largest interest group focusing on feminism and women's issues in the United States.
http://www.now.org
- Founded in 1972, the **Eagle Forum** is a conservative, pro-family, and antifeminist interest group.
http://www.eagleforum.org
- **Concerned Women for America** is a conservative Christian activist group focusing on pro-family issues.
http://www.cwfa.org
- **Independent Women's Forum** is an interest group whose mission is to increase "the number of women who value free markets and personal liberty."
http://www.iwf.org

CHAPTER 3

The Many Faces of Feminism

Feminism is a belief in the social, political, and economic equality of the sexes. In the fall of 2012, a reporter asked pop superstar Taylor Swift whether she considered herself a feminist, and she replied, "I don't really think about things as guys versus girls. I never have. I was raised by parents who brought me up to think if you work as hard as guys in life, you can go far." Two years later, Swift told another reporter that she was now a feminist. Swift explained her change of heart:

> As a teenager, I didn't understand that saying you're a feminist is just saying that you hope women and men will have equal rights and equal opportunities. What it seemed to me, the way it was phrased in culture, society, was that you hate men. And now, I think a lot of girls have had a feminist awakening because they understand what the word means. For so long it's been made to seem like something where you'd picket against the opposite sex, whereas it's not about that at all.

In the summer of 2015, Taylor Swift again faced an educational moment about feminism when she responded to hip-hop giant Nicki Minaj via social media in

NICKI MINAJ ✅
@NICKIMINAJ   2h

If your video celebrates women with very slim bodies, you will be nominated for vid of the year 😊😊😊😊😊😊😊😊😊😊😊😊

Taylor Swift ✅
@taylorswift13   🐦 Follow

@NICKIMINAJ I've done nothing but love & support you. It's unlike you to pit women against each other. Maybe one of the men took your slot..

6:13 PM - 21 Jul 2015

↩   ↻ 22,935   ★ 26,921

a way that many critics saw as insensitive to the issues of women of color. Minaj tweeted about her frustration with being overlooked for some of the top music video awards because she does not fit the thin standard of beauty in the pop music industry. Swift assumed the tweet was directed at her and responded in a way that dismissed Minaj's experience of both racism and sexism in the music industry.

Popular feminist blogs called out Swift for engaging in "white feminism" by not acknowledging Minaj's experiences of bias in the industry. They criticized Swift for making the issue solely about sexism with the comment that "maybe one of the men took your slot" instead of recognizing that race may have also influenced who was nominated for the top awards. Minaj replied to Swift with a clarification and request that Swift speak out about the biases women of color face in the industry: "Didn't say a word about u. I love u just as much. But u should speak on this." Social media lit up with the controversy as tens of thousands of people weighed in on the exchange. Swift issued an apology to Minaj two days later, and Minaj graciously accepted the apology and asked the world to move on.

Taylor Swift @taylorswift13   Following

I thought I was being called out. I missed the point, I misunderstood, then misspoke. I'm sorry, Nicki. @NICKIMINAJ

RETWEETS 49,706   FAVORITES 94,124

6:32 PM - 23 Jul 2015

Taylor Swift's feminist experiences tell us a lot about the contemporary state of feminism in the United States. Swift's evolution from rejecting the feminist label to accepting it is typical. Many people believe the myth that feminism equals "man hating," so many reject the label "feminist," even if they are in favor of gender equality. The disconnect between what feminism is and what many people believe feminism to be has evolved during the past four decades as feminism has challenged traditional family and social arrangements. We explore feminist myths and their origins in this chapter to better understand how beliefs about feminism may be shaped by larger social forces. Swift's "educational moment" with Minaj shows the importance of intersectional feminism today. This type of feminism acknowledges that in addition to gender, women's experiences also vary by race, class, and other factors. Swift's feminist stumble is part of a decades-long struggle to move feminism beyond the experiences of just white, middle-class women.

The rapid online response to Swift's comments about Minaj demonstrates the new energy and power of the feminist blogosphere, a collection of popular blogs that raise awareness of women's issues and call out sexism. Some scholars consider the rapid rise in online feminist activism so powerful that it constitutes a new wave of feminism (as discussed in Chapter 2). The goal of this chapter is to introduce the many faces of feminism. The ten primary types of feminism are described in the first section: liberal, radical, Marxist, socialist, psychoanalytic, eco-, postmodern, transnational, intersectional, and third wave. Most of these types of feminism were popularized during the second wave of the feminist movement in the 1960s and 1970s, but some (postmodern and third wave) emerged more recently in response to second wave feminisms. We then discuss the backlash against feminism from religious leaders, politicians, postfeminists, and the media that began in the 1970s and intensified in the 1980s. Next, we analyze negative stereotypes and myths about feminism. Finally, we examine the question of whether men can be feminists. This has long been debated by scholars, but today, men's participation in feminism is generally accepted and even encouraged.

TYPES OF FEMINISM

Feminism is not a singular way of thinking. Feminists tend to agree on the goal of achieving social, political, and economic equality of the sexes. But this is where the agreement ends. Different types of feminists have different ideas about the root causes of gender inequality, how other systems of hierarchy (e.g., class and race) influence gender oppression, whether sex and gender are biological or socially constructed, and the best ways to achieve gender equality. The ten types of feminism described overlap because they are not mutually exclusive. A single person may agree with multiple feminist approaches; that is, one may identify as a global feminist because of its focus on gender inequality around the world, but also favor the liberal feminist approach of using the law to achieve gender justice. It is also worth noting that this section provides only a general overview of the main branches of feminism. There are dozens of variations on each of the types of feminism examined here; this is simply an overview of the most basic elements of each feminist approach.

Liberal Feminism

The second wave of the feminist movement was initiated in the 1960s by liberal feminists who believe that female subordination is deeply rooted in social customs and laws. Liberal feminists consider the state the principal protector of individual rights, so they advocate for legal and policy reform to eradicate gender inequality. This branch of feminism is split between classic liberal feminists who believe that the state should ensure equality of *opportunity* through protecting civil rights and liberties (e.g., voting rights, freedom of speech) and egalitarian liberal feminists who believe that the state should ensure equality of *outcomes* through social programs (e.g., food stamps, equal pay).[1]

Early publications laid the groundwork for the liberal feminist idea that so-cietal customs and legal constraints are the biggest barriers to gender equality. British thinker Mary Wollstonecraft introduced liberal feminism in her book *A Vindication of the Rights of Woman*, published in 1792, in which she made the radical claim (for the time) that women have a right to be educated. Nearly a century later, John Stuart Mill's essay "The Subjection of Women," published in 1869, made a similar plea for a woman's right to be educated and her voice to be represented in political decision making. Another century after Mill's essay, Betty Friedan's book *The Feminine Mystique*, published in 1963, launched the second wave with its examination of women's unhappiness, "the problem that has no name."[2] As noted in Chapter 2, Friedan described a post–World War II campaign run by the federal government to convince women to return home from the factories to their roles as housewives and mothers to free up jobs for the men returning home from the war. Domestic life left many women dissatisfied, and Friedan proposed that women should get educated and join the paid work-force as a solution to their unhappiness.

Liberal feminists have passed many laws to address gender inequality. They lobbied for Title IX (1972) mandating equal pay for university employees, equi-table funding for women in sports, and a gender-equitable learning environment. Liberal feminists also campaigned against sexual harassment in the workplace and continue to press for laws against gender discrimination and sexual harass-ment in education and the workplace that disadvantage women today. Liberal feminists have been criticized by other feminists for focusing primarily on the concerns of middle-class, white women. For example, Friedan's *The Feminine Mystique* revolved around the experiences of white, middle-class women rather than that of black women and other women of color, most of whom already worked outside the home and did not have the economic "luxury" of being a housewife. Contemporary liberal feminists are more aware and inclusive in ad-vocating for the needs and rights of women of diverse races and class situations, but true inclusion of varied experiences is a constant struggle in any movement for social justice. Liberal feminists have also been criticized for judging women's progress based on male standards of competition, ambition, and achievement instead of questioning whether different standards of societal customs would make everyone happier.

Radical Feminism

Radical feminism also surfaced during the second wave of the feminist move-ment. Radical feminists believe that patriarchy is the oldest form of oppression and, as such, it serves as a template for relatively newer forms of oppression (e.g., racism and classism).[3] Patriarchy is a social system in which men are assumed to rightfully hold the primary positions of power in politics, society, and the family. While liberal feminists address women's oppression in unequal laws and liberties, radical feminists locate the root of gender oppression in deeper formal and informal patriarchal relations between the sexes. Radical feminists believe that because men have greater value than women in a patriarchal society, both men and women view men as the norm and women as "other," and this cannot be changed through laws.

Radical feminists go beyond liberal feminism by advocating for a reordering of society in which patriarchy is eliminated in both public and private spheres. The public sphere is the workplace and politics and the private sphere is the home. Liberal feminists focus their efforts on equality in the public sphere, while radical feminists focus on both the public and private life. Radical feminists popularized the second wave sentiment that "the personal is political." Many radical feminists came from the civil rights movement and brought a revolutionary perspective with them. One of the primary tools of radical feminist organizing in the 1960s was "consciousness-raising" groups that brought women of different race, class, and professional backgrounds together to discuss their shared experiences of gender oppression with the motto "sisterhood is powerful."

Radical feminism put sexual politics on the national agenda in the 1960s, including family planning and abortion, sexual violence, pornography, and prostitution. The most prominent voices in radical feminism during the second wave were scholar activists. In 1970, radical feminist Anne Koedt debunked "The Myth of the Vaginal Orgasm,"[4] and Kate Millet demonstrated how writings in literature, philosophy, and politics uphold patriarchy by masquerading it as "nature," science, and objectivity in *Sexual Politics*.[5] Professors Catharine MacKinnon and Andrea Dworkin wrote extensively about the violence, degradation, and deprioritization of women's sexual pleasure in pornography.[6]

Radical feminists were the first to propose that the sexual objectification of women in pop culture and porn diminishes women's power and pleasure. Sexual objectification is the act of reducing a person from a human being to an object that exists for one's sexual pleasure. Radical feminists argued that corporations were selling sexism under the guise of sexual liberation. For example, Playboy Enterprises took off as a result of the sexual revolution of the 1960s, and its founder, Hugh Hefner, opened Playboy Club franchises in major U.S. cities featuring women as "bunnies" wearing skimpy outfits to serve drinks to men. Radical feminists argued that these clubs reinforced the old notion that women's sexuality exists for men's pleasure, that this supposedly new and liberating sexuality reinforces the idea that women exist to serve men.

Beyond writing on the subject, radical feminists took radical action to challenge societal norms. For example, Dworkin and MacKinnon used their academic work to lobby for laws curbing pornography. They drafted the Minneapolis Anti-Pornography Ordinance, a law that allowed legal action to halt the sale of sexually explicit materials determined to promote the subordination of women through objectification. Similar ordinances were proposed in Indianapolis; Cambridge, Massachusetts; and Washington State. In 1968, radical feminists also gathered to protest the Miss America pageant by throwing their bras and heels into a garbage can in a public demonstration on the Atlantic City, New Jersey, boardwalk and unfurled a banner with the words "Women's Liberation."

Radical feminists staged countless other protests and public demonstrations, including a "burial of traditional womanhood" at the Arlington National Cemetery in Virginia.

Radical feminists faced stiff opposition from other feminists during the "sex wars" of the 1980s. The central disagreement was whether the new sexual permissiveness facilitated women's pleasure or degraded them. Radical feminists argued that images of female objectification in pornography, film, and advertising translated into real-life subordination and abuse of women's bodies: sexual harassment, rape, domestic violence, and prostitution. Robin Morgan summed up that argument with her quip that "pornography is the theory, and rape the practice."[7] On the other side of the debate, "pleasure" feminists argued that pornographic materials could have many different layers of meaning that women could use for their sexual exploration, and they argued that alternative sexualities, including those that involve bondage and discipline and sadomasochism, were pro-feminist. Pleasure feminists were highly critical of radical feminist proposals to use censorship on the grounds that it would restrict women's sexual pleasure.

This gulf between radical feminists and pleasure feminists reached a breaking point in 1982 at the Barnard Sexuality Conference themed "Pleasure and Danger." Trying to open space for a discussion of pleasure, conference planners had deliberately excluded "radical and revolutionary feminists" because they dominated feminist discourses on sexuality in the United States. Radical feminists responded by protesting their exclusion outside the conference. Protesters wore t-shirts with "For a Feminist Sexuality" on the front and "Against S/M" on the back, and they passed out leaflets promoting their position. The conference erupted in a verbal showdown that both reflected and furthered a chasm in the women's rights movement. Radical feminists ultimately lost the "sex wars" in the courts, the academy, and the media. All of their antiporn legislative efforts were eventually blocked by city officials or overturned by the courts. Meanwhile, in the university, radical feminist critiques fell off as postmodern feminist critiques emerged and third wave feminists embraced the idea of sexual objectification as empowering (discussed below). However, radical feminism is experiencing a resurgence in the 2010s as feminists across the globe are taking to the streets to protest prostitution and sexual violence in their respective countries.

Marxist Feminism

Marxist feminism was also popular during the second wave of the feminist movement, although it was more of an academic feminism than the activist branches of liberal and radical feminism. Marxist feminism locates the root cause of gender inequality in capitalism rather in than laws (liberal feminism) or patriarchy (radical feminism). Marxist feminists propose that gender inequality is the result of the economic, political, and social structures created by capitalism in which those who own the means of production exploit the labor of workers.[8] This branch of feminism draws from the writings of Karl Marx and Friedrich Engels, who trace men's dominance over women through the family to the control of private property by patriarchs and the passage of inheritance to male offspring.

Marxist feminists believe that capitalism shapes women's personal identities and labor in ways that ensure their subordination. People define themselves through their work, and the adage "a woman's work is never done" causes women to see themselves as obligated to constantly work in both the public and private spheres. Capitalism also encourages women to view housework and childrearing as a "labor of love" rather than a massive, hidden market that makes the paid labor force possible. Marxist feminists blame capitalism for splitting the public sphere, where men hold value as "insiders" in the economy, and the private sphere, where women are devalued as "outsiders." Marxist feminists believe the public/private split and its gender hierarchy are the template for women's broader subordination in society.

Marxist feminists advocate for a radical rethinking of the interdependence of the public and private spheres that reconsiders childrearing and household labor as valuable work, recognized as such through paid wages for housework. They also propose equal sharing of childrearing activities in the home so that this work is not seen as exclusively or predominantly "women's work." Marxist feminists also advocate for equal pay for men and women who are performing the same or similar work in the paid labor force. The ultimate goal of Marxist feminists is to replace capitalism with an economic system that recognizes and values all labor. Some scholars and activists have criticized Marxist feminism for focusing exclusively on the economic system as the cause of gender inequality in the United States. Socialist feminism was created by feminists who saw the benefits of Marxist feminist critiques, but concluded that this branch of feminism dismissed women's oppression as less important than the oppression of workers.

Socialist Feminism

Socialist feminism is a blend of radical feminism and Marxist feminism that arose during the second wave. While Marxist feminists believe that capitalism is the primary cause of women's second-class status in society and radical feminists believe that patriarchy is the root cause, socialist feminists blame both capitalism and patriarchy. Socialist feminists agree with Marxist feminists that capitalism divides the public and private spheres, but this theory comes up short in terms of explaining why men dominate the public sphere while women dominate the private sphere or why women are subordinate even in the sphere that they dominate.[9] Socialist feminists point out that Marxist feminism cannot explain these inconsistencies because it is gender blind. Combining capitalism and patriarchy, socialist feminists argue that women's financial dependence on men is the driving force of gender inequality in society.

The first socialist feminist organization, Radical Women, formed in 1967 in Seattle, Washington, is still active today. It emerged from a class taught by communist civil rights activist Gloria Martin at Seattle's Free University. The Chicago Women's Liberation Union published the first work on socialist feminism in

1972, entitled "Socialist Feminism: A Strategy for the Women's Movement." Socialist feminists work on a host of issues involving capitalism, sexism, racism, and other systems of hierarchy and oppression. They are just as likely to join a fight for racial discrimination in the workplace as a march for women's reproductive rights because they see these systems as interconnected. Socialist feminists were the first branch of feminism to formally prioritize the leadership of women of color in their ranks.

Socialist feminists locate gender oppression in both the public and private spheres, so their remedies address both the economic and cultural sources of women's second-class status. They agree with Marxist feminists that capitalism should be replaced with an economic system that acknowledges the work and value of all. They also call for gender equality in the home and workplace through unfettered reproductive rights, affirmative action, and other policies aimed at achieving gender equality. Women cannot achieve equality with men until they are no longer financially dependent on men.

Psychoanalytic Feminism
Psychoanalytic feminism materialized in the late 1970s in academic feminist circles. This branch of feminism proposes that women's oppression is rooted within deeply ingrained internal psychic gender dynamics that are developed in childhood and reinforced by societal norms. They propose that gender is not biological, but is instead socially constructed through psychosexual development influenced by social norms. Gender inequality, then, comes from early childhood experiences that lead men to see themselves as "masculine" and girls to see themselves as "feminine." Since society values masculinity more than femininity, girls and women come to see themselves as "other" to a male norm.

One branch of psychoanalytic feminists draws heavily from Sigmund Freud's stages of sexual development theories in the construction of masculinity and femininity. Freud, the founder of psychoanalysis, has been heavily criticized for his idea that girls suffer "penis envy" because it is based on the unquestioned assumption of male superiority, but Freudian psychoanalytic feminists find many of Freud's ideas to be revealing in explaining gender inequalities.[10] Another branch focuses on the power of language to construct these roles based on the work of Jacques Lacan. Lacanian psychoanalytic feminists believe that male dominance is created and reinforced through masculine/scientific language that shapes how girls and boys view gender roles and power.[11] The way we talk about masculinity over femininity from one generation to the next causes boys and girls to value masculinity more.

For psychoanalytic feminists, addressing gender inequality means addressing women's psychic internalization of their other, inferior status to men. This means altering family structures and early childhood experience that reinforce masculinity and femininity. For example, gendered roles in the household create boys who are prepared for work in the public sphere but are emotionally stunted and girls who have more of a capacity for intimacy but are less prepared for work in the public sphere. These gender norms could be addressed by coparenting in the household with both the mother and the father working outside the home, thus eradicating the implied hierarchy of men over women. Lacanian psychoanalytic feminists see language as the primary vehicle for reinforcing masculinity and femininity, so they propose replacing masculine/scientific language with the more feminine/subjective experience of the body to challenge gender inequalities.

Freudian psychoanalytic feminism has been criticized for its biological essentialism, that is, its assumption that gender inequality is ultimately based on biological differences. Both Freudian and Lacanian branches of feminism have been critiqued for their focus on male social development as the basis for social arrangements. The work of psychoanalysis feminists has also been challenged for the complexity of its language and ideas that are not accessible to lay readers. This latter critique means psychoanalytic feminism remains a mostly academic rather than an activist branch of feminism.

Eco-feminism

Eco-feminism became a popular form of both academic and activist feminism during the second wave of the women's rights movement. The term eco-feminism was originally coined by French writer Françoise d'Eaubonne in 1974 and popularized in the United States by women of color who drew connections among race, gender, class, and environmental exploitation and Mary Daly, the author of *Gyn/Ecology*.[12] This branch of feminism locates the root of gender inequality in both patriarchy and a human separation from nature that produces a culture where science and technology are used by men to exploit both nature and women. In the Western world, nature is considered inferior to culture in the same way that women are considered inferior to men because women are thought of as closer to nature as a result of their connection with birth and child care. For example, women's menstrual cycles are aligned with lunar cycles. According to eco-feminists, gender inequality is driven by the same ideas that cause humans to exploit the environment.

While radical and psychoanalytic feminists challenge the idea that gender differences are "natural" as opposed to socially constructed, some eco-feminists generally see women as inherently more nurturing because of their deeper connection to nature. Eco-feminists seek the liberation of women in a way that recognizes and values childbirth and caretaking while at the same time devalorizing male values of dominance and exploitation. Other eco-feminists argue that although women are more connected to nature, the connection is socially determined and men have just as much potential to establish such connections.

Eco-feminists call for people to reject the divide between "nature" and "culture" as a fundamental step toward addressing gender inequality. They see dualistic thinking that organizes the world in terms of dichotomies as one of the root causes of gender inequality, such as mind/body, reason/emotion, human/nature, and man/woman. For example, eco-feminists view the split between nature and culture as something that humans created rather than a naturally occurring split.

They challenge this dualistic thinking and call for new ways of framing the world that take into account that these dichotomies are complementary and interdependent. Eliminating the oppositional, binary approach to organizing the world is the first step in addressing cultural thinking that places men above nature and women.

Eco-feminists also believe the most effective ways to address gender inequality are to eliminate binary thinking, have humans reconnect with the natural world, and identify environmental degradation as inextricably entwined with gender oppression. Eco-feminists call for a radical reordering of the world centered on female values of caretaking over male values of competitiveness, individuality, and assertiveness. Some eco-feminists also call for "women-only" spaces where women can experience life free from patriarchal oppression. Eco-feminism has been criticized for reinforcing stereotypes about the nature of men and women and for essentialism in drawing connections between women and biology. Eco-feminism has also been challenged for being too theoretical and complex for lay readers to understand. This branch of feminism has also been questioned for its exclusion of men from women-only safe spaces.

Transnational Feminism

Transnational feminism emerged in the mid-1970s in response to the nearly exclusive focus of U.S. feminists on Western cultures that misrepresents and erases the experiences of women living in non-Western countries. The work of Chandra Talpade Mohanty first convinced scholars that understanding colonialism is crucial for identifying the origins of and remedies for gender inequality.[13] Colonialism is when one country takes over another country and its people. Transnational feminists call particular attention to the long history of British, French, Spanish, and U.S. colonialism and how it has shaped and continues to shape the experiences of women in postcolonial countries.

Transnational feminists attribute gender inequalities in the non-Western world to racism and the long-lasting economic and cultural effects of colonialism. Colonialism involved mostly white empires violently acquiring countries mostly populated by people of color. Colonization often led to a loss of language and cultural heritage and always involved the exploitation and mistreatment of the colonized people. According to transnational feminists, true understanding of gender inequality must take into account the ways in which the legacy of Western colonialism has shaped the cultures within formerly colonized countries. Transnational feminists emphasize the role played by nation-specific sociopolitical environments, race, sexuality, colonialism, and global economic exploitation of less developed countries by the Western world.

Transnational feminists are critical of mainstream forms of U.S. feminism because they are inherently aligned with colonialism and racism by virtue of their location and tradition of ignoring the experiences of women in less developed countries. Transnational feminists propose that people work together worldwide to address gender oppression, but reject the idea of global sisterhood in favor of building more equitable connections with women across borders and contexts.

According to transnational feminists, the best way to address gender inequality is to deal with it on a national or subnational level in ways that take intersectional issues into account. Gender inequalities are thus best addressed by incorporating the ideas of indigenous feminist movements with Western feminism.

PROFILE IN POWER

Malala Yousafzai

Malala Yousafzai is the youngest person to win the Nobel Peace Prize, and her extraordinary activism on behalf of girls in Pakistan has grown into an international movement. Born on June 12, 1997, Yousafzai was only 11 years old when the Taliban banned girls from attending school in her town. In response, Yousafzai wrote a blog about her ordeal living under Taliban rule, and she was featured

SOURCE: Southbank Centre

in a documentary about her life under the Taliban occupation in her region. She wrote under a pseudonym because her family was afraid that her school would be attacked and she would be harmed by the Taliban.

The Taliban responded by boarding Yousafzai's school bus on the afternoon of October 12, 2012, asking for her name, and then firing three gunshots at her. One bullet pierced her forehead, but she lived and recovered after months of rehabilitation. This attempted assassination sparked an international outpouring of support for the young activist. Protests were held over shootings in several Pakistani cities, and Yousafzai became a household name through international press coverage. Madonna dedicated her song *Human Nature* to Yousafzai the day after she was shot, and Angelina Jolie donated $200,000 to help the Malala Fund advance girl's educational opportunities. In the wake of the shooting, the United Nations launched a petition in Yousafzai's name calling for all children to have the opportunity to receive an education. More than two million people signed the petition, and it helped pass Pakistan's first Right to Education Bill.

Yousafzai was featured as one of *Time Magazine*'s "Top 100 Influential People in the World" from 2013 to 2015 and is also the winner of Pakistan's first National Youth Peace Prize. Yousafzai is the focus of the 2015 documentary *He Named Me Malala* (after Malalai, a Pakistani heroine). Although she was engaging in feminist activism, Yousafzai did not call herself a feminist until after she heard Emma Watson's speech before the United Nations in 2015 that launched the #HeForShe campaign. She and her father cofounded the Malala Fund, which is dedicated to enabling girls to complete a quality education without having to worry about their safety. Yousafzai celebrated her eighteenth birthday cutting the ribbon for the Malala Yousafzai All-Girls School near the Syrian border.

Intersectional Feminism

Like transnational feminism, intersectional feminism also appeared in the 1970s in response to the second wave's narrow focus. Driven by black feminist thought and Chicana feminism, intersectional feminists criticized the movement's emphasis on the experiences of white, middle-class women. As mentioned earlier, Friedan's *The Feminine Mystique* revolved around the experiences of white, middle-class women rather than that of black women and other women of color. Intersectionality is the idea that race, class, gender, ability, and sexuality all work together to define women's experiences of oppression. Intersectional feminists believe that to truly understand and address gender inequality, one must account for the wide variation in experiences of gender oppression based on intersecting identities.

Audre Lorde, Gloria Anzaldúa, Cherríe Moraga, and Barbara Smith were prominent intersectional feminists during the second wave of the women's rights movement. As a self-described black, lesbian, mother, poet warrior, and feminist, Lorde called for feminism to address the many ways in which different women face oppression through poetry and prose.[14] Anzaldúa, a Chicana, feminist, and queer theorist, focused on the intersectional experience of marginalization growing up on the Mexico–Texas border. Moraga was one of the first prominent Chicana/lesbian writers. In her work, Moraga made connections between the way she was treated for her sexuality and her race and her mother's experiences as a poor Latina.[15] Barbara Smith, a black, lesbian, socialist feminist, played a key role in building black feminism in the United States. After experiencing the sexism of organizing in the civil rights movement, she turned to feminist activism to address the intersectional experiences of racism and sexism for women of color.

In 1981, Anzaldúa and Moraga edited *This Bridge Called My Back: Writings by Radical Women of Color*, a now-classic book that was widely received at the time because it brought so many voices of feminists of color together in one place.[16] It had considerable influence in academic scholarship because it linked race, class, and gender and had great influence in real-world activism because it called existing feminist politics and practices into question. In 1982, Smith published the *Combahee River Collective Statement*, a powerful manifesto emphasizing class consciousness, sexuality, and race as integral to understanding and combating gender inequality.[17] The Combahee River Collective was active for nearly a decade, fighting against racism in the women's rights movement, stereotypes of black women in popular culture, sexual violence, prison reform, and violence against women. In 1989, nearly two decades after the first intersectional critiques, legal scholar Kimberlé Crenshaw coined the term "intersectionality" that is widely used in research and activism today.[18]

Intersectional feminists believe that the best way to address remedies for gender oppression is to recognize that different forms of oppression work together, and to tackle one, they must all be addressed. For example, feminists who push for pay equality for men and women would recognize that although white women make an average of 78 cents for every dollar a white man makes, African American women make 64 cents, while Latinas make 54 cents.[19] For intersectional feminists, the push for gender justice can only be effective if different forms of oppression that intersect with sexism are also addressed.

Womanism is a sophisticated response to intersectional feminism that was coined by poet and activist Alice Walker in 1983. Womanism is a feminist practice that celebrates black women's talents and contributions in ways that uphold African American community and traditions. Similar to eco-feminists, womanists believe that women and men have naturally inherent differences and that these differences should be recognized and respected. One key component of womanism is the belief that other oppressive forces, such as racism, take precedence over gender oppression, so feminist concerns are seen as integral but secondary to racial injustice. Womanism is a way to address gender oppression without directly critiquing black men, and the term womanism sets women of color apart from white women who are associated with the term feminism.

Intersectional critiques have been a prominent part of feminism since the second wave, but in the 2010s, intersectionality became part of public consciousness with two prominent hashtag campaigns. In the fall of 2013, the hashtag #SolidarityIsForWhiteWomen went viral on social media sites after black feminist Sydette Harry called out self-described male feminist Hugo Schwyzer on social media for mistreating women of color who criticized him online. Schwyzer responded with a social media "meltdown," which entailed posting more than 100 tweets in a single hour admitting his mistreatment of women of color and claiming to be a feminist fraud. He apologized for his behavior toward women of color in one tweet.

After Schwyzer's Twitter statements, Harry and others then called out prominent white feminists for providing Schwyzer a platform and for not criticizing him when feminists of color reported issues with his behavior five years earlier, in 2008. In response, thousands of people took to Twitter and other social media sites with #SolidarityIsForWhiteWomen to criticize how mainstream feminism continues to exclude the concerns of women of color. For example, hashtag creator Mikki Kendall pointed out that mainstream feminists often treat women of color as teaching tools or resources for white women.

Intersectionality was again part of a national conversation in 2015 when the hashtag #WhiteFeminism trended on social media after actor Patricia Arquette made an Oscar speech about the gender pay gap. During her speech, Arquette stated, "It's our time to have wage equality once and for all." Backstage, when asked to elaborate on her speech, Arquette stated, "It's time for all the women in America and all the men that love women, and all the gay people, and all the people of color that we've all fought for to fight for us now." This comment implies that the "women" Arquette is concerned about are heterosexual (loved by men) and white. She also suggests that white women have been fighting for the rights of gays and people of color, but to this point, gays and people of color have not joined the fight for women. In essence, Arquette erased the efforts of women of color and lesbians in the fight for gender justice and focused on white women in her call for wage equality. Arquette later said that she should have chosen her words more carefully. Her comments inspired a national conversation about the importance of an intersectional approach to feminism.

Postmodern Feminism

Postmodern feminism is the first of the feminisms that appeared after the decline of the second wave. This form of feminism is mostly an academic rather than an activist feminism crafted in response to the leading feminisms of the second wave. Postmodern feminists believe that language, whether in written, spoken, or symbolic form, shapes the way we perceive and experience the physical world. Postmodern feminism is distinct from other branches of feminism in that there is no absolute definition of "gender." Postmodern feminists argue that gender is not biological but instead is a category that we construct through language that simplifies the world in ways that uphold existing gender inequalities.

The roots of postmodern feminism can be seen in the work of Simone de Beauvoir, who posed the question of why women are seen as the "other" to the male norm in society. French feminists propelled postmodern work in the 1980s, and Judith Butler's 1990 book *Gender Trouble* popularized it in U.S. feminist circles.[20] Butler challenged the distinction drawn by previous feminists between sex (biological) and gender (socially constructed), arguing instead that both sex and gender are socially constructed. Butler argues that sex and sexual "difference" are constructed through language (how we label and talk about difference) and performance (everyday actions that reinforce the concept of sex differences) rather than biological fact. Postmodern theorists challenge the conflation of sex and gender and reject the idea that "men" and "women" are categories that simply exist in nature (essentialism). They also challenge the view of gender as fixed, binary, and determined at birth, rather than a fluid, mobile construct that allows for multiple gender expressions.

The abstract concepts of postmodern feminism may be difficult for some to grasp, but they become clearer through real-world application. For example, Butler points out that when doctors are confronted with a newborn baby with ambiguous genitalia, they often perform surgeries to make the body conform to "female" instead of recognizing that many human bodies do not fit neatly into two sex categories. Instead of pigeonholing infants into the category of male or female, postmodern thinking proposes that we allow the world to be as complex and complicated as it is. Postmodern feminists call for a radical rethinking of how our perceptions and experiences of the physical world are determined by how we describe the world, which is invariably an inaccurate and simplified version given its complexity.

Postmodern feminists see no single basis for women's subordination, so there is no single answer for addressing gender injustice and inequality. They propose resisting and reshaping the language that constructs the reality of gender inequality and seeing language as a political struggle that is always open to reinterpretation. For example, the rising profile of transgender people in popular culture challenges the fixity of the sex/gender binaries. Public conversation about Caitlyn Jenner and Laverne Cox breaks down binary thinking about gender and reveals that gender and sex are not the same. Instead of being natural categories, they are open to change and reinterpretation. However, postmodern feminists have been criticized for using language that is hard for laypeople to decipher and use in the everyday struggle for gender justice. Additionally, some critics have expressed concern that postmodern feminism discourages political action because it deconstructs gender to the point that it becomes impossible to advance political claims based on categories. In other words, it is difficult to press for policies that improve gender equality if gender is perceived as a real category on which political claims can be made.

Third Wave Feminism

Unlike the first and second waves of feminism, the label "third wave feminism" refers not to a heightened level of feminist activity, but to a relatively quieter era with a purposefully less extreme approach to gender justice than the second wave. Rebecca Walker, the daughter of Pulitzer Prize–winning author Alice Walker, first used the term "third wave" in a 1992 essay, and it was quickly adopted as *the* mainstream feminism in the United States. This branch of feminism is also unlike previous branches in that it does not advance a theory about the causes and remedies of gender justice.[21] It began as a push against what some saw as rigid expectations placed on women by second wave feminisms and quickly formed to be a highly individualistic approach to gender justice with an emphasis on "girl culture" and intersectionality.

Third wave feminism is distinct from second wave feminism in its focus on individual choice. This branch of feminism rejects the idea of false consciousness, a theory that people are manipulated by larger systems like capitalism and patriarchy in ways that harm them. An example of false consciousness for radical feminists would be when a woman undergoes plastic surgery because it makes her feel better about her body, but is actually upholding sexist beauty standards that made her feel bad about her body in the first place. Third wave feminists argue that women do not experience false consciousness and that suggesting that women are manipulated by larger systems of power is insulting to women. This emphasis on individual choice rather than structural causes of gender inequality is a fundamental characteristic of third wave feminism. If the motto of the second wave was "the personal is political," the unofficial motto of third wave feminism is "the personal and the political are whatever I decide is personal or political for me."

The intersectional feminism of the second wave in the 1970s became a core part of third wave feminism in the 1990s. This branch of feminism considers race, social class, and transgender issues core components of the struggle for gender justice. Third wave feminists have also incorporated postcolonial, transnational feminism into their work. They reject the idea that there is a universal experience for women and instead recognize the many differences that constitute the category "woman." Third wave feminists focus on concerns in the United States as well as the region- and culture-specific struggles of women in other countries.

Third wave feminism is also distinct from other types of feminism in its assertion that women can be empowered through sexual objectification. Contrary to radical feminist critiques of sexual objectification as harmful and disempowering for women, prominent third wavers Jennifer Baumgardner and Amy Richards write that "objectification is no longer our biggest problem" because women have reclaimed their sexuality.[22] They present sexy celebrities, such as Madonna, as evidence that women are now defining sexuality on their own terms. The influence of third wave feminism can be seen in young people today. Americans who came of age in the 2000s with a media influenced by third wave thinking are less critical of sexual objectification than are generations born earlier.

Third wave feminists are also distinct in the value they place on fashion and material luxuries as part of the girl culture experience. They disagree with many branches of second wave feminism that women should reject the "trappings" of femininity promoted by advertisers. *Bust*, a flagship third wave magazine, sums it up well that the third wave is about celebrating girl culture—"that shared set of female experiences that include Barbies and blowjobs, sexism and shoplifting,

Vogue and vaginas." Referred to as "lipstick" feminism or "girlie" feminism, third wave feminists celebrate the fashion, make-up, high heels, and other consumer displays of femininity that drew criticism from many second wave feminists.

Not all third wave feminists agree with the idea that women can be empowered through an emphasis on consuming products. For example, the Riot Grrrls, a hardcore punk feminist movement, was a collection of bands in the 1990s that addressed feminist issues, including sexual violence, domestic abuse, and racism. Musical artist Beth Ditto writes that the Riot Grrrls were "a movement formed by a handful of girls who felt empowered, who were angry, hilarious, and extreme through and for each other. Built on the floors of strangers' living rooms, tops of Xerox machines, snail mail, word of mouth and mixtapes, riot grrrl reinvented punk."[23] Bikini Kill, led by front person Kathleen Hanna, pioneered the Riot Grrrl movement with hard-hitting feminist lyrics. Beyond the music, Riot Grrrl bands also organized chapters with consciousness-raising groups and created do-it-yourself magazines and art. Bikini Kill published the *Riot Grrrl Manifesto* in 1991, calling for a greater inclusion of women in the creation of popular culture and a rejection of racism, classism, homophobia, sexism, and other interlocking systems of oppression. Although most third wave feminists celebrated girl culture through fashion and make-up, the Riot Grrrl movement actively rejected the consumerist lifestyle, which aligns them closely with the radical feminist perspective of the second wave.

Third wave feminists prefer to reclaim language rather than censor it. The multiple r's in Grrrl signify a reclaiming of the term "girl" that is often used to reduce grown women to children. The practice of reclaiming language is a third wave feminist project. Third wave feminists have attempted to reclaim "spinster," "bitch," "whore," "cunt," and "slut" with varying degrees of success. For example, Meredith Brook's 1997 hit song "Bitch" and Elizabeth Wurtzel's 1999 book *Bitch: In Praise of Difficult Women* were overt attempts to reclaim the term. In 2011, third wave feminists organized Slutwalks after a Toronto police officer publicly stated that "women should avoid dressing like sluts in order not to be victimized." The use of the term slut in Slutwalk is a tactic to reclaim a word that has historically been used to censure and shame women for being sexual.

Third wave feminism has been criticized for emphasizing individual choice over structural causes of gender inequality. Others are critical of third wave feminism for making collective action difficult because of its radically individual approach and lack of a coherent political agenda. This branch of feminism has also been criticized for allowing feminism to mean whatever the individual decides, to the point that the label feminist is no longer meaningful. Third wave feminism faced a challenge in 2008 when Republican vice presidential candidate Sarah Palin identified herself as a feminist. Palin's critics were quick to point out that she had opposed reproductive freedoms, cut funding to test rape kits, cut funding for teen mothers, and a host of other empirically anti-woman policies. Feminist Sarah Palin reveals the practical complexity of a feminism that relies on individuals to define its meaning.

Fourth Wave Feminism

Feminism in the fourth wave seems to be ideologically distinct from the ideas of the third wave and other forms of feminism. Online communication technology has produced a new type of feminism, one that combines intersectional feminism with postmodern critiques of the gender binary and transnational feminism in action. Unlike third wave feminism, this new feminism emphasizes structural critiques and collective activism. However, like the third wave, this new feminism remains highly individualistic and lacks a coherent set of theories about gender injustice. We label this new type #Feminism because it uses social media to raise awareness about the fluidity of categories, boundaries, and meaning in its quest for gender justice. This label is a way to distinguish the fourth wave, which describes eras of increased feminist activity, from *types* of feminism, of which there are many.

#Feminism is distinct from other forms of feminism in its everyday use of complex concepts previously used mostly by academics. For example, the concept of gender fluidity has also become commonplace. Gender fluidity refers to the idea that gender is a socially constructed performance that is malleable—a postmodern feminist idea. Gender fluidity is so commonly understood that in 2014, Facebook altered its gender status to include 58 different options, including "agender," "cisgender," "gender nonconforming," "genderqueer," "pangender," "transgender," and "two-spirit." Hashtag campaigns and viral articles have made intersectionality a part of everyday language in the United States. The term "intersectionality" was used ten times in major newspaper publications in the United States from 2000 to 2009 and 435 times from 2010 to 2015. Online communication technology has enabled fluid feminists to deradicalize previously "radical" feminist concepts like gender fluidity and intersectionality.

Online technologies have also changed the practice of mainstream feminism by putting transnational feminism into practice more easily. The global nature of the Internet means that feminists in the United States can now follow what is happening to women worldwide in real time. Fourth wave feminists have access to technology to realize the goal of transnational feminists to recognize the struggles of women across the globe and to network and organize in online solidarity. For example, in 2011, feminists from across the globe petitioned the government of South Africa to end the practice of "corrective" lesbian rapes where a man rapes a lesbian with the hopes of "turning" her into a heterosexual woman. The petition received nearly 200,000 signatures and received much media coverage. In response, the South African government launched a National Task Team to end the practice of "corrective" rape. Feminists in the United States continue to mostly focus on concerns that affect them directly, but online organizing tools have changed the face of feminism by opening the possibility of a truly transnational feminist focus.

One unique aspect of #Feminism is online call-out culture. Call-out culture refers to progressive activists "calling out" other people, leaders, corporations, and others for language and behavior that is sexist, racist, ableist, etc. Call-outs are a public action that impacts more than just the individuals involved, for example, when Nicki Minaj called out Taylor Swift and the feminist blogosphere called out Patricia Arquette for her narrow concern about white women's pay. Call-out culture continuously exposes underlying and explicit sexism and other "isms" in a way that holds people more accountable for their actions and words than in the past. Call-out culture also creates an environment built on social policing that silences some people who fear they will say the wrong thing in a world where the "proper" terms and concerns are constantly changing. Call-out culture alters the practice of mainstream feminism by holding those who identify as feminists to a higher standard of speech and conduct and possibility limiting debate on points of disagreement.

#Feminism is also marked by a confessional culture that has personalized the political in new and important ways. Confessional culture is one where people share private experiences with the world using (mostly social) media. Online technologies provide safe spaces where feminists can discuss issues that were rarely discussed in such wide and relatively anonymous forums, such as sexual violence and abortion. As discussed further in Chapter 12, after 30 years of activism around the issue, the new campus antirape movement finally succeeded in putting campus sexual violence on the national agenda in 2013 using online technology. Anonymous online forums allowed sexual assault survivors to anonymously share their stories, and the shocking details of survivor experiences brought survivors together and eventually led to President Barack Obama putting campus sexual violence on the national policy agenda. Confessional culture has changed mainstream feminism by providing an outlet for sharing common experiences of gender injustice, which serve as the basis for collective understanding and action.

THE BACKLASH AGAINST FEMINISM

In 1991, author Susan Faludi published the book *Backlash: The Undeclared War against American Women* that described efforts to discredit the women's rights movement and feminism. A backlash is a negative reaction to movements for social change. Every social movement that effectively challenges the existing social order, including the civil rights movement and the movement for LGBTQ rights, has faced a backlash. The backlash against feminism started in the late 1970s and intensified in the 1980s, and its effects are still being felt today as evidenced by the small number of people who identify as feminists. It came from four primary places—religious leaders, political leaders, postfeminists, and the media.

Conservative religious and political leaders initiated the backlash against feminism after *Roe v. Wade* (1973), the Supreme Court decision that legalized abortion. They decried the Court's decision and channeled their efforts into defeating the Equal Rights Amendment (ERA). The ERA stated that "equality of rights under the law shall not be denied or abridged by the United States or by any state on account of sex." After a decade of work to pass this amendment, the backlash against feminism ensured its defeat in 1982. One of the primary organizations working against the ERA was the Moral Majority. Created in 1979 by Reverend Jerry Falwell, the Moral Majority was a political organization intended to push back against the cultural shifts advocated by the women's rights movement. During the decade it operated, it was the most popular conservative lobbying group in the United States, attracting more than four million members and two million donors. The Moral Majority advocated for a "traditional" family arrangement that it saw as under threat by an "anti-family" feminist agenda. The organization advocated against abortion, homosexuality, and women working outside the home. The Moral Majority was instrumental in Ronald Reagan's election to the presidency in 1980.

The Republican Party was the first party to add the ERA to its party platform in 1940, but removed it 40 years later when nominating Reagan for president. Many of Reagan's policies while president reversed the progress feminists had fought for during the 1970s, including cutting welfare benefits and reducing funding for international family planning and investigating sexual harassment and discrimination in the workplace. Reagan also opposed equal pay legislation and helped to popularize the stereotype of the "welfare queen," a black woman who drives a Cadillac and wears fur coats with the money she gets defrauding welfare. Although this stereotype is inaccurate, it effectively stigmatized poor women. Reagan spokesperson Faith Whittlesey gave the White House's only policy speech on the status of women in the United States, titled "Radical Feminism in Retreat," in which she declared feminism a "straightjacket" for women.

The media backlash against feminism came in the form of describing feminism as a passé social movement, one that was no longer necessary because gender equality had already been achieved. Much news coverage throughout the 1980s furthered the claim that gender issues were a thing of the past. Media backlash against feminism also came in the form of framing equality as the source of women's unhappiness, not sexism. Faludi pointed out that instead of showing high-powered career women as successful and happy in films and television, throughout the 1980s they were almost always portrayed as single, pining for a man, burned out from work, and concerned about not having children. According to Faludi, news coverage in the 1980s "issued a steady stream of indictments against the women's rights movement, with such headlines as 'when feminism failed' or 'the awful truth about women's lib.' They hold the campaign for women's equality responsible for nearly every woe besetting women, from mental depression to meager savings accounts, from teen suicides to eating disorders to bad complexions." Feminism was framed in ways that discouraged some young people from identifying as feminists or recognizing the social, economic, and political gains of the movement.

The views of postfeminists also emerged in the 1980s, with academics and public commentators who argue that gender equality has been achieved and that pushing feminism further unnecessarily advantages women. Postfeminists point to the strides women have made in education and the workplace as evidence that feminist activism is no longer necessary. Some scholars consider postfeminists part of third wave feminism that champions empowerment through individual choice, consumer culture, fashion, and sexual pleasure, while other scholars classify postfeminists as outside the feminist label entirely. Camille Paglia is perhaps the most prominent postfeminist who believes that feminism has gone too far in its quest for gender equality. She laid out her argument to a news reporter: "Let's get rid of Infirmary Feminism, with its bedlam of bellyachers, anorexics, bulimics, depressives, rape victims, and incest survivors. Feminism has become a catch-all vegetable drawer where bunches of clingy sob sisters can store their moldy neuroses."[24] More recently, in 2014, a campaign called "Women against Feminism" on Tumblr and Facebook featured young women holding up signs about why they do not need feminism. Examples included, "I don't need feminism because I am not a delusional, disgusting, hypocritical man-hater!" or "I don't need feminism because I love men!" and "I don't need feminism because I don't need to belittle a man in order to lift myself up."

PROFILE IN POWER

Gloria Allred

Gloria Allred is the best known women's rights attorney in the world. During her 40-year legal career, she has won hundreds of millions of dollars in settlements and for plaintiffs in cases involving discrimination on the basis of sex, gender, race, physical ability, and sexuality. She has won many awards for her work, including the President's Award for Outstanding Volunteerism from the White House in 1986 and the highest award given by the National

SOURCE: uncatigger; Flickr

Association of Women Lawyers. In 2014, she received the Lifetime Achievement Award from the National Trial Lawyers for her pioneering work to fight gender discrimination. In addition to her legal work, Allred is also an outspoken advocate for gender justice as a television commentator, radio talk show host, and activist.

Allred, an only child, was born in Philadelphia in 1941. She earned an honors English degree from the University of Pennsylvania and went on to earn a master's degree from New York University and a law degree from Loyola Law School. She put herself through college as a single mother, and now she has three generations of feminist lawyers in the family—Allred, her daughter and television legal analyst Lisa Bloom, and her granddaughter, Sarah Bloom. Gloria first became interested in women's rights cases when she survived a rape at gunpoint that necessitated an abortion that nearly took her life because of medical complications.

One of her earliest cases was against the formerly all-male Friars Club. In 1987, Allred filed a sex discrimination lawsuit and ended up being the club's first female member. In recent years, she has become known for representing high-profile cases, including Nicole Simpson's family in the murder case against O. J. Simpson, actor Hunter Tylo's pregnancy discrimination case against the popular television show *Melrose Place*, plaintiffs in a lawsuit challenging Proposition 8 that outlawed same-sex marriage in California, transgender woman Jenna Talackova, who won the right to compete in the Miss Universe Canada pageant, campus rape survivors, and Bill Cosby survivors.

FEMINIST MYTHS?

Do myths about feminism exist, and do they help perpetuate negative stereotypes about feminists? Religious leader Reverend Pat Robertson encapsulated many stereotypes about feminists when he claimed in 1992 that the "feminist agenda is not about equal rights for women. Feminism is a socialist, anti-family, political movement that encourages women to leave their husbands, kill their children, practice witchcraft, destroy capitalism and become lesbians."[25]

One major stereotype about feminists is that they are man hating. Feminist scholars and activists have pointed out for years that feminism is not about hating men; it is instead about achieving social, political, and economic equality for all. Although different types of feminists pursue different paths to achieve gender justice and equality, feminist critiques are aimed at patriarchy and sexism, not individual males. As cultural commentator Jackson Katz points out, feminist efforts often benefit both men and women, such as campaigns to end domestic violence, address HIV/AIDS, destigmatize "feminine" career choices like teaching and nursing, and mandate more family leave time.

Another stereotype about feminists is that they are angry people who lack a sense of humor. This feminist myth has been challenged in recent years by the comedy of Margaret Cho, Tina Fey, Sarah Silverman, Wanda Sykes, Mindy Khaling, Amy Poehler, Ellen DeGeneres, Amy Shumer, Jessica Williams, and others who use comedy to launch searing, intersectional feminist critiques of sexism, racism, and homophobia. The most prominent feminist voices in popular culture are now comedians, and online feminist campaigns often use humor to expose sexism. For example, the popular hashtag #sorryfeminists was started after the editor of *The New York Times Style Magazine* tweeted, "The sexy (sorry, feminists), smart, sassy Katie Roiphe live on stage @nypl on Wednesday night." This humorous campaign made fun of the idea that feminists are not sexy or lack a sense of humor.

> **Elyse Anders** @dELYSEious   1h
> I think wearing a bra is more comfortable when it's not on fire.
> #sorryfeminists
> Expand
>
> **Rob Tannenbaum** @tannenbaumr   1h
> I clicked on your avatar. #sorryfeminists
> Expand
>
> **Jessica Valenti** @JessicaValenti   1h
> I'm an excellent cook. #sorryfeminists
> Expand

Another stereotype is that feminists are ugly lesbians. Feminists are a diverse group within the United States and appearance cannot determine whether someone is a feminist. In August 2014, the hashtag campaign #FeministsAreUgly poked fun at this stereotype. Within a month, more than 91,000 feminists had tweeted selfies with this hashtag to demonstrate the diversity of feminists' physical appearances. In terms of sexuality, there is an affinity between seeking equal rights for women and equal rights for LGBTQ individuals, but this does not mean

that all lesbians are feminists or that all feminists are lesbians. According to a 2013 study conducted by the National Institutes of Health, 96.6 percent of the population identifies as heterosexual, which means the vast majority of feminists are also heterosexual, although some identify as lesbian, bisexual, transsexual, pansexual, or another form of sexuality.

Some feminists argue that the negative stereotypes about feminism from conservative religious and political leaders, as well as media misrepresentations, have had a significant effect on the number of Americans who identify as feminists. According to a 2015 *Vox* poll, only 18 percent of people in the United States say they are feminists, while 52 percent say they are not feminists, and the remainder were not sure. In the same poll, 85 percent say they believe in "equality for women." This disconnection between support for the primary goal of feminism and use of the label feminism suggests that negative stereotypes have altered and, at times, distorted the basic definition of feminism and its goal of achieving gender equality.

CAN MEN BE FEMINISTS?

Since feminism is the belief in the social, political, and economic equality of the sexes, anyone who supports this idea is technically a feminist. Men have been a part of feminism in the United States since the early nineteenth century brought about the first wave of feminism that involved the fight for women's suffrage. They have provided key support in each successive wave of the women's rights movement by strategically leveraging their male privilege to further the cause. For example, minister Parker Pillsbury (1809–1898) was an abolitionist and a women's rights advocate who lectured and protested to achieve an end to slavery and equality for women. Pillsbury helped draft the constitution for the American Equal Rights Association in 1865, and he coedited the newsletter *The Revolution* with suffragette leader Elizabeth Cady Stanton.

Many men were involved in the second wave of the women's rights movement. Three men were among the 49 cofounders of the National Organization for Women in 1966, and men walked arm in arm with women at feminist protests and marches. Men's participation in the second wave was not without debate. Some feminist leaders, including the influential French thinker Simone de Beauvoir, argued that men cannot be feminists because they cannot truly understand women's oppression. Other feminists argued that men's identification as feminist is one of the strongest stands men can make in the struggle for gender justice and that excluding them from the movement suggests that women are solely responsible for ending sexism. Other feminists, such as bell hooks, argue that men's liberation from the constraints of societally proscribed gender roles is a vital goal for feminist scholarship and activism. Some men use the label "pro-feminist" as a middle ground in the debate to indicate that they are feminist allies.

The feminist movement of the 1960s produced the consciousness-raising Men's Liberation Movement of the 1970s that created spaces for men to challenge traditional gender roles. This movement pushed back against the social expectation that men had to be the breadwinners of a nuclear family as well as social pressure to hide one's emotions. The Men's Rights Activists of the 1980s were a backlash against the Men's Liberation Movement and the second wave of feminism. The Men's Rights Activists believe that feminists have emasculated men and overlooked men's suffering. More specifically, they cite men's shorter life expectancy and biases in favor of women, who are seen as the primary caregivers in the eyes of the law in divorce and custody cases. According to the Men's Rights Activists, these experiences mean that men are just as oppressed as or even more oppressed than women. The Men's Rights Activists have grown in size and scope since their inception.

The debate about whether men can be feminists has subsided in the past decade with the rise of #Feminism. The idea of whether men can identify as feminists is complicated by questions of gender fluidity and shifting notions of what it means to be a "man" or a "woman." For example, if only women can identify as feminists, does this include trans women? Today, people of diverse sexes, genders, sexualities, and other identities consider themselves feminists. In addition, many men today are involved in feminist scholarship and activism. In her book *Men and Feminism*, Shira Tarrant identifies a large group of men involved in men's studies from feminist perspectives, including Michael Kimmel, Jackson Katz, Kevin Powell, and Michael Messner.[26] Scholars have explored questions of how men can best be involved in the movement for women's equality without displacing women's voices and leadership. With the millennial generation, many young male and transgender activists have joined women in using social media to further gender equality. For example, avowed feminist blogger and activist Charles Clymer runs the popular Equality for Women page on Facebook, and John Kelly has been an influential activist in the new Campus Anti-Rape Movement.

CONCLUSION

Feminism is the belief in social, political, and economic equality of the sexes. There are ten major types of feminism that disagree on the root causes of gender inequality and the remedies for addressing it. The most popular forms of feminism during the peak of activism in the 1960s and 1970s were liberal feminism and radical feminism. We have entered a new era of feminism (the fourth wave) that is distinct in terms of ideology and tactics; #Feminism combines intersectional feminism with postmodern critiques of the gender binary and transnational feminism. Social movements invariably face a backlash because they challenge the existing social order. The backlash against the second wave of feminism started in the 1970s and primarily came from religious leaders, politicians, postfeminists, and media. This backlash was effective, and its effects can be felt today. Fewer than one in five Americans say they are feminists, although 85 percent say they believe in "equality for women." Feminism is a set of ideologies or a way of thinking about gender justice, so anyone who believes in the social, political, and economic equality of the sexes can identify as a feminist.

CHAPTER SUMMARY

- We described ten primary forms of feminism in this chapter: liberal, radical, Marxist, socialist, psychoanalytic, eco-, postmodern, transnational, intersectional, and third wave feminism. An ongoing debate exists about whether a fourth wave of feminism has begun.
- The second wave of the feminist movement was initiated by liberal feminists who believe that female subordination is deeply rooted in social customs and laws and the best way to achieve gender equality is through legal and policy reform.
- Radical feminists of the second wave locate the root of gender oppression in deeper formal and informal patriarchal relations between the sexes, and they seek to eliminate gender inequality by challenging societal norms and institutions that uphold patriarchal relations in both the public and the private spheres.
- Marxist feminists of the second wave locate the root cause of gender inequality in capitalism and advocate for a more equitable economic system as the best way to achieve gender equality.
- Socialist feminism of the second wave is a blend of radical feminism and Marxist feminism. They believe that when it comes to women's oppression, patriarchy and other forms of oppression are influential beyond capitalism because women's experiences of oppression vary by their social class and race.
- Psychoanalytic feminists of the second wave place the root of women's oppression in deeply ingrained internal psychic gender dynamics that are developed in childhood and reinforced by societal norms. They propose altering family structures and early childhood experience that reinforce masculinity and femininity to address gender inequalities.
- Eco-feminists of the second wave identify the root cause of gender inequality as the societal belief that nature is considered inferior to culture in the same way that women are considered inferior to men because women are thought of as closer to nature. This branch of feminism calls for humans to reconnect with nature and for new ways of seeing the world that are not based on oppositional dichotomies and hierarchies that place men above the natural world and women.
- Transnational feminism emerged in the mid-1970s in response to the nearly exclusive focus of second wave feminists on Western cultures that misrepresents and erases the experiences of women living in non-Western countries. Transnational feminists call for recognizing the role played by nation-specific sociopolitical environments, race, sexuality, colonialism, and global economic exploitation of less developed countries by the Western world.
- Intersectional feminism emerged during the second wave in response to the movement's almost exclusive focus on the experiences of white, middle-class women. Intersectionality is the idea that race, class, gender, ability, and sexuality all work together to define women's experiences of oppression. To address gender inequality, one must account for the wide variation in experiences of gender oppression based on intersecting identities.

- Postmodern feminists of the 1990s believe that "gender" is not biological but instead is a category that we construct through language that upholds existing gender inequalities. They propose that feminists resist and reshape the language that constructs gender.
- Third wave feminism from the 1990s is mislabeled in that it is a distinct type of feminism, but is not a new wave of heightened feminism activism. It began as a push against what some saw as rigid expectations placed on women by second wave feminisms and quickly formed to be a highly individualistic approach to gender justice with an emphasis on girlie culture and intersectionality.
- Feminism has entered a new wave of heightened activism through the use of new online and social media communication technologies. Cultural commentators have dubbed this the fourth wave of feminism (which is technically the third time feminist activism has peaked in the United States).
- We propose that a new type of feminism has emerged in the past five years that is distinct from third wave feminism in that it combines intersectional feminism with postmodern critiques of the gender binary and transnational feminism in action. We label this new type #Feminism because it prioritizes the fluidity of categories, boundaries, and meaning in its quest for gender justice.
- A backlash against the second wave of feminism started in the 1970s and primarily came from religious leaders, politicians, postfeminists, and media-generated negative stereotypes. The most prominent negative stereotypes about feminism are that feminists hate men, are angry people without a sense of humor, are ugly, and are lesbians.
- Fewer than one in five Americans now call themselves feminists, although 85 percent say they believe in "equality for women."
- The debate about whether men can be feminists has subsided in the past decade, and many men and transgender men and women identify as feminists today. Feminism is a set of ideologies or a way of thinking about gender justice, so it is not exclusive to women.

STUDY/DISCUSSION QUESTIONS

- How many different types of feminism exist? Why are there so many forms of feminism?
- Which form(s) of feminism are most appealing to you, if any, and why?
- The authors propose that fluid feminism is distinct from third wave feminism. In what ways are they distinct, and in what ways do they overlap?
- Has the backlash against feminism been successful in achieving its goal of discrediting feminism? Why or why not?
- Can anyone identify as a feminist? Why or why not? If not, what are your criteria for who can identify as a feminist?

CASE STUDIES

1. Is Beyoncé's brand of feminism empowering?

In February 2015, Beyoncé appeared on the Super Bowl halftime stage in a form-fitting, sequined bodysuit silhouetted against a glowing sign with the word "feminism." This image was seen by 114 million television viewers, and it quickly went viral. Beyoncé's public embrace of feminism inspired other celebrities and many young women to "come out" as feminists, but she also faced criticism for promoting the idea that being a sex object is empowering. These two different responses to Beyoncé's performance reflect two different approaches to feminism. What would radical feminists conclude about the empowerment in Beyoncé's Super Bowl performance? What would third wave feminists conclude?

2. Should celebrities be feminist spokespeople?

In November 2014, when actor Emma Watson launched the global solidarity movement for gender equality, #HeForShe, Taylor Swift responded, "I wish when I was 12-years-old I had been able to watch a video of my favorite actress explaining in such an intellectual, beautiful, poignant way the definition of feminism. Because I would have understood it. And then earlier on in my life I would have proudly claimed I was a feminist because I would have understood what the word means." Celebrities raise awareness about feminist concerns in a way that academics, activists, and others simply cannot. But as we saw in many examples in this chapter, celebrities sometimes lack a thoughtful approach to feminism or oversimplify complicated feminist issues. What do you see as the pros and cons of having celebrities serve as the primary spokespeople for feminism?

3. Are you a feminist?

People who identify as feminists can often recall the moment that they knew they were feminists. It can happen at work, at school, reading a book, watching a movie, or experiencing an event that inspired the moment they knew they were feminists. Some feminists have labeled this the "click" moment, the moment their feminist light bulb turned on. If you identify as a feminist, when was your click moment, and what inspired it? If you are a feminist, which type(s) of feminist are you?

RESOURCES

- The **Young Feminist Activist Program** fosters young women's activism across ages and countries through hands-on activism.
  http://yfa.awid.org
- **Feminist.com** is a great resource for information about feminism and activism opportunities.
- The **Campus Action Network of the National Organization for Women** is a national feminist activist network on colleges and universities across the country.
  http://now.org/getinvolved/campus-action-network/

- The **Global Grrl Zine Network** is a transnational network of do-it-yourself projects for feminists.
  http://www.grrrlzines.net/about.htm
- **Incite!** is a national network of radical feminists of color working to end violence against women, gender nonconforming individuals, and trans people of color.
  http://www.incite-national.org/

CHAPTER 4

Gender Representations in Popular Culture

Lady Gaga caused the nation to pause during the 2016 Academy Awards ceremony when she performed her Oscar-nominated song *Till It Happens to You,* which she cowrote with music giant Diane Warren for the campus rape documentary *The Hunting Ground.* Lady Gaga's performance was introduced by Vice President Joe Biden, who spoke about the White House's "It's on Us" initiative to combat campus rape. Lady Gaga was joined on stage by 50 campus rape survivors of all races, genders, and sexualities. The singer's powerful vocals pierced through public consciousness, and the tearful audience leapt to its feet for a standing ovation when the last note was played. After the Oscars, Lady Gaga revealed to her family that she was raped as a teenager.

Earlier in the week, Lady Gaga had publicly shown her support for pop star Kesha, who was involved in a legal battle with Sony. Kesha was suing the label to get out of her recording contract to avoid working with Dr. Luke, a producer who, according to Kesha, raped and abused her. Lady Gaga appeared outside the Sony headquarters in New York City to demand that the company "do what is right, not what is better for business."[1] #Feminists started the #FreeKesha hashtag, and Sony agreed to let her work with other producers. Lady Gaga's public support of a fellow survivor elevated the public conversation about sexual violence and modeled supportive behavior that many survivors often do not receive when they go public with their experience.

Lady Gaga's advocacy against issues of sexual violence speaks to the power of celebrities and entertainment media in shaping the public policy agenda. This was not the first time the pop singer used her star status to elevate policy issues. Lady Gaga has long advocated for the rights of LGBTQ individuals. For example, in 2010, she attended the MTV Video Music Awards flanked by four members of the military who were discharged because of their sexuality, and in 2011, she made history with the first song on the Billboard chart to include the word "transgender" in *Born This Way.* She is one of many celebrities who use their brand and name recognition to advocate for pressing political and social concerns.

This chapter examines the role that mass media play in shaping our society and political culture. We focus on entertainment media and its influence on society through film, music, television, radio, video games, books, and online content. Entertainment media is the primary source of popular culture, a term used to describe products, forms of expression, customs, attitudes, behaviors, and beliefs suited to the tastes of the general masses that define a society at a given time. In plain terms, pop culture is the culture of "the people" as opposed to high culture (e.g., opera, ballet), which is typically reserved for the socioeconomic elite. Pop culture are the blockbuster films we frequent, the magazines we see when we pay for our groceries, the TV series we binge on Netflix, the video games we play, the music we dance to, the music videos we watch, and countless other mediums.

We begin this chapter with a look at why pop culture matters. It is easy to dismiss the images and storylines in mass media as simply entertaining, harmless fun, but half a century of social science research reveals that media shapes our perceptions and priorities. In the second section, we present evidence that new communication technologies increase the influence of mass media. The third section examines the representations of women, men, and gender-nonconforming individuals in pop culture with an emphasis on harmful and damaging misrepresentations. Next, we analyze how leadership is presented in gendered ways in pop culture. Finally, we describe how the shift from traditional media to new online media has gendered implications.

WHY POPULAR CULTURE MATTERS

Pop culture matters because it reflects and shapes societal perceptions and priorities. However frivolous it may seem, pop culture is worth studying because it reveals the issues Americans pay attention to and what we value as a culture. Most Americans think that mass media profoundly influences other people, but that they are immune to media influence. U.S. society is saturated with media, so only people living without technology in the woods far, far away from civilization are immune to its effects. Researchers have asked whether and how media affects people since the 1920s, and this question is even more pressing today with the invention of online technologies. Based on nearly a century of research, we can say for certain that mass media is influential. Research by political scientist Shanto Iyengar shows that although media may not tell people what to think, it can tell people what to think about (known as agenda setting) and how to think about it (known as framing).[2] In other words, media play a vital role in shaping what matters to us and how we should think about these priorities.

Pop culture plays a powerful role in determining individual and collective consciousness. Songs, movies, books, and other forms of media tell stories, and as social creatures, humans are drawn to these stories to make sense of their lives. Media narratives provide people a blueprint for how they ought to behave. The pop culture trends of the time inform people's priorities, how they should spend their time, how they should spend their income, and many other aspects of their lives. They teach us about the proper role of science and technology in our lives, how people should behave in relationships, who deserves condemnation, who we should emulate, and how to overcome hardships. Movies and TV are able to present "reality" or something akin to it, or they can weave fantastic stories that bend time, space, gravity, and even tradition. Elusive ideas such as equality, justice, redemption, and democracy can be explored in fictionalized pop culture settings in ways that are not possible in the real world. But despite media potential to topple existing societal hierarchies, pop culture tends to reflect and therefore reinforce existing social hierarchies in overt and subtle ways. Novelty may pull in viewers, but bending accepted cultural norms too far will alienate mainstream audiences and work against the commercial end goal of the entertainment industry. Therefore, most media narratives uphold the existing social order rather than challenge it, which means that existing societal biases, like racism, sexism, and classism, are typically reinforced by pop culture content.

Notwithstanding pop culture tendencies to uphold the existing social structure, pop culture can also be a powerful tool for social change. Public opinion and perceptions must change to change the status quo in society, and shifting depictions of different groups in entertainment media influence public opinion about that group. For example, positive representations of LGBTQ individuals in pop culture shifted public perception in favor of gays and lesbians, a catalyst for policy change that brought about the legalization of same-sex marriage through a Supreme Court ruling in 2015.

NEW MEDIA INFLUENCE

Media are more influential than ever before because its use has become the most popular cultural pastime in the United States. Mass communication technologies have become relatively cheap, and most households have multiple media devices. According to the Kaiser Family Foundation, 99 percent of families own TVs, 97 percent own the technology to play videos, 86 percent have a personal computer in the home, 80 percent own at least one video game system, and 82 percent have cable or satellite TV. Typical Americans spend two-thirds of their waking hours plugged in to mass media.[3]

Children are also plugged in to media more than previous generations. The average child in the United States spends 45 hours per week consuming media—more time than one spends in school or any activity other than sleeping. Child cell phone use jumped from 39 percent to 66 percent in the past decade, while tablet access soared from 18 percent to 76 percent during that time. Children spend more time playing games and watching media on their cell phones than talking on them. Three-quarters of children ages eight and under use mobile devices to play games and watch media, and that number tripled in the past decade. Children have more access to pop culture and its influence than ever before, but 80 percent of parents say they have media restrictions that they do not actively enforce.[4]

Media affect many aspects of our life and have become more influential in recent years because most people are constantly connected to media communication devices. More than 75 percent of Americans have household access to the Internet, and the sheer volume of Internet content increased nine times over from 2010 to 2015.[5] Media exposure rapidly accelerated starting in 2005 with the invention of new smartphone and tablet technology that lets Americans access media continuously and on the go. Two-thirds of Americans use smartphones, and the average smartphone user reaches for his or her phone 150 times a day.[6] Most Americans now use the Web to accomplish nearly every goal of modern life—from scheduling to driving directions, fitness applications, finding a date, etc. College students today grew up in a world where social media as a normal part of life is so ubiquitous that its presence is invisible.

Mass media are more of a presence in our everyday lives than in the past, but most people do not recognize its influence. Half of teenagers in the United States say that TV does not influence them "at all," while one-third say it affects them "only a little." People hold similar beliefs about the influence of social media. Three in five (62 percent) Americans believe that marketing on social media, such as Facebook and Twitter, has no influence on their purchasing decisions, but corporations run aggressive online marketing campaigns because they are highly effective.[7] Young people are exposed to more advertising than any previous generation, but they are less critical of its effects than previous generations. Media expert Jennifer Pozner has observed a decline in young people's ability to think critically about the media they consume:

> I find stark differences in young people's responses to similar TV clips. Today's teens and young adults grew up watching reality shows as uncritically as their parents watched *The Cosby Show* in the 80s and *Happy Days* in the 70s . . . but many other young women and men tell me that shows like *The Bachelor* and *Flavor of Love* are "hilarious," "just TV, not a big deal," or more disturbingly, "realistic."[8]

GENDER REPRESENTATIONS IN MEDIA

Gender representations in media can determine power dynamics in society. Power is defined as a person's ability to control things or people. Power allows individuals to amass resources and improve their social value, and mass media representations reflect who has power in society and who lacks power. Media both reflect and shape who has power in U.S. society. It is a powerful teaching tool when it comes to "proper" gender roles and norms. Mass media teach us that women hold less social value in society through their relative scarcity in popular culture; that girls and women should derive their value from their physical appearance; and that boys and men should derive their value from their ability to amass wealth and achieve dominance over others. These are but a few of the lessons we learn from gender representations in pop culture, all of which vary by class and race in ways we explore below.

Media Representations of Girls and Women

Existing research on pop culture finds that media mostly limit and diminish the social status of girls and women. The most pernicious gender gap in pop culture is the general erasure of women's stories in favor of men's narratives. Men's lives and activities remain prioritized over women's lives and activities in pop culture. Basic cable offers more than two dozen sports channels primarily aimed at a male audience, but only three channels specifically for women (Oxygen, OWN, and Lifetime). Women's stories and faces are vastly underrepresented in film and TV, a gap that has not shifted in 60 years.

The most persistent way that women are represented in pop culture is to not be represented at all. According to a decade of research from the Geena Davis Institute on Gender in Media, women comprise 39 percent of speaking roles in prime-time TV programs and one-third of speaking roles in films. In general, women of color are less visible than white women in pop culture. Women of color are more likely to be shown in prime-time TV programs than white women, but less likely to have speaking parts in films. In 2014, only three women of color played the lead in the 100 top-grossing films.

In 2015, Viola Davis became the first black woman to ever win an Emmy for best actress in a drama. During her acceptance speech, she situated her win within the larger context of a lack of racial diversity in the entertainment industry:

> "In my mind, I see a line. And over that line, I see green fields and lovely flowers and beautiful white women with their arms stretched out to me, over that line. But I can't seem to get there no how. I can't seem to get over that line." That was Harriet Tubman in the 1800s. And let me tell you something: The only thing that separates women of color from anyone else is opportunity. You cannot win an Emmy for roles that are simply not there.

Similar gender gaps exist in children's programming. Boy characters in movies outnumber girl characters three to one, a ratio that has remained consistent since the 1950s.[9] This massive gender gap teaches children that boy's lives are more interesting and important than girl's lives and that their stories deserve to be told. Nearly three in four speaking parts in children's TV and film entertainment are male, and 83 percent of narrators for children's programming are male. This gap signals that the opinions of boys/men are more valuable than that of girls/women and that their voices matter more. At a young age, most children in the United States are taught that gender imbalance is acceptable and normal.

When women do appear in film and TV, they are far more likely than men to be sexualized. One-third of female characters in prime-time TV programs and family films are shown wearing sexy attire compared to eight percent of men.[10] This gender gap signals that girls/women should be judged based on this physical appearance and that they should strive to be attractive to gain attention and validation from others. As explored below, this puts women in a subordinate position rather than a position of power in social relationships. The gender gap in sexualization is also present in children's programming. When girl characters appear in TV and film, they almost always fit narrow beauty standards that reinforce body dissatisfaction: small waists, large breasts, and long legs. Girls and teen characters in film are just as likely to be shown in sexy attire as adult female characters in films.

Male characters in TV and film are significantly more likely to be shown as working professionals than are female characters. In family films, 67 percent of employed characters are male compared to 45 percent of female characters. More than half (55 percent) of males in prime-time TV programs are employed compared to 44 percent of female characters.[11] Female characters are also rarely presented in professional roles. In fact, men comprise 80 percent of working characters in children's programming. Media teaches children early on that men and women occupy different social positions in society. This gender gap reinforces separate-spheres ideology, the idea that the proper place for men is in public spaces in positions of power, while the proper place for women is in the home.

A lack of women driving media production partially accounts for persistent gender gaps in the way male and female characters are presented in pop culture. With regard to films, men outnumber women as content creators by a ratio of nearly five to one. According to the Center for Women in TV and Film, women comprised 19 percent of executive producers, 18 percent of editors, 11 percent of writers, and seven percent of directors for the top-grossing films of 2014.[12] Increasing the number of women behind the scenes increases the number of women on the small and big screens. For example, when a female writer works on a film, the number of female characters increases more than ten percent.

Beyond film and TV, the Representation Project reports that women hold only three percent of clout positions in media more broadly (i.e., telecommunications, entertainment, publishing, and advertising).[13] This means that nearly all of the media content Americans consume that plays a profound role in shaping values and priorities is produced by men who were raised in a media culture that mostly excludes women. It is no surprise that the number of female characters has remained largely unchanged in six decades.

Girls and women have become significantly more hypersexualized in media in the past decade for marketers and content producers to cut through the media "clutter." This clutter is the result of new media technology that exposes Americans to more advertisements and other images than ever before—about 3,000 a day.[14] Those who live in cities see an average of 5,000 ads a day compared to about 500 in 1971.[15] Americans get a barrage of advertisements from TV (through standard commercials and frequent product placement in programs), magazines, newspapers, and social media sites. We see advertisements when we leave the house on our digital devices, billboards, the sides of buses, our doctor's office, at the gas pump, in elevators, on airplanes, in product placements in movies, etc.: "Marketers used to try their hardest to reach people at home, when they were watching TV or reading newspapers or magazines. But consumers' viewing and reading habits are so scattershot now that many advertisers say the best way to reach time-pressed consumers is to try to catch their eye at literally every turn."[16] And they do.

One way that pop culture creators cut through the clutter is with more plentiful and more extreme images of sexualized girls and women. Objectification is the process of treating a human being like an object for use, and sexual objectification is the process of treating a human being as an object for sexual use. Female objectification has become such a normal part of U.S. culture that it is sometimes difficult to identify it in pop culture. The CHIPS test is useful to identify objectifying images. If the answer is "yes" to any of these five questions, then the image in question is sexually objectifying:

1. **Commodity**: Does the image show a sexualized body as a commodity that can be bought, sold, or traded? For example, this advertisement features a woman with her body parts marked like pieces of meat to be sold at a supermarket.

2. **Harmed**: Does the image show a sexualized person being harmed? For example, in this advertisement for a Ford car, reality television stars Kim, Kourtney, and Khloe Kardashian are bound and gagged in the back of a car being driven by socialite Paris Hilton.

3. **Interchangeable**: Does the image show a sexualized body as interchangeable with other bodies? For example, this advertisement for undergarments shows four women with similar body types all in a row, each body like the next body.

4. **Parts**: Does the image show only part of a sexualized body? For example, this advertisement from American Apparel shows six images of a woman's thighs, crotch, legs, and buttocks.

5. **Stand-in:** Does the image show a sexualized body as a stand-in for an object? For example, a woman's body is shown as a beer bottle.

Rates of female sexual objectification have shot up in the past decade, and social acceptance of objectification is the new social norm. Images from TV, video games, films, magazines, and many other sources almost exclusively use female bodies to sell products, and in TV shows and films, the camera frame often focuses on female body parts in an objectifying manner, rather than the whole picture.

Pop culture teaches women and girls a harmful lie that being a sex object is empowering. The key to understanding why it is not empowering lies in understanding the difference between being *sexy* and being *sexual*. Humans tend to see the world in dichotomies or two opposing groups, for example, good versus evil, us versus them, male versus female. Dichotomies are cognitive shortcuts that help us simplify a complex world, but they also constrain our thinking about groups into only two categories, and one category is always considered superior to the other. When it comes to sexuality, most of us think in terms of the subject/object dichotomy, where subjects act and objects are acted on. Subjects are *sexual*, while objects are *sexy*. Being *sexual* revolves around one's own sexual pleasure, while being *sexy* serves the sexual pleasure of others. In other words, sex objects are automatically in a subordinate societal position to sexual subjects. Girls and boys learn from an early age that men are sexual (that they have sexual desires) and women are sexy (that they are desired).

Young girls are especially susceptible to believing that being a sex object is empowering. They learn early that the holy grail of female existence is the production of a high-quality product (their body), while boys get the message that it is their job/right to consume these products. Psychologist Sarah Murnen and her colleagues point out that "girls are taught to view their bodies as 'projects' that need work before they can attract others, while boys are likely to learn to view their bodies as tools to use to master the environment."[17]

Pop culture teaches this message effectively. Nearly 70 percent of six-year-old girls want to be viewed as sexy, and one-third of the clothing items sold to girls have sexualizing characteristics.[18] Little girls get the message loud and clear from marketers that their primary value is their body and that they should view their body as a project to be constantly improved to get attention. Media scholar Gigi Durham identifies five messages that media corporations teach little girls through advertising and entertainment content:[19]

- Girls don't choose boys—boys choose girls—but only sexy girls.
- There's only one kind of sexy.
- Girls should work to be that type of sexy.
- The younger a girl is, the sexier she is.
- Sexual violence can be hot.

Young girls face a barrage of hypersexualized messages daily, long before they have the cognitive ability to understand them. Beyond media, the lie that being a sex object is empowering is reinforced early and often by strangers, friends, and family telling little girls "you look so pretty," by peers that socially "police" the way they look, and by grade school teachers who evaluate pretty girls as more competent in their classrooms. These little girls grow into women who cannot escape this consistent message from marketers, media producers, educators, parents, family, and friends. Some third wave feminists disagree with these critiques and believe that women can gain power by getting attention for being sexy.

Pop culture also teaches us that it is okay to degrade women using sex. We learn to deprioritize women's sexual pleasure from pornography where the "cum shot" almost always revolves around heterosexual male ejaculation; where women's pain is seen as desirable and erotic in pornography; where TV shows are replete with erotic sexual violence against women, including the all-too-common "sexy corpse." These lessons from pop culture affect sexual practices in the real world. "Hooking up" is often not sexually pleasurable for young women, as evidenced by the fact that men are twice as likely to orgasm during heterosexual hook-ups. Women report high rates of unwanted sex with hooking up, and they are often unable to shape the trajectory of sexual encounters once they have started. Men's sexual pleasure, then, is a higher priority to both men and women in heterosexual hook-ups, a pattern that mirrors the gender imbalance in pop culture porn and other entertainment media.

Some third wave feminists disagree with these critiques and believe that women can gain power by getting attention for being sexy and that being sexy for others can be a part of one's sexual pleasure. This may be the case, but female sexual objectification comes at a high personal cost to women. The most measurably harmful effect of female objectification in pop culture is what researchers call self-objectification: girls/women internalizing the idea that they are sex objects and view themselves through the lens of being sex objects. In 1996, psychologists Barbara Fredrickson and Tomi-Ann Roberts started tracking the harms of growing up in a culture where female sexual objectification is the norm.[20] They found that almost all women self-objectify to a greater or lesser extent.

Self-objectification is linked to a variety of mental health disorders, including clinical depression, "habitual body monitoring" (constant concern about one's body), body shame, diet restriction, symptoms of anorexia and bulimia, shame about menstrual cycles, and social physique anxiety.[21] Self-objectification has also been linked to lower cognitive functioning, less physical mobility, and a lower grade point average in college. Self-objectification also has direct consequences for politics. The more a woman sees herself as a sex object, the lower her external political efficacy—the belief that her voice matters in politics.[22] This finding has serious implications, considering that an increasing percentage of each generation of girls self-objectify, and political efficacy is linked to the likelihood of voting as well as running for office.

PROFILE IN POWER

Geena Davis

The Oscar award–winning actor Geena Davis is best known for her roles in *Beetlejuice* (1988), *Thelma and Louise* (1991), and *A League of Their Own* (1992). She played the first female president in a television series titled *Commander in Chief* (2005–2006). Davis is also known for being a champion for women in media. She founded the Geena Davis Institute for Gender in Media in 2007 after watching children's television programs with her daughter and noticing the gender imbalance of characters. The institute has produced the largest body of research on gender representations in entertainment media, and Davis shares these data with industry insiders to shape

SOURCE: itupictures; Flickr

content. In 2015, she also cofounded the Bentonville Film Festival, the first film festival that champions race and gender diversity in film.

Davis is also involved in other gender justice advocacy. She is the face of the *Geena Takes Aim* campaign for the Women's Sports Foundation Campaign in support of Title IX educational opportunities for women. She served as a role model for many young women when she took up archery in the late 1990s and made it to the semifinals berth for the 2000 Summer Olympics in Sydney.

Born in Massachusetts in 1956, Davis graduated from Boston University and moved to New York to work as a fashion model. She made her film debut in 1982 with *Tootsie* and has worked in the industry since. She won an Academy Award for *The Accidental Tourist* in 1988. Davis is a member of Mensa, an organization for people in the top two percent of intelligence.

The Impact of Women's Representations in Pop Culture

In addition to teaching viewers that women's stories and voices are less important than men's and teaching girls and women to self-objectify, pop culture also affects male viewers. Male viewers see objectified women as a collection of body parts rather than as a whole person. Furthermore, when a man sees a sexually objectified woman, his brain sees her in the same way it sees an inanimate tool—a thing that exists for his use. According to psychologist Susan Fiske, he sees her as less than fully human because he does not conceive of her as an entity with a "fully experiencing mind."[23] The routine dehumanization of women as sex objects causes both men and women to view women as a collection of parts instead of a whole human being. Both men and women view sexually objectified women as less warm, less moral, and less competent. Men and women are also less concerned about the pain and suffering of sex objects, which they see as less worthy of empathy. It is no surprise, then, that men who watch more TV are more likely to hold dysfunctional beliefs about relationships with women and are more accepting of sexual harassment against them.

As discussed above, sexual objectification is dehumanizing, and socially accepted dehumanization of a group is often the first step in enacting violence against that group. In other words, pop culture objectification contributes to a culture of sexualized violence against women. One in six women in the United States will face sexual assault or rape in her lifetime, and one in four women of color and one in three Native American women will experience it. Research indicates that viewing ads where women are portrayed as sex objects increases rape-supportive attitudes in men, and men who view objectified women in video games are more likely to believe rape myths, such as the idea that sometimes women "deserve" to be raped. Men who are exposed to objectified women in pop culture are also more likely to hold sexist beliefs, such as the idea that men are more capable leaders, that women deserve less freedom than men, and that women should be subservient to men.

Norms of female objectification also directly affect female candidates. Once they gain positions of power, women are still expected to maintain a physically pleasing (object) status, but this diminishes their electability. The pressure to be physically appealing on the campaign trail works against candidate viability and perceptions of competence. Psychologists Nathan Heflick and Jamie Goldenberg find that female candidates and political leaders who are sexualized and considered feminine are judged to be incompetent.[24] For example, Sarah Palin was harmed by her sex-object status in 2008 when the press focused on her body and appearance. Republican voters who focused on Palin's physical appearance during the campaign were less likely to vote for the McCain–Palin ticket than other Republicans.

Gendered press coverage exacerbates the existing practice of emphasizing dress and appearance for female candidates and leaders by focusing on those aspects in media coverage. For example, media focused more on the dress and appearance of 1984 Democratic vice presidential candidate Geraldine Ferraro, 2000 Republican presidential candidate Elizabeth Dole, 2008 Republican vice presidential candidate Sarah Palin, and 2008 Democratic presidential contender Hillary Clinton than on that of their male competitors. Clinton acknowledged that she had to spend more time getting ready each morning than her male competitors because of gendered expectations that women will wear make-up and style their hair, and a now defunct website dedicated to the First Lady's appearance was one of the most popular websites during the early years of the Internet. Clinton commented, "If I want to knock a story off the front page, I just change my hairstyle."

Media Representations of Boys and Men

The expectations and lives of boys and men are also profoundly affected by representations in pop culture. Like women, men learn how they should act and how they should treat other men, women, and children. By and large, pop culture pigeonholes men into narrow social roles that diminish their health and happiness. Media both elevates some types of masculinity and denigrates others, so viewers are taught which forms of masculinity are best or preferred at a given time. We see the recurring fearless action hero, the housework-averse sitcom dads with wives who are far more attractive than they, the crass but ultimately "good guy" who inexplicably hooks up with the beautiful girl in bro-comedies, the bad boy womanizer who also turns out to be redeemable, etc. Media present men as primary providers and protectors, but often as failed parents. Male characters are rarely shown as playing a key role in home life, which reinforces the separate-spheres ideology.

The most prominent depiction of men in entertainment media is a macho guy stereotype that is encouraged to solve problems using threat, force, and violence. Male characters have been associated with violence since the dawn of mass entertainment media more than a century ago, but the violence has become more common and extreme in the past decade. Before the age of 18, a typical American child will view more than 200,000 acts of violence in media, including more than 26,000 murders.[25] TV programs display more than 800 violent acts per hour, so viewers will encounter acts of violence whether they are viewing one program or channel surfing.

One in three male characters in advertisements, film, and media fit the macho guy stereotype, and men of color are disproportionately represented as violent.[26] For example, in the most played video games, black male characters are more likely than other characters to carry a gun. They are also disproportionately likely to be portrayed as a "gangsta" or a "thug" and much more likely to be shown as an athlete than white men. In TV shows, men of color are more likely to experience personal problems than white men, and they are far more likely to use physical aggression to solve those problems. Men in general are misrepresented as stereotypes in media, but men of color are especially misrepresented.

The Impact of Men's Representations in Pop Culture

The primary impact of media representations on boys and men is prevailing notions of masculinity. Media establishes norms of masculinity—what it means to be a "real man"—and boys learn this lesson early. Masculinity in media is often associated with emotional detachment, competition, aggression, and violence. Media scholar Jackson Katz argues that media are the primary way "millions of boys and men learn early on that acting like a man means you don't complain, you don't admit weakness, you don't ever let others see the anxious man behind the curtain."[27] Katz and other scholars are critical of this brand of masculinity because it encourages boys and men to engage in high-risk behaviors that could be fatal. It also causes men to shut off basic human emotions to be a real man. Young boys learn that to maintain the social order that awards them gender privilege, they should conform to the dominant mode of masculinity presented in the media. It is no surprise, then, that the more children watch TV, the more they hold sexist ideas about traditional male and female roles in society.

The pressure to be hypermasculine is particularly acute for poorer men who lack resources but are able to earn respect by emanating threat. Men of color are disproportionately affected by this pressure, but poor and working-class white men who lack the opportunities available to more privileged males are also more likely to embrace a hypermasculine pose they learn from media to perform authority and control through physical threat. Katz and others have deemed contemporary American masculinity "toxic" because it shortens men's life spans. Masculine pressure to downplay pain and vulnerability is driving the nearly ten-year difference in longevity between men and women. Men die at higher rates at every age because they tend to treat their bodies as though they are invulnerable, engage in more high-risk behaviors, wait longer to admit that they are sick, wait longer to get help for sickness, and have lower rates of compliance with treatment than women. These behaviors stem from societal norms of masculinity that are constantly shaped and reinforced by pop culture.

Masculinity also leaves many men traumatized and often depressed without knowing it. Psychologist Terry Real presents numerous studies finding that although infant boys and girls are equally emotional and expressive, parents often unconsciously begin to project "manliness" on male infants and speak to them less, comfort them less, and nurture them less. In other words, parents unwittingly fail to respond to the emotional needs of male infants because of deep-seated ideas about masculinity, ideas that are fostered by pop culture. Real's research suggests that boys start hiding their emotions as young as three years old to conform to gender expectations, and this behavior continues as they mature. The pressure to conform to masculinity leaves boys and men afraid to show weakness, emotionally distant, and often unable to recognize or process their feelings in healthy ways. Instead, men tend to externalize stress and act out their emotions through more socially approved means, such as drug addiction, working too much, and violence.

Men are twice as likely as women to suffer from rage disorders, and they are more likely to abuse substances that lead to hospitalization and death.[28] Men also commit nine in ten murders and comprise 77 percent of murder victims. They commit suicide at four times the rate of women and make up 93 percent of the prison population. James Gilligan, the former director of the Center for the Study of Violence at Harvard Medical School, stated, "I have yet to see a serious act of violence that was not provoked by the experience of feeling shamed and humiliated, disrespected and ridiculed, and that did not represent the attempt to prevent or undo that 'loss of face'—no matter how severe the punishment, even if it includes death." The brand of masculinity being projected in popular culture exacts a great toll on men and boys.

In addition to damaging men's health and happiness, the violent masculinity presented in pop culture is also linked to real-world violence. Studies conducted in the 1950s first discovered a link between viewing violent media content and aggressive behavior. The Surgeon General's Scientific Advisory Committee on Television and Social Behavior was created in 1969, and a decade later the committee produced a report identifying the major effects of violence on TV. The more children watch violence on TV, the less sensitive they become to the pain and suffering of others, the more fearful they are of the world, and the more likely they are to act in harmful or aggressive ways. Research in the 1980s linked TV violence to higher rates of arrest as adults.

In the 1990s, researchers turned their focus to the impact of violence in video games, a new type of media that was quickly gaining popularity with young people, especially boys. Nine in ten teens play video games on a regular basis on a smartphone, tablet, or gaming console, and more than half play video games on a daily basis. A 2010 study by researcher Craig Anderson and colleagues finds that violence in video games increases aggressive thoughts and behaviors and decreases empathy and prosocial behaviors.[29] Violence in music videos has been linked to an increase in aggressive thoughts and feelings in male viewers. Images of violence against women in music videos increases male viewers' acceptance of adversarial sexual beliefs and relationship violence. The empathy of incoming college students has decreased a surprising 40 percent in the past decade, and video games and the constant interaction with online content rather than humans is driving this troubling trend. According to clinical psychologist Jeanne Brockmyer, young people who play video games are initially "horrified by things they see, but we can't maintain that level of arousal. Everyone gets desensitized to things."

Gender-Nonconforming Individuals in Media
Pop culture rarely features characters that do not fit within the male/female, heterosexual, gender-conforming binary, but this has dramatically changed in the past decade. It is important to note that gender (a performance involving the masculine/feminine spectrum), sex (genitalia involving the female/intersexed/

male spectrum), and sexuality (the gender/sex a person is sexually attracted to) are three distinct things.

A vast majority of characters in film, TV, and other forms of pop culture are heterosexual. LGBTQ characters did not appear in pop culture until the 1970s, and since that time, their representations have rapidly increased in recent years. ABC aired the first show portraying LGBTQ people in a sympathetic light in 1972 with the made-for-TV movie *That Certain Summer* about a gay male relationship. A few gay and lesbian characters were featured in film and TV in the 1970s and 1980s, but when *L.A. Law* included a lesbian kiss in an episode in 1991, it caused a public uproar and companies threatened to pull their ads. Episodes with LGBTQ characters and plotlines multiplied in the 1990s, and in 1997, *Ellen* became the first TV show to feature a LGBTQ person in a leading role. *Will & Grace*, the second show to feature gay leads, aired in 1998. In the 2000s, many shows on TV and cable depicted LGBTQ casts and leads, such as *Queer as Folk* and *The L Word*, but the 2010s are marked by the inclusion of LGBTQ characters in the leading prime-time shows, such as *Modern Family* and *Glee*.

Hollywood films also started featuring LGBTQ leads in wide-release films in the past two decades. The acclaimed films *Boys Don't Cry* (1999) and *Brokeback Mountain* (2005) demonstrated the bankability of stories about LGBTQ protagonists, but an analysis of the top-grossing films from 2007 to 2014 found that only 0.4 percent of leading characters were LGBTQ and only 14 percent of films feature an LGBTQ character.[30] Furthermore, when LGBTQ characters are included, they are rarely shown in healthy or stable relationships or raising a family. In other words, LGBTQ individuals are still mostly invisible in pop culture, and when they are cast, their characters tend to be stereotypes. The lingering symbolic annihilation and "othering" of LGBTQ people in pop culture signal and shape their relative lesser social worth and value in the United States.

On a positive note, pop culture has played an important role in kick-starting a national conversation about the fluidity of gender. In 2013, Netflix aired *Orange Is the New Black*, featuring Laverne Cox as Sophia Burset, a transgender inmate who is struggling with family and identity issues. Cox's character is presented as a complex person for whom gender identity is but one aspect of her life. In 2015, Amazon aired *Transparent*, a series about an older father now living as a woman. In 2015, Olympic gold medalist transgender icon Caitlyn Jenner appeared on the cover of *Vanity Fair* and launched her new reality show, *I Am Cait*. In 2015, *Glee* character Coach Beiste was revealed as transgender. That year was also the first time the word "transgender" was used in a State of the Union address, when President Barack Obama condemned violence against transgender people. According to the National Center for Transgender Equality, at least one transgender person is killed each month because of gender identity, and pop culture paved the way for Obama to address this issue.

Pop culture has played a prominent role in elevating awareness of transgender people, but not all representations are positive. The Gay and Lesbian Alliance against Defamation analyzed transgender characters in media from 2002 to 2014 and found that 54 percent were negatively portrayed, while only 12 percent were shown positively.[31] They also found that transgender people are cast as victims 40 percent of the time and as killers or villains 21 percent of the time. One in five transgender characters were depicted as sex workers, by far the most common profession shown for gender-nonconforming characters. Sixty-one percent of the storylines with transgender characters included antitransgender language. For example, *Nip/Tuck* dedicated an entire season to a psychopathic, baby-stealing, sexually predatory trans woman. Pop culture, then, is a double-edge sword when it comes to social justice and progress. It is a powerful tool for reinforcing existing gender biases that harm women, men, and gender-nonconforming individuals. It can also be a powerful force for raising awareness of issues and shifting public perceptions and behaviors.

PROFILE IN POWER

Laverne Cox

Laverne Cox is an actor and LGBTQ activist who is best known for her portrayal of Sophia Burset in the popular Netflix series *Orange Is the New Black*. Cox has a list of "firsts" to her name. She is the first transgender person to be nominated for an Emmy Award in the acting category, the first transgender person to have a wax figure likeness at Madame Tussauds wax museum, and the first transgender person to be featured on the cover of *Time Magazine*.

SOURCE: Taylor Pecko-Reid/KOMU 8

Cox uses her celebrity to advance transgender rights. She speaks and writes about transgender rights in a variety of media outlets. In 2014, Cox joined a campaign against an Arizona law that allows people to arrest anyone they think is "manifesting prostitution" because it has been disproportionately applied to transgender women of color. Cox has also been involved in efforts to address the mistreatment of transgender women in prison. In 2014, she won the Stephen F. Kolzak Award from the Gay and Lesbian Alliance against Defamation for her work as an advocate for the transgender community.

Cox was born in Mobile, Alabama, and she has an identical twin brother. She experienced severe bullying in school for her gender nonconformity, and at age 11, she attempted suicide. She graduated from the Alabama School of Fine Arts with an emphasis in dance and went on to study acting at the Marymount Manhattan College in New York City. Today, Cox is the most visible transgender celebrity in the nation, and she has used her celebrity to build a platform to fight for the rights of transgender individuals.

POLITICAL LEADERSHIP IN POP CULTURE

Pop culture shapes our perceptions of leadership in gendered ways that influence who is seen as worthy and capable of occupying positions of power. In this section, we focus on depictions of presidential leadership, a position of particular significance because it is the most powerful political position and because Americans have projected their hopes and desires onto the office for the past two centuries. Who is "allowed" to occupy this office in entertainment media reveals a lot about societal level of comfort with leaders of different identities. An examination of pop culture reveals that fictional leaders are mostly male, media conflates leadership with masculinity, reporters cover actual candidates in ways that reflect gender bias, and experts are typically cast as male. These media biases translate into double standards for male and female political candidates and leaders.

Leaders Are Portrayed as Men

Women are mostly missing in pop culture portrayals of leadership, and gender-nonconforming individuals are missing altogether. Fictional storylines in film and TV almost exclusively present leaders as men. Male characters comprise 96 percent of criminal leaders, 89 percent of business leaders, 89 percent of government and military leaders, and 81 percent of scientific and intellectual leaders.[32] This lopsided presentation of leadership in entertainment media reinforces the idea that men are better suited for formal positions of power. This bias is especially apparent with higher political offices, such as the presidency.

Pop culture both helps and hinders traditionally excluded groups from gaining access to the White House by shaping popular perceptions. Political scientist Lilly Goren studies the representation of men of color and women as presidents in pop culture, and she concludes that fictional black presidents paved the way for Barack Obama's election to the White House in 2008. She also finds that white women's presidential representations lag about 30 years behind those of African American men. The first black male president in entertainment media appeared in the 1933 film *Rufus Jones for President*, while the first white woman appeared three decades later in *Kisses for My President* (1964). The plot of *Kisses for My President* is a running joke about the "feminine" responsibilities of the first gentleman, which undermines the viability of her fictional candidacy. Overall, wide-release films have prominently featured 139 fictional presidents from 1960 to today, 97 of whom are white men compared to 14 men of color and one white woman. Although men of color are making inroads in pop culture depictions of the presidency, women of all races are rarely shown in this role.

The path candidates take to the White House in film and TV storylines also matters. Goren points out that black and Latino men have been elected to the presidency outright in the past 15 years (e.g., *24*, *Deep Impact*), while they previously ascended to the office through accidental means, like the death of a president.

She also finds that women are still portrayed as gaining the White House accidently rather than through election, which signals that they are not truly suited for the job.

More women are represented as fictional presidents in TV than film, but with mixed success. *Hail to the Chief* aired in 1985 with President Julia Mansfield, but was canceled two months later. Two decades later, President Laura Roslin appeared in the remake of *Battlestar Galactica* (2004) and Geena Davis starred as President Mackenzie Allen in *Commander in Chief* (2005), which was canceled after one season. Allison Taylor played a female president in later episodes of the hit TV series *24* (2009–2010) and fictional vice president Selina Meyer eventually ascends to the presidency in HBO's *Veep* (2012–present).

Most of these characters ascended to the office "accidently," through an unusual series of events rather than an election, for example, the president suffering a cerebral aneurism (*Commander in Chief*), being the highest ranking official left after a Cylon attack (*Battlestar Galactica*), or the president stepping down to care for his sick wife (*Veep*). This unusual pathway to the White House sends the message that women are not electable leaders, and when they do manage to land in the White House, their leadership is fundamentally illegitimate.

White women lag behind men of color, and both groups are far behind white men, who occupied the presidency for the first 220 years of our nation, but no group is more erased than women of color. All of the female presidents mentioned above are white women. More women of color are appearing as leading characters in prime-time TV, for example, Kerry Washington in *Scandal*, Viola Davis in *How to Get Away with Murder*, and Gina Rodriguez in *Jane the Virgin*, but they remain woefully underrepresented, especially in leadership roles. The only black female president in film or TV was Oprah Winfrey (playing herself) in CBS's futuristic legal drama *Century City*, which was canceled after just four shows in 2004. The symbolic annihilation of women of color as political leaders in pop culture both reflects and reinforces societal discomfort with this idea. This deep-seated bias against minority female leadership is best demonstrated by considering the implausibility of a black woman winning the presidency after spending just two years in the U.S. Senate (Obama's path to the White House).

Leadership Is Portrayed as Masculine

According to Pippa Norris and Ronald Inglehart, "patterns of domination, subordination, and the exclusion of women are core elements to the historical development of our most basic institutions."[33] Pop culture contributes to these patterns by establishing men as "natural" leaders, and it also promotes a specific type of hypermasculine leadership that limits public perceptions of who can be president. Jackson Katz notes that every presidential contest is a competition over competing visions of masculinity, a competition to see who is "man enough" to be president. This requirement for the presidency excludes many qualified candidates, particularly women, and encourages presidents to make decisions based on projecting a masculine image to stay in office.

Political scientist Meredith Conroy finds that candidates with more masculine traits win election, and candidates routinely feminize their opponents to win.[34] For example, George H. W. Bush's campaign chided Michael Dukakis for not being manly enough during a photo op with a tank during the 1988 campaign, and Bush was then feminized during the 1992 election when he got sick and vomited at a state dinner. Whether it is allegations of John Kerry getting Botox injections in the 2004 general election or John Edwards's expensive haircuts in the 2008 Democratic primaries, the presidential contest is inherently a contest of who is the most masculine candidate. In general election contests, the tallest of the two candidates wins most of the time. Both male and female candidates feel pressure to adopt masculine characteristics during elections, but women are at a disadvantage because "it is difficult for women to prove their allegiance to and mastery of the masculinist ideology."

The link between masculinity and the presidency can be drawn back to Teddy Roosevelt (1901–1909) and his use of pop culture at the time to craft a masculine persona. Roosevelt was an aristocratic, sickly child whose asthma plagued him his whole life, and although he led an active lifestyle as an adult, it was far from the rough and rugged image he projected. Roosevelt understood the power of pop culture, and he projected a masculine "cowboy" image through elaborate photo shoots that were published in the popular newspapers of the day. Presidential candidates since Roosevelt continue to link the presidency with masculinity, and this is especially true since the advent and widespread adoption of TV in the 1950s. Mass media is an effective way for candidates to project a masculine image on the campaign trail and while in office.

Entertainment media play a key role in linking leadership with masculinity. The most notable examples are Bill Pullman's president in *Independence Day* (1996), who uses his fighter pilot skills to save the world, Harrison Ford's president in *Air Force One* (1997), who personally foils a terrorist attempt, and Jamie Foxx's president in *White House Down* (2013). This popular archetype of the "warrior" president underpins the undemocratic bias of the presidency as a bastion of masculine leadership.

Gender Bias in Media Coverage of Candidates

In addition to leaders and leadership being presented as mostly male and masculine, respectively, reporters cover actual candidates in ways that reflect gender bias. Researchers have found bias in two areas: the type of coverage and the tone of coverage that male and female candidates receive.

In terms of the type of coverage, reporters give female gubernatorial and senatorial candidates less issue-related coverage than male candidates, which signals that their candidacy is less serious.[35] Additionally, reporters generally associate male candidates with "male policies" and traits and female candidates with stereotypically "female policies" and traits.[36] This bias has negative electoral consequences for female candidates because the public places a higher priority on issues that are stereotypically associated with men, such as the economy and national security, compared to issues associated with women, such as health care and education.

Reporters also pay more attention to personality traits and focus more on the personal lives, dress, and appearance of female candidates.[37] For example, in one study of gubernatorial and senatorial races in 2002, eight percent of news stories about female candidates mentioned their marital status compared to only one percent of stories about male candidates.[38] Similarly, reporters mentioned appearance in six percent of news stories about female candidates compared to one percent for male candidates. Press coverage of Elizabeth Dole's dress and appearance was more intense than that of her male contenders in 2000, and in 2008, Hillary Clinton also received an unusual amount of attention focused on her appearance—from her "cackle" and cleavage to her pantsuits and the size of her bottom.[39]

When it comes to the tone of coverage, female candidates receive significantly more negative coverage than male candidates.[40] In Erica Falk's analysis of nine female presidential candidates from 1800 to 2008, she finds that reporters use negative stereotypes that trivialize women's candidacies.[41] Female candidates also receive more coverage questioning their viability in ways that cause voters to see them as less viable candidates.[42] Sexist language is also a normal part of the political environment for female candidates. For example, in 2008, media host Glenn Beck described Hillary Clinton as a "stereotypical bitch" and commentator Tucker Carlson joked that when she comes on television, "I involuntarily cross my legs." In 2016, media and social media commentary derided Clinton in gendered ways about her voice (#Shrillary), not smiling enough (host Joe Scarborough tweeting to Clinton, "Smile. You just had a big night"), smiling too much (commentator David Frum tweeting, "Who told Hillary Clinton to keep smiling like she's at her granddaughter's birthday party?"), and being too ambitious for staying in a race she was winning (#DropOutHillary).

Gender biases in press coverage have electoral consequences in that they affect voter perceptions in ways that disadvantage female candidates. Although the media do not tell readers what to think directly, they tell us what topics to think about through agenda setting and how to think about these topics by framing them in certain ways with emphasis placed on some aspects and not others.[43] For example, by disproportionately covering issues such as national security or military crises, which are perceived to be "men's issues" by the public, the media are priming their audience to think less seriously about a female candidate. Gender biases in media coverage may also discourage women from running for office themselves.[44]

Professionals/Experts Are Portrayed as Men
Pop culture also hinders the leadership potential of women and gender-nonconforming individuals by linking expertise to men. Women are vastly underrepresented when it comes to who is featured as experts in politics and economics. People who deliver the news and comment on contemporary events are disproportionately male and mostly white. According to the Women's Media Center, women constitute 32 percent of the anchors in evening news broadcasts, 37 percent of print news, and 42 percent of online news.[45] Only one in four political pundits on cable news programs are female, and male commentators

outnumber female commentators nine to one on Sunday news programs. Male voices and perspectives dominate news coverage and send the message to viewers that expertise is a male domain. Media biases in who gets to be an expert both reflect and reinforce deep-seated biases about who holds knowledge in society. Philosopher Lorraine Code studies societal notions of knowledge and concludes that "it is no exaggeration to say that anyone who wanted to *count* as a knower has commonly been male."[46]

Another way that pop culture fundamentally shapes ideas about female leadership is by limiting representations of fictional experts in film and television. Experts are almost exclusively shown as male and are mostly shown as white, while women are mostly identified in terms of their roles as lover, wife, and mother. According to Martha Lauzen's research at the Center for the Study of Women in Film and Television, male characters are twice as likely as female characters to be identified by professional work-related roles, such as chief executive officer or doctor (62 percent compared to 34 percent).[47] Three in five female characters (58 percent) are identified only by a personal life role, such as wife or mother.

Gendered ideas of knowledge derive from the separate-spheres ideology, the idea that women are better suited for private affairs, while men are better suited for public life. This fundamental belief persists despite women moving into social, economic, and political spheres in the United States. A majority of Americans still believe that women should be the primary caregivers of children and responsible for family social obligations. Separate-spheres ideology is evident in the fact that women face more questions about their family responsibilities on the campaign trail than do men, and voters are concerned that female candidates will neglect their families if they gain public office. Similar concerns are not generally raised for male candidates at any level of office. The second wave of the feminist movement made public-sphere activities attractive, but did little to valorize private activities. Thus, although women have moved *en masse* into the public sphere, few men have moved into the private sphere, and women who work outside the home do twice the amount of housework as their husbands.[48]

Separate-spheres ideology is of particular significance to the highest political offices, such as the presidency, because these positions are analogous to the head of the household. It is difficult to envision anyone other than a masculine father figure as the head of the household, and, thus, it is difficult to imagine a woman as the symbolic head of the national household. The mismatch of being a woman and being a patriarchal protector is seen in the lack of female protector roles in pop culture. There are rare exceptions, such as Sigourney Weaver's character Ripley in the *Alien* franchise, where women are cast as the protector. Instead, women are cast as the love interest of the hero, the sidekick, or the damsel in distress.

Biases against female expertise and leadership have consequences for real-life female leaders in political and corporate settings. Female leaders are demonstrably effective and profitable in the corporate sector, but both men and women still prefer male bosses over female bosses. Additionally, stereotypes about gender and leadership caused both men and women to evaluate female leaders more negatively than their male counterparts, regardless of their leadership style. A Catalyst study of countries across the globe found that although different countries value different types of leadership, "male" leadership was valued more than "female" leadership across the board. For example, in some countries, the ideal leadership skill was problem solving, while in others, the ideal skill was team building; regardless, "whatever was most valued, women were seen as lacking it."[49]

OLD MEDIA AND NEW MEDIA

The rapid growth in Internet use has blurred the line between traditional news and entertainment media in gendered ways that affect power in U.S. society. Old or legacy media refers to traditional modes of media such as radio, cable TV, newspapers, magazines, and books. It is distinguished by its editorial filters, meaning that content has been approved through a formal, top-down process. New media refers to online content such as blogs, wikis, and social media. It is marked by a lack of editorial filter, user-generated content, and interactive user feedback. New media emerged in the mid-1990s with the widespread adoption of personal computer technology, and its use accelerated in the mid-2000s with the invention of social media.

New media has not eclipsed old media, but most Americans now access online sources for information in addition to or in lieu of traditional media. According to the American Press Institute, most Americans still get their news from local TV (81 percent) or national network news (72 percent), and a majority of Americans also watch cable news (61 percent).[50] Two-thirds (66 percent) of Americans get their information from printed or online newspapers, while more than half (56 percent) get their news from radio sources. Just under half (47 percent) obtain news from online-only reporting sources, such as the Huffington Post or Buzzfeed. According to the Pew Research Center, one in three Americans use Facebook as a source for news, while one in ten report the same for Twitter and YouTube.

New media shifts the balance of who is in control of information, which has implications for gender equality. Editors and writers no longer have exclusive purview of the content, and readers can provide feedback in the comments and commentary about news articles in social media reposts. The number of producers, distributors, and consumers of media has multiplied in the age of new media. New technologies have increased news consumption and produced the habit of "news snacking"—users viewing news content for short periods throughout the day. Digital media increases both political knowledge and political participation, but it has also contributed to party polarization in the United States.

New media has implications for gender equality because news media has become more sensationalized, infused with pop culture content. Hybrid news organizations that combine both "hard" news and "soft" celebrity and gossip "news" have become commonplace, for example, the Huffington Post and the Daily Beast. This means that photos of objectified celebrities now run next to articles about the trade deficit and health-care policy. This hybridization and lack of editorial filters has also changed the content of political news coverage in ways that hamper female candidates and political leaders.

Research on old media coverage of female candidates finds that newspaper articles are twice as likely to mention the appearance and families of women who are running, and female candidates are four times more likely to receive sexist coverage than male candidates. Female candidates are also discussed in more negative terms than are male contenders. The volume of gendered and sexist coverage is even more pronounced in new media, which means that new media is a more hostile environment for women trying to gain political leadership positions. Without editorial filters and the outward pursuit of objectivity, the misogyny quotient and negativity in new media is heightened.

As discussed in Chapter 3, new media has positive implications for gender justice through #Feminism. New media produced the feminist blogosphere that elevates the voices of women and feminist perspectives. Websites like Jezebel, the Feminist Wire, Ultraviolet, Feministing, Ms. Blog, and many others have created a culture where overt and subtle sexism can be called out, recognized, and addressed. New online media technologies have put feminist concerns on the public agenda in a way that arguably signals a new wave of feminism.

The shift from old media to new media has mixed implications for gender justice. Fewer editorial filters mean that greater sexism and other forms of bias work their way into media content. However, online spaces mean that biases can more quickly and readily be "called out." The question is whether grass-roots and alternative media geared toward gender justice are an effective counter to massive media companies that generate the images and content consumed the most.

CONCLUSION

In this chapter, we explored how mass media shape our society and political culture in gendered ways. Media have become even more influential recently because most people are constantly connected to media communication devices. Stories of women's lives are mostly absent in popular culture, and this has remained relatively constant since the 1950s. When women are shown, it is rarely in leadership positions, but more often as love interests and sex objects. This portrayal diminishes women in general. Entertainment media also portray leadership as a masculine pursuit. Most leaders in film and TV are men, and female leaders are shown as "accidental." Women are underrepresented and misrepresented in media because they hold only three percent of decision-making positions.

Pop culture also portrays men in ways that harm them by showing characters that are emotionally detached, aggressive, and violent. The norms of masculinity cause men to die at higher rates at every age because they tend to treat their bodies as though they are invulnerable, engage in more high-risk behaviors, and wait longer to admit that they are sick or seek treatment. It also causes higher rates of depression, addiction, and suicide.

Pop culture also misrepresents gender-nonconforming individuals. Most are portrayed as social deviants, killers, villains, and sex workers. These media representations matter because they shape who is seen as a qualified leader, who is a possessor of knowledge, and who is worthy of status within society.

CHAPTER SUMMARY

- This chapter examined the role that mass media play in shaping our society and political culture in gendered ways.
- It is easy to dismiss pop culture as simply entertaining, harmless fun, but half a century of social science research reveals that media shape our perceptions and priorities.
- Media affect many aspects of our life and have become more influential in recent years because most people are constantly connected to media communication devices through new technologies like smartphones.
- Women's representations in mass media mostly diminish their social status. Stories of women's lives are generally missing in pop culture, and this underrepresentation has not changed much since the 1950s.
- Women in pop culture are also less likely than men to be shown in professional or leadership positions. They are typically defined by their roles as love interest, wife, or mother.
- When women do appear in film and TV, they are far more likely than men to be sexualized. Female sexual objectification has increased in the past decade as marketers and content producers try to cut through the clutter of images in new media to reach viewers/consumers.
- We introduced the CHIPS test as a quick way to determine whether an image is sexually objectifying. Does the image show a sexualized body as (1) a commodity, (2) harmed, (3) interchangeable, (4) body parts, or (5) a stand-in for an actual object?
- Female sexual objectification diminishes women's power by setting up a society where their worth is determined by their bodies and the validation of others. Objectification culture has been linked to depression, eating disorders, lower cognitive functioning, diminished physical mobility, and a lower grade point average.
- Viewers see an objectified image as a collection of body parts rather than a whole person and as a tool that exists for their use. They are less concerned about the pain and suffering of an objectified woman. Societal acceptance of this dehumanization of women is linked to high rates of sexual violence against them.
- Mass media focus on the dress and appearance of female candidates, which diminishes their electoral success. Female candidates and political leaders who are sexualized and considered feminine are judged to be incompetent.
- Women hold only three percent of clout positions in mass media, and when women are decision makers, the representation of women improves.

- Pop culture misrepresents men in ways that diminish their health and happiness. Male characters are shown as solving problems by maintaining control and enacting violence, and masculinity in media is often associated with emotional detachment, competition, aggression, and violence, which encourages boys and men to engage in high-risk behaviors and shut off their emotions.
- This brand of masculinity shortens men's life span. Men die at higher rates at every age because they tend to treat their bodies as though they are invulnerable, engage in more high-risk behaviors, wait longer to admit that they are sick, wait longer to get help for sickness, and have lower rates of compliance with medical treatment than women.
- Masculinity also leaves many men traumatized and often depressed without knowing it. Men tend to externalize stress and act out their emotions through more socially approved means, such as drug addiction, working too much, and violence. This is linked to higher rates of rage disorders, substance abuse, violent crime, and suicide.
- Studies conducted in the 1950s first discovered a link between viewing violent media content and aggressive behavior. More recently, research indicates that violence in video games increases aggressive thoughts and behaviors and decreases empathy and pro-social behaviors.
- The representation of gender-nonconforming individuals has dramatically improved in the past decade, but the vast majority of characters in film, TV, and other forms of pop culture still fit the male/female binary and identify as heterosexual.
- Pop culture sparked a national conversation about the fluidity of gender with the prominence of transgender celebrities such as Laverne Cox, Janet Mock, and Caitlyn Jenner. This conversation put violence against transgender individuals on the national political agenda.
- Pop culture representations of gender-nonconforming individuals are improving, but they still have a long way to go. Although we are seeing more transgender characters in mass media, they are mostly portrayed as social deviants, killers, villains, and sex workers.
- Pop culture shapes our perceptions of leadership in gendered ways that influence who is seen as worthy and capable of occupying positions of power. Fictional storylines in film and TV almost exclusively present leaders as men.
- Fictional black presidents in film and TV paved the way for Barack Obama's election to the White House in 2008, but white women's presidential representations lag about 30 years behind those of African American men, and female leaders of color are virtually nonexistent in entertainment media. Black and Latino men have been elected to the presidency outright in the past 15 years, but women get to the office accidently rather than through election, which signals that they are not truly suited for the job.
- Pop culture presents leadership as masculine, which also disadvantages many men and all women. In politics, every presidential contest is a competition to see who is "man enough" for the job. Entertainment media shape this expectation with the "warrior" president archetype.

- Pop culture also hinders the leadership potential of women and gender-nonconforming individuals by linking expertise to men. News anchors and pundits who analyze politics are overwhelmingly male. This bias in who is seen as an expert reinforces bias about who holds knowledge in society.
- Gendered ideas of knowledge derive from the separate-spheres ideology, the idea that women are better suited for private affairs, while men are better suited for public life. This fundamental belief persists despite women moving into social, economic, and political spheres in the United States.
- Pop culture biases against female expertise and leadership matter. Both men and women still prefer male bosses over female bosses, and both men and women evaluate female leaders more negatively than their male counterparts, regardless of their leadership style.
- New media has implications for gender justice because news media has become more sensationalized, infused with pop culture content. This means that photos of objectified celebrities now run next to articles about the trade deficit and health-care policy. Also, the volume of gendered and sexist coverage of female candidates is more pronounced in new media. However, new media also produced the feminist blogosphere that elevates the voices of women and feminist perspectives.
- Pop culture is a double-edge sword when it comes to gender justice. It is a powerful tool for reinforcing existing gender biases that harm women, men, and gender-nonconforming individuals. It can also be a powerful force for raising awareness of issues and shifting public perceptions and behaviors.

STUDY/DISCUSSION QUESTIONS

- How does popular culture influence our lives? Has this influence increased or declined in the past decade?
- How are women typically represented in mass media? How does this vary by race?
- How are men typically represented in mass media? How does this vary by race?
- How are transgender people typically represented in mass media? How does this vary by race?
- How is leadership depicted in pop culture, and why do these biases matter?

CASE STUDIES

1. **How can we improve intersectional representations in pop culture?**
   Women and gender-nonconforming individuals have been vastly underrepresented in pop culture for more than half a century, especially people of color. Does this mean that society has accepted this behavior for so long that it is invisible to most people? As nearly six decades of activism around this issue demonstrate, increasing awareness of the issue is not enough to change it.

What are some ways to effectively shift such deep-seated societal beliefs that some people matter less than others?

2. **Do transgender representations in the media reinforce the binary?**
There is no doubt that 2015 was a breakthrough year for transgender women. Janet Mock, Laverne Cox, Caitlyn Jenner, and other trans women celebrities earned awards, graced the covers of popular magazines, and landed prominent roles in TV and film. The high profile of trans people and issues in pop culture represents progress in the struggle for gender justice, but the most prominent trans celebrities fit the male/female binary and are conventionally attractive. What does this tell us about societal comfort with gender fluidity? Why haven't trans men and gender-androgynous individuals received the same attention and accolades as transgender women who conform to traditional notions of femininity and women being sexy?

3. **What would it mean to address toxic masculinity?**
Women's misrepresentation in media and its numerous harmful effects have been the subject of scholarly analysis, documentaries, and public debate since the 1970s, but the role of media in spreading toxic masculinity has only recently received public attention. Why have men's harmful media misrepresentations received less attention? Is this a reflection of society caring less about the health and happiness of men, societal assumptions of male invulnerability, or something else? What would it mean if we as a culture took toxic masculinity seriously? How would it challenge men's patriarchal power to adopt a different brand of masculinity or eliminate the masculine/feminine binary altogether?

4. **Is new media an effective tool in the struggle for gender justice?**
As demonstrated in this chapter, mass media both reinforce gender hierarchies and provide a forum to challenge these hierarchies. New media has exacerbated gender injustice with online gender harassment, more sexist coverage of female candidates, an increase in female sexual objectification, more violent content, pressure for boys to be more hyperviolent, etc. However, the blogosphere gives feminist, critical race, and queer activists more of a voice in the national conversation. Is this seat at the table enough to counterbalance the harmful gendered effects of mass media?

RESOURCES

- The **Representation Project** provides documentaries, curriculum, and other resources about the misrepresentations of women and men in popular culture. http://therepresentationproject.org
- Dr. Jackson Katz's **Mentors in Violence Prevention** program is a gender violence and antibullying program that educates participants about the role of media in promoting unhealthy masculinity. http://www.mvpnational.org/

- **Trans Media Watch** is a nonprofit organization dedicated to improving the representations of transgender and intersexed people in media through research and advocacy.
  http://www.transmediawatch.org
- Founded by the Academy Award–winning actor Geena Davis, the **Geena Davis Institute on Gender in Media** produces annual reports on the representation of women in entertainment media.
  http://seejane.org
- The mission of the **Women's Media Center** is to get more women in media through advocacy campaigns, monitoring of media sexism, and training of female experts.
  http://www.womensmediacenter.com

CHAPTER 5

Women as Political Participants

In February 2012, George Zimmerman shot and killed 17-year-old African American high school student Trayvon Martin. The teenager was walking back from 7-Eleven to his father's house in Sanford, Florida, having purchased a bag of Skittles and an Arizona Ice Tea. Moments before the shooting, Zimmerman had placed a call to police from his sport utility vehicle to report a "suspicious person." The police instructed Zimmerman to stay in his vehicle and not approach Martin; Zimmerman disregarded the instructions and confronted Martin, and an altercation ensued. Police did not initially arrest Zimmerman because his actions were deemed self-defense. Within weeks of the shooting, a Change.org petition calling for Zimmerman's arrest garnered 1.3 million signatures, and on the one-month anniversary of Martin's death, protesters took to the streets in cities across the United States demanding a full investigation of the shooting. Zimmerman was charged with murder and acquitted in July 2013. In response, protests were staged in more than 100 cities in the United States, with many protesters wearing hoodies, the outfit Martin was wearing when he was shot. This was the beginning of a major new national social movement started by three women.

Alicia Garza, Patrisse Cullors, and Opal Tometi formed the #BlackLivesMatter (BLM) movement in the days following Zimmerman's acquittal, and it quickly became the largest social movement in the United States. Organizers held more than 1,000 protests and demonstrations in the first year of its existence, some of which shut down subway systems and major freeways. They also organized an annual Black Friday boycott at stores and malls across the United States on the busiest shopping day of the year to demonstrate the economic power of African Americans. In the fall of 2015, BLM inspired students at colleges and universities across the United States to demand more equitable treatment on campus through demands, demonstrations, and occupations. Three queer women of color launched BLM, but their contributions and leadership have mostly been erased in mainstream media coverage of the movement. Male leaders have become the most prominent voices in BLM, and the subcampaign #SayHerName was organized in response to BLM overlooking police and vigilante violence targeting black women. According to cofounder Garza,

> Straight men, unintentionally or intentionally, have taken the work of queer Black women and erased our contributions. Perhaps if we were the charismatic Black men many are rallying around these days, it would have been a different story, but being Black queer women in this society (and apparently within these movements) tends to equal invisibility and non-relevancy.[1]

The marginalization of the BLM cofounders is indicative of a broader trend of political participation. Women often play key organizing roles in political movements and campaigns, but their contributions tend to be overshadowed by male organizers. This is especially true for women of color whose very identity conflicts with ingrained notions of who is a "real leader." In this chapter, we explore these issues within a larger examination of women's electoral and nonelectoral participation.

Men and women have different pathways to politics, and they engage in politics in different ways. The purpose of this chapter is to examine how political participation is gendered, why it is gendered, and how gender affects political outcomes.[2] We organize the chapter into three different parts focusing on childhood political socialization, political preferences, and political participation. In the first section, we look at the different ways in which girls and boys are raised to think about politics. We find that boys are encouraged to view politics as their domain, and girls receive the opposite message. In the second section, we examine how gender differences in political preferences affect policy positions, party identification, and vote choice. We show that women are more liberal than men and are more likely to identify with the Democratic Party and vote for Democratic candidates. In the third section of this chapter, we examine gender gaps in political participation—voting, making a campaign contribution, working for a political party, community organizing, signing an online petition, and boycotting for political reasons. We find that women and men participate in politics at about the same level, but in group organizing, men tend to dominate leadership positions. This chapter provides a detailed overview of the gender gaps in political ambition, political ideology, party affiliation, voting, and other aspects of politics.

CHILDHOOD POLITICAL SOCIALIZATION

Gender is one of the foundational ways in which we organize politics, meaning that gender matters when it comes to elections, political activism, resource allocation, and policymaking. Women and men approach politics in different ways and through different paths. Gender gaps in politics can be traced back to political socialization, defined as the process by which individuals in a society learn about their political culture. Girls and boys are taught different messages about whether and how they should be active in politics, and this translates into differences in political interest, political knowledge, political efficacy, and political ambition. We address each of these topics in turn. We report broad differences between men and women, but there is great diversity within these groups in terms of race and class that we report on whenever data are available.

Political Interest

Political interest is measured by how much a person pays attention to contemporary political events. Researchers have documented a persistent gender gap in political interest, with men showing significantly greater interest. For example, at the high end of political interest, 26 percent of men are "very interested in politics and current events" compared to only 15 percent of women.[3] Political interest is an important building block of democracy because people with higher political interest levels participate at higher rates. People with higher rates of interest in politics are more likely to follow political news, and this leads to higher rates of political ambition. Political interest also translates into greater involvement in politics. Young people who visit political websites every day are twice as likely as those who rarely or never visit such sites to express an interest in holding public office. Researchers have identified many social, political, and psychological causes of the political interest gender gap. The root cause is gendered political socialization. Politics has been defined by societies as a primarily male pursuit since its inception in Greece more than 2,000 years ago, and from a young age, boys are encouraged to be interested in and knowledgeable about politics. This positive democratic message is reinforced over the life course for men but not for women. Similar to being able to speak the language of sports, men are rewarded socially for being knowledgeable about current political events.

Boys and girls in the United States learn that politics is a white male domain by seeing mostly white male leaders in positions of power and in popular culture depictions of leadership. We know that these depictions impact political interest because women who live in states with a higher proportion of women in the state legislature have higher levels of political interest knowledge than women living in states with fewer female leaders.[4] Female voters reasonably expect that female political leaders will be more responsive on issues that matter more to women, so they pay more attention to politics and policies in general when represented by a woman.

Political Knowledge

A persistent gender gap also exists for political knowledge. Men exhibit higher levels of knowledge about basic political facts and processes than do women in the United States and across the globe.[5] The political knowledge gender gap does not vary by how progressive the country is when it comes to gender equality, which means that men possess more political knowledge even in countries with relative gender equality. The political knowledge gender gap tends to be overstated because women are less likely than men to guess on survey questions when they are unsure of the answers, but the gap is persistent and large.

The knowledge gap encompasses knowledge differences in how political institutions work, contemporary public policy issues, political leadership, and political events. Political knowledge is measured by a series of questions that ask people to identify political leaders based on photographs, provide basic knowledge about which party controls Congress or the number of Supreme Court justices, and identify details of current political events such as wars or natural disasters. Men offer the correct answers about 15 percent more often than women. The gender gap in political knowledge is not caused by differences in intelligence, intellectual ability, or academic preparation.[6]

One root of the knowledge gap is that news consumption is primarily a male activity, which means that men are encouraged to keep up with political news. College men are twice as likely as college women to regularly visit political websites and nearly ten percent more likely to take a political science or government class. Men are also more likely to view televised political events, such as presidential debates and State of the Union addresses. When it comes to news consumption, women are more interested in stories about health, safety, natural disasters, and celebrities, while men are more interested in stories about sports and politics.

Another factor that contributes to the political knowledge gender gap is a bias in who presents political news. Women are more likely to tune in to radio and television programs when female anchors and contributors are delivering the news, but political news is dominated by white male faces and voices. According to the Women's Media Center, men generate 62 percent of the news. In television news, men are on camera 68 percent of the time, and male experts are relied on twice as often as female experts.[7] Women are less likely to be interested in and knowledgeable about politics as the result of a male bias in media coverage of politics. Women also have time constraints that affect their acquisition of political knowledge relative to men. Researchers find that women have less time to devote to politics because they are more likely than men to be working outside the home and carry domestic and child-care responsibilities within the home. In short, women have less time to devote to activities that do not directly pertain to paid employment and domestic responsibilities.

Political Efficacy

Political efficacy is the perception that one's voice matters in politics. There are two types of political efficacy—internal and external. Internal political efficacy is defined by the belief that a person can understand and therefore participate in politics, while external political efficacy is the belief that the government will be responsive to a person's demands. Men and women look remarkably similar when it comes to external political efficacy, but they differ significantly on measures of internal political efficacy.[8] Women are less likely to have confidence in their personal ability to influence politics than men. People of color have lower political efficacy and higher rates of cynicism than white people, and this is especially pronounced for women of color.[9]

There are many psychological, social, and political causes of the gender gap in internal political efficacy. One primary cause is the gender gap in political knowledge. Women have less confidence in their ability to have a political impact because they have less knowledge about political processes and events. Additionally, women start with lower overall levels of self-esteem than men, which translates into lower confidence in the political realm. Another cause of the gap in political efficacy is the cultural norm of female sexual objectification. Women who score higher on measures of self-objectification, as discussed in Chapter 4, have significantly lower rates of internal political efficacy.[10] This finding stands even when education, income, and other factors that affect political efficacy are taken into account. In other words, the pop culture norm of female sexual objectification affects both the personal and the political lives of women in the United States.

Positive reinforcement can reduce or eliminate the internal efficacy gap.[11] In experimental settings, women who receive positive feedback on political knowledge tests reported higher levels of political interest and confidence in their ability to influence politics. Men were not affected by positive feedback, and their interest in politics declined when they were given accurate feedback on their performance. This demonstrates that men and women have distinct psychological approaches to politics, what Jennifer Lawless and Richard Fox call a "gendered psyche." Men are overly confident about their political knowledge and their efficacy suffers when they are shown their shortcomings, while women start with low confidence and their confidence increases with positive feedback.

PROFILE IN POWER

Alicia Garza, Patrisse Cullors, and Opal Tometi

Alicia Garza, Patrisse Cullors, and Opal Tometi are three queer, black activists who founded the #BlackLivesMatter campaign in 2012 after neighborhood watchperson George Zimmerman shot and killed 17-year-old Trayvon Martin as he was walking home from a convenience store. The #BlackLivesMatter campaign is critical of the structural racism that persists in the United States, especially as it manifests in the killing of unarmed black people by law enforcement and vigilantes. This movement has grown since 2012, and hundreds of protests have taken place in cities and towns across the United States to protest against police brutality toward black Americans.

Garza, who lives in Los Angeles, devised the hashtag that would become the campaign name with the Facebook post: "Black people, I love you. I love us. Our lives matter. Black Lives Matter." Prior to this campaign, Garza had worked on campaigns for worker rights, antiracism, antigentrification, and antiviolence against trans and gender-nonconforming people. She is the director of special projects for the National Domestic Workers Alliance, the leading advocacy organization fighting for the rights of nannies, housekeepers, and elderly caregivers. Garza has earned many awards for her activism, including the Bayard Rustin Community Activist Award for her work fighting against gentrification in San Francisco.

Cullors is also a lifelong social justice advocate. As a child, she witnessed family members experience policy brutality, and this inspired her to work on law enforcement accountability initiatives. Cullors was born in Los Angeles, and she was forced to leave her home at age 16 when she told her parents she was queer. She went on to earn a college degree in philosophy and religion from the University of California, Los Angeles, and was awarded a Fulbright Scholarship. Cullors was the executive director of the Coalition to End Sheriff Violence in LA Jails and she co-founded Dignity and Power Now, a prison activism organization. In 2007, she was awarded the Mario Savio Young Activists of the Year Award, and in 2015, she was named an NAACP History Maker.

Tometi, the daughter of Nigerian immigrants, is a writer based in New York. She worked as an immigrant rights organizer prior to creating most of the social media infrastructure for #BlackLivesMatter. She also serves as the executive director of the Black Alliance for Just Immigration, a national advocacy organization to further immigrant rights and racial justice together. Tometi grew up in Phoenix, Arizona, and she earned a bachelor's degree in history and a master's degree in communications from the University of Arizona. Prior to directing the Black Alliance for Just Immigration, she worked as a case manager for survivors of domestic violence. In 2014, she was featured as a new face in civil rights leadership in *Essence* magazine and the *Los Angeles Times*.

Garza, Cullors, and Tometi met one another through a national organization that trains community organizers. After Zimmerman's acquittal, they began to communicate with one another via social media about the best way to respond. #BlackLivesMatter has emerged as the new civil rights movement that has inspired millions of people across the globe to take action against police brutality and state-sanctioned violence that disproportionately targets people of color.

Political Ambition

A gender gap also exists when it comes to political ambition. Men have higher rates of political ambition than women, which means that men are more likely to consider running for public office.[12] Women think they are less qualified to run for political office than men with the same or comparable qualifications. According to Lawless and Fox, men are almost twice as likely as women to have thought about running for public office "many times." Nearly half of men (48 percent) have considered running for public office at some point, compared to 35 percent of women. The political ambition gap starts at a young age, when men's political interests and ambition are piqued and encouraged in a way that women's are not. Teen boys are also significantly more likely to have considered running for office before they graduated from high school than teen girls (15 percent compared to nine percent). It is important to note that the gender gap in political ambition is not the result of women having different aspirations than men in general or women having less of a sense of civic duty. Young men and women today are roughly equally likely to want to have children, get married, achieve career success, and earn a lot of money. Young men and women are also equally likely to want to improve their communities, but women are less likely to see running for public office as a viable way to do so.

There are many causes for the gender gap in political ambition. One primary cause is that women are less likely than men with similar qualifications to be encouraged to run for public office.[13] In other words, friends and family members give men more encouragement to run for public office because politics is seen as a male domain. Family members are especially important in influencing a person's political ambition. Someone who is encouraged to run for political office by at least one family member is 43 percent more likely to have high political ambition than a person who receives no encouragement from family. Another reason women possess lower political ambition than men is that they see the electoral environment as biased against them. They view campaigns as hyper-competitive and biased in ways that will not give them a fair shake should they pursue politics. For example, sexist media coverage of Hillary Clinton and Sarah Palin in the 2008 election discouraged girls and women from running.[14] Women tend to be more risk averse than men to begin with, so perceived biases significantly dampen political ambition. The gender gap in political ambition starts early in life as a result of educational and peer experiences that politicize young people. Participation in competitive activities in grade school and junior high school, such as the debate team or student government, significantly increase a person's interest in running for public office. In general, teachers, coaches, and other adults encourage boys to participate in these competitive activities more than girls.

The gender gap for political ambition is also caused by differences in self-confidence for young women and men. Girls and women have lower self-confidence than boys and men in every country, and it tends to emerge between ages four and 14. Differences in self-confidence come from patriarchal ideas that men and their activities are more important and worthy than women and their activities, which leads men to significantly overestimate their intelligence and abilities. For example, men tend to overestimate their IQ, while women underestimate theirs,[15] and both mothers and fathers tend to think that their sons have higher IQs than their daughters. In other words, we raise our girls to underestimate their skills and abilities in ways that translate into overall lower confidence levels. One interesting point about political ambition is that the gender gap becomes larger during the college years for people who are privileged to further their education beyond high school. Men have experiences during college, such as affirmation from professors and encouragement to participate in competitive activities, which improve their political ambition. Young women's political ambition declines during college, which means they are not getting the same messages from campus professionals during these formative years.

POLITICAL PREFERENCES

Women and men have different interests and experiences in life that shape their political preferences in ways that are also affected by experiences of race, class, sexuality, and other characteristics. These political precursors lead to significant gender gaps on policy positions, party identification, and vote choice. In this section, we examine how political attitudes shape the policies that people support and the candidates they vote for.

Policy Positions

According to the Center for American Women in Politics, women and men hold different views on a host of domestic and foreign-policy issues.[16] On the domestic side, men are less supportive than women of national health care, poverty assistance programs, and restrictions on firearms. Men are also less supportive of programs aimed at addressing social and economic inequalities such as same-sex policies, affirmative action, equal pay laws, and laws banning LGBTQ discrimination in the workplace and the military. Women are generally more supportive of policy issues that directly affect them. Men and women are equally supportive of abortion rights, but women are more supportive of abortion under any circumstances. Women are also more likely to favor employer-mandated birth control, laws curtailing sexual harassment in the workplace, and women in combat roles in the military. Men and women were equally supportive of the Equal Rights Amendment (ERA) when it was hotly contested in 1970s and 1980s, but women were more active in trying to get it passed.

When it comes to fiscal issues, men are more individualistic in their approach than women. Women are far more likely than men to favor a national minimum wage. They prefer raising taxes to balance the budget rather than cutting benefit programs, while men prefer program cuts. Women are more likely to attribute the growing gap between rich and poor to an economic system favoring the wealthy, while men are more likely to attribute it to overregulation of the free market. When asked whether the United States is more successful when the government emphasizes self-reliance versus community, women generally favor community, while men favor self-reliance.

A gender gap also exists when it comes to environmental issues. Women are more risk-averse than men and thus more supportive of environmental regulations to reduce health risks. Women are eight percent more likely to believe that the country should do whatever it takes to protect the environment (75 percent compared to 67 percent) and eight percent less likely to think the country has gone too far in efforts to protect the environment (20 percent compared to 28 percent).[17] Men are significantly more supportive of the use of nuclear power and offshore oil and gas drilling as a way to address the nation's energy needs. Women (65 percent) are slightly more likely than men (60 percent) to believe that climate change is happening.

Women and men also differ in terms of their general outlook on government. Women are more likely to favor an activist role for government, especially in terms of social services for those in need, guaranteeing jobs, and providing for a standard of living. Women perceive government programs to be more effective than do men. This difference in perceptions of government can be attributed to the fact that, on average, women are more economically vulnerable than men and are more likely to receive government support because of child-care roles. In other words, women have greater support for government programs because they are more likely to personally benefit from them.

The largest and most consistent policy gender gap is on national defense. In general, women are less supportive than men of military spending and war. Gendered support for war is strongly dependent on the context of a given war. Women are less likely than men to support unilateral wars initiated for economic reasons, but the gender gap disappears for wars approved by the United Nations with a humanitarian goal. When it comes to foreign policy, a greater percentage of men than women believe that the best way to ensure peace is through military strength (35 percent compared to 27 percent).[18] More women (62 percent) than men (53 percent) believe that diplomacy is the best way to ensure peace.

Gender gaps in policy support vary depending on political and economic conditions, but they are significant and persist over time. Early feminist theorists attributed gender gaps in policy support to women's natural superiority or differences in ethical reasoning. Theorist Carol Gilligan proposes that women are more oriented toward interpersonal relationships, while men are concerned with rights and rules. This translates into a gender gap in ethical reasoning where women are more concerned about caring for others, while men emphasize fairness in their moral assessments. Theorist Sarah Ruddick proposes that women have "maternal thinking" from raising children that causes them to be more caring toward others in general. These early theories seem to suggest biological origins, but more recent scholarship focuses on gendered socialization as the origin of the policy gender gap.

One experience that produces the gender gap in policy is the societal expectation that women are primary caregivers. Women are more oriented toward caretaking—an "ethic of care"—and as a result, women are more supportive of policies that do the same. Women are more concerned about social safety nets because they are more aware of issues affecting their family and friend network. Women are also more supportive of policies that address inequality because of firsthand experiences of inequality. In employment, for example, the vast majority of adult women report that they have been paid less for performing the same work as their male colleagues, have been denied a promotion based on their gender, and have experienced sexual harassment. Women are also more likely to be poor and elderly than men, so they are more likely to be beneficiaries of social programs.

Feminist identification also shapes the policy gender gap. Women who identify as feminists are linked to lower rates of racism, a greater sense of egalitarianism, and expressions of empathy for the disadvantaged. The gender gap that emerged in voting, partisanship, and policy positions in the 1980s was driven by the women's movement of the 1970s that raised feminist identification rates. According to Pamela Conover, "there is not so much a gap between men and women as there is a gap between men and feminists."[19]

Women have many experiences and interests in common, but it is important to point out that not all women share the same policy positions. As discussed in Chapter 2, conservative women who are strongly influenced by religious beliefs and a desire to maintain traditional gender roles organized in the late 1970s in response to the second wave of the feminist movement. Concerned Women for America, the largest conservative women's organization, mobilized against *Roe v. Wade* (1973), the ERA and what members perceived as threats to women's traditional roles as wives and mothers. The Independent Women's Forum, founded by a group of women working in the George H. W. Bush administration in 1992, focuses on economic issues and advocates for individual freedoms and self-governance, such as opposition to Title IX and affirmative action programs, on the basis that women can gain gender equality without government interventions.

Party Identification

Until 1964, women favored the Republican Party over the Democratic Party, but the second wave of the women's movement and the conservative backlash against the movement attracted men to the Republican Party while women flocked to the Democrats. The Republican Party was more inclusive of the women's rights agenda than the Democratic Party for most of the twentieth century. They were the first to support the ERA while worker's unions, a major Democratic voting bloc, opposed the amendment until the late 1960s. During the second wave of the women's movement, both parties supported policies aimed at gender rights, including the Equal Pay Act (1963), the addition of Title VII to the Civil Rights Act (1972), congressional approval of the ERA (1972), and the addition of Title IX to the Educational Amendments (1972). The seismic culture shift of the late 1970s that culminated in the election of Ronald Reagan in 1980 solidified the Democratic Party as the champion of progressive women's rights and the Republican Party as the domain for conservative women's issues. Walter Mondale added Geraldine Ferraro to his presidential ticket in 1984 in an attempt to woo female voters in the wake of their new alliance with the Democratic Party.

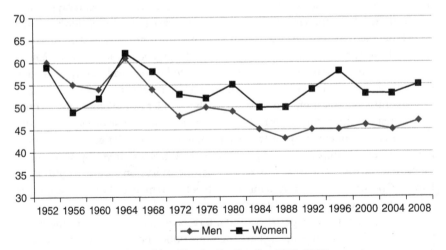

Figure 5.1 Democratic Party Identification by Gender: 1952–2008

Today, 52 percent of women identify as Democrats versus 36 percent who identify as Republican.[20] Compare this to 44 percent and 43 percent of men who identify as Democrats and Republicans, respectively. Women are more likely to contribute money to the Democratic Party, while the opposite pattern is found with men. The partisan gender gap is directly related to the respective policy positions of the two major parties. There is wide intersectional variation in party identification by race. Women of color are significantly more likely than white women to identify as Democrats. About 55 percent of white women identify and vote Democratic on a consistent basis, while more than 90 percent of black women, 67 percent of Latinas, and 65 percent of Asian American women vote Democratic. In other words, the female Democratic voting bloc is driven by women of color.

Women's partisanship and voting patterns have remained relatively stable since the early 1980s, while men's patterns generally fluctuate in response to growth in the size of government. For example, when presidents enact major policies that expand the size and scope of government (e.g., public health care), men in particular react by becoming more conservative and supporting the Republican Party, which stands for smaller government. Political scientists speculate that men fluctuate more in their partisanship and vote choice than women because men are generally more informed about what is happening in politics.

Vote Choice

When women won the right the vote in 1920, many people speculated that a distinct women's voice would emerge in the electorate that reflected women's greater support for social services and health care, but the gap did not become a permanent fixture of U.S. politics for another six decades. Women slightly favored the Democratic candidate in presidential elections since 1964 starting with Lyndon Johnson, but the gap solidified in the 1980 presidential election when Reagan alienated many female voters with his hawkish stance on military force, proposed cuts to social welfare programs, and his opposition to the ERA. Reagan's opposition to abortion and the ERA, as well as his support for "traditional" family values, also alienated many women, who left the Republican Party and did not return.

The party gender gap is now a predictable fixture in presidential politics, and Republicans have lost the female vote in every presidential contest since 1988. The 11-point gender gap in the 1996 election between incumbent Bill Clinton (55 percent) and challenger Robert Dole (38 percent) was the largest in history. In 2012, Mitt Romney would have beaten Barack Obama in a landslide if only men had voted, and Obama received only 36 percent of the white male vote. Obama was reelected with a ten-point gender gap, with 55 percent of female voters casting a vote for him compared to 44 percent of men. In 2016, the gender gap was 11 points, with 54 percent of women supporting Hillary Clinton and 41 percent supporting Donald Trump.

The gender gap in vote choice varies by marital status, race, and social class. In the 2008 presidential election, a majority of white women (53 percent) voted

Table 5.1 Gender Gap in Vote Choice, 1980–2016

YEAR	PRESIDENTIAL CANDIDATES	WOMEN	MEN	GENDER GAP
2016	Donal Trump (R)	41%	52%	11 pts.
	Hillary Clinton (D)	54%	41%	
2012	Barack Obama (D)	55%	45%	10 pts.
	Mitt Romney (R)	44%	52%	
2008	Barack Obama (D)	56%	49%	7 pts.
	John McCain (R)	43%	48%	
2004	George W. Bush (R)	48%	55%	7 pts.
	John Kerry (D)	51%	44%	
2000	George W. Bush (R)	43%	54%	
	Al Gore (D)	54%	43%	10 pts
	Ralph Nader (Green)	2%	3%	
1996	Bill Clinton (D)	55%	44%	
	Bob Dole (R)	38%	45%	11 pts.
	Ross Perot (Reform)	7%	10%	
1992	Bill Clinton (D)	45%	41%	
	George H. W. Bush (R)	38%	38%	4 pts.
	Ross Perot (Reform)	17%	21%	
1988	George H. W. Bush (R)	50%	57%	7 pts.
	Michael Dukakis (D)	49%	41%	
1984	Ranald Reagan (R)	56%	62%	6 pts.
	Walter Mondale (D)	44%	37%	
1980	Ranald Reagan (R)	47%	55%	
	Jimmy Cater (D)	45%	36%	8 pts.
	John Anderson (I)	7%	7%	

Source: Gender Gap Fact Sheet, Center for American Women and Politics (CAWP), Eagleton Institute of Politics, Rutgers University.

for John McCain over Obama (46 percent). The same pattern emerged in 2012 when 56 percent of white women voted for Romney compared to 42 percent who voted for Obama. A majority of white women did not support Obama in either of his elections, but historically high turnout from women of color ensured that Obama received the women's vote in each election. Black women voted for Obama at a rate of 96 percent, 76 percent of Latinas voted for him, and 66 percent of other women of color, including Asian Americans, did the same. Women of color now constitute one in six voters, and their overwhelming support for Obama was enough to negate the reverse gender gap among white women.

Single women have the largest gender gap in vote choice, whether or not they have children, because they rely more on social services than other Americans. Exit polls from the 2008 presidential election indicate that 74 percent of single women with children supported Obama compared to 68 percent of single men with children. Additionally, 69 percent of single women with no children voted for Obama compared to 56 percent of unmarried men with no children.

The gender gap in voting is not as large as the race or class gap in partisan voting. For example, in the 2012 election, Obama was elected with 54 percent higher support from African Americans than from white Americans; 80 percent of those making $150,000 or more voted compared to 47 percent of those making $10,000 or less per year, and 63 percent of households making $30,000 or less voted for Obama compared to 35 percent that voted for Romney. The gender gap in vote choice matters in politics, but race and class matter more.

Women have become an important voting bloc in presidential elections. Electoral competition at all levels of government intensified starting in the early 1990s as many white southerners aligned themselves with the Republican Party. The 1994 Republican Revolution was a response to the 1992 election of Bill Clinton and what was framed as ultraliberal policies, and it gave control of both houses of Congress to the Republicans for the first time in more than 40 years. Since then, swing voters have held particular significance in national contests, and female voters are especially important because they are more likely to be undecided voters. Dole and Clinton made specific appeals to married, suburban white women, also known as "soccer moms," in the 1996 election, and in 2004, this same demographic was cast as "security moms" concerned about terrorism and the safety of their families. Incumbent presidents often pass policies that appeal to women leading up to elections, such as pay equity initiatives, policies addressing sexual violence, and new child-care laws. In the 2008 election, candidates made explicit appeals to "hockey moms"—women with a college education and middle-class means who identify as independents. McCain's addition of Sarah Palin as his vice presidential candidate was an overt appeal to that population.

Do women vote for women? It depends. The biggest factor in predicting how someone will vote is party identification. Voters who identify as Democrats are highly likely to vote for the Democratic candidate, while voters who identify as Republicans are highly likely to vote for the candidate from their party. Other factors also come into play in vote choices, including incumbency, the issue environment of the election, and personal candidate characteristics. When it comes to Congress, voters reelect the incumbent about 90 percent of the time because they have higher name recognition, more resources, and a record of constituent service in their state or district.

Women are more likely to vote for female candidates than men, especially during elections when gender is a salient issue. For example, 1992 was dubbed the Year of the Woman in politics given the record number of women running for political office that year. This issue environment gave female candidates a boost in media coverage and positive focus on their gender, which translated into higher levels of support among female voters. Women are more likely to support female candidates than were men, but party identification and incumbency mattered more. According to Democratic pollster Celinda Lake, Democratic women are more likely to vote for a male Democrat than for a female Republican, and Republican women favor male Republican candidates over female candidates from the opposite party. This indicates that for women, policy positions matter more in their vote choice than shared gender identification with a candidate.

POLITICAL PARTICIPATION

Early political socialization sets the stage for gendered approaches to politics later in life. In this section, we examine how men and women differ in their engagement with politics in the electoral realm and beyond. We operate on the basic assumption that higher levels of political participation are desirable. Accountability in our political system can only be accomplished with an active and vocal citizenry, so high levels of voting and other types of involvement in politics are necessary components of a healthy democracy. Political scientists do not agree on a definition of democracy, but most concur that it is a system of government where power lies with the people who rule through free elections of representatives. The three primary pillars of U.S. democracy are political equality (one person, one vote), political liberty (freedom from unnecessary government intervention), and popular sovereignty (government authority derives from the consent of the people). Citizen engagement in politics is vital in the struggle to maintain these pillars of democracy, so when a class of citizens is discouraged from engaging in politics, this becomes a democratic problem.

Prior to discussing gender gaps in political participation, it is important to understand what we mean by the term. Some political scientists define participation in politics narrowly to include only government-related activities. For example, Sidney Verba, Kay Lehman Schlozman, and Henry Brady define political participation as activities that have "the intent or effect of influencing government action—either directly by affecting the making or implementation of public policy or indirectly by influencing the selection of people who make those policies."[21] Other political scientists define political participation more broadly, to include activities that do not directly involve government but have political implications. For example, Steven J. Rosenstone and John Mark Hansen provide a broader definition of political participation as actions "directed explicitly toward influencing the distribution of social goods and social values." In other words, they consider any actions that seek to alter existing arrangements of social goods (resources) or values (norms) political.[22]

In this section, we describe activities that go beyond voting and participating in elections to provide the most comprehensive picture of the different ways in which women and men participate in politics. It is important to note that we miss women's ways of engaging when we focus only on voting. In the 1990s, feminist scholars, including Carol Hardy-Fanta and Martha Ackelsberg, argued that the public life/private life distinction in political science segregates and overlooks the actions of women and others who engage outside of the conventionally defined "public" sphere of electoral politics. According to Ack-elsberg, "it remains the case that a focus on the electoral arena, and on tradi-tional forms of participation, offers us only a partial view of politics and participation in this country, and, in particular, the participation of women."[23] For example, modes of participation that are dominated by women of color, such as building alternative institutions when government institutions fail, are deemed private social work instead of political work or political boycotts. Women vote at higher rates than men and are most likely to engage with their communities and with the political system at the grass-roots level and in service or volunteer-related groups.[24] Men engage more in direct political action and volunteering with political organizations.

Electoral Participation

There are many ways to be involved in electoral politics. The most popular activ-ity and the one political scientists have studied the most is voting. We begin with an overview of the gender gap in voter turnout, followed by an assessment of campaign and party work, contacting a public official, professional lobbying, and running for office.

Voting is one electoral activity where women typically outpace men. Women have turned out to vote at higher rates than men in every presidential election since 1984. The gap is generally about four percent, meaning that about ten mil-lion more women than men go to the polls to vote on Election Day. According to the Center for American Women in Politics, more women than men are also registered to vote: 81.7 million compared to 71.4 million in 2012. Women are the largest voting bloc in the United States, and women of color are the fastest grow-ing part of the bloc. According to Harvard analyst Maya L. Harris, women of color account for 74 percent of the growth in female voters since 2000.

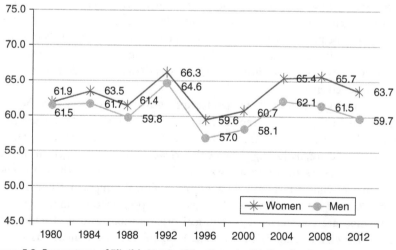

Figure 5.2 **Percentage of Eligible Voters Who Reported Voting, by Gender**

Gender is only one factor that influences a person's likelihood of voting. Race is also important. African Americans turn out to vote at the same rates as white voters of the same economic class, and in the 2012 election, they voted at higher rates than whites. Asian Americans and Latinos vote at consistently much lower rates than African Americans or whites. For example, in the 2012 election, blacks (66.2 percent) and whites (64.1 percent) had the highest turnout, followed by Latinos (48 percent) and Asian Americans (47.3 percent). Starting in the 2000s, women of color have turned out to vote at historically high rates that have influenced the outcome of elections. As noted above, a majority of white women did not support Obama in either of his elections, but historically high turnout from women of color ensured that Obama received the women's vote each time.

From an intersectional perspective, turnout for black women in 2012 was higher than that of any other gender or race group, and since that time, more than two million women of color have registered to vote. In 2013, women of color turned out to vote at historically high rates in the Virginia gubernatorial contest that elected Democrat Terry McAuliffe. McAuliffe lost the white women's vote in that election, but women of color emerged as a voting bloc that delivered the election. The voices and concerns of women of color rarely take center stage in politics, but their growing political power requires political parties and campaigns to make them a priority.

Another way to participate in electoral politics is to affiliate with a political organization. Citizens have thousands of options, such as EMILY's list, which stands for Early Money Is Like Yeast (in that it makes the dough rise). It was started by Ellen R. Malcolm in 1985 to raise early money for pro-choice, Democratic female candidates to attract later donations. On the other side of the political aisle, citizens can volunteer with the National Federation of Republican Women, an organization founded in 1938 with the mission of recruiting and training candidates. According to the Citizen Participation Survey, more men (53 percent) than women (44 percent) are affiliated with a political organization. The gender gap disappears when it comes to volunteering for a political organization. Men (nine percent) and women (eight percent) are equally likely to volunteer with a political organization, which is surprising since women consistently volunteer in general at significantly higher rates than do men (28 percent compared to 22 percent).

A gender gap also exists for paid campaign work. According to the New Organizing Institute, 55 percent of national paid campaign staffers are male compared to 45 percent who are female.[25] Nearly 17 percent of campaign workers are women of color, including 11 percent African American, five percent Latina, and one percent Asian American women. This indicates that although women and men are equally likely to volunteer for a political campaign, women, especially women of color, are less likely to hold a paid position on a campaign.

Women are concentrated in political organizations aimed at addressing women's issues. For example, the National Women's Political Caucus was formed in 1972 to get more women into political offices. Early on, prominent second wave feminist leaders ran the organization, including Gloria Steinem, Betty Friedan, Shirley Chisholm, and Bella Abzug. The National Women's Political Caucus continues to work today to elect both Republican and Democratic women to office. The National Organization for Women is also active in electing female candidates to public office. A number of organizations raise money for female candidates to make them more competitive in electoral contests. The Women's Campaign Fund (founded in 1974) works to elect pro-choice female candidates of both parties, and EMILY's List (founded in 1985) raises money for electing pro-choice Democratic women to office. SHE-PAC (founded in 2012) supports conservative female candidates. According to the Center for American Women in Politics, 58 organizations with the mission of electing female candidates to office exist, 17 at the national level and 41 at the state and local levels.

One particular type of political organization that warrants special attention is political parties. Although women have been involved in social movement politics since before the founding of the nation, the political parties have historically been seen as a male domain. The modern party system dates back to the 1820s, when the election of President Andrew Jackson saw white male citizens voting and engaging in politics at high rates, regardless of whether they owned property. In response, the political parties redefined their role as winning elections by conducting campaigns that mobilize voters. The political parties quickly became a primary source of entertainment and bonding for white men, and women were informally excluded for the most part. Women initially participated through third parties, such as the Prohibition Party and the Progressives, which were aligned with reform (i.e., prohibiting alcohol, reforming government corruption). When women gained the right to vote in 1920, the parties aggressively recruited women, but not for party leadership positions. Alice Paul, the leader of the National Women's Party, authored the original Equal Rights Amendment, and the National Women's Party unsuccessfully lobbied Congress to pass it.

Both major political parties have been criticized for having few women in their leadership ranks and for running female candidates mostly in races where there is little chance of winning. Both the Republican and Democratic parties have developed programs to do a better job of recruiting and supporting female candidates, and in 2011, Debbie Wasserman Schultz, a Democratic member of Congress from Florida, became the first female head of a major party. Men are more likely than women to work in volunteer and paid positions on political campaigns. For example, women comprised 40 percent of overall staff for the 2012 presidential campaigns, but held only 32 percent of senior positions.[26] Democratic campaigns were more gender balanced than Republican campaigns, and Democratic staffers are more likely to be paid more than Republican staffers.

Another way that a person can engage in electoral politics is through campaign contributions. Men are more likely to contribute money to campaigns than are women (27 percent compared to 20 percent), and men also make bigger campaign contributions on average than women. Women make up only 30 percent of donors who contribute $200 or more to campaigns. At the high end of donor generosity, the top ten male donors contribute about five times more than the top ten female voters. It is telling that despite a persistent wage gap that puts women at a relative disadvantage to men when it comes to contributions, women of all backgrounds are more likely to donate to charity than men, but not when it comes to politics. When they do contribute, women are more likely to make a donation to a female candidate. For example, 52 percent of Hillary Clinton's contributions during the 2016 primary came from women, a rare exception to the gender gap in campaign contributions.

Discussing political events and happenings with others is another way to engage in electoral politics. Research finds that men tend to talk more about politics than women do, and they derive greater enjoyment from political talk. According to Pew Research, about three in four men (77 percent) discuss politics at least a few times a month, compared with 60 percent of women. When asked about their level of enjoyment, 63 percent of men say they enjoy it some or a lot compared to 45 percent of women.[27] Among people who discuss politics on a regular basis, women are more likely to discuss politics with a family member (85 percent compared to 76 percent of men), while men are more inclined to have political conversations with non–family members (79 percent compared to 70 percent of women). This pattern is true for men and women of all ages and across races. Men are more likely to discuss politics, and when they do, it is often with friends or work colleagues rather than with family members.

Another way to participate in electoral politics is to contact a public official to voice a concern or influence a policy decision. In general, men (38 percent) are more likely than women (30 percent) to contact a public official, and this is especially true for women of color. The medium matters when it comes to the gender gap in contacting public officials. Women are less likely than men to contact public officials through direct means, such as a phone call, e-mail, or letter. However, women are more likely to send a more indirect message to public officials through online petitions. This means that although public officials hear less often from women, especially women of color, through direct means, their concerns may be getting through in the form of petitions calling for action.

Lobbying is another way that an individual can influence electoral politics. Men dominate the ranks of paid lobbyists at all levels of government. In Washington, DC, where professional lobbying has become a $3 billion industry, men constitute 66 percent of the more than 11,000 registered lobbyists.[28] Female lobbyists look remarkably similar to male lobbyists in their techniques and strategies, and once they gain access to lawmakers, they are taken seriously. This indicates that although women are still outnumbered in the ranks of lobbyists, when they do arrive, they are equally effective. In addition to being outnumbered, female lobbyists have fewer average contracts than male lobbyists, which means they are drawing smaller salaries. At the high end, only 15 percent of lobbying firms are headed by women, and female chief executive officers make an average of $600,000 less than their male counterparts—$1.31 million for women compared to $1.93 for men in 2013.

Running for office is the most direct way a citizen can be involved in electoral politics. According to Lawless and Fox's work, men and women are equally likely to aspire to improve their communities, but men are far more likely to see running for elective office as the best way to do so (26 percent compared to 17 percent). They attribute this to the fact that potential female candidates are less confident, less competitive, and more risk averse than potential male candidates. It has been more than four decades since the second wave of the women's rights movement, when women began to move en masse into corporate high rises and the halls of federal, state, and local government. Yet, the most elite positions of leadership in politics and business continue to be disproportionately held by men. Women have moved into more elected positions, but the rapid progress of previous decades has slowed and, in some cases, even reversed. In 2016, women held 17 percent of the seats in the House of Representatives and 20 percent of the seats in the Senate. Except for a small spike in the Senate, these numbers have stagnated for a decade. At the state level, less than a quarter of legislative seats and statewide elective offices are held by women, a percentage that peaked at nearly 30 percent in 1992 and has slowly fallen since. Although it is important to keep in mind that the number of female state legislators has increased fivefold since the 1970s, the number of women elected to state and federal positions of leadership in government reached its height in the late 1990s and has now leveled off.

Origins of the Electoral Participation Gap

As noted previously, participation in electoral politics is gendered. Men tend to engage at higher rates than women overall because of differences in political socialization. Starting at a young age, boys are encouraged to acquire basic civic skills such as public speaking and directing group activities that are the building blocks for later political participation. People who master civic skills in nonpolitical settings have higher rates of political efficacy that enable them to engage politics at higher rates. In addition to civic skills, boys are encouraged to learn about politics and participate in student government at much higher rates than girls.

The gender gap in political participation can also be traced to differences in financial resources. People with higher incomes participate more in politics, which means that women are disadvantaged because they make less money on average. This is especially true of women of color. Along these lines, the more a woman contributes to her overall household income, the higher her rate of participation in politics. In other words, the more economic power she has in the household and the greater her overall earnings, the more she participates in politics outside the household.

PROFILE IN POWER

Bree Newsome

Brittany Ann Byuarium "Bree" Newsome is a social justice activist and a filmmaker. She gained substantial media attention on June 27, 2015, when she scaled the flag-pole in front of the South Carolina state capitol to remove the Confederate flag. Newsom's political demonstration came 10 days after a shooter with ties to white supremacist ideas stormed the Charles-ton AME Church and gunned down nine black congregants. The Confederate flag is seen by many as a sign of hatred because it symbolizes the Southern fight to maintain slavery. The National Association for the Advancement of Colored People had been running a boycott of South Carolina since 2001 to compel state legislators to remove the flag, but with no success.

SOURCE: REUTERS/Adam Anderson

As Newsom climbed the pole, a group of police officers gathered at the base and demanded that she get down. She replied, "In the name of Jesus, this flag has to come down. You come against me with hatred and oppression and violence. I come against you in the name of God. This flag comes down today." With the flag in hand, she then came down the pole, announced that she was ready to be arrest-ed, and was escorted to a nearby police car. A crowd of people who did not expect this act of civil disobedience applauded her as she was put into handcuffs. The flag was raised again within an hour, but it was permanently removed a few weeks later.

Newsom's act of civil disobedience garnered national and international coverage, and within a day, a crowdfunding campaign had raised more than $60,000 for her bail and legal expenses. The local chapter president of the National Association for the Advancement of Colored People, Reverend Dr. William Barber II, compared Newsom's actions to those of Rosa Parks and other civil rights icons. Then–presidential candidate Hillary Clinton praised Newsom's activism during a speech in the state for Dr. Martin Luther King Day. In 2016, Newsom was awarded the NAACP Image Award–Chairman's Award for her activism.

Newsom was not involved in political issues until she was a young adult. She grew up in Maryland, where she developed an early interest in filmmaking. She had talent at a young age, and a short animated film she created in high school won her a scholarship to the prestigious New York University's Tisch School of the Arts. She was the first black undergraduate student to be nominated for the Wasserman Award (which Spike Lee won as a graduate student). Newsom credits the racism and sexism she experienced as a young filmmaker in the horror and sci-fi genres as her inspiration for social justice activism.

Nonelectoral Participation

Men and women engage in nonelectoral forms of participation at roughly equal rates. This gender equality is important because rates of nonelectoral activities are on the rise in the United States. For example, more Americans are attending demonstrations (16 percent in the past year), signing a petition (28 percent), and occupying a building (two percent) than in previous decades, and protests have moved from the margins to the mainstream.[29] Voting, the hallmark of political participation, has seen double-digit declines in the United States since 1960, and although the 2008 presidential election caused presidential voting to spike to nearly 60 percent of the eligible electorate, turnout is in a long-term decline. Voter turnout in the 2014 midterm election was the lowest it has been in 72 years, with less than half of the eligible electorate turning out to vote.

Political scientists offer several explanations for this decline in electoral participation: lower feelings of "external political efficacy"; older Americans not passing their civic-mindedness on to their children and grandchildren; the declining role of the political parties as providers of political cues; and an erosion of social capital, the "networks, norms, and social trust that facilitate coordination and cooperation for mutual benefit."[30] According to political scientist Robert Putnam, social capital "has been shrinking for more than a quarter of a century," and this recent erosion is washing away the exceptional American political bedrock of civic engagement through churches, unions, parent–teacher associations, civic groups, and fraternal organizations that determine levels of political participation. Putnam concludes that television and other forms of mass communication have radically "privatized" the way we spend our leisure time, and this in turn has caused social capital and conventional political participation to shrink. Television now absorbs 40 percent of the average American's disposable free time, a 33 percent increase since 1965.

With all of the hand wringing about the decline in electoral participation, most scholars have overlooked the crucial fact that modes of participation are not simply falling, they are also shifting. Citizens have made a dramatic shift toward more individualized civic activities, such as political boycotting, at the expense of electoral action. Political scientist Pippa Norris finds that electoral engagement has been replaced by newer types of participation, including online activism, networked social movements, and transnational policy networks: "Political energies have diversified and flowed through alternative tributaries, rather than simply ebbing away." Women are roughly as likely to be involved in these newly popular modes of nonelectoral participation as men.[31]

Social movements are group actions aimed at addressing specific social or political issues. Men and women are equally likely to be involved in social movement work and are also equally likely to engage in a political protest (six percent). However, the ways in which men and women are involved in social movements reflects gendered patterns. Men are also more likely to run community meetings, speak up in community meetings, and hold key decision-making roles in community organizing campaigns. Secretarial, child-care, and clean up jobs, as well as other domestic tasks, disproportionately fall on the shoulders of women.

Sexist divisions of labor in social movements of the 1970s caused many women to leave and start their own social movement. These gender roles persist in social movements today. For example, in the movement to rebuild New Orleans post-Katrina in 2005, although 60 percent of the volunteers were women, almost all of the leadership positions in the grass-roots organizations that formed after the storm were held by men. According to sociologist Ian Breckenridge-Jackson, women who were in leadership positions experienced routine challenges to their expertise and leadership that men did not experience. Furthermore, 62 percent of female volunteers experienced more gender harassment on the worksite. But things have improved for women in social movements. When the Occupy Wall Street movement that began in 2011 informally elevated male leaders and male voices in the press, feminists in the movement acted swiftly to hold it accountable. According to professor and long-time activist Jackie DiSalvo, decades of consciousness-raising on the left now prevent the "very macho leadership" of social movements from the 1970s.

Community organizing is one type of social movement when people who live close to one another carry out campaigns to further their shared interests. For example, residents might come together to protest the building of a nuclear reactor nearby or the erection of a freeway through their neighborhood. Community organizing could entail negotiating with public officials, nonviolent disruption, boycotts, strikes, public shaming, mass lobbying, and a variety of other tactics to achieve specific policy goals. In addition to resolving specific issues, the goal of community organizing is to develop a body that represents the interests of the community in any political decisions affecting it. While men typically acquire civic skills through political organizations, women are more likely to acquire such skills through volunteer work with civic organizations.[32]

Community organizing is linked to Saul Alinsky, an early community organizer who began his career to combat juvenile delinquency in Chicago in the 1930s, but female organizers have mostly been overlooked as such. For example, Ida B. Wells organized against the rape of black women and the lynching of black men in the late nineteenth century, and African American women organized black women's clubs that funded nursing homes, orphanages, and day-care centers. Starting in the latter half of the nineteenth century, women have dominated civic projects and groups, such as parent–teacher associations, water commissions, and library boards. Political scientist Krista Anderson notes that women initially became active as community organizers because they were formally and informally excluded from electoral politics.

Today, men and women are equally likely to work as community organizers and to volunteer in the nonprofit sector. Women in general, and women of color in particular, are more likely than men to engage in alternative institution building, defined as the creation of new nonprofit organizations and less formal organizations to fill a need in the community.[33] For example, in post-Katrina New Orleans, local women of color opened women's homeless shelters, domestic violence shelters, and health clinics to fill the pressing demand left when government services were cut. Similarly, Carol Hardy-Fanta documents how Latinas from the Dominican Republic, Puerto Rico, and Central and South America create alternative community institutions to serve the unique needs of their neighborhoods in Boston.

Women and men are equally likely to use consumer activism as a political tool. Consumer activism comprises actions aimed at corporate entities for political purposes. For example, the documentary *Blackfish* (2013) inspired a massive outpouring of consumer activism against the popular SeaWorld theme park for its treatment of captive killer whales (orcas) that led to a dramatic 84 percent drop in SeaWorld profits[34] and a ban on orca captivity by the San Francisco Board of Supervisors.[35] Consumer activism comes in four primary forms: political purchasing actions (boycotting and buycotting); investment actions (responsible investing, shareholder resolutions, divestment); direct actions (consumer protests, culture jamming, vandalism); and public shaming social media campaigns.

The United States has had a long and unique relationship with consumer activism. It was sewn into the fabric of our national identity during the founding when colonists used market channels to express political concerns (e.g., the Boston Tea Party, the sugar boycotts), and in the intervening centuries, this form of activism has been used as a complementary political tool in different social movements. Rates of consumer activism have steadily increased since the 1970s, but they surged in the 2000s as the result of new online organizing tools that made this form of activism easier and more attractive.[36] Social networking sites, such as Facebook, Twitter, Instagram, and Tumblr, blogs, and petition sites make it simple to share information about a corporation and to quickly organize a petition, boycott, or protest. In addition, new communication technologies make consumer activism more effective by conveying a unified message to corporations more quickly, and corporations are more likely than ever to quickly respond.

According to political scientists Benjamin Newman and Brandon Bartels, about one in five Americans boycott (18 percent) each year. Political purchasing is far more popular with younger Americans than with older Americans. Nearly 60 percent of people under the age of 30 have boycotted at some point in their lives, and half have boycotted in the past year. Rates of boycotting vary by race, ideology, and education, but not by gender. Liberal, educated, white Americans are more likely to engage in political purchasing than other Americans. According to psychologist Monroe Friedman, women have led consumer activist efforts, and they have historically "complemented on the consumption side of the economic coin their husbands' activities on the production side." Today, men and women are equally likely to become involved in a political boycott, but these actions are more often initiated and directed by female activists.

CONCLUSION

In this chapter, we examined the different ways in which women and men approach politics. Gender gaps in politics can be traced back to political socialization. Boys and girls are taught that politics is a white male domain by seeing mostly white male leaders in positions of power and in popular culture depictions of leadership. It is no wonder, then, that persistent gender gaps exist for political knowledge, internal political efficacy, political ambition, and plans to run for public office.

When it comes to political participation, women are more likely than men to vote, while men are more likely to engage in direct action, contribute money, contact an elected official, and run for office. When women are involved in political organizing, they are less likely to hold leadership or paid positions. Women and men are equally likely to use consumer activism as a political tool, such as boycotting, socially responsible investing, consumer protests, and public shaming social media campaigns.

The gender imbalance in politics matters because women and men hold different views on a host of domestic and foreign-policy issues. On the domestic side, men are less supportive of national health care, poverty assistance programs, bans on LGBTQ discrimination, affirmative action, and equal pay laws. Women are more supportive of poverty safety net programs, environmental regulations, and restrictions on firearms. In terms of foreign policy, women are less supportive than men of military spending and military interventions in general, unless they have a humanitarian goal. Since 1964, women have favored the Democratic Party over the Republican Party, and women of color are especially likely to identify as Democrat. Women are more likely to vote for female candidates than are men, especially during elections when gender is a salient issue, but partisanship trumps candidate gender. Women are the largest voting bloc in the United States, and women of color are the fastest growing part of the bloc.

CHAPTER SUMMARY

- Gender is one of the foundational ways in which we organize politics, meaning that gender matters in terms of elections, activism, resource allocation, and policy-making. Women and men approach politics in different ways and through different paths.
- Gender gaps in politics can be traced back to political socialization, defined as the process by which individuals in a society learn about their political culture. Girls and boys are taught different messages about whether and how they should be active in politics.
- Researchers have documented a persistent gender gap in political interest, with men showing significantly greater interest. Boys and girls in the United States learn that politics is a white male domain by seeing mostly white male leaders in positions of power and in popular culture depictions of leadership.
- A persistent gender gap also exists for political knowledge. Men exhibit higher levels of knowledge about basic political facts and processes than women in the United States and across the globe. The knowledge gap encompasses knowledge differences in how political institutions work, contemporary public policy issues, political leadership, and political events. The gender gap in political knowledge is not a result of differences in intelligence, intellectual ability, or academic preparation. It is caused by consumption of political news, bias in who presents the news, and the fact that women have less time to devote to politics because of domestic responsibilities.

- Men and women look remarkably similar when it comes to external political efficacy, but they differ significantly on measures of internal political efficacy. There are many psychological, social, and political causes of the gender gap in internal political efficacy, including the political knowledge gap, lower overall levels of self-esteem in women than in men, and the cultural norm of female sexual objectification.

- A gender gap also exists when it comes to political ambition. Men have higher rates of political ambition than women, which means that men are more likely to consider running for public office. Women think they are less qualified to run for political office than men with the same or comparable qualifications and are less likely to have considered running for office. The political ambition gap is not the result of women having different aspirations than men in general or women having less of a sense of civic duty. Instead, it is the result of differences in friends and family members encouraging political ambition, women's lower self-confidence, perceived biases in the electoral environment, and different experiences with competitive activities in childhood.

- Women and men hold different views on a host of domestic and foreign-policy issues. On the domestic side, men are less supportive than women of national health care, poverty assistance programs, and restrictions on firearms. Men are also less supportive of programs aimed at addressing social and economic inequalities such as same-sex policies, affirmative action, equal pay laws, and laws banning LGBTQ discrimination in the workplace and the military. Women are generally more supportive of policy issues that directly affect them, safety net programs, and environmental interventions.

- In foreign policy, women are less supportive than men of military spending and war. Gendered support for war is strongly dependent on the context of a given war. Women are less likely than men to support unilateral wars initiated for economic reasons, but the gender gap disappears for wars approved by the United Nations with a humanitarian goal. Women are less supportive of military interventions and more supportive of diplomacy for maintaining peace.

- Not all women share the same policy positions. Conservative women who are strongly influenced by religious beliefs and a desire to maintain traditional gender roles organized in the late 1970s in response to the second wave of the feminist movement.

- Since 1964, women have favored the Democratic Party over the Republican Party. Women are more likely to contribute money to the Democratic Party, while the opposite pattern is found with men.

- There is wide intersectional variation in party identification by race. Women of color are significantly more likely than white women to identify as Democrats.

- The gender gap in voting is not as large as the race or class gap in partisan voting.

- Women are more likely to vote for female candidates than are men, especially during elections when gender is a salient issue, but partisanship is more important than candidate gender. Democratic women are more likely to vote for a male Democrat over a female Republican, and Republican women favor male Republican candidates over female candidates from the opposite party.

- Women are more likely than men to vote and engage in "private" and non-electoral forms of participation, while men are more likely than women to be involved in direct actions and political organizations.
- Women have turned out to vote at higher rates than men in every presidential election since 1984. Women are the largest voting bloc in the United States, and women of color are the fastest growing part of the bloc. The voices and concerns of women of color rarely take center stage in politics, but their growing political power requires political parties and campaigns to make them a priority.
- More men than women are affiliated with a political organization. The gender gap disappears when it comes to volunteering for a political organization.
- Although women have been involved in social movement politics since before the founding of the nation, the political parties have historically been seen as a male domain. Men are more likely than women to hold paid staff positions and leadership positions on campaigns.
- Men are more likely than women to work in volunteer and paid positions on political campaigns and more likely to hold leadership and well-paid positions.
- Men are more likely to contribute money to campaigns than are women, and men also make bigger campaign contributions on average than do women.
- Men tend to talk more about politics than do women, and they derive greater enjoyment from political talk. Men are also more inclined to have political conversations with non–family members, while women primarily discuss politics with family.
- Men are more likely than women to contact a public official, and this is especially true for women of color. Women are less likely than men to contact public officials through direct means, such as a phone call, e-mail, or letter. However, women are more likely to send a more indirect message to public officials through online petitions.
- Men dominate the ranks of paid lobbyists at all levels of government, and female lobbyists draw significantly smaller salaries.
- Men and women are equally likely to aspire to improve their communities, but men are far more likely to see running for elective office as the best way to do so.
- Gender gaps in electoral participation are a result of early political socialization, where boys are encouraged to acquire basic civic skills such as public speaking and directing group activities that are the building blocks for later political participation and differences in financial resources.
- Men and women engage in nonelectoral forms of participation at roughly equal rates. This gender equality is important because rates of nonelectoral activities are on the rise in the United States, while electoral participation is in decline.
- Men and women are equally likely to be involved in social movement work and are also equally likely to engage in a political protest. However, men are more likely to be seen as movement leaders.

- Men and women are equally likely to work as community organizers and to volunteer in the nonprofit sector. Women in general, and women of color in particular, are more likely than men to engage in alternative institution building.
- Women and men are equally likely to use consumer activism as a political tool, such as boycotting, socially responsible investing, consumer protests, and public shaming social media campaigns.

STUDY/DISCUSSION QUESTIONS

- Why are there gender gaps in political interest, knowledge, efficacy, and ambition?
- Why are there gender gaps in policy positions, partisanship, and vote choice?
- In what ways do women and men differ when it comes to electoral politics?
- In what ways do women and men differ when it comes to nonelectoral politics?
- What measures can be taken to eliminate gender gaps in politics?

CASE STUDIES

1. **Why haven't the female cofounders of #BlackLivesMatter received much recognition for their work in media coverage of this social movement?**
   In this chapter, we examined gender gaps in nonelectoral political participation, including work in social movements. Women's contributions to social movements have often been overlooked in U.S. history. How does intersectional identity bias come into play with the founders of the #BlackLivesMatter movement?

2. **How would you characterize progress toward gender equality in political socialization and participation?**
   Women have made great strides when it comes to increasing representation in political positions, but gender gaps persist in virtually every aspect of political socialization, perceptions, and participation. How far have women come in the struggle for gender equality in pathways to politics? How is this complicated by intersectional issues of race and class?

3. **Has your political socialization encouraged or discouraged you from running for public office?**
   We laid out a number of factors that affect political ambition in this chapter, including women's perception that they are less qualified to run for political office, differences in friends and family members encouraging political ambition, women's lower self-confidence, perceived biases in the electoral environment, and different experiences with competitive activities in childhood. How have each of these factors increased or decreased your political ambition?

4. **In what ways are you involved in electoral and nonelectoral politics?**
   In this chapter, we provided many different ways a person can participate in politics. Are you involved in politics? If so, does your participation tend toward electoral participation? Nonelectoral participation? Both? How does your participation reflect broader trends in gender gaps when it comes to participation?

RESOURCES

- The mission of the **Women and Politics Institute** at American University is to close the gender gap in political leadership through research and training. http://www.american.edu/spa/wpi
- **Pathways to Political Leadership for Women of Color** at the University of Boston, Massachusetts, provides leadership training for women of color. https://www.umb.edu/cwppp/womens_political_leadership/pipeline
- The **Public Leadership Education Network** provides leadership training for young women who are interested in public service. http://plen.org

CHAPTER 6

Women as Political Candidates

Some political pundits called the 2012 election cycle the second "Year of the Woman." The first, in 1992, saw a record number of women running for and winning political office at all levels, in part because of the large number of open seats that came from retirements and redistricting. In 2012, during a campaign where policy issues relevant to women were front and center (including abortion, contraception, pay equity, and preventing violence against women), voters in Wisconsin elected the first open lesbian to the Senate (Democrat Tammy Baldwin), voters in Hawaii elected the first Asian American woman to the Senate (Democrat Mazie Hirono), and New Hampshire became the first state with an all-female congressional delegation, which included Senators Jeanne Shaheen (D, elected in 2008) and Kelly Ayotte (R, elected in 2010), in addition to having a woman governor, speaker of the state house, and chief justice of the state supreme court.[1] That distinction lasted only two years, however, because Representative Carol Shea-Porter (D) lost her reelection bid to Republican Frank Guinta in 2014 (although she beat him in a rematch in 2016).

Although American citizens continue to witness many notable "firsts" among women in politics, the overall progress remains slow when it comes to electing women to public office. Although women have made tremendous progress in gaining access to positions of political power in recent years, the United States "is still not even near gender parity in the percentage of women holding elective legislative positions; it is likely to be many years, at best, before parity can even be on the horizon."[2] If women make up slightly more than half of the population in the United States, which translates into more than half of eligible voters, then why are women still so underrepresented in elected political office? Since gaining the right to vote in 1920, women have been making up for lost time in many areas of the political process. For example, women outnumber men as voters; in the 2012 presidential election, 71.4 million women voted, while only 61.6 million men voted, and in 2016, 72.6 million women voted compared to 64.4 million men.

Despite the gains made in recent decades, women candidates still face barriers to achieving electoral success. Although public perceptions of women as active participants in the political process have broadened, many argue that various factors continue to restrict political opportunities for women, including sexual division of labor (women are still predominantly responsible for child care and household chores); work structures and sex-role expectations (lack of "flex time" and other career advancement opportunities for women with family responsibilities); ambivalence about women exercising power; and perpetual issues such as how the media can portray women leaders in a negative light.[3] The electoral process itself can also create barriers for women candidates, like the high rate of incumbency and fewer open seats for challengers and the fact that most women start their political careers later than most male candidates, in part because of family demands. In addition to the structural impediments, one of the most important barriers for women to overcome is simply making the decision to run for office; the perception for many potential women candidates that they do not have a strong chance of winning, even if it is untrue, is what contributes to the failure of women "to toss their hats in the ring" and hold more seats at all levels of government.[4]

Yet, a compelling argument can be made as to why more women should become public officeholders and why their leadership at the national, state, and local levels can make an important difference in terms of public policies. Women politicians offer an ideological advantage (regardless of party affiliations, women are often in a better position to address certain societal needs relating to the overall welfare of citizens or to protest other policies such as war). An increase in women's representation can also help to legitimize the political system and provide societal benefits as well, with increased competition for public office.[5] Evidence is also starting to emerge that suggests electing more women to public office can be contagious, meaning that "contagion is the influence of women's participation and political gains in one institution on others." Increase in political participation can be a slow-building process in some countries, "but even small gains in the percentage of women can have significant effects down the road."[6] Important influences on women's representation in other countries comes from sources such as the level of development within the country, the level of political participation and the work force, the type of electoral or selection system, the characteristics of the institution, and ideology/region. The adoption of quota laws, at either the party or national level, can also significantly increase women's participation in parties, legislatures, and all political institutions.[7] Although the adoption of such quotas in the United States seems highly unlikely, it is important to point out that as of 2016, the United States ranks 97th among 189 countries when ranked in terms of the number of women in the national legislature (down from 84th in 2014).[8]

In this chapter, we consider women as political candidates, including the unique challenges that women face in running for office at all levels of government. Breaking into the system to become a political leader is not an easy task for women candidates, particularly given the challenges that women have faced within the party structure and in raising adequate funds to finance campaigns. Also, since the incumbency factor is so prevalent in allowing members of Congress and other elected offices (like legislatures in states without term limits) to hold such a strong advantage in getting reelected, women and minority candidates often face an uphill battle in reaching some level of parity in terms of representation. First, we will look at how women candidates are recruited to run for office, followed by the institutional barriers within the electoral arena with which women candidates must contend. Then, we turn to the role of money in campaigns, followed by the all-important image created for women candidates through the watchful eyes of the news media.

RECRUITING WOMEN CANDIDATES

Understanding the first step in the electoral process—recruiting candidates—is a good place to start when considering why, despite gains made in some areas, the numbers of women holding political office are still relatively low. Are there barriers, either institutional or informal, that exist for women candidates? According to political scientists Susan Carroll and Richard Fox, American elections are "deeply gendered" in many ways. Not only do men constitute a large majority of the candidates running for president, Congress, and state governors, but also those who work behind the scenes in campaigns—strategists, pollsters, fundraisers—are mostly men. In the news media, most anchors and reporters covering presidential elections are men, the language used during campaigns is dominated by war and sports metaphors, and campaigns often rely on gender-specific strategies to attract votes (with the "women's vote" receiving significant attention in recent years).[9]

Do women receive adequate encouragement and support to run for political office? The initial decision to run is perhaps the most difficult for women to make for their own careers in the short run, yet the most crucial in the longer-term goal of placing more women in positions of political power. Although women candidates in recent elections have shown that they can raise money competitively compared to male candidates and that women can win both congressional and statewide elections, there is still resistance for many potential women candidates to run. According to political scientist Ruth B. Mandel, many young women today have decided to shun the high-pressure, brutally competitive lifestyle that comes with many leadership opportunities, including those within the political arena. As a result, the number of women in elected positions has leveled off in the past few years (compared to the yearly increases during the early 1990s of the percentage of women holding congressional and state positions), as many women are thinking twice before committing to becoming a political candidate. As Mandel states, "There is a continuing conundrum here. Nothing will change the picture of leadership and perhaps the practices of leadership unless women themselves choose to pursue leadership. In the United States, far and away, this matter of women's choices stands as the single greatest remaining challenge to achieving parity for women in leadership. . . . [as] women must choose to walk the path."[10]

Anecdotal evidence about women's political experiences, either while being recruited to run for office or when running, present a mixed story. Although some women report facing hostility at trying to break into a traditionally male-dominated sphere like politics, other women have received tremendous enthusiasm and support from male political elites in their pursuit of public office.[11] Party leaders in both the Democratic and Republican parties during the 1970s and 1980s were not overly committed to recruiting female candidates for Congress. And, when the parties did recruit women, they were often doing little to facilitate their election to office once the campaign began. Patterns emerged in the relationship between female candidates and party leaders to show that contacts between the parties and potential women candidates were less frequent, and women were often recruited to run as "sacrificial lambs" in a district where there was no hope of winning. The reluctance of both the Democratic and Republican parties' to "approach women and to present them with the opportunity to run in races [with] at least some chance of general election victory [has been] an important feature of the political opportunity structure that inhibits substantial increases in the numerical representation of women among elective officeholders."[12] More recent analyses that include congressional data into the early 1990s, however, show that women no longer run disproportionately for unwinnable seats and that women are just as likely as men to have party leaders encourage their candidacies.[13]

Women seeking office in state legislatures face similar situations regarding candidate recruitment. The likelihood that a woman will run for a state legislative seat varies from state to state and ties in with other factors like incumbency, the number of eligible women in the recruitment pool, and the perceived viability of women candidates by party leaders. However, party recruitment can and does play a significant role in electing women legislators in some states. This process often begins at the local level because local party leaders can provide important information to those candidate gatekeepers at the state level regarding which candidates may have the highest probability of winning an election. Therefore, party leader evaluations of potential candidates play a large role in determining who runs for office. According to political scientist Kira Sanbonmatsu, "where the parties recruit candidates to run or formally or informally support candidates in the primary, party leaders can play a major role in shaping the social composition of the legislature. . . . In states with an organized recruitment process, whether that process yields women candidates very much depends on party leaders' perception of the quality and electability of women candidates and their personal knowledge of or access to names of potential women candidates."[14]

In terms of being eligible to run for political office, most women candidates have the necessary qualifications for the job—most are well educated and have professional or managerial careers (although few tend to be lawyers, perhaps because women were in many respects barred from the legal profession until the 1970s). Most women candidates also have some party and organizational experience, although these types of qualifications in general appear to have little effect on election outcomes. Yet, with most political offices still dominated by men, the one qualification that many women still lack is prior officeholding experience. This seemed to represent an important barrier for women candidates, particularly throughout the 1970s and 1980s. According to political scientist Susan Carroll, "It is not the case that those who are more qualified win while those who lack qualifications lose. The only variables that seemed to discriminate between winners and losers with any consistency were some measures of party activity and former officeholding."[15] Prior political experience, particularly at the local level, can be a critical indicator of the number of women who will be seen as credible candidates for higher office. Therefore, the "pipeline" or "bottleneck" that allows women to enter the political arena as candidates can explain one of the factors accounting for previous and current shortfalls, since "experience in one elected office is seen as providing credentials for other offices."[16]

Recent studies by political scientists have attempted to better understand the factors that may keep women from running for elected office. Incumbency, as we will discuss in the next section, dominates much of the electoral process in Congress and state legislatures and serves as a structural barrier for all candidates, not just women. Yet there are still specific barriers to elected office that appear to be unique for potential women candidates. The primary reason for women's underrepresentation at all levels of government stems from the simple fact that women choose to run less frequently than men, although when they are similarly situated to male candidates (in terms of party and financial support), they are just as likely to win. The factors that seem to contribute to a woman's choice not to run include political gender role socialization, a lack of political confidence, family responsibilities, and a lack of visible women role models in politics.[17] Also, a critical gender difference exists in the candidate emergence phase because of a substantial winnowing process that yields a smaller ratio of women than men candidates. Women may be less likely to receive encouragement from party officials at this crucial phase, yet women candidates who do choose to run tend to receive similar amounts of support from party leaders and other political activities. Women are also less likely to deem themselves qualified to run for political office, even when they have achieved great professional success. This suggests that "recruitment patterns—or lack thereof—appear to solidify women's self-perceptions."[18] In addition, women are often less interested in running for public office than men, and when women do run for office, they tend to choose lower level offices.[19]

THE ELECTORAL PROCESS

Regardless of the sex of the candidate, the roles that incumbency, redistricting and the creation of "safe seats," and campaign finance play in American political campaigns can explain a lot about who is elected.

Incumbency and Safe Seats

The incumbency advantage, which includes a sizable fundraising advantage over challengers, can translate into high reelection rates. In Congress, since 1964, incumbent members in the House of Representatives have averaged a reelection rate of 93 percent, and incumbent members of the Senate have averaged a reelection rate of 85 percent. In certain years, those percentages are even higher. In 2004, for example, 98 percent of incumbents in the House of Representatives and 96 percent of incumbents in the Senate were reelected. The lowest that number has been since 1964 is 85 percent in the House (in both 1970 and 2010) and 55 percent in the Senate (in 1980).[20] Many factors contribute to the incumbency advantage, including name recognition, the ability to provide services for their constituents (done with the help of congressional staffers) as well as the ability to send free mail (known as franking) to voters within their district, the ability to support legislation that their constituents also support, and the advantage over challengers in raising large amounts of money to fund their campaigns. In addition, congressional races receive little news media coverage, which leaves voters uninformed about the candidates and the relevant issues, and they instead rely on name recognition or party loyalty when casting a vote. With all of these factors combined, challengers tend to be weaker candidates. This is ironic since Americans tend to resoundingly dislike Congress as an institution, yet they never seem to blame their individual representatives for the problems of government waste and legislative gridlock.

The creation of so-called safe seats in recent years has also contributed to the high rates of incumbency. With the help of redistricting, which occurs at the state level, political parties who hold the majority in state legislatures have been able to create safe districts through partisan gerrymandering, where the opposing party has little or no chance of defeating an incumbent. As a result, nearly one-fourth of all congressional seats in the most recent elections have seen incumbents running unopposed in the general election. This is particularly problematic for women candidates and helps to explain why women tend to do better in open-seat elections where there is no incumbent on the ballot. The bottom line is that since so few women candidates are incumbents and nonincumbents rarely win elections, the rate of women in political office has remained low.[21]

Although we do know that women candidates can successfully compete on the campaign trail and win elections, incumbency often stands in the way of more opportunities for new faces to enter public office, regardless of gender. One study of women candidates showed that women's success rates were identical to men's when comparing incumbent women and men, when comparing women and men running for open seats, and when comparing female challengers to male challengers. The challenge for women candidates is more about incumbency than about gender: "Incumbents, most of whom are men, win much more often than challengers. For women to have a level playing field, they have to wait for men to retire, resign, or die, and then run for the open seat."[22] Other studies have shown that congressional districts with women representatives tend to be those that had open-seat opportunities (no incumbent running), those with a history of female candidates and representatives, and those that are mostly outside of southern states.[23] Women candidates also tend to face more competition in the primary process for seats in the House of Representatives, although women do not win primaries at lower rates than their male counterparts.[24]

All of this helps to explain the success of women candidates in 1992, known as the "Year of the Woman," because the electoral environment offered numerous opportunities for political newcomers. Not only were American voters in a strong anti-incumbent mood following scandals involving the House post office and bank, but also several open seats were created by retirements and redistricting from the 1990 census. In addition, women's interest groups were strongly motivated to nominate and elect women candidates following the U.S. Supreme Court confirmation hearings of Clarence Thomas during the fall of 1991, which included testimony from law professor Anita Hill that Thomas had sexually harassed her while he served as her boss at the Equal Employment Opportunity Commission. As a result, women candidates won a record number of seats in both the House of Representatives and the Senate. In the House, 106 women ran for congressional seats on a major party ticket, and 47 won seats in the general election. In the Senate, 11 women ran and six were elected, which contributed to the largest ever one-time increase in candidates and winners. Gains were also made in state legislatures; prior to 1992, women made up six percent of Congress and 18 percent of state legislatures, with those numbers increasing to ten percent in Congress and 20 percent at the state level following the 1992 election.[25]

Women have experienced a higher rate of electoral success in state legislatures because of a higher turnover rate for incumbents, since state legislators are more likely to return to their previous careers or run for higher office, thereby creating more open seats for challengers. This is also, in part, because some states, like Texas, have part-time legislators with low salaries, making it difficult to create a long-term career in the state capitol. Other states like California do have full-time, well-paid state legislators, but their time in office is governed by mandatory term limits.

Campaign Finance

Money also plays a prominent role in American political campaigns, and the costs associated with running for political office continue to escalate. Since Congress first passed the Federal Election Campaign Act in 1971 (followed by major amendments to the act in 1974, many Supreme Court rulings both increasing some and loosening other restrictions, and numerous political battles to reform campaign finance), women candidates have developed effective strategies to raise money to fund their campaigns. Initially, as women first began to run for political office in larger numbers during the 1970s and 1980s, women struggled to raise adequate campaign funds. Since women were underrepresented in both politics (political action committees, known as PACs, give proportionately more money to incumbents) and the corporate world (where many large single donations come from), they were often at a huge disadvantage in terms of fundraising. Most also assumed that potential donors were reluctant to give money to women candidates and that women were "psychologically less predisposed to ask for donations." However, by the 1990s and continuing today, women candidates now raise and spend as much or more than their male counterparts.[26] According to political scientist Barbara Burrell, "The new story is [women's] emergence as operators and leaders in the financing of campaigns for public office."[27] Incumbents still enjoy a sizable advantage over challengers in this area, however; regardless of sex, challengers have a more difficult time raising money because they are often not seen as competitive. For example, in 2016, Senate incumbents raised an average amount of $12,708,000, while challengers only raised an average of $1,599,714. In the House, incumbents raised an average of $1,582,625, while challengers only raised an average of $231,727.[28]

Recent campaign finance data have shown that women still lag behind men in contributions from large moneyed interests (such as business PACs) because they rely slightly more on contributions from both individuals and single-issue/ideological PACs. However, this also allows women candidates to find alternate pathways to financial viability while building a broader base of electoral support.[29] In addition, women's PACs have made important financial contributions to women candidates in addition to providing training, consultation, and workers in support of the campaign. The timing of financial contributions also plays an important role because "early money" is crucial for building and maintaining momentum during the primary campaign. These donor networks that target women donors to support women candidates, including EMILY's List for Democratic pro-choice women candidates (EMILY stands for "early money is like yeast," in that it "helps the dough rise"), the WISH List for Republican pro-choice women candidates (WISH stands for Women in the Senate and House), and the Susan B. Anthony List for Republican pro-life women candidates, have created a gender gap in fundraising that gives an advantage to women congressional candidates. The advantage is greater for Democratic women, however.[30] As a result, since women's PACs give early money disproportionately to Democratic women candidates, Republican women candidates "face a more daunting task of establishing early viability."[31]

Nonetheless, women running for Congress in recent years have matched and, at times, outpaced their male counterparts. For example, Senator Kirsten Gillibrand (D-NY) is considered one of the top fundraisers on Capitol Hill and part of a growing class of women "powerhouse" fundraisers.[32] Whether giving by women to women candidates has contributed to this trend is still somewhat unclear, but fundraising within the women's community (particularly from national women's PACs) has played a significant role in the level of success in this area of campaigning.[33] The recent success among women candidates of both parties for congressional seats may provide an important harbinger for future women presidential candidates. Although Elizabeth Dole cited a lack of money for her early departure from the Republican presidential primary race in late 1999, the fundraising data from recent congressional campaign cycles "seems to suggest that the traditional economic structural barriers to a woman running for the presidency are beginning to dissipate."[34] Hillary Clinton raised a total of $223 million for her first presidential campaign in 2008, which was second only to the $750 million raised by Barack Obama during his presidential campaign the same year (Obama's totals include both the primaries and the general election, while Clinton's totals reflect only the primaries). And in 2016, Clinton raised nearly $500 million (with Super PAC funds totaling nearly $200 million) during her primary and general election campaigns. In both years, Clinton shattered any myth about women candidates not being able to raise significant amounts of money to fund a presidential campaign.

PROFILE IN POWER

Geraldine Ferraro

Type the name Geraldine Ferraro in any Internet search engine and you will find web page after web page that labels her an "American political leader"[35] or states how she "forever reshaped the American political and social landscape."[36] Although young women today may not be as familiar with Ferraro or her historic run for the vice presidency in 1984, she remains an important symbol in American politics for older genera-

SOURCE: Joe Haupt; Flickr

tions of women who saw her as a groundbreaking candidate on the national level. The first woman to be nominated on a major party ticket, the congresswoman from Queens, New York, was also the test case for the news media on how to handle a female candidate on the presidential campaign trail.

In her six-year tenure in the House of Representatives, Ferraro gained a reputation for pursuing legislation beneficial to women's causes, including working for passage of the Equal Rights Amendment, sponsoring the Women's Economic Equity Act ending pension discrimination against women, and seeking greater job training and opportunities for displaced homemakers. In 1984, under pressure from women's rights advocates and women's organizations such as the National Organization for Women to place a woman on the ticket, Democratic presidential nominee Walter Mondale made history by picking Ferraro as his running mate. Despite her strong reputation as a legislator, Ferraro was considered a gamble by some political analysts, but a necessary one for Mondale to have any chance of upsetting incumbent President Ronald Reagan that November. To

Democrats, Ferraro represented the candidate who could close the gender gap—by the summer months of 1983, polls showed that 17 percent fewer women than men supported the president and his policies—making party leaders believe that the powerful voting bloc of women could make the difference. Instead, Reagan walked away with a resounding victory, winning every state except Mondale's home of Minnesota.

Although the race between Mondale and Reagan was never close during the fall of 1984, Ferraro's presence on the ticket as the "first" woman vice presidential candidate made headlines up until election day. One of the biggest stories of the campaign became the business dealings of Ferraro's husband, John Zaccaro. When Ferraro revealed that her husband had decided not to release his tax returns because it might compromise his business dealings, the press had a field day. Never before had a candidate's spouse been subjected to such scrutiny by the press. In her book about the campaign, *Ferraro: My Story*, Ferraro recalls stating at a press conference, "He's not the candidate, I am." More than 250 reporters jammed the "disclosure" press conference only to learn that both Ferraro and her husband had overpaid, not underpaid, their federal income taxes.[37] The scrutiny by the press continued throughout the campaign, on issues ranging from Ferraro's views on abortion as a Catholic (she was pro-choice) to how a "lady" candidate was supposed to act (for example, should she and Mondale hug in public or merely shake hands?) to whether, because of her Italian heritage, her family had ties to organized crime (no evidence ever surfaced). Ferraro also recalled that conservative columnist George Will of the *Washington Post* wrote a scathing column about her family finances prior to the press conference at which the tax returns were disclosed. Ferraro challenged him on a national news show, saying he would have to apologize when the tax forms were revealed. Instead, Will sent her a dozen roses with a card that read, "Has anyone told you you are cute when you're mad?"[38]

Throughout the campaign, novel—and somewhat odd—stories about Ferraro kept appearing. Even before the Democratic convention had come to a close, the *Los Angeles Times* ran a "Convention Notebook" column that included an interesting commentary on a new problem Mondale and Ferraro would face: with so many Secret Service agents around, which candidate would go down the elevator first and be forced to wait in the garage for the other? The headline gave away the answer, "During Drafty Delay in a Garage, Protocol Rules It's Ladies First."[39] Many media outlets also could not help but talk about fashion in their political reporting. The *New York Times*'s story on Ferraro's nomination described her appearance and clothing three separate times: "Mrs. Ferraro, dressed in a white suit, gave the thumbs-up sign in response to the convention" began the second paragraph of the story. Later, the story reported on Ferraro's appearance at a fundraiser earlier in the day, "dressed in a bright turquoise dress," and called Speaker of the House Tip O'Neill's comments about Ferraro "avuncular." The third reference to Ferraro's appearance stated, "Clad in white and wearing a string of pearls about her neck, Mrs. Ferraro bounced in time to the beat of the song, 'New York, New York,' as, with a broad grin, she accepted waves of applause." The news of Ferraro hugging several House colleagues whom she had not seen since Mondale had announced her candidacy was also included in the story.[40] Ferraro's campaign, and her resulting relationship with the press, also got off to an auspicious start during an August appearance in Mississippi. Jim Buck Ross, the state agriculture commissioner, quizzed Ferraro on whether she could bake blueberry muffins. When she responded, "I sure can. Can you?" she was informed that men in the South don't cook. The exchange made headlines for several days in newspapers across the nation.[41]

After the loss in 1984, Ferraro did not return to politics until 1992, when she sought the Democratic nomination in New York for the U.S. Senate. One of four candidates for the nomination, Ferraro believed that much of the press coverage focusing on her novelty as the first woman to run for vice president, as well as the attacks on her family, were behind her. However, allegations concerning her husband's business connections and questions about their tax returns surfaced again. The stories once again made national headlines, this time mostly because of who was raising the issues—one of her challengers for the nomination, New York comptroller and former congresswoman Elizabeth Holtzman. Like Ferraro, Holtzman was known as a feminist politician supportive of women's rights and had beaten a veteran incumbent in 1972 to first get elected to Congress. Trailing Ferraro in the early polls, Holtzman went on the attack using negative television ads—like many candidates do—in an attempt to slow down the frontrunner's momentum. But a feminist woman attacking another feminist woman was too good of a story for the national press to pass up and represented a unique double standard within the news media in that "the women weren't acting the way women were supposed to act" since they were behaving more like male politicians.[42] In the end, neither Ferraro nor Holtzman earned the Democratic nomination, and New York did not participate in the "Year of the Woman" by sending its first elected woman to the Senate (that did not happen until Hillary Clinton's election in 2000).

Ferraro again ran unsuccessfully for the U.S. Senate in 1998, losing the Democratic nomination to the eventual winner of the seat, Representative Charles Schumer. She also worked as a political analyst for CNN and served as the ambassador to the United Nations Human Rights Commission during Bill Clinton's administration. Ferraro made headlines during the 2008 presidential campaign; an early supporter of Hillary Clinton, Ferraro caused a stir when she commented on the success of Barack Obama's campaign during the Democratic primaries: "If Obama was a white man, he would not be in this position. And if he was a woman (of any color) he would not be in this position. He happens to be very lucky to be who he is. And the country is caught up in the concept."[43] Ferraro was accused by many of making a racist comment, although she insisted that she was only speaking about historic candidacies. Nonetheless, within days of the story, she resigned her position on the Clinton campaign finance committee. On the nomination of Sarah Palin later that year as the second woman to run on a major party ticket for vice president, Ferraro stated her pleasure in no longer being the only woman to run for the office: "Every time a woman runs, women win."[44] Ferraro died of complications from blood cancer in 2011 at the age of 75; her political legacy remains intact as the woman "who strode onto a podium in 1984 to accept the Democratic nomination for vice president and to take her place in American history as the first woman nominated for national office by a major party" and for removing "the 'men only' sign from the White House door."[45]

MEDIA COVERAGE OF WOMEN CANDIDATES

Like money, media coverage of candidates plays a significant role in the electoral process. Not only are voters reliant on information provided by the news media about who is running and what is at stake during an election, but also candidates must spend a great deal of time developing effective media strategies. Much research in recent years has been devoted to how women candidates are portrayed in news media coverage and whether a gender bias exists that stands in the way of more women being elected to public office. Traditionally, women politicians have been viewed in the news media as an anomaly—a unique occurrence that deserves attention because it is outside the norm.[46] Trivialization of women in the mass media through portrayals on television and in movies also leads to "symbolic annihilation" of women in general, as well as the stereotyping that occurs in news coverage of women candidates and politicians.[47] Early research also revealed stereotypes about both male and female political candidates. Women, who were considered more compassionate, were seen as more competent in the traditional "female" policy areas of health care, the environment, education, poverty, and civil rights. Men, who were considered more aggressive, showed stronger competencies in the traditionally "male" policy areas of military and defense matters, foreign policy, and economic and trade issues.[48]

Early research on news coverage of women candidates suggested that negative stereotyping of women candidates hurt their efforts to win an elected office. Political scientist Kim Fridkin Kahn found in the early 1990s that the news media pay more attention to style than substance when covering female candidates and that news coverage that downplays issues and highlights personal traits develops less favorable images for female candidates.[49] Other early studies found similar results in the negative stereotyping of women candidates. A study by the White House Project that included several gubernatorial candidates found that not only did women candidates receive more coverage of style than of substance, but also male reporters more often focused on the personal than did female reporters.[50] In a similar study on women candidates in U.S. Senate races, the results showed that news media coverage on television "disadvantaged women candidates in the eyes of voters" by providing more favorable coverage of male candidates than of women candidates.[51] However, although these studies and others show that media biases and negative stereotyping of women candidates still exist, "it does appear that coverage is becoming more equitable" in terms of quantity and substance.[52] Often, a more subtle gender bias can exist in coverage, such as inserting details about appearance in news stories about women candidates or describing women politicians "in ways and with words that emphasize women's traditional roles" that "perpetuate stereotypes of women politicians as weak, indecisive, and emotional."[53] Women politicians can also be trivialized by the gender-specific words journalists commonly use to describe them, such as "plucky," "spunky," or "feisty."[54]

The results of these studies suggest that negative stereotyping of women candidates by the news media can be particularly problematic for women presidential or vice presidential candidates. During Geraldine Ferraro's run for the vice presidency in 1984 (with Democratic nominee Walter Mondale) and Elizabeth Dole's short-lived campaign for the Republican nomination in 1999–2000, gender was a significant label in the news coverage of both women candidates; "the most pernicious coverage for both campaigns was the 'lipstick watch,'" with almost 30 percent of Ferraro's coverage and more than 40 percent of Dole's coverage containing references to clothing, make-up, hair, and other feminine categorizations.[55] Other studies also suggested that although the news media are usually quick to herald the fact that American voters seem ready to elect a woman president, women running for elected office at all levels of government are still viewed as a political anomaly, that a disproportionate amount of coverage is devoted to clothing and hairstyles, and that the mass media in general still often rely on negative stereotyping of women.[56]

More recent studies point out that presidential elections are "gendered" spaces that focus on masculinity, toughness, and whether potential candidates have "presidential timber." Although the candidacies of Clinton in 2008 and Michele Bachmann (R-MN) in 2012 began to shift the definition of masculinity on the campaign trail, more progress is needed to "regender" presidential campaigns to provide acceptance for styles of leadership that do not evoke hypermasculinity.[57] News media emphasis on candidate sex, appearance, marital status, and masculine issues in news coverage "still haunts female candidates," particularly when considering the coverage of Clinton and Palin in the 2008 presidential race. New media (online and social media sites) included some of the most offensive/sexist coverage, as the "online universe of political commentary operates outside of traditional media editorial boundaries and is sometimes incisive but often offensive and unsubstantiated."[58]

However, according to political scientist Dianne Bystrom, there is some good news for women candidates: "Despite continuing stereotypes held by voters and the media, women candidates can manage campaign communication tools in ways that improve their chances of success. Women candidates who present themselves successfully in their television ads and on their websites may be able to capitalize on these controlled messages to influence their media coverage for a synergistic communication effort."[59] In addition, despite the attention paid to the appearance and dress of a female candidate, recent research suggests that "appearance effects are likely to occur only when the news media portray candidates in unflattering ways." Furthermore, women are at no greater risk in this regard than men because voters often react similarly to appearance coverage regardless of gender, and "when Americans go to the polls, they are far more likely to vote based on the candidates' party affiliation or ideological leanings than on the lines around their eyes or the size of their waistline."[60]

Many gender stereotypes come from the way women are portrayed in the mass media, and although there has long been an assumption that voters rely on gender stereotypes when evaluating candidates, little empirical evidence exists to back up the claim. Recent research instead suggests that although stereotypes do exist in the abstract, gender stereotypes in the real world "are not major forces but instead are, like many things, context-bound and episodic, appearing in some races but not others." Partisanship and ideology still matter more than voter-gender stereotypes when it comes to supporting a candidate.[61] A similar study found that gender stereotypes were not a key component of candidate evaluations or voter decisions, but that the political party of women candidates can instead play a more significant role in voter decisions.[62] It is also important to remember that women candidates do not automatically attract or win the support of women voters. Although women do tend to support women candidates by a slight advantage in most elections, partisanship among voters is still a better predictor of the outcome of a race as opposed to the sex of the voter when a woman candidate is on the ballot.[63] Although bias against women candidates is "largely a thing of the past," a candidate's sex is not irrelevant because "hostility toward women has been replaced by a more complex set of considerations that involve people's social and political reactions to candidate sex and gendered issues."[64]

In addition, the conventional wisdom about how women face a "double bind" (for example, they are penalized by voters if they appear unfeminine or too "tough") may not be accurate. According to political scientist Deborah Jordan Brooks, women "benefit from toughness more than men with respect to their perceived effectiveness . . . [and] although all candidates should be in touch with their empathetic, 'feminine' side, [women candidates] do not have to be more attuned to it than men. . . . Indeed, the more general point to underscore is that to be judged as a leader and not as a lady is not necessarily a wholly positive experience; it simply means that women and men are not judged by different standards."[65] Brooks also points out that women politicians are judged more harshly as "politicians" as opposed to "women" and that women are no longer tokens or anomalies in American politics, at least at the legislative level: "The genie of female leadership will not go back in the bottle. The fact that a candidate is a woman is not an oddity, problem, or all-defining characteristic that it may once have been."[66] She does not suggest, however, that women no longer face challenges on the campaign trail, but indicates that gender alone is not the defining factor in whether a candidate wins or loses, since "it is very hard for any candidate, man or woman, to win a race, especially a race for national or statewide office. The public has challenging expectations for any candidate."[67]

CONCLUSION

How we elect politicians in the United States plays an important role in determining the number of women who serve in public office. Although women candidates, especially those running for Congress, have succeeded in recent years in the area of fundraising, the incumbency advantage still hurts the chances of any new or "outsider" candidates (particularly women and minorities) winning seats and thereby possibly bringing a different perspective to the policymaking process. For more women to be elected to public office, they must be encouraged to do so by political parties and other political activists, and perhaps more important, they must believe that they have a strong chance of winning, which will encourage more women to enter the eligibility pool. Although feminist/pro-choice women candidates made substantial gains in both congressional and state races in 1992, it is worth noting that two years later in 1994 (known as the "Year of the Angry White Male" as the Republican Party captured both houses of Congress for the first time in 40 years), several conservative, pro-life women were also elected to Congress, reminding us that a monolithic view of "women politicians" does not exist. Since the mid-1990s, the gains for women winning elections to public offices at all levels of government have slowed tremendously, with only modest and incremental increases. Perhaps future research by political scientists and other interested observers should continue to consider what changes to both public institutions and public policy result from women at both ends of the political/ideological spectrum running for, and eventually holding, public office.

Political attitudes toward women in politics have changed as more women have been elected to office, moving away from the outdated belief that women did not belong in public life. Although scholars have documented numerous barriers that have traditionally existed for women candidates, some institutional and some informal, newer research by political scientists is beginning to show that gender stereotypes may not be as harmful as once thought. According to political scientist Kathleen Dolan, although much work still must be done in the study of gender stereotypes for both women and men, "Given the increasing number of women candidates who run for a wide range of offices, we should acknowledge that women's uniqueness as candidates may be on the wane. And as public opinion data suggest that stereotypes of women and men may be easing, we should consider whether women candidates have successfully neutralized the impact of stereotypes through their decisions and actions."[68] The bottom line is that as more women win campaigns and hold political office, the view of women as political leaders will more than likely continue to shift public attitudes about the efficacy of women in public life.

CHAPTER SUMMARY

• Inadequate recruitment of women candidates helps to explain why the numbers of women holding political office remain relatively low, and there is still resistance for many potential women candidates to run. Many young women today shun the high-pressure, brutally competitive lifestyle that comes with many leadership opportunities, including those within politics.

- The number of women in elected positions has leveled off compared to the yearly increases during the early 1990s in Congress and at the state level. However, women no longer run disproportionately for unwinnable seats and women are just as likely as men to have party leaders encourage their candidacies.
- The likelihood that a woman will run for a state legislative seat varies from state to state and can be affected by factors such as incumbency, the number of eligible women in the recruitment pool, and the perceived viability of women candidates by party leaders. However, party recruitment plays a significant role in electing women legislators in some states.
- Most women candidates have the necessary qualifications for the job, being well educated and having professional and/or managerial careers. Most also have some party and organizational experience.
- Prior political experience, particularly at the local level, can be a critical indicator of the number of women who will be seen as credible candidates for higher office. The "pipeline" that allows women to enter the political arena as candidates is crucial.
- The main reason for women's underrepresentation at all levels of government stems from the fact that women choose to run less frequently than men, although they are just as likely to win. The factors that contribute include political gender role socialization, a lack of political confidence, family responsibilities, and a lack of visible women role models in politics. A critical gender difference exists in the candidate emergence phase because of a substantial winnowing process that yields a smaller ratio of women than men candidates.
- The incumbency advantage, which includes a sizable fundraising advantage over challengers, leaves fewer opportunities for women to win seats. The creation of "safe seats" has also contributed to the high rates of incumbency.
- The success of women candidates in 1992, known as the "Year of the Woman," was in part a result of the number of open seats during that election cycle. Women's interest groups were also motivated to nominate and elect women candidates following the U.S. Supreme Court confirmation hearings of Clarence Thomas during 1991, which included testimony from law professor Anita Hill that Thomas had sexually harassed her while he served as her boss at the Equal Employment Opportunity Commission.
- Women candidates won a record number of seats in both the U.S. House of Representatives and the Senate. In the House, 106 women ran for congressional seats on a major party ticket, and 47 won seats in the general election. In the Senate, 11 women ran and six were elected, which contributed to the largest ever one-time increase in candidates and winners. Gains were also made in state legislatures.
- Women have experienced a higher rate of electoral success in state legislatures because of a higher turnover rate for incumbents, since state legislators are more likely to return to their previous careers or run for higher office, thereby creating more open seats for challengers.

- Money also plays a prominent role in American political campaigns, although women candidates now raise and spend as much as or more than their male counterparts.
- Recent campaign finance data have shown that women still lag behind men in contributions from large moneyed interests (such as business PACs) because they rely slightly more on contributions from both individuals and single-issue/ideological PACs. However, this also allows women candidates to find alternate pathways to financial viability while building a broader base of electoral support.
- Women's PACs have made important financial contributions to women candidates in addition to providing training, consultation, and workers in support of the campaign.
- Media coverage of candidates also plays a significant role in the electoral process. Traditionally, women politicians have been viewed in the news media as an anomaly—a unique occurrence that deserves attention because it is outside the norm. Trivialization of women in the mass media through portrayals on television and in movies also leads to "symbolic annihilation" of women in general, as well as the stereotyping that occurs in news coverage of women candidates and politicians.
- Early research on news coverage of women candidates suggested that negative stereotyping of women candidates hurts their efforts to win an elected office.
- Emphasis on candidate sex, appearance, marital status, and masculine issues in news coverage is still present, although women candidates can develop successful communication strategies to mitigate the effect. New media (online and social media sites) include some of the most offensive/sexist coverage.

STUDY/DISCUSSION QUESTIONS

- What factors contribute to the successful recruitment of women candidates? Why, even with other successful examples, do some women still believe that they cannot win an election?
- How do party leaders and other political activists impact the recruitment of women candidates? What can they do to encourage more women to run for public office?
- What role does incumbency play in congressional elections, and why does this serve as such an imposing barrier for women getting elected?
- Why is early money so important for women candidates, and how have women's PACs helped to alleviate this financial burden?
- In what ways does the news media perpetuate negative stereotypes of both women candidates and women politicians?

CASE STUDIES

1. **Does descriptive representation matter?**
In this chapter, we fleshed out the structural challenges that explain why there are so many men but few women in politics. The focus here is on descriptive

representation, the idea that elected officials should somewhat match politically relevant characteristics, such as gender, race, and geographic region. Another form is substantive representation, the idea that elected officials should advocate for the interests of politically marginalized groups, such as women or people of color, regardless of their identity. Analyze how these two types of representation might be connected. How does identity influence the substance of an official's policy? Is it necessary to elect more women to better represent women's interests? Why or why not?

2. **How can we get more women into politics?**
   In Chapter 5, we analyzed the early childhood origins of why so few women run for public office. In this chapter, we examined the structural barriers that discourage women from entering politics. Now that you have a good sense of the challenges, how can we get more women to run for and win public office? If you had a magic wand, what social beliefs, social practices, institutional processes, governmental structures, etc., would you change to get more women to run for public office?

3. **Have you considered running for public office?**
   If you are a typical college student enrolled in a class on gender in politics, the answer to this question is likely "no." If the answer is "yes," analyze what beliefs and experiences led you to consider running for public office. If the answer is "no," analyze what experiences and beliefs have discouraged you from wanting to run for public office. What people or situations in your life have discouraged or encouraged your political ambition, how, and why?

RESOURCES

- The **Federal Election Commission** administers and enforces federal laws that govern the financing of federal elections.
  http://www.fec.gov
- The **Center for Responsive Politics** is a leading research group tracking money in U.S. politics and its effect on elections and public policy.
  http://OpenSecrets.org
- The **Democratic Senatorial Campaign Committee** works to elect Democrats to the U.S. Senate.
  http://www.dscc.org
- The **National Republican Senatorial Committee** works to elect Republicans to the U.S. Senate.
  http://www.nrsc.org
- The **Democratic Congressional Campaign Committee** recruits candidates, raises funds, and organizes races to help elect Democrats to the House of Representatives.
  http://www.dccc.org

- The **National Republican Congressional Committee** recruits candidates, raises funds, and organizes races to help elect Republicans to the House of Representatives.
http://www.nrcc.org

CHAPTER 7

Women as Legislators

Still remembered as the "Year of the Woman," the American political landscape shifted dramatically in 1992 as more women ran—and won—legislative seats at both the national and state level than ever before. The progress of electing more women to public office was particularly notable in California as the largest state in the nation made history by electing two women to the U.S. Senate that year— Barbara Boxer and Dianne Feinstein. Boxer, a Democrat who had served ten years in the House of Representatives, won an open seat following the retirement of fellow Democrat Alan Cranston after four terms in the Senate. Feinstein, the former mayor of San Francisco, won a special election to fill the Senate seat vacated a year earlier when Senator Pete Wilson (R) resigned after being elected governor of California. Since their respective wins in 1992, Boxer and Feinstein have remained dominant political figures in California. Each has been reelected four times with few serious challenges, each has been a prolific fundraiser, and each will leave a strong legacy—Boxer as a liberal senator known for her staunch support of reproductive rights, environmental protection, health-care reform, and her vote against the Iraq War in 2002 and Feinstein as a more moderate Democrat who is known for serving on the Senate intelligence and judiciary committees and for authoring the federal assault weapons ban passed in 1994.

When Boxer announced that she would not seek a fifth term in 2016, it marked the end of an era. Many Californians have a hard time remembering when they were not represented in the U.S. Senate by Boxer and Feinstein; in fact, anyone born after 1992 has never been represented by a male senator. That trend continued as the two candidates on the general election ballot in November 2016 to fill Boxer's seat were two women—California Attorney General Kamala Harris (D) and Representative Loretta Sanchez (D). Because of California's open primary and the fact that California is a strong Democratic state, Harris and Sanchez each advanced to the general election after they were the two top vote-getters in the primary, thus ensuring that California would send another woman to the Senate. Harris won the general election, defeating Sanchez 63 to 37 percent.

The legacy of the "Year of the Woman" continues to shape current legislative campaigns. Since 1992, women have made great strides in getting elected to legislative positions, both at the federal and state level. These seats of power within the American system of government represent a crucial aspect of policymaking as legislators are directly responsible for writing the laws at all levels of government. There are now more women serving in the U.S. Congress and in state legislatures across the country than ever before. At the start of the 115th Session of Congress in 2017, a total of 104 women were serving in the U.S. Congress (19.4 percent), with 21 in the Senate (21 percent) and 83 in the House of Representatives (19.1 percent). Along with California, Washington and New Hampshire hold the distinction of being represented by two women in the Senate, an institution long regarded as an exclusive all-male club in Washington, DC. Maine had also been within this exclusive group before Olympia Snowe's (R) retirement in 2012. And in the House of Representatives, Nancy Pelosi (D-CA) made history in 2007 with her election to the top leadership post as Speaker of the House. She has served as House minority leader since 2011 after Republicans won control of the House in the 2010 midterm election. To date, California has sent the most women to Congress with 41, followed by New York with 28.[1]

But despite the progress since 1992, women are still nowhere close to reaching parity with men as members of Congress or state legislators. Women still make up less than 20 percent of Congress and 25 percent of state legislatures. While 321 women have served in Congress, that represents only two percent of the more than 12,000 members since the first session of Congress in 1789.[2] In addition, two states as of 2017—Mississippi and Vermont—have yet to elect a woman to Congress. This serves as an important paradox for women, who make up 51 percent of the voting population: how to translate that voting strength into proportional representation within state and national government. Why is progress so slow in getting women elected to legislative positions? And when women do get elected to office, why do so few rise to leadership positions within the party ranks? Another important question to consider concerns the leadership style of women legislators and whether they make a difference in terms of both the policymaking process and policy outcomes. In this chapter, we will discuss women and legislative leadership, the history of women serving in Congress, the impact of women legislators on the policy agenda, and the number and impact of women serving in state legislatures.

WOMEN AND LEGISLATIVE LEADERSHIP

Why study women as legislators, and what can we learn about women's style of leadership in this political venue? First, it is important to understand how a legislature functions to achieve its ultimate goal of lawmaking. Individual members of a legislature are elected to represent an equal number of citizens (or, in the case of the U.S. Senate, states are represented equally with two members each) in the policymaking process. While some members may have more seniority or may be members of the majority party, which may in turn provide them more powerful committee or leadership positions, all legislatures within the United States operate on the simple premise of "one person, one vote." In most areas of the decision-making process, a simple majority among the members in both houses is required to pass a bill that will then be sent to the executive branch to be signed or vetoed by the president or state governor. (Exceptions in Congress include, for example, a two-thirds vote to override a presidential veto or to approve a constitutional amendment to then be considered by the states). As a result, consensus-building and cooperation among members is necessary to pass legislation.

Cindy Simon Rosenthal, in her study of women state legislators, explains that the study of legislative leadership has mostly considered men and, as a result, has failed to acknowledge the contribution of women to lawmaking in recent decades. "Congressional studies, which dominate the legislative literature, remain mostly about men. Might it be that male behavior has been conflated as institutional behavior?"[3] If women traditionally exhibit leadership traits that are more openly democratic, cooperative, and promote a group-centered mode for decision making, then one might assume that women have had a positive impact on how legislatures function. Rosenthal's study, which consisted of surveys of legislative committee chairs from 50 states, focus groups, interviews, and an extensive study of the state legislatures in Colorado, Ohio, and Oklahoma, demonstrated that "sex, the social understandings of gender, and gendered institutions all influence leadership style."[4] She categorizes legislative leadership as having two distinct styles: aggregative (also known as transactional; a style that is leader centered and hierarchical, with leaders exercising power over others) and integrative (also known as transformational; a style that is nonhierarchical and stresses mutuality and community, empowering others, and a common purpose among members).[5] Aggregative/transactional leadership is considered the norm within legislatures, in part due to the study of institutions as historically dominated by men. The integrative/transformational leadership style has also been present in legislatures as women have gained a more prominent role, yet researchers have mostly ignored this until recently.

By examining institutions in which both men and women occupy leadership roles, modest differences in leadership traits among men and women become apparent. For example, women committee chairs often exhibit leadership styles closer to the integrative/transformational model. As Rosenthal states, "Leadership is a complex phenomenon of individual experiences, circumstances, and relationships. Nonetheless, on a wide variety of individual measures of leadership traits, motivation, or behavior, women and men differ in ways that are substantively and statistically significant."[6] In a later writing, Rosenthal also concludes there is evidence from states across the nation to indicate that "women committee chairs in state legislatures adopt styles that emphasize both getting things done and getting along, but that getting things done predominates." And while women legislators are now more assertive in terms of leadership thanks to more women holding positions of power in the legislative arena, their continued effectiveness and inclusion within the institutional setting demands that more women achieve leadership positions.[7]

Many other studies have been conducted since the early 1990s that consider the role gender may play in legislative strategies. As we will discuss later in this chapter, several studies have shown that women legislators are more likely to sponsor bills dealing with so-called women's issues such as health care, education, and child care. In addition, some evidence suggests that women legislators may be equally or even more effective than their male colleagues in advancing successful legislation,[8] particularly when they exert high effort, consensus-building, and issue specialization under certain circumstances (such as when they are members of the minority party).[9] Another study found that gender can help explain different styles of representation due to women's persistent underrepresentation in Congress, as women in both parties are more likely to speak on the House floor: "In a male-dominated institution, and in a political arena where gender stereotypes call into question women's leadership, congresswomen of both parties have extra incentives to increase their visibility and prove their expertise to their colleagues and constituents alike, leading them to give more speeches on the House floor."[10]

PROFILE IN POWER

Nancy Pelosi

In 1925, Representative Mae Ella Nolan (R-CA) became the first woman to chair a congressional committee when, during the 68th Congress, she chaired the Committee on Expenditures in the Post Office Department. Nearly eight decades later, another representative from California, Democrat Nancy Pelosi, became the highest-ranking women to ever hold a leadership position when her Democratic colleagues supported her as the House minority leader in 2003. Four years later, Pelosi made history again when she became Speaker of the House in 2007 at the start of the 110th Congress. When her party lost control of the House during the 2010 midterm elections, Pelosi remained the top Democrat and resumed her role as House minority leader. While more women than ever before are now serving in Congress, the top leadership positions have remained an important and elusive glass ceiling for women in politics. Pelosi served as the Democratic whip, the number two leadership position for the minority party, prior to her ascension to Democratic leader and then Speaker of the House, yet she remains the only woman to hold such a leadership position in either house of Congress.

Why are leadership posts so important within Congress? As a political institution, Congress is dominated by party politics. And the U.S. Constitution helps to maintain our two-party system of government with single-member congressional districts. That means that to win a congressional seat, a candidate needs a simple majority (or plurality if more than two candidates are on the ballot) to win the seat and represent all citizens within the district. The difficulty in a third-party candidate winning the majority of votes in a congressional district preserves the two-party system. As a result, the two major parties—Democrats and Republicans—control the rules that govern the policymaking process within Congress.

In the House of Representatives, the Speaker of the House comes from the majority party. The Speaker refers bills to committees, appoints members to special committees, and grants members the right to speak during debates. After the Speaker, the top leadership posts in the House include the majority leader and whip and the minority leader and whip. The party leaders and whips try to organize their members to support or oppose legislative proposals. Whips are usually selected from among the most experienced members of the House. Majority party members also chair and hold a majority of seats on both the House and Senate standing committees and subcommittees. The Senate is similar, with positions of majority and minority leaders and whips, but does not have a Speaker.

Pelosi, who has five children, did not seek elective office until her children were mostly grown; she has been in the House of Representatives since 1987, representing California's 8th District (which includes most of San Francisco). Her father, Thomas J. D'Alesandro Jr., was a former congressman and mayor of Baltimore. Since first taking over the position as House minority leader in 2003 and then Speaker of the House in 2007, Pelosi has earned a reputation as a pragmatic leader who is not afraid to speak her mind in public. Throughout her congressional career, she has also been known as a top Democratic fundraiser and policy strategist. However, the Democrats' choice of Pelosi for minority leader in 2003 was questioned by many political commentators, even those sympathetic to the party's policy positions, due to her image as a San Francisco liberal. She took over the job from Richard Gephardt, a more centrist Democrat from Missouri, but her voting record seems to be in line with a majority of House Democrats, even if it does not represent the views of mainstream Democratic voters nationwide.[11] While moderate Democrats preferred the leadership style of Gephardt, who was always careful not to offend anyone with his positions, liberals within the party liked Pelosi's style of "coming out swinging" with clear positions for the Democratic Party. In May 2004, frustrated by the Bush administration's policies in the war in Iraq, Pelosi criticized President George W. Bush by saying, "I believe that the president's leadership and the actions taken in Iraq demonstrate an incompetence in terms of knowledge, judgment and experience."

In 2006, Pelosi was candid with the press about her intention to help the Democrats regain control of the House so that she could become the first woman Speaker. After achieving that historic feat and with the Democrats in the majority in both houses of Congress, Pelosi announced her plan to push through major items on the Democratic policy agenda within the "first hundred hours" of the 110th Congress. Nearly all of the items on the legislative plan were passed, including an increase in the federal minimum wage, a reduction in student loan interest rates, new rules for Medicare prescription drug costs, increased funding for stem cell research, stricter rules for lobbyists, "pay-as-you-go" spending to reduce the national deficit, ending tax subsidies for oil companies, and increasing port security (as recommended by the 9/11 Commission). In addition, Pelosi continued to be an outspoken critic of many of the Bush administration's policies, particularly the war in Iraq. However, she disappointed many liberals in the Democratic Party when she announced after becoming Speaker that impeachment proceedings would not be pursued against Bush or Vice President Dick Cheney over the decision to invade Iraq in 2003. As a leader of the Democratic Party, Pelosi's support of then–presidential candidate Barack Obama in 2008 helped to solidify his support among Democratic voters, and Pelosi campaigned tirelessly that year to also increase the Democratic majority in the House. In 2009, her outspoken style of leadership continued as she publicly charged the Central Intelligence Agency with misleading Congress since 2001 on torture and other issues related to the Bush administration's war on terror, and in 2010, she was crucial in gathering enough votes among Democrats to pass the Affordable Care Act, Obama's signature health-care reform.

Pelosi, who broke an important glass ceiling for women in Congress as the first woman to lead her party, has been called an "elegant and energetic" politician who has "the kind of star quality that many say makes them again excited to be Democrats. Young women come to the Capitol to have their picture taken in front of her office."[12] The question remains as to whether a woman Speaker makes a difference in terms of the legislative agenda or the day-to-day functions of the House (on issues such as bipartisanship or collegiality among members), and it is important to remember the institutional limitations, traditions, and procedures within the House, as well as the role of party politics, that may leave little room for change based on gendered leadership. However, as Speaker of the House from 2007 to 2011 and second in line for succession to the presidency (after the vice president), Pelosi was the highest-ranking woman politician in the history of the United States.

WOMEN IN CONGRESS

The main argument put forth by suffragists in the struggle to secure the vote for women centered on the belief that women should not be prevented from civic participation and duties and that women should be allowed to select their own representatives. When women did secure the right to vote with the ratification of the Nineteenth Amendment to the U.S. Constitution in 1920, many assumed that women would voice their political preferences by electing other women. However, not all women rushed to the ballot box to participate in the electoral process. Other factors came into play as well to contribute to the many obstacles that women politicians would face in the following decades. Few women sought elective office during the first half of the twentieth century, and of those who did, several were nominated by the minority party in a district where the candidate had little chance of winning.

History

The first woman to serve in the U.S. Congress was elected before women nationwide had the right to vote. Jeannette Rankin, a Republican from Montana, served two terms in the U.S. House of Representatives, the first from 1917 to 1918 (Montana had granted women's suffrage prior to 1920) and the second from 1941 to 1942. Rankin, a pacifist, was the only member of Congress to vote against American entry into both World War I and World War II. Rebecca Latimer Felton, a Georgia Democrat in her 80s, became the first woman to serve in the U.S. Senate in 1922. She was appointed as a temporary replacement to a vacant seat and only served for two days before giving up her seat to the man who had been elected to it. Hattie Wyatt Caraway, an Arkansas Democrat who was appointed to the U.S Senate to succeed her late husband in 1931, was the first of many women to take this path to the Senate. After her appointment to the office, Caraway later became the first woman elected to the Senate in her own right, where she served two full terms. She was also the first woman to chair a Senate committee—the minor position of chair of the Committee on Enrolled Bills.

While women succeeding to the Congress as widows was a common occurrence throughout the twentieth century, it is now more often the exception than the rule. When a vacancy occurs in the House of Representatives, a special election must be held. As such, a widow had the advantage of name recognition. In the Senate, a vacancy is usually filled through a gubernatorial appointment until the next regularly scheduled federal election (which occurs every even-numbered year). However, three more recent examples show that this practice is still in effect. Doris Matsui, widow of 26-year House veteran Robert Matsui, won a special election to her late husband's district in California in March 2005. Mary Bono, the widow of entertainer and former Palm Springs, California, mayor Sonny Bono, won a special election to fill his House seat following his accidental death in 1998. And in the Senate, Jean Carnahan represented the state of Missouri for two years after her husband posthumously won election in 2002. Mel Carnahan, a Democrat, died in a plane crash two weeks prior to the election, where he was challenging the incumbent Republican senator John Ashcroft. His wife Jean was then appointed to fill the Senate seat by the state governor, but she lost her reelection bid in 2004.

Major growth in the number of women seeking legislative office at the national level, and as a result women being elected to office, did not occur until the late 1960s and early 1970s. The modern women's rights movement began to change the political environment, albeit slowly, which encouraged more women to seek political office in an effort to change public policies that affected them directly. One woman who arrived in Congress during this time was Patricia Schroeder, who served 24 years in the House of Representatives as a Democrat from Colorado. Schroeder was elected to Congress in 1972 at the age of 32. Her first campaign, run out of her own house, focused on ideas rather than on money. She also beat the political odds to win the seat, since her campaign was also short on political support and endorsements. The only endorsements she received came from the few African American elected officials in Colorado at the time. Not only did the Democratic Party refuse to support her campaign, but also the Colorado Women's Political Caucus, which she had helped to found, denied her an endorsement. The average contribution to her campaign was a mere $7.50, which came from several individual supporters within the congressional district.[13] Schroeder, who defied the critics and naysayers when she was first elected, always maintained a leadership style focused on her outsider status, as opposed to the many women she would later see in Congress who tried to move things along and play by the rules: "It's not that they lack vision, but they want to remain players. Whereas I arrived realizing I would *never* be a player—so I would play the outsider game."[14]

By 1984, the number of women nominated by their party to run for the House of Representatives had increased dramatically. That same year, U.S. Representative Geraldine Ferraro of New York became Democrat Walter Mondale's running mate in the presidential election. A total of 65 women ran for the House that year; however, only 22 women were elected, and most who won were incumbents. Many political observers concluded that while Ferraro's candidacy had been symbolic for women, real progress in the number of women elected had not occurred.

In 1986, Barbara Mikulski of Maryland became the first Democratic woman elected to the Senate without first being appointed to the seat. Mikulski, who was known as a master strategist in getting bills passed before she retired in 2016, spent her early years in the Senate learning as much about the institution and its processes as possible. She also respected the Senate traditions and its rules and sought the guidance and advice of the Democratic men with whom she served:

> I was at an initial disadvantage as a woman coming to the Senate, and it wasn't just that the gym was off-limits. I didn't come to politics by the traditional male route, being in a nice law firm or belonging to the right clubs. Like most of the women I've known in politics, I got involved because I saw a community need. And it was tough, absolutely. I didn't have any natural mentors to show me the ropes. I had to seek out my mentors. So when four women finally joined me in the Senate in 1993, I was very gratified. I gladly took on the role of mentor and adviser.[15]

A nomination to the U.S. Supreme Court in the fall of 1991 served as a catalyst for more women running for office, more women getting elected, and the start of a grass-roots effort among women's advocacy groups to change the gender balance on Capitol Hill. When President George H. W. Bush nominated Clarence Thomas to fill a vacancy on the Supreme Court due to the retirement of Associate Justice Thurgood Marshall, no one could have predicted the national firestorm over sexual harassment that would be unleashed. When law professor Anita Hill's claims of sexual harassment against Thomas, for whom she had worked at the Equal Employment Opportunity Commission, were leaked to the press, Hill was called to testify before the all-male Senate Judiciary Committee. Prior to the Senate investigation into the charges, it was unclear as to whether the Senate would take the accusations seriously.

Seven women in the House of Representatives were outraged over the apparent indifference to such a charge by their male colleagues in the Senate. On October 8, 1991, the women, led by Schroeder and including then-member of the House Barbara Boxer (D-CA), Louise Slaughter (D-NY), Eleanor Holmes-Norton (D-DC), Nita Lowey (D-NY), Patsy Mink (D-HI), and Jolene Unsoeld (D-WA), along with several reporters in tow, marched up the steps to the Senate on the opposite side of the Capitol to demand that their concerns be heard by the Democratic leadership. Boxer recalled later that the women wanted to help Democratic senators, who were attending their regular Tuesday Democratic caucus lunch, understand the importance of the issue. At the time, only two women (Mikulski and Nancy Kassebaum, a Republican from Kansas) were serving in the Senate. The women believed that their perspective would be welcomed; instead, they initially found themselves outside a closed door they were not allowed to enter. Finally, with the threat of negative press coverage from the reporters present, Senate Majority Leader George Mitchell agreed to meet with the women in a side room.

Further testimony and investigations did follow into Hill's allegations against Thomas. However, Thomas was confirmed by the full Senate in a vote of 52–48 (the second closest vote ever to confirm a Supreme Court nominee). More important, for many women across the nation, the event proved to be galvanizing in the sense that women were not a visible part of the political elite within Washington. Boxer recalled, "It was humiliating to be so summarily dismissed—to have to beg for a hearing. But we kept demanding to be heard until [Mitchell] agreed to meet with us. And so we got our hearing. It turned out to be a travesty. It was shameful. But it was also a wake-up call. All over the country, women watched those hearings, and reacted to seeing that long row of white male senators. It was made painfully clear that they just 'didn't get it.'"[16]

As a result, the presidential and congressional election year of 1992 became known as the "Year of the Woman." Many more women ran for Congress than in years past, in part due to the Hill–Thomas controversy. As a result, the number of women in Congress rose from 32 at the end of the 102nd Congress to 52 during the 103rd Congress, including 20 new women members in the House and four new women senators. (The new senators included Democrats Boxer and Feinstein of California, Patty Murray of Washington, and Carol Moseley Braun of Illinois; Republican Kay Bailey Hutchison of Texas increased the number to seven when she won a special election in June 1993 to replace Democrat Lloyd Bentsen, who had been appointed treasury secretary in the new Clinton administration). More than 60 million women had voted in the general election in November 1992, which played a crucial role in the largest increase in the number of women elected to Congress in history. The success of women candidates in 1992 can also be attributed to many other factors, including redistricting, a record number of retirements from the House in 1992, and the House post office scandal in 1991 and the House bank scandal in 1992. These issues, as well as legislative gridlock between a Democratic-controlled Congress and a Republican White House, contributed to the public desire in 1992 for a change in the membership and policies on Capitol Hill. Women capitalized on this situation as relative newcomers; "with a strong reputation for honesty and integrity on the one hand, and expertise on many domestic issues on the other, women were looked upon to initiate reform."[17]

Since 1992, the number of women serving in Congress has steadily yet slowly increased. As of 2017, there are currently 104 women serving in Congress—83 in the House and 21 in the Senate (see Table 7.1). In addition, women hold five of the six nonvoting seats in the House (the District of Columbia, Puerto Rico, Guam,

Table 7.1 Women in the 115th Congress–U.S. Senate

SENATOR	STATE (PARTY AFFILIATION)	YEAR ELECTED
Tammy Baldwin	Wisconsin (D)	2012
Maria Cantwell	Washington (D)	2000
Shelley Moore Capito	West Virginia (R)	2014
Susan Collins	Maine (R)	1996
Catherine Cortez Masto	Nevada (D)	2016
Tammy Duckworth	Illinois (D)	2016
Joni Ernst	Iowa (R)	2014
Dianne Feinstein	California (D)	1992
Deb Fischer	Nebraska (R)	2012
Kirsten Gillibrand	New York (D)	2009*
Kamala Harris	California (D)	2016
Maggie Hassan	New Hampshire (D)	2016
Heidi Heitkamp	North Dakota (D)	2012
Mazie Hirono	Hawaii (D)	2012
Amy Klobuchar	Minnesota (D)	2006
Claire McCaskill	Missouri (D)	2006
Lisa Murkowski	Alaska (R)	2002
Patty Murray	Washington (D)	1992
Jeanne Shaheen	New Hampshire (D)	2008
Debbie Stabenow	Michigan (D)	2000
Elizabeth Warren	Massachusetts (D)	2012

*Gillibrand was appointed to fill the vacant Senate seat in 2009 and won election in 2010.
SOURCE: Center for American Women and Politics, Rutgers, State University of New Jersey.

American Samoa, and the U.S. Virgin Islands). Thirty-two states are now represented by at least one woman in the House. Among the largest states, California has 17 women representatives, New York has nine, Florida has seven, and Illinois has three. Texas, the second most populous state in the nation, only has three women in its House delegation, as does Ohio, ranked seventh in population. Pennsylvania, the sixth most populous state, has no women members in its House delegation (see Table 7.2). Of the 104 women currently serving in Congress, a total of 38 (36.5 percent) are women of color, and 11 of those women represent California (the most populous state in the nation with the greatest racial and ethnic diversity among its citizens).[18]

The Policy Agenda

When it comes to policymaking, many assume that women officeholders automatically support and prioritize what are often referred to as "women's issues"—domestic policy issues including education, health care, welfare, and reproductive rights, among others. However, party affiliation (Democrat or Republican) and political ideology (liberal, moderate, or conservative) are still the most important predictors for bill sponsorship or the actual vote on a particular bill for women in Congress or state legislatures. A recent study on the role of gender and how it influences policymaking in state legislatures shows that party identity and

Table 7.2 Women in the 115th Congress–U.S. House of Representatives

STATE	NO. OF WOMEN REPRESENTATIVES	PERCENTAGE
Alabama	2/7	28.6
Arizona	2/9	22.2
California	17/53	32.1
Colorado	1/7	14.3
Connecticut	2/5	40.0
Delaware	1/1	100
Florida	7/27	25.9
Hawaii	2/2	100
Illinois	3/18	16.7
Indiana	2/9	22.2
Kansas	1/4	25.0
Maine	1/2	50.0
Massachusetts	2/9	22.2
Michigan	2/14	14.3
Minnesota	1/8	12.5
Missouri	3/8	37.5
Nevada	2/4	50.0
New Hampshire	2/2	100
New Jersey	1/12	8.3
New Mexico	1/3	33.3
New York	9/27	33.3
North Carolina	1/13	7.7
Ohio	3/16	18.8
Oregon	1/5	20.0
South Dakota	1/1	100
Tennessee	2/9	22.2
Texas	3/36	8.3
Utah	1/4	25.0
Virginia	1/11	9.1
Washington	4/10	40.0
Wisconsin	1/8	12.5
Wyoming	1/1	100

Source: Center for American Women and Politics, Rutgers, State University of New Jersey.

institutional partisan structure "fundamentally shape how women represent women." Party identity determines how women candidates stake out a position during the election, and this continues when participating in the legislative policymaking process; majority party control of the chamber also "shapes the alternatives to women's issues offered by women legislators into a legislative agenda. Votes on this agenda are largely partisan or near unanimous; it is quite rare to see women legislators cross party lines to support the same women's issues bill with their roll call votes in an otherwise partisan chamber vote. . . . Thus, for women legislators, representing women is an inherently partisan endeavor."[19]

Other studies, however, have shown that having more women serve in legislatures, as well as their visibility within the institution (leadership positions, access to the news media, etc.), *does* positively impact the success of legislation that affects women.[20] Data on bill sponsorship and roll call votes suggest a strong correlation between women holding legislative seats and the gender orientation of policies introduced and adopted.[21] Another recent study suggests that women citizens may be more active politically when represented by women senators.[22] Yet, not all women in Congress are homogeneous, in terms of either style or the substance of their policy agendas. Yet, most women members of Congress "perceive of themselves as surrogate representatives for women and share some common perceptions about the experiences and ties that bind women together," although they differ in their party affiliation, political ideologies, racial and ethnic backgrounds, and the districts or states they represent.[23] In addition, studies have shown that women are "having a distinctive impact on the congressional agenda" and that both Democratic and Republican women are "more likely to advocate women's issue bills than are their male partisan colleagues, particularly feminist legislation."[24]

Gender, however, is not the only factor when it comes to issues relevant to women. There has long been an assumption that due to the small number of women serving in Congress, women are also underrepresented regarding relevant policies. However, research shows that, in general, "women appear to experience policy representation that is on a par with that of men." Partisan affiliation, as opposed to gender, determines more about how a member of Congress will vote on an issue. Democratic members of Congress more often support so-called women's issues than do Republican members, regardless of gender.[25] Also, male and female members of Congress representing the same constituency "amass virtually indistinguishable voting records on the liberal–conservative policy dimension," although when it comes to voting on women's issues, "female senators tend to be more supportive than the male senators they replace and male senators tend to be less supportive than the female senators they replace."[26]

The political environment in which women members of Congress find themselves can also make a difference in the type of legislation they pursue, including seniority on a committee and whether their party is in the majority or minority. Membership in a political party "can enhance or constrain women legislators' efforts," as can the presence of a women's caucus or whether women serve in committee leadership positions.[27] The most diversity among women members of Congress in recent years has occurred among Republican women, as the Republican Party on the national level has taken a more social conservative stance on many issues, which has placed pressure on moderate Republican women who differ with the majority view within their party on women's issues (for example, reproductive rights).[28]

However, women politicians can bring different priorities into the policymaking arena than their male colleagues, and some evidence suggests that women can also be more likely or willing to work across party lines to achieve policy goals. One example is the leadership style of female members of the U.S. Senate, who at times make their collective voices heard on bipartisan issues affecting women. Beginning in the mid-1990s, when the number of women in the Senate had first increased, such initiatives included the Homemaker Individual Retirement Account (cosponsored by Democrat Barbara Mikulski of Maryland and Republican Kay Bailey Hutchison of Texas, which allows homemakers to invest as much money in these tax-free retirement accounts as their working spouses) and a resolution in support of mammograms for women in their 40s (cosponsored by Mikulski and Republican Olympia Snowe of Maine).[29] More recently, three Republican women— Susan Collins (R-ME), Lisa Murkowski (R-AK), and Kelly Ayotte (R-NH)—abandoned their party's position and joined Democrats in pushing to end the 2013 budget shutdown.[30] Yet, despite these and other examples of bipartisanship, the women in the Senate are still beholden to party loyalty on many other issues. As the Senate transformed from an "old boys club" into a more "individualist and a more partisan institution" by the late 1990s, the demands of state constituencies and increasing partisanship meant that all senators must often be team players when it comes to their party's ideological goals.[31]

As former senator Olympia Snowe once pointed out, the women in the Senate are all different "in our political positions, our styles, our life experiences. However, women just come from a different place than men do in terms of being more relationship-oriented and more collaborative. In fact, many of the skills women develop in life actually work pretty well in this institution . . . where collaboration is an essential ingredient in getting things done."[32] Despite partisan affiliations, most women in Congress have forged a sense of collegiality that comes from their experiences as women in a traditionally male-dominated institution. The women in the Senate, for example, get together for regular informal dinners in Washington. The purpose of the dinners is not behind-the-scenes deal making; they serve as a "familiar ritual among women colleagues everywhere— that uniquely female manner of lending support by sharing experiences, describing challenges, and talking about the issues they care about."[33]

The women in the House have a more formal method of discussing important issues and collaborating on pieces of legislation dealing with women's issues. The Congressional Caucus for Women's Issues, a bipartisan group founded in 1977, has fought for the passage of many bills dealing with economic, educational, and health-care issues, among others. One of the biggest challenges the caucus has ever faced came in 1995, when Republicans gained control of both houses of Congress for the first time in 40 years. With a commitment to reduce the cost and size of government, the Republican leadership eliminated all legislative service organizations (including the Women's Caucus). Such organizations could still exist, but were to be renamed congressional member organizations and would no longer receive public funding to pay for office space and staff. As a result, the co-chairs of the organization (one woman from each party) now take on the responsibilities of the caucus in addition to their regular duties as a member of the House.

Most, but not all, women in the House are members, and legislative priorities that became laws in recent years have included stronger child-care funding and child-support provisions as part of the welfare reforms in 1996; increased spending for and the eventual reauthorization of the Violence Against Women Act programs; contraceptive coverage for women participating in the Federal Employee

Health Benefits Program; Medicaid coverage for low-income women diagnosed with breast cancer; bills to strengthen stalking, sex offender, and date rape laws; and many other pieces of legislation dealing with women's issues. With the exception of a few years during the 1990s, the bipartisan membership of the caucus has agreed to take a neutral stand on the issue of abortion to keep the organization more inclusive. However, one critique of the bipartisan approach suggests that due to policy differences on issues such as reproductive rights between the two parties, the caucus has produced "a somewhat narrow range of discursive representations of women's interests that could be translated into policy."[34] The caucus also continues to pursue alliances with women senators, as well as the House and Senate leadership in both parties, other caucuses, and the White House. While more than 200 caucuses have existed in the House in recent years focusing on a variety of policy issues, the Women's Caucus has remained (along with the Congressional Black Caucus) one of the most resilient and successful caucuses. For the caucus to continue to succeed, it must "celebrate its diversity while channeling the tremendous energy and talent of the growing membership into concrete legislative action."[35]

PROFILES IN POWER

Republican Women in the U.S. Senate

Although the overall number of women serving in Congress remains low, so does the number of Republican women elected to the House and Senate. Through 2017, a total of 321 women have served in Congress, but only 111 (34.5 percent) have been Republican. Currently, of the 21 women serving in the Senate, only five (24 percent) are Republican. In the House, of the 83 women currently serving, only 22 are Republican (26 percent). This can be explained by any number of factors, including the gender gap that tends to favor the Democratic Party and its policy agenda. However, this is perhaps the only category in recent years that provides good news for Democrats regarding federal and state representation. Despite Barack Obama's success as a presidential candidate in 2008 and 2012, through 2016, Democrats lost control of the White House, the House (including 69 seats), and the Senate (including 13 seats), 12 governorships, control of state legislatures in 30 states, and more than 900 state legislative seats. And while Republican women in Congress still lag behind Democrats, three of the current Republican women in the Senate were elected during Obama's presidency—Deb Fischer (NE), elected in 2012; and Joni Ernst (IA) and Shelley Moore Capito (WV), both elected in 2014. (Kelly Ayotte of New Hampshire was elected in 2010, but lost her reelection bid in 2016).

While the three newest Republican women in the Senate represent more conservative policy agendas, the two senior Republican women—Susan Collins (ME), elected in 1996, and Lisa Murkowski (AK), appointed in 2002 and elected in 2004, have at times been more moderate on various positions. Collins is known for her bipartisanship and is considered one of the most moderate Republicans currently holding public office.[36] She is pro-choice, supports same-sex marriage, and has pushed for campaign finance reform. Murkowski has also showed a strong independent streak during her time in the Senate. She is mostly pro-choice and, as of 2013, supports same-sex marriage. During her reelection campaign in 2010, despite losing the Republican primary to Tea Party candidate Joe Miller, she ran as a write-in candidate in the general election and defeated Miller and Democrat Scott McAdams to retain her Senate seat.

The voices of women senators on both sides of the aisle became especially salient during the 2012 election cycle as Democrats claimed that Republicans were waging a "war on women" by supporting legislation to restrict reproductive rights, access to contraception, and protections against workplace discrimination. According to political scientist Michele Swers, "The women of the Senate played key roles in this quest for the hearts and minds of female voters" regarding the so-called war on women. For example, Ayotte became a prominent Republican spokesperson to argue that issues involving contraception were about religious freedom and not a war on women.[37] Swers argues that gender *does* have a strong influence on legislative behavior as it "affects the policy priorities of individual senators and the intensity of their commitment to issues. Beyond the preferences and perspectives of individuals, policy entrepreneurs recognize the association between gender and issue preferences. These entrepreneurs, ranging from fellow senators to interest group leaders, recruit women to their cause as they seek to build a support coalition for policy initiatives."[38]

Gender is also politically symbolic over divisive public policy issues as "Democrats and to a lesser extent Republicans turn to their female members to deliver party messages designed to capture the women's vote or defend the party against criticism that the party's policies will hurt women."[39] This role differs for Republican women in the Senate since women's issues are not a central part of the national Republican Party brand, since it instead focuses its messages on lowering taxes, reducing regulation on business, and strengthening national security. As a result, Republican women in the Senate "cannot leverage their connection to women's interests and women voters into power and authority with the Republican caucus as easily as Democratic women can." In addition, as the number of moderate Republican women continues to decrease, focusing on issues like reproductive rights "alienates the social conservative base of the Republican Party and puts these more moderate women in an uncomfortable position." The smaller number of GOP women in both houses of Congress also means less leverage for women members when it comes to demanding a seat at the party leadership table.[40] However, while they comprise only a small percentage of the membership in the Senate, Republican women—either individually or as a group—can still represent an important and powerful voice in the legislative process.

WOMEN IN STATE LEGISLATURES

Historically, state legislatures have served as an important political opportunity for women, and it has been at the state level that women have made greater gains in achieving parity with men in terms of representation. Women began to make substantial progress during the 1970s in getting elected to state legislatures, and that progress continued through the 1990s. When serving in leadership positions in state legislatures, women tend to differ from their male colleagues in important ways, namely that they "approach politics with an understanding and skills that have been shaped by family, community, volunteerism, and education. . . . Women are older, defer political careers until past their primary years of childrearing and family responsibilities, and hone their leadership ability in the classroom and community center rather than in the boardroom and locker room."[41] Women also engage in different legislative activities than men, including spending more time on constituent concerns, building coalitions both within and across party lines, and studying proposed legislation, making "women appear to be better team players with the legislature than are men." However, women legislators spend equal amounts of time as men do on traditional legislative activities such as campaigning, fundraising, seeking pork-barrel legislation (which brings state funds home to their district), and introducing new legislation.[42] There is also evidence of a trend among women in state legislatures that suggests a "professionalization gap," meaning that women are "more likely than men to perceive their legislative careers as a full-time rather than a part-time job."[43]

Research in recent years has also shown that, in general, women legislators at the state level serve as "agents of policy-related change" in representing those constituents who are economically disadvantaged, changing expenditure priorities for their state, and conducting business in public as opposed to old-style backroom political negotiations. Women legislators have also given more priority than their male colleagues to legislation dealing with health care, welfare issues concerning families and children, and promoting policies to help other women;[44] women legislators are also more liberal across the board than their male colleagues, regardless of partisan affiliation.[45] As the number of women in state legislatures has grown in recent decades and as women legislators have worked together through political caucuses, they have been able to move issues of greatest concern to women (like family leave, domestic violence, and comparable worth) into the legislative mainstream of state policy agendas.[46]

State legislatures represent an important function for women in politics for several reasons. First, state legislatures are an important entry point for women who seek higher political office. Second, the rate of gains for women at the state level directly impacts the percentage of women serving in the Congress and in other executive branch positions. And third, state legislatures decide many of the policy issues that are historically of direct concern to women (such as education, health care, and workplace policies).[47] Like their counterparts in Congress, many women in state legislatures pay considerable attention to domestic and women's issues, yet as a group, their policy choices are diverse and they do not represent a voting bloc committed to women's issues alone.[48] Historically, legislative sessions were scheduled to accommodate the schedules and economic responsibilities of men, including the cycles of planting, growing, and harvesting crops when the nation had a primarily agricultural economy. Based on the tradition that legislatures were run by men, the legislative schedule can still create a burden for women, who "experience the schedule of legislative life differently. . . . Even in contemporary times, as women participate in larger numbers in the paid labor force, the weight of household obligations continues to discourage women from legislative service. Women legislators are significantly more likely to serve in districts that are closer to the state capital, commuting daily to balance public and private duties."[49]

The first women to serve as state legislators were elected prior to the turn of the twentieth century. In 1894, three women—Clara Cressingham, Carrie C. Holly, and Frances Klock—were elected to the Colorado House of Representatives as the first women elected to any state legislature. Two years later in 1896, Martha Hughes Cannon was elected to the Utah State Senate, becoming the first woman state senator. More than a century later, many more women had followed in the paths of these early women politicians. According to the Center for American Women and Politics, in 2017, 1,842 (24.9 percent) of the 7,383 state legislators in the United States were women (women hold 443, or 22.5 percent, of the 1,972 state senate seats and 1,399, or 25.9 percent, of the 5,411 state house or assembly seats). Since 1971, the number of women serving in state legislatures has increased fivefold. Of the women state legislators serving in 2017, nearly one-fourth (23.7 percent) were women of color.[50]

In the past few years, however, progress has slowed in electing women to state political positions in all three branches of government—legislative, executive, and judicial. The number of women in state elective office has leveled off nationwide. Not many clear patterns exist across states to explain the number of women serving in state legislatures. However, two trends do emerge—a majority of women legislators are Democrats, and states in the South lag behind other states in electing women to state legislatures. Democratic women outnumber Republican women in state legislatures despite recent nationwide voting trends of more Republicans being elected than Democrats. Of all women state senators, 57.1 percent are Democrats, and of all women state representatives, 61.4 percent are Democrats. However, in 2009, those percentages were higher, at 70.2 and 70.8, respectively. With regard to southern states and the dearth of women legislators, Table 7.3 shows that many of the states with the smallest percentage of women legislators are found in this region of the country. Only two southern states—Florida and Georgia—have remained competitive with other top-ranked states in electing women to state legislative office.[51]

Beginning in the 1990s, women began to make substantial progress in holding state legislative leadership positions. In 2017, 67 (19.3 percent) of the 348 state legislative leadership positions are held by women; women hold 28 (17.3 percent) of the 162 leadership positions in state senates and 39 (21 percent) of the 186 leadership positions in state houses.[52] A strong relationship exists between states electing more women to state legislatures and those same states placing more women in positions of leadership, either as party leaders or committee chairs.[53] A "feminization" of state legislative leadership has also occurred. Not only has the increased number of women legislators led to more women holding leadership positions, but also a more "feminine" leadership style that emphasizes consensus and compromise has emerged for both women *and* men in

Table 7.3 Women in State Legislatures, 2017

STATE	NO. OF WOMEN/TOTAL	PERCENTAGE
Alabama	20/140	14.3
Alaska	18/60	30
Arizona	35/90	38.9
Arkansas	25/135	18.5
California	26/120	21.7
Colorado	39/100	39
Connecticut	52/187	27.8
Delaware	13/62	21
Florida	41/160	25.6
Georgia	61/236	25.8
Hawaii	21/76	27.6
Idaho	32/105	30.5
Illinois	64/177	36.2
Indiana	29/150	19.3
Iowa	34/150	22.7
Kansas	47/165	28.5
Kentucky	23/138	16.7
Louisiana	22/144	15.3
Maine	64/186	34.4
Maryland	60/188	31.9
Massachusetts	52/200	26
Michigan	35/148	23.6
Minnesota	65/201	32.3
Mississippi	24/174	13.8
Missouri	44/197	22.3
Montana	43/150	28.7
Nebraska	13/49	26.5
Nevada	25/63	39.7
New Hampshire	122/424	28.8
New Jersey	36/120	30.0
New Mexico	34/112	30.4
New York	58/213	27.2
North Carolina	42/170	24.7
North Dakota	26/141	18.4
Ohio	31/132	23.5
Oklahoma	19/149	12.8
Oregon	30/90	33.3
Pennsylvania	47/253	18.6
Rhode Island	35/113	31
South Carolina	23/170	13.5
South Dakota	21/105	20
Tennessee	22/132	16.7
Texas	37/181	20.4
Utah	20/104	19.2
Vermont	72/180	40
Virginia	27/140	19.3
Washington	54/147	36.7
West Virginia	18/134	13.4
Wisconsin	31/132	23.5
Wyoming	10/90	11.1
Total	1,842/7,383	24.9

SOURCE: Center for American Women and Politics, Rutgers, State University of New Jersey.

leadership positions.[54] Women have also capitalized on legislative power through holding committee chairs, which emphasizes "getting the job done" in terms of passing legislation as opposed to positional authority through a higher leadership position such as the House (or Assembly) or Senate leader; in these positions, women committee chairs "appear to be more comfortable developing their influence through group efforts aimed at solving a problem or achieving a desired outcome."[55]

CONCLUSION

Building on the progress that has been made in recent years, an increase in the number of women legislators in both the state and national government is inevitable. Women benefit the political process with "access to a greater diversity of ideas and experiences that fuel definition of problems and the creation of solutions."[56] For the number of women serving in legislatures at both the state and national level to continue to increase, strong recruitment efforts must be undertaken. Any political candidate needs an adequate amount of money as well as support from relevant interest groups and party leadership to be competitive in a campaign. Incumbent women also must identify and mentor other women to run for similar offices.[57]

Research conducted in recent years on both Congress and state legislatures has shown that women do make a difference in policy outcomes, particularly in those policies directly affecting women. However, women have yet to have a significant impact on legislative norms and practices and how legislatures operate on a day-to-day basis. Nonetheless, women, "though few in number and relatively new to positions of institutional power, are transforming our understanding of the nature of representation and are dramatically reshaping the agenda and representation of interests in Congress."[58] The same trend has emerged at the state level as well, as women continue to gain access to the legislative process in their quest to be equal participants in policymaking at all levels of government.

CHAPTER SUMMARY

- Individual members of a legislature are elected to represent an equal number of citizens (or, in the case of the U.S. Senate, states are represented equally with two members each) in the policymaking process. All legislatures within the United States operate on the simple premise of "one person, one vote."
- Studies have shown differences in legislative leadership traits among men and women, as well as legislative strategies related to policies that are pursued.
- After women secured the right to vote in 1920, few women sought elective office during the first half of the twentieth century, and of those who did, several were nominated by the minority party in a district where the candidate had little chance of winning.

- The first woman to serve in the U.S. Congress was Jeannette Rankin, a Republican from Montana, who served two terms in the U.S. House of Representatives, 1917–1918 (Montana had granted women's suffrage prior to 1920) and 1941–1942. A pacifist, she was the only member of Congress to vote against American entry into both World War I and World War II.

- Rebecca Latimer Felton, a Georgia Democrat in her 80s, became the first woman to serve in the U.S. Senate in 1922. She was appointed as a temporary replacement to a vacant seat and only served for two days.

- Major growth in the number of women seeking legislative office at the national level and, as a result, women being elected to office did not occur until the late 1960s and early 1970s.

- By 1984, the number of women nominated by their party to run for the House of Representatives had increased dramatically. That same year, U.S. Representative Geraldine Ferraro of New York became Democrat Walter Mondale's running mate in the presidential election. A total of 65 women ran for the House that year; however, only 22 women were elected, and most who won were incumbents.

- In 1986, Barbara Mikulski of Maryland became the first Democratic woman elected to the Senate without first being appointed to the seat.

- The largest increase came in 1992, known as the "Year of the Woman," thanks to many open seats, support from women's interest groups targeting women candidates, and the Supreme Court confirmation hearings of Clarence Thomas in 1991 that highlighted the dearth of women on Capitol Hill. Since 1992, the number of women serving in Congress has steadily yet slowly increased.

- Many assume that women officeholders automatically support and prioritize "women's issues"—domestic policy issues including education, health care, welfare, and reproductive rights, among others. However, party affiliation and political ideology are still the most important predictor for bill sponsorship or the actual vote on a particular bill. Yet, studies have shown that having more women serve in legislatures, as well as their visibility within the institution, has a positive impact on the success of legislation that affects women.

- Women politicians can bring different priorities into the policymaking arena than their male colleagues, and evidence suggests that women can be more likely to work across party lines to achieve policy goals.

- The Congressional Caucus for Women's Issues, a bipartisan group founded in 1977 for women in the House of Representatives, has fought for passage of many bills dealing with economic, educational, and health-care issues.

- State legislatures serve as an important political opportunity for women, and women have made greater gains in achieving parity with men in terms of representation at the state level. Research shows that women state legislators serve as "agents of policy-related change" in representing those constituents who are economically disadvantaged, changing expenditure priorities for their state, and conducting business in public as opposed to old-style backroom political negotiations. State legislative seats are also an important entry-level position for women seeking higher elective office.

STUDY/DISCUSSION QUESTIONS

- Why is integrative/transformational leadership more effective in legislatures, and why might women legislators benefit from this strategy?
- Why did women gaining the right to vote in 1920 not automatically translate into more women running for and being elected to political office?
- How does the Congressional Caucus for Women's Issues impact the legislative agenda in Congress?
- Why are leadership positions in Congress so important? How might women impact policymaking by holding these positions?
- Why are state legislatures such important venues for women's issues? How do state legislatures benefit women seeking a political career?

CASE STUDIES

1. **What factors explain gender differences in legislating?**
   As documented in this chapter, female legislators tend to use an integrative/transformational leadership approach that is more effective in legislative decision making that requires collaboration. Analyze the origins of gender differences in leadership styles. What early childhood experiences and gendered societal expectations account for the different ways in which men and women approach legislating?

2. **Does using the term "Year of the Woman" help or hurt women's progress?**
   Media headlines hailed 1992 the "Year of the Woman" because of the unprecedented number of women who ran for and were elected to Congress. Some commentators were quick to critique the use of this term because it suggests that women's small gains are more significant than they are, and it reinforces the idea that women are atypical in politics. As legal professor and Democratic strategist Susan Estrich put it, "when men exercise power, we don't call it 'men's day' or 'men's year.' We call it Tuesday." What are your thoughts on highlighting moderate gains for women in politics? Should we be celebrating small improvements? And does this subtly suggest that women are political outsiders?

3. **Will progress remain this slow?**
   It has been about 100 years since Jeannette Rankin was the first woman to serve in Congress, and women are still vastly underrepresented in national legislative positions. Today, only one in five members of the U.S. House and Senate are women. According to a 2014 report from the Institute for Women's Policy Research, gender parity in Congress will not be achieved for another century—in 2121. It is easy to think that gender justice happens "naturally" as time progresses, but the backlash against feminism and the constant struggle for elusive gender justice indicate otherwise. Given what you know about political struggle and challenges to women's representation, what changes do you recommend to achieve gender parity in Congress sooner?

RESOURCES

- The home page for the **U.S. House of Representatives**.
  http://www.house.gov
- The home page for the **U.S. Senate**.
  http://www.senate.gov
- **Women in Congress** is a congressional web page detailing the history of women in Congress.
  http://history.house.gov/Exhibition-and-Publications/WIC/Women-in-Congress/
- **Women's Policy, Inc.,** is a nonpartisan public policy organization whose mission is to bring women policymakers from both parties together to work on issues of importance to women and their families.
  http://www.womenspolicy.org

CHAPTER 8

Women as Executive Leaders

For years, political experts have speculated about when the United States would elect its first woman president. Most predictions and analysis focused on just one woman—Hillary Clinton. When she announced, while still first lady, that she would run for the U.S. Senate to represent New York in 1999, the assumption was that she was setting herself up to run for president in the not-so-distant future. When she passed on the 2004 presidential campaign, she immediately catapulted into the role of Democratic frontrunner for 2008 once George W. Bush secured reelection. Beginning in 2005 and throughout much of 2007, Clinton remained the presumptive frontrunner and Democratic nominee, until Barack Obama began to show his skill at fundraising and exciting large crowds on the campaign trail. When Obama won the Iowa caucuses in January 2008, the storyline of Clinton's political inevitability began to erode; this continued throughout the spring as Obama wrapped up the Democratic nomination. Despite Clinton's own declarations in the fall of 2008 that she would not run for the presidency again, she announced a second campaign for the White House in 2015.

Initially, the 2016 presidential campaign looked as if Democrats would have an easy path to picking their nominee (Clinton), while Republicans, with an initial field of 17 candidates, were supposed to battle it out until the last primary contest or even into the national convention. Instead, the strong anti-establishment mood of the electorate helped real estate mogul and reality television star Donald Trump wrap up the Republican nomination in early May, while Clinton struggled to fend off the surprisingly strong challenge from Vermont senator Bernie Sanders. While Clinton ultimately earned enough delegates to secure the Democratic nomination following a win in the California primary in June, Sanders nonetheless won a total of 22 primary and caucus contests and 1,879 delegates (of the 4,765 available) and raised a total of $222 million. The 2016 campaign presented Clinton with a frustrating sense of déjà vu, as her campaign tried to hold on to its "inevitability" as challenges—both real and potential—threatened to change the predicted storyline again of Clinton as frontrunner, Democratic nominee, and first woman president. Not only did Clinton face scrutiny, as well as an investigation by the Federal Bureau of Investigation over her use of a private e-mail server while secretary of state (2009–2013), but also other news stories surfaced about potential conflicts of interest involving contributions to the Clinton Global Initiative and speaking fees that both she and her husband, former president Bill Clinton, received. That, coupled with the enthusiasm for Sanders's progressive agenda and the public's disdain for political insiders, left Clinton and her long government resume struggling to prove to voters that she was trustworthy and honest. Even the idea of becoming the first woman president did not seem to work for her campaign; in May 2016, campaign research conducted by EMILY's List found that the Clinton campaign should "de-emphasize the 'first' talk" with voters and donors since "they already know she'd be the first woman president, but we don't get anything by reminding them." If anything, the message seemed to fall on deaf ears with younger women, who throughout the Democratic primaries overwhelming supported Sanders over Clinton.[1]

Clinton is not the only woman to ever run for president, nor was she the only women running in 2016. Even before any votes were cast, history had already been made—for the first time, a woman ran for president for both the Democratic and Republican parties. On the Republican side, former Hewlett–Packard chief executive officer (CEO) Carly Fiorina enjoyed a surprising surge in popularity in the fall of 2015 as a political outsider. Fiorina gained momentum in the polls following her impressive performance in the first of several Republican debates. As the only woman in the crowded Republican field, Fiorina focused on her corporate experience and the need to put a non-career politician in the White House. However, Fiorina ended her campaign in February 2016 after failing to earn significant voter support in the early contests of Iowa and New Hampshire.

When considering the question of electing more women to executive leadership positions, there has long been an assumption that "a viable woman presidential candidate (that is, a candidate who could legitimately compete in primaries and caucuses and have a real chance at her party's nomination) would help to further break down barriers for woman candidates at all levels of government."[2] While a woman has yet to win, the efforts of all women presidential and vice presidential candidates serve as an important milestone for women in American politics. Unfortunately, while women have made strides in achieving legislative office, there is still a dearth of women executive leaders in government, business, and all institutions within American society. From the top executive spot in the Oval Office, to governor's mansions and city halls, to corporate boardrooms across the country, executive leadership positions are still dominated by men.

In this chapter, we discuss executive political leadership and the barriers faced by women politicians in gaining access to these seats of power. First, we will look at how women in the corporate world have defined successful leadership to determine whether there are any lessons to be learned for women seeking political executive positions. Then we will consider the potential of electing a woman president and vice president, as well as the impact of women in other prominent executive positions—cabinet members and other White House staff positions, first ladies, state governors, and mayors.

GENDER AND EXECUTIVE LEADERSHIP

The job of the American president is often compared to that of a CEO of a large corporation. Unlike positions in legislatures, which by their very nature require cooperation on some level with other members in an equal position, a president or CEO has no counterpart within the organization and is ultimately responsible for making executive decisions. Several corporate executives in recent years have sought either the presidency or the position of state governor based on their successful business careers. Former business executives often reason that if they can run a major corporation, those same skills should transfer into running a government bureaucracy. The presidential candidacies of Donald Trump and Carly Fiorina in 2016, along with Mitt Romney's campaigns in 2008 and 2012, are just three recent examples of business leaders equating their many years of corporate executive experience with the skills necessary to be a successful executive leader in government.

Whether a successful CEO could also effectively run the executive branch of the federal government remains to be seen. However, both the political and business sectors share many masculine traditions in their structure, environment, and culture. Women have also been slow to make substantial gains in each field, as executive positions of power have always been male dominated. As a result, gender plays an important role in determining successful leadership traits, as a woman "cannot enter a post previously held by a male and be entirely interchangeable with him—in meaning at least."[3] Much has been written about how women's leadership styles in the business world—those based on building inclusive relationships—was better for business than the traditional, hierarchical system. Management literature has embraced the notion of women's unique leadership qualities, as well as their emotional intelligence (the ability to recognize and control one's emotions).[4] Many leadership experts also suggest that female leadership characteristics and principles—communication, personal relationships, community building, and ignoring the rigid hierarchy of most corporations—provide an important advantage to women in the corporate world.[5] However, many of these same women fear that acknowledging a difference exists between male and female leadership traits will be the same as admitting to inequality. As a result, women are often "wedged into stereotypes, often acting against female values, trying to fit the male definition of leadership."[6]

The old paradigm of leadership, defined as masculine within a hierarchical, command-and-control structure, shows an opposition to change. This style of leadership is also defined by individual (as opposed to group) efforts, with indirect communication trickling down through the organization's vertical structure.[7] However, many successful women in business have adopted a new paradigm of leadership that has moved away from this more traditional approach. Women used to try to succeed by trying to be more like men, including dressing like men and managing in a structured, top-down approach that limited their access to colleagues and customers—a "command-and-control style long associated with the masculine mind-set." But by the mid- to late 1990s, successful female corporate executives, like Meg Whitman of eBay, Inc., and Marcy Carsey of Carsey–Werner Company, began developing new strategies to grow their businesses. These new paradigm leaders were "noted for their abilities to blend feminine qualities of leadership with classic male traits to run their companies successfully, and become some of the most powerful women in American business."[8] Women who adopt the new paradigm of leadership succeed for three main reasons: self-assurance compels new paradigm leaders to stay motivated and take risks; an obsession with customer service helps them anticipate market changes; and new paradigm leaders use "feminine" traits to their advantage (empathy, collaboration, cooperation—acknowledging differences between men and women and their leadership styles make more approaches available).[9]

Like women in politics, women in business careers also face barriers in reaching the top of the corporate ladder. Childrearing and other family responsibilities top the list, as well as incorrect stereotypes that women just are not tough enough, aggressive enough, or ambitious enough to make it to the corner office. Studies have also shown that men are often reluctant to place women in positions of power over others in work settings.[10] In her role as CEO of Hewlett–Packard, Fiorina exhibited a leadership style during her six years (1999–2005) at the helm of the computer giant that even other women corporate officers admitted was a tough act to follow. Fiorina succeeded in gaining her position not by promoting her difference as a woman but by following the more traditional male path to power through drive and ambition, not the new paradigm of leadership. But most women in business have not followed Fiorina's model. Currently, women hold only a small percentage of the top-level jobs in major U.S. companies, and few women have ever risen to the level of CEO of major U.S. corporations. In 2015, only 22 women (4.4 percent) served as CEOs of Fortune 500 companies, including Mary Barra at General Motors, Meg Whitman at Hewlett–Packard, and Virginia Rometty at IBM.[11]

According to Marie Wilson, long known for her work with the White House Project and its goal of not only electing a woman president but also placing more women in all leadership positions, "Ambition in men is an expectation and a virtue. In women, it can be a kiss of death, guaranteeing isolation, ending relationships (personal and professional), pushing entire families into therapy, and making even the most self-assured CEO wonder what she was thinking."[12] Some studies suggest that women may be happier if they give up positions of power in return for more quality time in their lives for family, friends, and other nonbusiness pursuits.[13] In addition, other studies suggest that women, more often than men, are not willing to make family sacrifices to climb the corporate ladder. Nonetheless, women are often conflicted about such decisions, believing that they have somehow failed other women in their profession if they choose family over career. But many of those reports have been challenged as not being representative of the larger population of women, as other evidence suggests women are just as competitive as men and equally aspire to be CEOs, regardless of whether they have children and family responsibilities.[14] In addition, women corporate executives are still viewed as anomalies, just as many women in politics, and an inordinate amount of media attention is paid to a woman CEO who leaves a position, particularly if she is fired (although the firing of a CEO happens regularly in the business world).[15]

In recent years, there has been no shortage of books written on women and leadership, with many so-called experts weighing in with their solutions to the problem of the shortage of women in positions of authority, whether in politics or the corporate world. Facebook chief operating officer Sheryl Sandberg generated much debate with her suggestion that women simply need to "lean in" to fill the gender gap in leadership. Sandberg argues that women create internal barriers to leadership through self-doubt and worry too much about being liked, while external barriers include "blatant and subtle sexism, discrimination, and sexual harassment." Stereotypes about women leaders can lead to women being marginalized, and so few women leaders can lead to inaccurate generalizations about women, particularly regarding leadership: "A truly equal world would be one where women ran half our countries and companies and men ran half our homes. I believe that this would be a better world. The laws of economics and many studies of diversity tell us that if we tapped the entire pool of human resources and talent, our collective performance would improve."[16]

Debora Spar, president of Barnard College, takes a somewhat different approach, arguing that too many women of the postfeminism generation pursue perfection, which goes against the original goals of the feminist movement. With so many life choices now available, women tend to place unreasonable expectations on themselves. Feminism was supposed to "liberate women from the unreasonable, impossible standards that had long been thrust upon them. . . . As feminist ideals trickled and then flowed into mainstream culture, though, they became far more fanciful, more exuberant and trivial—something easier to sell to the millions of girls and women entranced by feminism's appeal." This has created "highly unrealistic expectations" for women in trying to combine personal and professional obligations.[17] According to Anne-Marie Slaughter, an attorney and academic, "women can't have it all,"[18] and author Hanna Rosin has declared "the end of men," arguing that women have begun to surpass men in numerous statistical trends in the workforce and in college graduation rates.[19] While only a small sample of the current debate about women as leaders, these arguments highlight the fact that there is no "one-size-fits-all" definition for how women should lead and/or make career choices. However, as women continue to gain more prominence in both the business and political arenas, it becomes even more important to understand how leadership is defined by gender.

ELECTING MADAM PRESIDENT

Conventional wisdom in recent years has suggested women still face an uphill battle as presidential candidates. The presumed barriers include the inherent masculinity of the office of the presidency, prevalent negative stereotypes of women leaders, gender bias in news coverage of woman candidates, and a lack of potential women candidates due to so few women holding political positions.[20] Yet, while being a woman running for president may require a unique strategy in fundraising, messaging, and creating a narrative that presents a strong leader capable of handling the job of president, these strategic areas "are not permanent structural barriers that stop a woman from winning the White House."[21]

The executive branch is perhaps the most masculine of the three branches of government, mostly due to its hierarchical structure, the unity of command, and the ability for a president to act decisively when the need arises. The presidency also "operates on the great man model of leadership," which leaves women defined as the "other" in the executive branch.[22] Creating a strong image of presidential leadership in the minds of Americans is an essential aspect of political success for any politician who aspires to the Oval Office. Strong leadership has historically been defined as an attempt to exert one's will over a situation, a societal view that "has been conditioned by the interpretation of American history as written." This, in turn, affects how the public will view other aspiring leaders, particularly women.[23] Also not helpful to women seeking the presidency is the notion of "presidential machismo," which is the image desired by many Americans to have their president exhibit tough and aggressive behavior on the international stage. Even though the unilateral actions of a president to wage war or carry out other military actions may run "counter to aspects of democratic theory of governance," public opinion polls routinely show that Americans admire this type of behavior by presidents, forming "the basis of a cult that often elevates presidents, primarily those regarded as strong and who waged successful wars, to the status of heroes."[24]

Once in office, presidents must remember that their job, by constitutional design, is one of both shared and limited powers. A paradox exists for presidential power, in that Americans expect great things from their presidents, but "the resources at the disposal of the president are limited and the system in which a president operates can easily frustrate efforts at presidential leadership."[25] As such, presidents must maximize their opportunities to gain influence and achieve success with their policy agendas, in dealing with Congress, and certainly in the eyes of the American public in determining job approval. Other factors must also be considered if presidents are to maximize their leadership potential, including effectiveness as a public communicator, organizational capacity (staffing and leadership style within the White House), cognitive style (intellectual curiosity coupled with either attention to detail or abstract thinking skills), and emotional intelligence.[26] If we assume that women tend to exhibit a leadership style based on cooperation, compromise, and emotional intelligence, a woman president would be no more constrained in this area than her male counterpart and might even enjoy a strategic advantage.[27]

Aside from the constitutional requirements for the office of the presidency—being at least 35 years old, a 14-year U.S. resident, and a natural-born citizen—no other formal criteria exist to run for president. However, several informal qualifications exist that limit the pool of potential nominees, with factors such as religion, race, and gender making the pool of viable candidates for both president and vice president almost exclusively Protestant, white, and male.[28] The health and age of the candidate, as well as family ties and personal relationships (particularly marital status and fidelity), are also important characteristics for candidates.[29] Leadership qualities are also considered. Leadership has routinely been defined on male, as opposed to female, terms. In American politics, business, and military circles, this view has been indoctrinated into the consciousness of most Americans through the traditional interpretation of our national history. This view of leadership, in turn, affects how the public will view other aspiring leaders, particularly women,[30] and it has often left women with a "double standard and a double bind" as men are still more readily accepted as leaders than women.[31]

Gender stereotypes can also influence how women candidates and their campaigns are covered in the news media. Potential women presidential and vice presidential candidates have not always been portrayed as authoritative or as strong leaders in the press. For example, in 1999 Elizabeth Dole "was covered more as a novelty than a serious candidate," what the White House Project referred to as the "hair, hemlines, and husbands" approach to coverage.[32] Other studies in recent years have also showed this trend of gender bias, making gender a significant, and not always positive, label in news media coverage for women candidates.[33] Public opinion in recent years suggests support for electing a woman president, at least in theory. However, in the two years following 9/11, support for electing a woman president in polling had declined, suggesting that women may face tougher public scrutiny during times of war.[34] In addition, while public opinion polls consistently show support for a qualified female presidential candidate, there is evidence to suggest that responses to this polling question may suffer from what researchers call "social desirability effects"—that is, respondents may be purposely giving false answers to avoid violating societal norms.[35]

Research has also shown that the gender, education, and political ideology of the respondents in polls about electing a woman president seem to be the most prominent factors that shape public opinion, followed by age, race, and party identification,[36] and that the character, personality, and style of presidential candidates are crucial in how voters evaluate those seeking the White House. While party affiliation and policy preferences remain important factors among voters, the decline of partisan loyalty and the desire for party nominees to appeal to moderate, middle-of-the-road voters during the general election campaign has placed more emphasis on the candidate as an individual. Political news reporting has become more cynical, sensationalized, hypercritical, and fragmented, which has led to an increased focus on the "cult of personality" during presidential campaigns.[37]

Perhaps the most tangible problem when considering the prospects of electing a woman president is simply that so few women are in the "on-deck circle"—a
short list of presidential candidates, put together in part by the news media
through speculation as well as the behavior and travel patterns of notable politicians (for example, who is traveling to Iowa and New Hampshire or speaking at
high-profile party events, in the months leading up to the first nomination contests). This circle exists of roughly 30 to 40 individuals in any given presidential
election year and can include governors, prominent U.S. senators, a few members
of the House of Representatives, and a handful of recent governors or vice presidents who have remained prominent in the news media.[38] Given that four of the
last seven presidents were former governors, this type of political experience tends
to elevate many candidates in the eyes of the news media. While serving as a state
governor is not the only path to the White House, the dearth of women who have
executive experience—either in politics or business—leaves fewer women on the
presidential short list. In addition, while the women currently serving in the U.S.
Senate enjoy high profiles in American politics, the Senate is traditionally not the
place to look for a presidential candidate. Barack Obama became the first president elected directly from the Senate since John F. Kennedy's election in 1960 and
only the third in U.S. history (the other being Warren Harding, elected in 1920).
The lack of women leaders in Congress also tends to keep women off the presidential short list; despite the historic House speakership of Nancy Pelosi, she remains
the only woman from either political party to ever hold a prominent leadership
position in the House of Representatives or the Senate.

The most glaring problem in electing a woman president may simply be that
so few women hold the appropriate leadership positions within our government
that allow them access to the on-deck circle. In addition, recent research has
shown that the candidate emergence phase of a campaign—moving from a potential to an actual candidate—represents one of the biggest hurdles for women,
particularly in seeking the presidency. A gender gap seems to exist in political
ambition, which is attributed to the fact that women are significantly less likely
than men to receive encouragement (either from a current or former politician or
from a financial supporter) to run for office or to deem themselves qualified to
run for office.[39]

Electing the first woman vice president would also break through a significant political barrier. To date, 14 vice presidents have gone on to become president, through either succession (following the death or resignation of the
president) or election in their own right. Since Geraldine Ferraro's historic bid for
the vice presidency as Democrat Walter Mondale's running mate in 1984, only
one other woman has been nominated for vice president—Alaska governor Sarah
Palin in 2008. In addition to the real-life campaigns of women seeking the presidency or vice presidency, the "woman as president" theme has also continued to
appear with regularity within pop culture. Both before and after 2008, American
movie and television viewers have seen many diverse portrayals of women as
president, vice president, secretary of state, and numerous other executive branch

positions. This trend is important in that "Hollywood decided to elect minorities and women to the presidency some time before reality moved in that direction."[40] The significance is that although these characters are fictional, they can function "as a propositional argument that women can serve as chief executives equal to men and that, to the extent that sexism endures in US society, it is recognized as anachronistic, ridiculous, or corrupt."[41] As Marie Wilson, founder of the White House Project, has long argued, the portrayal of women in all types of political leadership positions, even if fictional, helps one to imagine that it is possible.[42]

PROFILE IN POWER

Women Presidential Candidates

Prior to the presidential candidacies of Hillary Clinton and Carly Fiorina in 2016, what other women have sought the White House? The first female candidate for the presidency dates back to 1872, when Victoria Woodhull, a stockbroker, publisher, and protégé of Cornelius Vanderbilt, ran for president on the Equal Rights Party ticket. She was followed by Belva Lockwood, the first woman admitted to

Woodhill   Lockwood

practice law before the U.S Supreme Court and an active participant in the women's suffrage movement, who ran for president on the same party ticket in 1884 and 1888. Eight decades passed before the next woman officially sought the presidency. Senator Margaret Chase Smith, a Maine Republican, dropped out of the race after placing fifth in the New Hampshire primary. Smith, who made history by becoming the first woman to serve in both houses of Congress (elected to the House of

Smith

Representatives in 1940 to replace her dying husband and to the Senate in 1948), was also nominated for the presidency by Vermont senator George Aiken at the Republican national convention in 1964.

Shirley Chisholm, the first black woman to serve in Congress (a Democrat in the House of Representatives from New York), ran for president in 1972. In doing so, Chisholm stunned friends and colleagues with her decision, yet used her candidacy to raise awareness of issues such as education and other social

Chisholm

programs within the Democratic presidential primary. Although Chisholm's name was placed on the ballot in 12 primary states, she never received more than seven percent of the vote in any of the primary contests.[43] Until Clinton's campaign in 2008, no woman in either major political party had sustained a presidential campaign long enough to have

Schroeder   Dole

SOURCE: Lockwood: Brady-Handy Collection at the Library of Congress; Smith: U.S. Senate Historical Office; Chisholm: Thomas J. O'Halloran, U.S. News & World Reports. Light restoration by Adam Cuerden

a vote cast in her favor in the earliest contests—the Iowa caucuses and the New Hampshire primary. Pat Schroeder seriously considered a run for the presidency in 1988 after Democratic frontrunner Gary Hart dropped out of the race in the spring of 1987. Her campaign, however, never made it out of the exploratory mode and had officially ended by September 1987. Elizabeth Dole had a much stronger campaign organization going into the 2000 Republican primaries, yet when money and positive news coverage both became elusive in the fall of 1999, she too withdrew from the presidential race.

Unlike Schroeder and Dole, who both fared well enough in early public opinion polls to give their campaigns temporary credibility, Carol Moseley Braun's campaign for the 2004 Democratic presidential nomination was a long shot from the outset. Nonetheless, while she dropped out of the race in January 2004, prior to the Iowa caucuses, Moseley Braun made it onto 20 primary ballots, more than any other woman, Democrat or Republican, had ever achieved. She also performed well in several televised debates as the only woman in a field of mostly

Moseley Braun

white men and was credited with bringing a unique voice to the political discussion in the early days of the 2004 presidential race. She also had a major player within the women's rights movement as her campaign manager—Patricia Ireland, prominent feminist author and former president of the National Organization for Women. Moseley Braun's favorite line while out on the campaign trail told voters why they should take her candidacy seriously: "The final reason to vote for me is that I'm the clearest alternative to George Bush. I don't look like him. I don't talk like him. I don't think like him. And I certainly don't act like him."[44]

Then, in 2008, Clinton made history. She became the first woman to win a presidential nominating contest (when she won the New Hampshire primary in January 2008) that also resulted in earning delegates to the national convention.[45] In total, Clinton won 21 primaries (Arizona, Arkansas, California, Florida, Indiana, Kentucky, Massachusetts, Michigan, New Hampshire, New Jersey, New Mexico, New York, Ohio, Pennsylvania, Puerto Rico, Rhode Island, South Dakota, Tennessee, Texas, Utah, and West

Clinton

Virginia) and one caucus (Nevada),[46] earned 1,896 delegates (of 4,934 total, with 2,118 needed for the nomination) prior to the Democratic National Convention, and amassed a total of 18,046,007 popular votes[47] during the Democratic nomination process.

In 2012, only one woman ran for president—Representative Michele Bachmann (R-MN). Bachmann dropped out of the Republican primary race soon after a poor showing in the Iowa caucuses, finishing sixth with just under five percent of the vote. However, she performed well during the prenomination phase in 2011, becoming the first woman to win the Ames Straw Poll hosted by the Iowa Republican Party in August 2011 and giving her frontrunner status for a few

Bachman

weeks in the press. A founder of the House Tea Party Caucus, Bachmann was popular among conservative voters and had a history of fundraising success, which contributed to some in the news media considering her a viable presidential candidate. Despite her own campaign, when asked in early 2014 about electing a woman president, Bachmann said that she thinks many

SOURCE: Clinton: United States Department of State; Bachmann: Office of Congresswoman Michele Bachmann

Americans "aren't ready" for a female president, stating, "I don't think there is a pent-up desire."[48] Three women ran for the presidency in 2016. In addition to Clinton, the Democratic Party nominee, former Hewlett–Packard chief executive officer Carly Fiorina ran for the Republican Party nomination. Fiorina had a strong showing early in the primary after excelling in several Republican debates, but she suspended her campaign in February 2016 after it lost steam. Dr. Jill Stein also ran in the 2016 presidential election as the Green Party candidate. She garnered one percent of the popular vote in the general election.

Fiorina

Stein

SOURCE: Fiorina: Gage Skidmore; Stein: Gage Skidmore

WOMEN IN THE EXECUTIVE BRANCH

While no woman has yet served as president or vice president, women have taken an increasingly prominent role in other positions throughout the executive branch. Beginning in the 1960s and continuing through the 1970s, the link between the presidency and women—both in terms of appointments within the executive branch and in terms of policies relevant to women—became much stronger. During the 1980s, despite Ronald Reagan's appointment of the first woman to the U.S. Supreme Court, the number of overall appointments of women to positions within the administration declined. With George H. W. Bush's election in 1988, the numbers again increased, as well as the attention paid to women's issues.[49] The next two presidents, Bill Clinton and George W. Bush, appointed women to executive posts in record numbers, in part as recognition for the political importance of women voters and interest groups devoted to women's issues. This trend continued with the Obama administration. Three avenues of influence for women within both the White House and the federal bureaucracy include presidential appointments to cabinet and other cabinet-level positions, as well as posts within the White House as presidential advisors.

The Cabinet

Since the presidential cabinet was established in 1789, few women have held cabinet positions. Frances Perkins became the first woman to serve in the cabinet when Franklin D. Roosevelt appointed her secretary of labor. Madeleine Albright, who served as secretary of state during Bill Clinton's administration (1996–2001), became the highest-ranking woman to ever serve in the cabinet. The rank of cabinet offices is based on presidential succession, as well as the four "inner" cabinet positions that have been designated as such by presidency scholars in recent years due to the influence of the positions in national policymaking. The "inner" cabinets include the Departments of State, Justice, Defense, and Treasury. According to the Presidential Succession Act of 1947, cabinet members follow the vice president, speaker of the House of

Representatives, and the president pro tempore of the Senate based on the date their offices were established. The first four cabinet members in line for succession include, in order, secretary of state, secretary of treasury, secretary of defense, and the attorney general.

During the mid-part of the twentieth century, women cabinet appointments were usually viewed as tokenism within an administration. By the 1990s, however, the political climate had changed and public expectations had shifted as women cabinet appointments began to be seen as a more routine presidential practice. At the start of his administration in 2001, George W. Bush appointed three women to his cabinet—Elaine Chao (Labor), Gale Norton (Interior), and Ann Veneman (Agriculture)—and also appointed Christine Todd Whitman to a cabinet-level position as head of the Environmental Protection Agency. Bush sought to follow the example set by his predecessor, Bill Clinton, in appointing a cabinet that looked like America in terms of gender and ethnic diversity. Five women had served in cabinet positions during Clinton's two terms in office. Bush also included two women appointees to his second-term cabinet, including moving Condoleezza Rice from national security advisor to secretary of state (See Table 8.1). Similarly, Barack Obama appointed four women to his cabinet in 2009, including Hillary Clinton (State), Hilda Solis (Labor), Kathleen Sebelius (Health and Human Services), and Janet Napolitano (Homeland Security). Donald Trump appointed two women to his cabinet in 2017, Betsy DeVos (Education) and Elaine Chao (Transportation).

A president's nomination to a cabinet post is a signal of representation—the nominee for a cabinet position reflects the president's agenda in that area of policy. As such, the cabinet secretary represents the president's policy agenda to relevant constituents (voters, interest groups, Congress, state and local governments). While many of the women who have served in the cabinet have done so in positions of influence over "women's issues," particularly in the departments of Health and Human Services and Labor, appointments in recent years suggest that women are now being considered for a wider variety of posts within an administration. However, based on news media coverage and treatment during the confirmation process in the Senate, many of these women cabinet members are still viewed as token appointments within the administration. One recent study suggests "women have yet to be perceived as full participants in the cabinet, either as office holders or as constituents."[50] In addition, although there is now greater diversity (both gender and race/ethnicity) in presidential cabinet appointments, more integration, as opposed to tokenism, of diversity is needed within the executive branch to ensure that a message is sent that the president "is open to a variety of opinions on policy" and that voices reflecting a variety of backgrounds be heard."[51]

White House Staff
The White House staff has grown dramatically during the past century. With the creation of the Executive Office of the President in 1937, a formal staff put

Table 8.1 Women in the Cabinet: 1933 to the Present

State
Madeleine Albright, 1996–2001 (Clinton)
Condoleezza Rice, 2005–2009 (Bush)
Hillary Clinton, 2009–2013 (Obama)

Treasury
None

Defense
None

Justice
Janet Reno, 1993–2001 (Clinton)
Loretta Lynch, 2015–2017 (Obama)

Interior
Gale Norton, 2001–2006 (Bush)
Sally Jewel, 2013–2017 (Obama)

Agriculture
Ann Veneman, 2001–2005 (Bush)

Commerce
Juanita Kreps, 1977–1979 (Carter)
Barbara Franklin, 1992–1993 (Bush)
Penny Pritzker, 2013–2017 (Obama)

Labor
Frances Perkins, 1933–1945 (Roosevelt)
Ann McLaughlin, 1987–1989 (Reagan)
Elizabeth Dole, 1989–1991 (Bush)
Lynn Martin, 1991–1993 (Bush)
Alexis Herman, 1997–2001 (Clinton)
Elaine Chao, 2001–2009 (Bush)
Hilda Solis, 2009–2013 (Obama)

Health and Human Services (formerly Health, Education and Welfare)
Oveta Culp Hobby, 1953–1955 (Eisenhower)
Patricia Roberts Harris, 1979–1981 (Carter)
Margaret Heckler, 1983–1985 (Reagan)
Donna Shalala, 1993–2001 (Clinton)
Kathleen Sebelius, 2009–2014 (Obama)
Sylvia Mathews Burwell 2014–2017 (Obama)

Housing and Urban Development
Carla Anderson Hills, 1975–1977 (Ford)
Patricia Roberts Harris, 1977–1979 (Carter)

Transportation
Elizabeth Dole, 1983–1987 (Reagan)
Mary Peters, 2006–2009 (Bush)
Elaine Chao, 2017–Present (Trump)

Energy
Hazel O'Leary, 1993–1997 (Clinton)

Education
Shirley Mount Hufstedler, 1979–1981 (Carter)
Margaret Spellings, 2005–2009 (Bush)
Betsy DeVos, 2017–Present (Trump)

Veterans Affairs
None

Homeland Security
Janet Napolitano, 2009–2013 (Obama)

in place during FDR's second term in office to help with the implementation of New Deal policies, the president's inner circle of advisors has grown in both numbers and influence. With the increase in the role of the federal government in policymaking in the post–New Deal era, White House staffers now perform "integral and influential roles in both presidential policymaking and politics."[52] Women have made substantial gains in obtaining White House staff positions in recent years, particularly during the administrations of Bill Clinton, George W. Bush, and Barack Obama. However, a glass ceiling still seems to exist in allowing women access to the president's inner circle of closest advisors. Even when women are appointed to White House staff positions, their positions tend to be more political than related to the policymaking process within the White House.[53]

As Bush's national security advisor during his first term and moving into the job of secretary of state in his second term, Condoleezza Rice was a prominent exception to that rule. Rice played an integral role in drafting the Bush administration's foreign-policy strategy in the war on terrorism as well as the invasion of Iraq following the terrorist attacks on September 11, 2001. During the first Bush term, Rice was "by far the closest [advisor] to Bush" and was of "critical importance" in helping Bush reach foreign-policy decisions, particularly when other senior advisors were at odds over proposed courses of action. As a result, Rice "operated at the interface between the President and his political advisors, on the one hand, and his foreign policy team, on the other."[54] However, despite Rice's prominent White House role, along with Communications Director Karen Hughes, who represented one of the other most powerful and influential advisors in the early years of the Bush administration, no woman has yet served as a chief of staff and only a handful of women have ever earned the title, as Hughes did, of "special assistant to the president."

Dee Dee Myers, who served as Clinton's first press secretary (and the first woman to hold the job), was a visible member of the Clinton team through daily press briefings. However, she had difficulty performing her duties as she was routinely excluded from the inner-circle access to information found among Clinton's closest advisors. Situational and structural barriers also exist for women seeking

top staff positions within the White House. Not only do women with family responsibilities realize many political career opportunities somewhat later in life
than their male counterparts, but also much of the White House staff comes from
the president's campaign staff, where women rarely play a major role.[55] Hughes,
who was a close advisor to Bush in her capacity as communications director both
in his 2000 campaign and in the first two years of his administration, opted to
leave her position to return to her home state of Texas during her son's high school
years. (She did, however, continue to play an advisory role from afar during the
president's reelection campaign during 2004 and later served as undersecretary of
state for public diplomacy from 2005 to 2007).[56] Similarly, Valerie Jarrett also
served as a close aide to Obama during his presidential campaign prior to her
position as a senior advisor in the White House, and Kellyanne Conway served as
Trump's campaign manager before joining his White House staff as a senior
advisor.

First Ladies
There is no constitutional role for the president's family, yet there is no avoiding
the public role that comes from marriage to the president of the United States.
For most of the country's history, the president's wife has served as hostess in
chief. In the modern era, the duties of the first lady include some or all of the following: wife and mother, public figure and celebrity, the nation's social hostess,
symbol of U.S. womanhood, White House manager and preservationist, campaigner, champion of social causes, presidential spokesperson, presidential and
political party booster, diplomat, and political and presidential partner.[57] The
extent to which the first lady adopts any, or all, of these roles depends on private
negotiations with the president and to some extent public negotiations with the
country. The Office of the First Lady has become part of the official organizational structure of the Executive Office of the President. One of the main responsibilities of the first lady's staff is in the day-to-day dealings with the news media.
In addition to a press secretary, most first ladies have also employed a chief of
staff, a social secretary, a projects director (for causes that a first lady may adopt),
and several other special assistants. Since the 1970s, first ladies have employed
anywhere between 12 and 28 full-time employees for their staffs.[58] First ladies
also have an office in the White House; to date, only one—Hillary Clinton—
chose to have her office in the West Wing, as opposed to the East Wing, of the
White House, which was a clear indication of the advisory role that she planned
to play within her husband's administration. Regardless of the role that they
play, first ladies are often "complicated women" who are "called upon to clarify
and calm, or to inspire and motivate, projecting a voicing of confidence, reason,
and balance."[59]

The public role for first ladies has mostly been a social one, yet several first
ladies since Eleanor Roosevelt's tenure provide distinct examples of the power
and influence that can come with being the first spouse. Both Rosalynn Carter
and Hillary Clinton opted for active involvement in policy decisions and publicly

acknowledged their political role within the administration. Carter became an advocate for numerous causes, most notably research in the area of mental health issues. As the request of her husband, she also sat in on cabinet and other policy meetings, acted as one of his closest advisors, and even served as an envoy abroad in Latin America and other areas. Clinton, perhaps rivaling only Eleanor Roosevelt in the politically significant role that she played in her husband's administration, was a successful attorney and long-time advocate for children's issues before moving into the White House. As first lady, she acted as one of Bill Clinton's top policy advisors (hence the office in the West Wing) and most notably headed up the Clinton administration's health-care reform policy initiative (first introduced in 1993, but which failed to achieve congressional approval in 1994). After the failure with health-care reform, Clinton lowered her political profile and embraced more traditional activities for a first lady, as well as focusing on social issues, particularly those dealing with women and children.[60] Other first ladies, like Mamie Eisenhower, Lady Bird Johnson, Barbara Bush, and Laura Bush, opted for a more traditional, nonpublic role in their husband's White House.

Regardless of the public versus private role of the first lady, several have played unique roles in their husband's administrations. Jackie Kennedy, a former debutante, is remembered for her trend-setting fashions, redecorating the aging White House, bringing art and culture into Washington political circles, and providing glamor to the Kennedy administration at the start of the television age of politics. Betty Ford was an outspoken advocate for women's rights and is also remembered for raising public consciousness about addiction by publicly acknowledging her own problems with alcohol. While mostly a traditional first lady while in the public eye, Nancy Reagan was a formidable presence in the Reagan White House in protecting her husband's best interests. President Reagan trusted her judgment supremely and even consulted her regarding staffing decisions in the White House and major policy objectives. Michelle Obama, a Princeton and Harvard–educated attorney who put her career on hold during her husband's presidential campaign in 2008, chose the more traditional role of first lady by supporting nonpolitical causes, such as support for military families and fighting obesity in America's children. And, like several of her predecessors, she was tasked with raising two young daughters while living in the White House. Melania Trump is also raising a young son in the White House and has indicated that one issue on which she will focus while first lady is to combat the rise in cyberbullying.

GOVERNORS AND OTHER STATEWIDE POSITIONS

While it is no longer considered an anomaly for women to run for Congress or state legislative positions, women governors are still the exception rather than the rule. When it comes to executive political positions, "men are the ones who have historically made the decisions for the country" at both the national and state level.[61] Women have not had an easy time winning their state's highest political office, and many women gubernatorial candidates have been harmed by negative attitudes and stereotypes that suggest a woman cannot succeed in such a powerful executive position. With so few women having served as state governors, research to determine leadership styles of women in this position or trends in their impact on policymaking has yet to provide definitive answers. However, the face of the state governor is starting to change.[62] Recent trends have shown that most women running for governor have previous political experience at either the local or state level and that women candidates are most successful when running in open-seat elections (as opposed to an attempt to unseat an incumbent).[63] Another study also considered the impact of gender on gubernatorial personality and how governors exert political power. Female governors were more likely than male governors to express a more feminine approach to their public duties (empowering others in the political process as opposed to wielding power over others), yet they were also just as likely to take a more "masculine, power over" approach when necessary to adapt to the traditionally male-dominated political environment.[64]

As of 2016, six women were serving as state governors (three Democrats and three Republicans). That number reached its peak at nine in 2004 and 2007, which represented the most women who have ever served in this position simultaneously.[65] A total of 37 women have served as governor in 27 states (22 Democrats and 15 Republicans). Arizona is the only state where a woman governor has ever been succeeded by another woman and boasts the largest number—four—of women to hold the position. Rose Mofford, a Democrat, was elected secretary of state in 1986 and succeeded to governor in 1988 after the impeachment and conviction of Governor Evan Mecham. Mofford served as governor until 1991. Jane Dee Hull, a Republican, also began her ascent to governor as the Arizona secretary of state and succeeded to governor in 1997 on the resignation of Fife Symington, who had been convicted of fraud. Hull was elected to a full term in 1998, when Arizona became the only state to have an all-female line of succession with women holding the offices of governor, secretary of state (Betsey Bayless), attorney general (Janet Napolitano), treasurer (Carol Springer), and superintendent of public instruction (Lisa Graham Keegan). Janet Napolitano, a Democrat who made Senator John Kerry's short list for a running mate in the 2004 presidential contest, succeeded Hull as governor in 2003. Then, in 2009, when Napolitano became secretary of homeland security, she was succeeded by the lieutenant governor, Jan Brewer, who served until 2015.[66]

While the governor's office of large states is one of the most likely stepping stones to the White House, only one of the six largest electoral states (California, New York, Texas, Florida, Illinois, and Pennsylvania) has ever elected a woman as governor—Democrat Ann Richards served one term as Texas governor, elected in 1990 but defeated by George W. Bush in her reelection effort in 1994. (Richards is the second woman governor in Texas; Miriam Amanda "Ma" Ferguson, a Democrat, served as governor from 1925 to 1927 and 1933 to 1935, replacing her husband, who was impeached). Nellie Tayloe Ross, a Wyoming Democrat, became the nation's first woman governor in 1925 when she replaced her husband after he died in office. Ross served for two years and later became vice chair of the Democratic National Committee and director of the U.S. Mint. At the 1928 Democratic National Convention, she received 31 votes on the first ballot for vice president. Ella Grasso, a Democrat from Connecticut who served from 1975 to 1980, was the first woman elected as governor in her own right. Republicans did not elect their first woman governor until 1986, with the election of Kay A. Orr of Nebraska.

More recently, Democrat Wendy Davis ran for governor in 2014 but lost to Republican Greg Abbott. No woman has ever served as lieutenant governor or attorney general of Texas. California and New York offer similar records in electing women to statewide executive positions. California has seen three women gubernatorial candidates in the general election—Democrat Dianne Feinstein in 1990, Democrat Kathleen Brown in 1994, and Republican Meg Whitman in 2010—all of whom lost. No woman has ever been elected lieutenant governor, although Democrat Mona Pasquil served as acting lieutenant governor for nearly six months in 2009–2010 as an interim appointment. The former California attorney general, Democrat Kamala Harris, is the only woman to ever hold that post and the highest-ranking woman ever elected to a statewide position. In New York, no woman has ever been nominated on either the Democratic or Republican ticket to run for governor, and no woman has ever served as attorney general. Three women, however, have served as lieutenant governor; most recently, Republican Mary Donohue held the position from 1999 to 2006.

The dearth of women holding statewide executive positions matters since the governor's office of large states is one of the most likely stepping stones to the White House (four of the last seven presidents were state governors), and serving as lieutenant governor and/or attorney general is often a stepping stone to being elected governor. State governors are also key players in the implementation of public policy at the state level and serve as an important liaison in the creation of federal policy that effects state funding of programs (a crucial role as Congress has given more control and responsibility to states in the implementation of major federal programs). Governors perhaps hold more power and influence now than ever before, not only in overseeing their state budgets and bureaucracies but also in policymaking within Washington. With so few women having served as state governors, research to determine leadership styles of women in this position has yet to provide definitive answers. However, recent trends have shown that most women running for governor have previous political experience at either the local or state level and that women candidates are most successful when running in open-seat elections (as opposed to an attempt to unseat an incumbent).[67] In addition, partisanship can also affect the policy priorities of women governors. While the data are limited regarding the low number of women who have served as state governors, a recent study suggests that women governors from both parties emphasize issues of economics and education, but women governors who are Democrats "systematically concentrated more on health policy areas while Republicans emphasized social welfare."[68]

MAYORS

Historically, women have played a much larger role in the political process at the local level. Many women who would go on to have successful political careers at a much higher level began their careers in elected positions at the city level. In 1887, Susanna Salter was elected mayor of Argonia, Kansas, to become the nation's first woman mayor. Bertha K. Landes, the Republican city council president at the time, became acting mayor of Seattle in 1924, the first woman to lead a major American city. Two years later, she was elected mayor in her own right in a campaign run by women, but lost in her bid for a second full term. As of 2017, a total of 262 women (18.8 percent) were serving as mayors of cities with a population of 30,000 or more. Of these, the woman who heads the largest city within that group is Ivy R. Taylor of San Antonio, Texas, which has a population of more than 1.3 million (see Table 8.2). Houston, Texas, is the largest city in the United States to ever elect a woman mayor (Houston currently ranks fourth among the

Table 8.2 Largest U.S. Cities with Women Mayors (2017)

Ivy R. Taylor	San Antonio, TX	1,327,407
Betsy Price	Fort Worth, TX	741,206
Jennifer W. Roberts	Charlotte, NC	731,424
Muriel Bowser	Washington, DC	601,723
Megan Barry	Nashville, TN	601,222
Catherine E. Pugh	Baltimore, MD	620,961
Carolyn G. Goodman	Las Vegas, NV	583,756
Jean Stothert	Omaha, NE	408,958
Nancy McFarlane	Raleigh, NC	403,892
Libby Schaaf	Oakland, CA	390,724
Betsy Hodges	Minneapolis, MN	382,578
Karen K. Goh	Bakersfield, CA	347,483
Paula Hicks-Hudson	Toledo, OH	287,208
Nancy Barakat Vaughan	Greensboro, NC	269,666
Mary Casillas Salas	Chula Vista, CA	243,916
Jenn Daniels	Gilbert, AZ	208,453
Hillary Schieve	Reno, NV	225,221
Beth Van Duyne	Irving, TX	216,290
Sharon Weston Broome	Baton Rouge, LA	229,493
Lily Mei	Fremont, CA	214,089

SOURCE: Center for American Women and Politics, Rutgers, State University of New Jersey

largest cities with a population of more than 2.2 million), and it has done so twice. Kathy Whitmire served as mayor from 1982 to 1992, and more recently, Annise Parker served as mayor from 2010 to 2016 (she was also the first openly gay mayor of Houston).

Recent studies on the impact of women mayors suggests that there may be more gendered expectations for a woman to lead differently than there are measurable gendered differences. Given the nature of local politics and the types of social issues that mayors must deal with, policy issues at the city level could be more easily labeled feminine as opposed to "masculine." For example, education and social welfare programs are critical issues for cities and often benefit from leadership qualities associated with femininity and nurturing. This view of leadership at the city level calls into question the notion of masculine executive leadership.[69] A study of mayoral candidates also found that press coverage is not biased against female candidates, although the range of issues covered expands, suggesting "the presence of a female candidate enhances representation as the scope and depth of issue discussion is much greater, providing more issue options for voters to consider in making their vote choice."[70] Like research on women in higher executive political positions, future research as more women enter mayoral and other city and county positions will provide a clearer picture of the impact that women may bring to the political process as executive leaders at the local level.

CONCLUSION

While women have made progress during the past decade in breaking down more barriers to executive positions of political power, reaching gender parity within these leadership positions is still many years away. However, having women in such integral national positions as secretary of state (Madeleine Albright, Condoleezza Rice, and Hillary Clinton), attorney general (Janet Reno and Loretta Lynch), and national security advisor (Condoleezza Rice) can go a long way in changing social and cultural attitudes toward women in positions of power within our government. The election of more women state governors is also crucial to increase the number of women in the on-deck circle for potential presidential or vice presidential candidates in future campaigns. Recent studies have begun to focus more intently on the consequences of masculinism dominating executive politics. These consequences include a loss of talent by limiting the candidate pool to men only, a constrained worldview with a limited set of experiences for solving problems, and a loss of legitimacy for the government itself with women voters. An absence of women in executive political positions also perpetuates the myth that this is a male-only arena.[71]

Despite the progress for women seeking political careers, the United States still lags behind several other countries, some with much more conservative political cultures, in terms of electing women to executive leadership positions. While no other national system of government matches the constitutional uniqueness found within the American system of government, other countries have nonetheless selected women as their chief executives (including Argentina, Australia, Brazil, Chile, Costa Rica, Croatia, Great Britain, Iceland, Ireland, Israel, Liberia, New Zealand, Nicaragua, Pakistan, the Philippines, and Sri Lanka, among others). Many of these women were elected prime minister through a parliamentary system of government, which means that they did not have to win election through the support of a national constituency of voters. Instead, they only needed to win their local legislative seat and then gain the support of their party colleagues within parliament to be elevated to prime minister. However, different societal expectations are beginning to emerge for women in American politics, and the recent trend of women entering more executive political positions, whether through election or appointment, suggests that progress in this area continues.

CHAPTER SUMMARY

- We discuss the different leadership traits and styles among men and women executive leaders. Many leadership experts suggest female leadership characteristics and principles—communication, personal relationships, community building, and ignoring the rigid hierarchy of most corporations—provide an important advantage to women in the corporate world.
- Many successful women in business have adopted a new paradigm of leadership that has moved away from the more traditional approach of trying to be "like men." Like women in politics, women in business careers also face barriers in reaching the top of the corporate ladder, such as childrearing and other family responsibilities.
- Conventional wisdom in recent years has suggested women still face an uphill battle as presidential candidates. Presumed barriers include the inherent masculinity of the office, prevalent negative stereotypes of women leaders, gender bias in news coverage of woman candidates, and a lack of potential women candidates. However, no permanent structural barriers exist that stop a woman from winning the White House.
- The executive branch is the most masculine of the three branches of government due to its hierarchical structure, the unity of command, and the ability for a president to act decisively when the need arises. Creating a strong image of presidential leadership in the minds of Americans is an essential aspect of political success for any presidential candidate.
- Aside from the constitutional requirements for the office of the presidency—being at least 35 years old, a 14-year U.S. resident, and a natural-born citizen—no other formal criteria exist to run for president. However, informal qualifications

exist, including religion, race, and gender, making the pool of viable candidates for both president and vice president almost exclusively Protestant, white, and male.

- Gender stereotypes can also influence how women candidates and their campaigns are covered in the news media. Potential women presidential and vice presidential candidates have not always been portrayed as authoritative or as strong leaders.
- The biggest hurdle in electing a woman president is that so few women hold the appropriate leadership positions within our government to put them in contention for the presidency. Electing the first woman vice president will also break a significant political barrier.
- Women have taken an increasingly prominent role in other positions throughout the executive branch in recent years. The Clinton, Bush, and Obama presidencies saw record numbers of women appointed to executive posts within the cabinet, other federal executive agencies, and White House staff positions.
- First ladies have served as influential advisors as well as providing an important public link to the presidency. In the modern era, the duties of the first lady have included wife and mother, public figure and celebrity, White House manager and preservationist, campaigner, and champion of social causes. The Office of the First Lady has become part of the official organizational structure of the Executive Office of the President.
- Despite the progress made for women seeking legislative positions, women governors are still the exception rather than the rule. In the nation's history, only 37 women have served as governor in 27 states. While the governor's office of large states is one of the most likely stepping stones to the White House, only Texas has ever elected a woman governor (California, New York, Florida, Illinois, Ohio, and Pennsylvania have not).
- Historically, women have played a much larger role in the political process at the local level. Many women who go on to have successful political careers at a higher level began their careers in city politics.

STUDY/DISCUSSION QUESTIONS

- How do executive political positions differ from legislative positions? Why is the executive branch known as a male-dominated institution?
- What obstacles do women face in pursuing executive leadership positions, both in the corporate world and in national and state politics?
- What changes might a woman president bring to the executive branch and White House?
- How important are cabinet members and presidential advisors in the day-to-day operation of the White House? How have women made a difference in these positions in recent years?
- How influential should a first lady be in her husband's administration? What will be the role of the eventual "first husband?"

- Why have so few women ever served as state governors? What impact do women governors have on the political process?
- Why does the job of a mayor call into question the notion of masculine executive leadership?

CASE STUDIES

1. **What does the 2016 Republican primary tell us about gender and the presidency?**
Seventeen candidates vied for the presidency on the Republican side in 2016, and Donald Trump eventually emerged as the party nominee. During the campaign, the candidates performed acts of hypermasculinity to appear more macho than the next guy. Trump and Marco Rubio had a heated exchange over "hand" size, the media had a field day with the heels on Rubio's shoes and Ted Cruz painting his face and going duck hunting with Phil Robertson, the patriarch of the popular *Duck Dynasty* series. Masculinity plays a role in presidential contests, even when there are no (or in this case, few) female candidates. Why do these appeals work? What do they tell us about how the presidency is constructed in the imaginations of everyday Americans?

2. **What does the 2016 general election tell us about gender and the presidency?**
We expect our president to be macho in some basic ways, so when a viable female candidate enters the race, this complicates things. As noted in this chapter, female candidates who seek executive offices cannot escape the masculine expectations that come with executive office, but they walk a fine line in disaffecting voters by not also appearing "properly feminine." How did Clinton achieve this balance in the 2016 general election? In what ways did she perform masculinity befitting the presidency, and how did she simultaneously signal femininity? How did Donald Trump's presence in the election determine the ways in which she navigated this fine line?

3. **Why are legislative and executive positions viewed differently?**
There is a distinct difference in legislative versus executive positions when it comes to progress. A moderate number of women have moved into legislative positions in a relatively short period of time, but far fewer have been elected to executive positions, and that number declined at the state level in the past decade. What explains the slower progress on the executive side? What makes these positions relatively less available or viable for women who enter public life?

RESOURCES

- The **Institute for Women's Leadership** partners with multinational corporations, federal governments, global nonprofits, and emerging businesses to help women leaders grow and develop.
http://www.womensleadership.com

- The **Institute for Women's Leadership** at Rutgers, State University of New Jersey, provides interdisciplinary leadership educational opportunities that deepen understanding of critical issues affecting women.
  http://iwl.rutgers.edu
- **The First Ladies Gallery** is a White House web page that provides a history of first ladies from Martha Washington to Michelle Obama.
  http://www.whitehouse.gov/history/firstladies

CHAPTER 9

Women in the Judiciary

Former associate justice of the U.S. Supreme Court Sandra Day O'Connor once wrote, "I have been called the most powerful woman in the United States." Today, several women in both the political and corporate worlds top the list of most powerful women; when she served on the Supreme Court (1981–2006), O'Connor would have certainly been among them. She has stated that many people believe that as the first women appointed to the nation's highest court, she wielded tremendous power within the governing process. During the 1980 presidential campaign, Ronald Reagan promised that if he were elected, he would nominate the first woman to the U.S. Supreme Court. His first year in office, he made good on that promise by nominating O'Connor, who at the time was a member of the Arizona State Court of Appeals. Despite having graduated third in her class at Stanford Law School in 1952, perennially one of the top law schools in the nation (former chief justice William Rehnquist graduated first in the same class), O'Connor had difficulty finding work as an attorney in private practice. Instead, she embarked on a career of mostly public positions, including assistant state attorney general and a state senator in Arizona.

On O'Connor's historic appointment to the Supreme Court, Reagan was criticized by both liberals and conservatives for his choice. Liberals were happy to see the first woman join the high court, but feared that her positions, particularly on women's issues, would be too conservative. Conservatives, on the other hand, feared that she lacked adequate federal judicial experience and knowledge of the U.S. Constitution and that she would uphold abortion rights (Reagan had campaigned to make abortion illegal). When she retired from the Supreme Court nearly 25 years later, O'Connor had earned a reputation as a pragmatic and often centrist voice as an important swing vote on issues like abortion, affirmative action, and privacy rights.[1] She remained the only woman to serve on the high court until Ruth Bader Ginsburg, appointed by President Bill Clinton, joined her in 1993. Ginsburg, an often-outspoken justice on the issue of equal rights for women, complained of being "lonely" on the Court in 2007 as the only women following O'Connor's retirement two years prior.[2] She was joined by two other women during President Barack Obama's first term, with Sonia Sotomayor's confirmation as the first Latina to sit on the nation's highest court in 2009 and Elena Kagan's confirmation in 2010.

Women's ability to lead within the judicial branch of government is somewhat different than in other political arenas. While many judges at the state level are elected, the president nominates all judges at the federal level. Judges also have distinct responsibilities and a formal process in interpreting and applying the law, as opposed to creating the laws as legislators do, which sometimes limits their ability to directly shape public policy. A good judge is also supposed to be impartial and independent, not relying on his or her partisan or ideological viewpoints, when deciding a case. Whether or not this is true in all cases is difficult to determine; however, one would assume that a feminist judge would have a harder time changing the legal culture in America if she were staying true to her impartial judicial traditions. In terms of recruitment, judges are also not as high profile as other politicians, which makes providing female role models within the judiciary more difficult. This chapter will consider the progress women have made within the legal profession in recent decades, the history of women serving as judges at both the federal and state level, and the impact that women make on the judiciary as a whole. What is the historical relationship between women and the law in the United States? What barriers, if any, still exist for women entering the legal profession or seeking a judicial post? And, most important, do women judges make a difference in their interpretation and application of the law?

WOMEN AND THE LAW

The rule of law, which is the adherence to the basic legal foundation and rules that govern society, is fundamental to the U.S. constitutional system of government. Yet, for most of the nation's history, women did not have access to the law and the tools that it provided in shaping the political system. As we discussed in Chapter 2, not only did women have no voice in the writing of the U.S. Constitution, but also women were not specifically mentioned anywhere within the document. In addition, since the founding era, the "legal status of women has been shaped by an ideology grounded in cultural and physical differences between the sexes."[3]

The legal disenfranchisement of women in American life lasted throughout the nineteenth and well into the twentieth century, despite ratification of the Fourteenth Amendment in 1868 that included clauses declaring "equal protection" and "due process" of the laws. In 1875, the U.S. Supreme Court "dismissed out-of-hand" the claim that women had a constitutional right to vote as equal citizens. Also in the late nineteenth century, the Court upheld state laws barring women from practicing law and even from working as a bartender unless the woman was a member of the owner's immediate family. These rulings only enhanced the view of women as second-class citizens.

In the early twentieth century, the Supreme Court also handed down rulings, now seen as paternalistic, to protect women in the workplace regarding hours, working conditions, and wages. At the time, it was commonly assumed that women were not equals to men in the workplace and therefore, the "problem" of women working outside the home needed to be dealt with. The Court would not begin to reverse its views of gender-based discrimination in the workplace until the early 1970s.[4] Women were also the victims of discrimination in various other legal forms until the latter part of the twentieth century. Based on common-law traditions brought with the original American colonists from England, women lost all legal and property rights on marriage. Married women were denied equal custody rights, the right to keep their wages, and the right to divorce; single women also had few legal rights. Up until the early twentieth century, when many of these state laws began to be rescinded, married women were viewed as the legal property of their husbands, highlighted by a 1905 ruling by the U.S. Supreme Court that stated a husband could sue for property damages if his wife committed adultery. By losing their legal identity on marriage, women were also banned from entering into legal contracts (which precluded them from pursuing opportunities as business owners), and they could not file a suit in a court of law.

In addition, women were excluded as jurors for decades after women received the right to vote in 1920, even though jury duty is considered one of the most important civic responsibilities of American citizens. Even into the 1960s and 1970s, several states granted automatic exemptions to women for jury service, which meant that states had laws excluding women as jurors. The issue was finally settled in 1975 when the U.S. Supreme Court ruled in *Taylor v. Louisiana* that excluding women violated the Sixth Amendment to the U.S. Constitution, which mandated a jury of one's peers (eliminating women did not adequately represent a cross-section of the population).

Only in recent decades have women gained access to the law as equal citizens, as a profession, and as a means to enact political changes. Spurred on by the second wave of the women's rights movement in the 1960s and 1970s, laws (either through congressional action or rulings by the U.S. Supreme Court) finally began to reflect a woman's legal status as equal to men in the areas of property and economic rights, employment rights, and educational rights. As radical feminist and legal scholar Catharine A. MacKinnon notes,

> Law in the United States is at once a powerful medium and a medium for power. Backed by force, it is also an avenue for demand, a vector of access, an arena for contention other than the physical, a forum for voice, a mechanism for accountability, a form for authority, and an expression of norms. Women seeking change for women have found that all these consequences and possibilities cannot be left to those elite men who have traditionally dominated in and through law, shaping its structures and animating attitudes to guarantee the supremacy of men as a group over women in social life. Women who work with law have learned that, while a legal change may not always make a social change, sometimes it helps, and law *un*changed can make social change impossible.[5]

WOMEN AND THE LEGAL PROFESSION

While many career paths can lead people into a political career, a legal career—either as an attorney or judge—is a common path to elected or appointed office at the state and national levels. However, just as women had been excluded from voting for decades, women had also long been excluded in many ways from the legal profession. In addition to the suffrage movement during the late nineteenth century, a small group of women attorneys in the United States was blazing a trail for women who wanted to practice law. In 1890, there were only approximately 200 women attorneys in the United States. One member of this elite group, Ellen Martin, gathered with three dozen of her colleagues at the 1893 World's Fair in Chicago to hold the first Congress of Women Lawyers convention. Also in attendance was Belva Lockwood, who was the first women to run for president in 1884 on the National Equal Rights party ticket. This first generation of women attorneys in the United States fought for many things, including the inclusion of women students at more law schools (in 1870, only a handful of law schools accepted women, including Washington University, the University of Michigan, and Union College), granting bar privileges to women, and simply gaining acceptance in the profession.[6] While much of their work was in civil and family law and many were committed to political reform, this group of female attorneys was "smart, bold, and defiant. Its members were charming and argumentative. They debated whether to wear hats in court as well as fundamental questions of service and professional identity."[7]

Most barriers for women entering the legal profession did not disappear until the 1970s. Title IX of the Education Act of 1972, which guaranteed equal access to academic and athletic resources regardless of gender, dramatically increased the number of women attending law school. By 2014, women represented nearly half (47.7 percent) of all first-year law students in the United States and 34 percent of all attorneys.[8]

Recent studies and surveys within the legal profession have shown that women attorneys face many obstacles in achieving top leadership positions within law firms, corporations, and governmental agencies. While overt sexual discrimination may not be the biggest problem that women attorneys face in career advancement, there are organizational, institutional, and systemic obstacles that exist, including gender-based assumptions and practices, a lack of mentoring, and family–work conflicts.[9] In a recent study by the American Bar Association's Commission on Women in the Profession, women's opportunities within the legal profession, like those within the political and corporate worlds, are limited by unconscious stereotypes, inadequate access to support networks, inflexible workplace structures, sexual harassment, and bias in the justice system.[10] For example, in 2014, women held only 21 percent of general counsel positions in Fortune 500 companies, and women attorneys earn only 78.9 percent of the salaries earned by their male colleagues.[11]

Gender stereotypes are particularly problematic for women attorneys, who "often do not receive the same presumption of competence or commitment as their male colleagues."[12] A majority of women within the profession believe they are held to higher standards than men (a problem compounded for minority women). The lack of balance between work and family life also hampers career paths for women, including a double standard for working mothers who are criticized for a lack of commitment if they are not willing to sacrifice family needs for work. While no evidence exists to suggest that women attorneys with family responsibilities are any less committed to their careers, these same women are more likely to leave large law firms for a different job that offers a more flexible work schedule.[13]

Systemic gender bias within the justice system has long remained a problem for women, not only as attorneys but also as litigants. Beginning in the 1980s, several initiatives began to address some of these problems. Courts as institutions are traditional and formal in their practices and changes often occur slowly. For example, some courts used to sanction women attorneys who were married and refused to use their husbands' last names. While most cases of blatant discrimination are now rare, subtle discrimination still occurs in issues regarding the demographics of the bench (judges), bar (attorneys), and court personnel; differences in the outcomes for men and women during bail hearings or custody awards; and the general perception of participants based on gender (and also race).[14]

Most often, bias in the justice system falls into one of three categories: disrespectful treatment (for example, female attorneys being addressed by their first name while male attorneys are not, female attorneys being mistaken for support staff or being dismissed or ignored as insignificant to the proceedings); devaluation of credibility and injuries (dismissive attitudes about the importance of cases dealing with sexual harassment, employment discrimination, or acquaintance rape, for example); and stereotypical assumptions about gender, race, ethnicity, disability, and sexual orientation (domestic violence victims are somehow responsible for provoking their abuse, or mothers who work full-time are less deserving of child custody, for example). As a result, many states have implemented codes of conduct and educational programs to eliminate gender and racial bias in the courtroom.[15]

WOMEN AS FEDERAL JUDGES

Today, more than 100 courts make up the federal judicial branch. The lowest federal courts are the district courts, which serve as trial courts with juries and where most federal cases originate. If district court cases are appealed, the next step is a federal court of appeals. There are 12 federal judicial circuits (or territories), and each has its own court of appeals. With the exception of the District of Columbia, which has its own circuit, each of the other 11 circuits includes at least three states. Nine justices sit on the U.S. Supreme Court (eight associate justices and the chief justice), and, like other federal judges, all are appointed to life terms. Justices and federal judges can be impeached by a majority vote in the House of Representatives and removed by a two-thirds majority vote in the Senate. The latter has never happened to a Supreme Court justice, since all have served until retirement or death. When a vacancy occurs on any federal court, a potential judge or justice is first nominated for the position by the president. Next, the Senate judiciary committee considers the nomination and, if approved, it then goes to the entire Senate, with confirmation occurring by a simple majority vote. Since justices and federal judges serve a life term, this is an important opportunity for presidents to enjoy a lasting political legacy long after they leave office.

When considering women appointees, however, the "integration of women into the federal judiciary has been achingly slow."[16] President Franklin D. Roosevelt appointed the first woman to a federal bench. Florence Ellinwood Allen, appointed in 1934, served on the Sixth Circuit Court of Appeals for 25 years. No other woman would be appointed to a court of appeals for 34 years, when in 1968 Lyndon Johnson nominated Shirley Ann Mount Hufstedler to the Ninth Circuit Court of Appeals (where she served until 1979). Burnita Shelton Matthews became the first woman to serve on a U.S. district court when Harry Truman issued her a recess appointment to the district court for the District of Columbia in October 1949. The Senate confirmed her nomination in April 1950. John F. Kennedy appointed one woman to a district court position, and Johnson appointed two women to district courts. Richard Nixon and Gerald Ford appointed one woman each to a federal judgeship, both to a district court, with no appointments to an appeals court.

Jimmy Carter was the first president to seriously increase the number of women serving in the judiciary, and as president, he had "both the interest and the opportunity to diversify the federal courts" in terms of gender, race, and ethnicity.[17] He appointed 40 women to the federal judiciary (29 to district courts, which equaled 14.3 percent of his appointments, and 11, or 19.6 percent, to courts of appeal). Carter would not have the opportunity to appoint a justice to the Supreme Court during his four years in the White House, even though historically, presidents have an opportunity to make an appointment, on average, every two years. Yet, the legacy of Carter's appointment of women to federal district and appellate courts is significant in several ways: these women took different career paths to their appointments than their male colleagues (more experience as state judges or law professors and less experience working for large law firms or in politics); it is presumed they brought a "gendered perspective" to the federal bench, counterbalancing the historic perspective of mostly white males; yet, their decisions do not differ dramatically from those of their liberal male colleagues; and these women judges influenced the justice system through their activities outside of the courtroom, including the creation of gender bias task forces in the profession.[18]

Carter's immediate successors, Ronald Reagan and George H. W. Bush, appointed fewer women to the federal bench. Reagan, who disapproved of using affirmative action policies in judicial appointments, named 30 women to federal judgeships (24, or 8.3 percent, to district courts and six, or 7.2 percent, to courts of appeal). Bush appointed 36 women to the federal bench (29, or 19.6 percent, to district courts and seven, or 16.7 percent, to courts of appeal).

Table 9.1 Presidential Appointments of Women to the Federal Judiciary, 1933 to 2016

PRESIDENT	DISTRICT COURT (NO., %)	APPEALS COURT (NO., %)	SUPREME COURT (NO., %)
Franklin D. Roosevelt	0/134, 0	1/51, 2.0	0/8, 0
Harry S. Truman	1/101, 1.0	0/27, 0	0/4, 0
Dwight D. Eisenhower	0/129, 0	0/45, 0	0/5, 0
John F. Kennedy	1/102, 1.0	0/21, 0	0/2, 0
Lyndon B. Johnson	2/126, 1.6	1/40, 2.5	0/2, 0
Richard Nixon	1/181, 0.6	0/46, 0	0/4, 0
Gerald Ford	1/50, 2.0	0/11, 0	0/1, 0
Jimmy Carter	29/203, 14.3	11/56, 19.6	n/a
Ronald Reagan	24/290, 8.3	6/83, 7.2	1/3, 33.3
George H. W. Bush	29/148, 19.6	7/42, 16.7	0/2, 0
Bill Clinton	88/305, 28.9	20/66, 30.3	1/2, 50
George W. Bush	54/261, 20.7	17/62, 27.4	0/2, 0
Barack Obama	110/268, 41.0	26/55, 47.3	2/2, 100
Total percentage	340/2,298, 14.8	89/605, 14.7	4/37, 10.8

SOURCE: Federal Judicial Center, "Biographical Directory of Federal Judges."

Bill Clinton, however, reversed that trend by appointing 108 women to serve in federal judicial posts (88, or 28.9 percent, to district courts and 20, or 30.3 percent, to courts of appeal). During his eight years in office, George W. Bush appointed 71 women to the federal bench (54, or 20.7 percent, to district courts and 17, or 27.9 percent, to courts of appeal) (see Table 9.1). He also became the first president to nominate a woman to the Supreme Court who would not be confirmed (as we will discuss below). Through the end of his second term, Barack Obama had appointed 136 women to the federal bench (110, or 41.0 percent, to district courts and 26, or 47.3 percent, to courts of appeal).

Historically, few women have been appointed to federal judicial positions. The main reason for the small number of women being appointed stems from the fact that until the 1970s, few women were entering the legal profession. As such, like women seeking leadership positions within the legislative and executive branches, a limited pool of qualified women existed for presidential consideration for such posts. Bias has also existed in the selection and confirmation process. Applicants whose careers have focused on public service or public interest law are assumed to be activist on certain policy issues, which means that as judges, they go beyond merely interpreting the law to actively participate in making new law. Judicial activists can adhere to either a liberal or conservative political ideology. For example, liberal activists view the Constitution as a broad grant of freedom to citizens against government interference, particularly those issues involving civil rights and civil liberties. As a result, judicial activism is not always viewed favorably during the confirmation process, particularly by those politicians who believe that judges should not seek new principles that can change the existing law, but should instead leave policymaking to elected officials. Women, particularly women of color, disproportionately come from public service backgrounds and, as a result, are often overlooked for appointments.[19]

Two other important factors have contributed to the small number of women being appointed to judicial positions. First, high standards exist in terms of education and experience for judicial office. Most candidates must not only hold a law degree, but also have several years of trial experience. Second, the judicial selection process is complicated and is often linked to building strong professional ties and reputations within male-dominated legal circles. As a result, many women do not find themselves on the short lists for consideration of these positions.[20] Two recent nominations to the Supreme Court—George W. Bush's nomination of Harriet Miers and Barack Obama's nomination of Sonia Sotomayor—provide interesting and somewhat contradicting examples of how many of these factors play out in the confirmation process.

The Supreme Court

Let's consider the many issues at play when the president is faced with a vacancy on the high court. Presidents rely on many factors in their decision to nominate someone, including objective qualifications, policy preferences, political and personal reward, and building political support. The president's "situation" also affects the confirmation process, including political strength in the Senate, level of public approval, mobilization of interest group activity, and the importance of the nomination (for example, will a new justice change the ideological balance of the Court?).[21] Nominees are always attorneys, although this is not a constitutional or statutory requirement, and most attend top law schools (of the current justices, Anthony Kennedy, Stephen Breyer, John Roberts, Elena Kagan, and Neil Gorsuch attended Harvard University; Clarence Thomas, Samuel Alito, and Sonia Sotomayor attended Yale University, and Ruth Bader Ginsburg graduated from Columbia University after spending her first two years at Harvard). Previous jobs usually include appellate judges (state or federal), jobs within the executive branch, jobs within the Justice Department, or highly elected office. All but one of the current justices were nominated while serving on a U.S. Court of Appeals; Kagan was serving as the U.S. solicitor general when she was nominated. Most justices are older than 50 when nominated, and a majority are from upper- or middle-upper-class families (Thomas and Sotomayor are exceptions to the latter, both having grown up in poorer, working-class environments).[22]

In addition, despite attempts to keep the Court an unbiased and independent institution, presidential appointments are nonetheless political, and a "myth of merit" exists when a president makes their selection. As a result, several highly qualified individuals have been passed over for appointment. The political climate also plays a large role in who is selected, as do race, gender, religion, and geography. Several other factors can also contribute to the outcome of a confirmation vote, like whether the president is from the same party as the Senate majority and whether the president and their nominee might face a tough confirmation battle.[23] While the nomination process has been democratized since 1968, it has also become "disorderly, contentious, and unpredictable," which can be attributed to changes in political institutions in the past 30 years that now allow greater public participation in the selection process.[24] This means that what used to happen mostly behind closed doors in the Senate to determine whether the president's selection was qualified to serve on the Supreme Court has now become a more political, campaign-like process, with both opponents and supporters (most notably well-funded interest groups) making a claim about whether a nominee's ideological perspective should disqualify him or her from service. In this environment, unanimous or near-unanimous confirmation votes in the Senate have become the exception rather than the rule, with senators in the minority party often voting against the nominee just to score political points with their constituents or supporters instead of judging the nominee based on qualifications.

In the fall of 2005, George W. Bush nominated White House Counsel Harriet Miers to the Supreme Court to fill the vacancy created by Sandra Day O'Connor's retirement. Initially, John Roberts had been nominated to fill O'Connor's seat, but he was then nominated for chief justice following the death of William Rehnquist in September 2005. Miers was a surprise pick by Bush for several reasons, most notable among them the fact that she had never served as a judge, she had a lack of experience with constitutional issues, and she had close personal ties to Bush (an expectation exists that justices are to remain independent, with no close ties to the president). While both liberals and conservatives voiced opposition regarding Miers's nomination, social conservative groups were most vocal; socially conservative, evangelical voters had played a significant role in Bush's reelection in 2004, and in return, they wanted conservative, strict-constructionist judges who would not engage in what they believed amounted to judicial activism. While the Roberts nomination was cheered by conservative groups, the Miers nomination was not; while Roberts had a long judicial track record with service on both federal district and appellate courts, along with an impressive legal resume, Miers had no such track record and no judicial experience. After she fared poorly in terms of her knowledge of the U.S. Constitution in interviews with U.S. senators and on the questionnaire provided to nominees by the Senate Judiciary Committee, Miers withdrew her nomination in October 2005 only three weeks after Bush had nominated her and prior to the Senate holding any confirmation hearings.[25] Appeals court judge Samuel Alito was then nominated and confirmed to fill O'Connor's vacancy.

As a result, Ginsburg remained the only woman on the Supreme Court for nearly four years until the confirmation of Sonia Sotomayor in August 2009. After the surprise retirement of Justice David Souter in May 2009, Barack Obama had an opportunity for a Supreme Court nomination within the first few months of his presidency. Obama made clear that empathy was an important qualification for his first Supreme Court nomination: "I will seek someone who understands that justice isn't about some abstract legal theory or footnote in a case book. It is also about how our laws affect the daily realities of people's lives—whether they can make a living and care for their families; whether they feel safe in their homes and welcome in their own nation. I view that quality of empathy, of understanding and identifying with people's hopes and struggles as an essential ingredient for arriving at just decisions and outcomes."[26]

Many pundits predicted that the President would nominate a woman, while others predicted that Obama would make history by nominating the first Hispanic judge to the high court. Obama opted for both with Sotomayor, whose impressive resume included experience on the U.S. District Court for the Southern District of New York (nominated by George H. W. Bush in 1991) and the U.S. Court of Appeals for the Second Circuit (nominated by Bill Clinton in 1997). In addition, Sotomayor, who is of Puerto Rican descent, earned her bachelor's degree with honors from Princeton University and her law degree from Yale Law School, where she also served as an editor of the Yale Law Review. Prior to her appointment to the U.S. District Court, Sotomayor worked as an assistant district attorney in New York and worked for several years in private practice. She has also been an adjunct law professor at both New York University and Columbia University.

In effect, Sotomayor represented an outstanding nominee in terms of education and experience. Yet, her nomination did receive opposition from many conservative Republicans in the Senate with charges of judicial activism (even though assessments of her time on the federal bench suggested she was more of a moderate, as opposed to liberal, judge) and criticism of her now-famous "wise Latina" remark. In 2001, while giving a talk at Berkeley Law School, Sotomayor remarked, "I would hope that a wise Latina woman with the richness of her experiences would more often than not reach a better conclusion than a white male who hasn't lived that life." While taken somewhat out of context by her critics, Sotomayor answered questions about the remark during her confirmation hearings before the Senate Judiciary Committee, stating that while personal experiences help to shape a judge's perspective, ultimately the law is the only guide for making a decision. Sotomayor was confirmed by the Senate on August 6, 2009, by a vote of 68–31 (all opposition votes came from Republicans). The final vote in the Senate to confirm Sotomayor represents how the confirmation process has become more politicized and ideologically contentious since O'Connor's confirmation in 1981, when she was confirmed with a unanimous vote of 99–0, and since Ginsburg's confirmation in 1993 with a vote of 96–3. Many observers of the Supreme Court suggest that it would be hard to imagine the high court ever returning to an all-male club.

PROFILE IN POWER

Ruth Bader Ginsburg

Unlike other political leaders, Supreme Court justices are not easily recognizable to a majority of the American public. There are no cameras allowed in the Supreme Court, and justices rarely give interviews or make media appearances; since all federal judges serve for life terms, they do not need to face the voters or worry about public opinion to keep their jobs. Yet, in recent years, Ruth Bader Ginsburg has proven that even a Supreme Court justice can become an iconic figure thanks to social media. What started out as a Tumblr page has become a book[27] and an Internet sensation: Notorious RBG, the moniker given to Ginsburg as a champion of equal rights and social justice.

The presence of Notorious RBG across the Internet is ironic given that Ginsburg's nomination as the second woman to serve on the Supreme Court in 1993 was not nearly as high profile as Sandra Day O'Connor's appointment in 1981. Nonetheless, Ginsburg did represent the first woman appointed to the Court by a Democrat, President Bill Clinton. Her appointment also guaranteed that the makeup of the Court would include more

SOURCE: Collection of the Supreme Court of the United States, Photographer: Steve Petteway

than just one "woman's seat" on the bench (although she was the only woman on the Court when O'Connor retired in 2006 until Sonia Sotomayor was confirmed in 2009). Ginsburg received her law degree from Columbia University in 1959 after completing her first two years of study at Harvard University. Like O'Connor, despite graduating at the top of her prestigious law school class (Ginsburg tied for the number one spot), Ginsburg's first job was as a legal secretary. She then received a clerkship with a U.S. district court judge and worked for many years as a law school professor at both Rutgers University and Columbia University. She also worked as the general counsel for the American Civil Liberties Union from 1973 until 1980, when Jimmy Carter appointed her to the U.S. Court of Appeals for the District of Columbia. She served as an appellate judge for 13 years prior to her appointment to the Supreme Court in 1993.

When Clinton had his first opportunity to appoint a Supreme Court justice in 1993, Ginsburg's name appeared on the initial list of more than 40 potential candidates being considered by the White House. Ginsburg's chances for appointment were improved by a campaign waged by her husband. Unknown to Ginsburg at the time, her husband Martin worked extensively behind the scenes to garner support for her among legal scholars and those within major women's advocacy groups. Martin Ginsburg's public relations campaign helped to secure his wife's position on Clinton's short list of candidates receiving serious consideration.[28] Ginsburg also made a lasting impression on Clinton when they met prior to her nomination. Clinton was impressed by Ginsburg's family struggles (her mother died of cancer when she was 17 and her husband had also endured a battle with cancer early in their marriage) as well as her commitment to women's issues, in particular fighting gender discrimination. Clinton stated that she was the perfect candidate for the high court due to her distinguished judicial career, her advocacy work on behalf of women's issues, and her "demonstrated ability as a consensus builder [and] healer."[29]

Compared to the contentious and divisive confirmation process of Clarence Thomas in 1991, Ginsburg's confirmation to the Supreme Court was relatively smooth, with a 96–3 confirmation vote in the Senate. The Senate Judiciary Committee had also welcomed two new members in 1993—newly elected senators Dianne Feinstein (D-CA) and Carol Moseley Braun (D-IL). Ironically, despite Ginsburg's long support of women's issues and her pro-choice stance on the issue of abortion, several women's groups were critical of her nomination due to her belief, published within a law journal article, that the Court used the wrong rationale in its 1973 *Roe v. Wade* decision that legalized abortion. Ginsburg supported the outcome of the case, but argued that a stronger constitutional argument could have been made. This worried some pro-choice groups that she might support overturning the Roe decision (an outcome that has not occurred).

According to legal scholar Lawrence Baum, Ginsburg has had little impact on the overall ideological balance of the conservative-leaning Rehnquist (1986–2005) and Roberts (2005–Present) courts. Ginsburg, a moderate liberal, is similar to the justice whom she replaced in terms of ideology (Associate Justice Byron White, appointed by John F. Kennedy in 1962). And, along with Stephen Breyer, a fellow moderate liberal who joined the Court in 1994, "the proportion of pro-civil liberties decisions has increased only slightly since they joined the Court, and the Court's doctrinal positions continue to be conservative in most respects."[30] Nonetheless, Ginsburg has strongly supported pro–affirmative action cases before the Court and has also continued her fight against gender discrimination. One of her most notable majority opinions in a case came in 1996 in *United States v. Virginia*, in which the Court stated that the state-funded Virginia Military Institute's exclusion of women was unconstitutional and a violation of the equal protection clause of the Fourteenth Amendment.

Ginsburg, now in her third decade of service on the Court and seemingly not ready to retire, has been an excellent role model for other women in the legal profession who aspire to high-ranking judicial positions. Legal scholar Lawrence Abraham gives Ginsburg high praise for her time on the Court: "Always well prepared, an articulate, incisive questioner in oral argument, a clear and often elegant writer, Ruth Bader Ginsburg has proved herself to be a genuine asset on the Court."[31] As Ginsburg herself stated at her inauguration to the Court on August 10, 1993, "A system of justice will be richer for diversity of background and experience. It will be poorer, in terms of appreciating what is at stake and the impact of its judgments, if all of its members are cast from the same mold."

WOMEN, COURTS, AND THE POLICY AGENDA

Women judges within the federal branch represent important political actors for women's rights. Like other areas of politics, a woman's voice within judicial policymaking has the potential to bring a different perspective to the law. However, recent studies have not shown significant differences between the actions of female and male judges. According to legal scholar Anita Hill, "Empirical and anecdotal accounts do not conclusively establish the idea that individual women judge differently or that women as a group judge differently from men."[32] Still, a diverse judiciary in terms of sex, race, and ethnicity is important for symbolic reasons. Possible explanations for the results may be the fact that so few women have served as judges, as well as the fact that gender differences may be neutralized by the act of judging, which is bound to legal traditions and processes.[33] Diversity on the bench is also important "because the federal judiciary has been arguably the most important actor in women's rights." Both reproductive rights and gender equality are "judicially created rights," since they are not specifically guaranteed in the U.S. Constitution, but have been interpreted by the Supreme Court to exist.[34] A ruling by the Supreme Court can only be overturned by a constitutional amendment or if the Court overturns itself with a new decision.

The legal system provides many institutional constraints in the exercise of power for the members of the Supreme Court. These constraints include precedent, the parameters of constitutional and statutory law, concern for the integrity of the Court as an institution, and the decision-making process of the nine individuals who sit on the Court. Yet, as Justice O'Connor points out, having women on the bench can bring an important diversity to the selection of cases as well as the outcomes that affect policy: "None of this is to say that women do *not* differ from men in the way they exercise power, only that the differences are subtle. We all bring to the seats of power our individual experiences and values, and part of these depend on our gender."[35]

As discussed in Chapter 2, women have been viewed through the public versus private sphere dichotomy since the nation's founding. Legally, women were denied their property and their identity (separate from their fathers or husbands), as well as other rights as equal citizens, into the twentieth century. The judicial system, and particularly the U.S. Supreme Court, relied on "biological essentialism" to rule that women only belonged within the private sphere for nearly 200 years before changing course in the 1970s. With several decisions dealing with women's economic rights, workplace rights, and most notably reproductive rights by the mid-1970s, the Court began to legally view women on a more equal standing with men.[36] As a result, the Supreme Court, in several cases throughout the 1970s and 1980s, developed what is known as the "intermediate" or "heightened" scrutiny test to deal with sex-based discrimination. This judicial test means that any law passed that places women in a separate category from men must be substantially related to the achievement of an important government objective. As a result, the courts, and in particular the Supreme Court, have been sensitive in recent years to problems that women face in the workplace and in dealing with financial matters and have struck down certain discriminatory standards for women as unconstitutional.

WOMEN AS STATE AND LOCAL JUDGES

As part of the federal system of government, each state has its own system of courts. While some states vary in the exact structure of its judicial branch, all state courts have a similar structure to the federal branch with lower trial courts, intermediate appellate courts, and a court of last appeal at the highest level (called supreme courts in most states). Only cases that deal with a federal issue can be appealed from a state supreme court to the U.S Supreme Court. While many people believe that the federal judiciary is the most important court system in the country, nearly 95 percent of all cases are heard in state courts. The selection of judges varies in each state, with methods ranging from partisan elections (for example, Texas) to nonpartisan elections (for example, Oregon and Washington) or political appointment with judicial retention (for example, California, where voters decide with a simple "yes" or "no" to keep a governor's choice on the bench).

In 2016, 5,596 women were serving as state judges (31 percent of the 18,006 positions). Of those, 122 (35 percent) were serving on state courts of last resort (usually the state's supreme court), with 344 (35 percent) on intermediate appellate courts, 3,502 (30 percent) serving on general jurisdiction (district) courts, and 1,628 (33 percent) serving on limited and special jurisdiction courts.[37] In 1976, 20 states had no women judges. During the Carter administration, when the President was actively appointing women and minorities to federal judicial positions, states began a similar trend. By 1979, each of the 50 states had at least one woman serving as a judge. And, between 1980 and 1991, the percentage of women state judges increased from four to nine percent. By 1991, there were 14,094 judges on state courts, including 1,230 women.[38] The states with the highest current percentage of women judges include Oregon and New Mexico, each at 43 percent; 47 percent of the judges in the District of Columbia are women.[39]

The increase in the number of women judges at the state level indicates a change in attitudes among voters in the states that either elect or retain judges through the ballot box. This also suggests that the eligible candidate pool for state judicial positions has broadened in many states to include the career paths of women attorneys, which can differ from that of their male colleagues (for example, more public-sector work or working as a government lawyer). Of the women now serving on state courts of last resort, the demographics of this group suggest that these women are more often selected from a lower state court and have more experience as a prosecutor than their male counterparts. This trend suggests that "extensive judicial experience [may persuade] judicial selectors that non-traditional candidates are capable, despite the dissimilarity in their legal careers to more traditional white, male candidates."[40] Outside factors can also increase the likelihood that women are seated on the state bench. For example, heightened attention to notable appointments on the U.S. Supreme Court of a woman or minority can encourage such appointments at lower levels. Institutional factors can also play a role in encouraging diversity on the bench, such as the number of seats on a court, the length of term, if there is a mandatory retirement age, and the selection process (judicial election vs. appointment).[41] A recent study on state trial court judgeships in Florida and Georgia found that women are frequently successful when they run for these positions and that the best way to increase gender diversity on the bench is when women seek an open seat as opposed to challenging an incumbent or waiting for a gubernatorial appointment.[42]

The increasing number of women and minorities serving on state and local courts has also contributed to a broader understanding of diversity and how that relates to treating all participants within the judicial system fairly and equitably. According to Judge Sophia A. Hall, Circuit Court of Cook County, Illinois, diversity among judges is important when dealing with the complexity of cases at the state and local levels: "The changes have confronted the culture of the judiciary. Diversity has caused judges to realize that fairness cannot be assumed. The complicated social issues affecting families appearing in court have caused judges to realize that effectiveness is not a given."[43] Others have also argued that the judiciary at all levels should "reflect the community that it serves" as it should be able to relate to and understand the life experiences of all participants.[44]

PROFILES IN POWER

Women on the California Supreme Court

As the largest and most diverse state in the nation and as a state often noted for its progressive brand of politics, it is surprising that California has yet to elect its first woman governor. However, the state's highest court cannot be criticized for having a male-dominated bench. Currently, four of the seven justices on the Supreme Court of California are women. They include Chief Justice Tani Gorre Cantil-Sakauye, appointed by Governor Jerry Brown in 2011 and only the second woman to ever hold the position; Associate Justice Kathryn Mickle Werdegar (appointed in 1994), Associate Justice Carol A. Corrigan (appointed in 2005), and Associate Justice Leondra R. Kruger (appointed in 2014). Corrigan, appointed by Governor Arnold Schwarzenegger, replaced Janice Rogers Brown, who now serves on the U.S. Court of Appeals for the District of Columbia Circuit. While Brown served on the California Supreme Court, she was the only African American justice on the Court, was notably more conservative than her other moderate Republican colleagues (there were six Republicans total), and clashed often with moderate Chief Justice Ronald M. George. As a result, she gained the attention of the George W. Bush White House for a possible federal court position. Bush first nominated Brown to the appeals court in 2003, but Senate Democrats successfully blocked her nomination (along with a handful of other conservative Bush appointees to the federal bench) until 2005.

The most notable woman jurist in California's history, however, would have to be the state's former Supreme Court Chief Justice Rose Elizabeth Bird. As the first woman ever to serve on California's highest court on her appointment in 1977, she served on the bench until January 1987. From the start, Bird had a distinguished career in both the law and public service. She received her law degree in 1965 from Boalt Hall School of Law at the University of California, Berkeley (a time when only a handful of women were accepted to top law schools). She clerked for the chief justice of the Nevada Supreme Court after graduation, and in 1966, she became the first woman hired as a deputy public defender in Santa Clara County. She taught at Stanford Law School from 1972 to 1974, and then in 1975, Governor Jerry Brown appointed her as the first woman to serve as a cabinet member in California. As secretary of the agriculture and services agency, she had administrative responsibility over 12 different state agencies.

Under Bird's leadership, the Supreme Court strengthened environmental laws, consumer rights, and the rights of women and minorities. Her accomplishments also included the 1984 adoption of the first rule to permit television and photographic coverage of court proceedings in trial and appellate courts with the consent of the presiding judge. Bird also introduced the first use of word and data processing to the Supreme Court and Courts of Appeal. In 1987, she appointed the Committee on Gender Bias in the Courts, which began the trend for more studies in the years to follow on state courts' treatment of people based on gender, race and ethnicity, sexual preferences, and disabilities.[45]

But more important, Bird received national attention for her opposition to the death penalty, becoming a lightning rod on the issue by invalidating every one of the 58 death penalty cases that she heard on appeal. Supporters of Bird claimed that she had been "appropriately circumspect, cautious, and thorough" in her review of all 58 death penalty cases, and she was joined by at least one other justice in overturning each sentence. Opponents of Bird and her death penalty decisions claimed that she used a "series of minute legal technicalities . . . to prevent the implementation of California's death penalty" as the only California Supreme Court jurist between 1978 (when California's death penalty statute went into effect) and 1986 who had not voted to affirm a single death penalty case.[46] Bird's opponents were eventually victorious, as California voters removed Bird and two of her liberal colleagues from the Court in a two-to-one vote in 1986. The election marked the first time that Californians had voted not to retain a Supreme Court Justice. Bird died in 1999 at the age of 63 from complications of breast cancer. Since leaving the high court, she had remained completely out of the public spotlight. Regardless of one's opinion on the death penalty, perhaps Bird's legacy can be found in the fact that California continues to have the largest backlog of death row inmates in the nation.

DO WOMEN JUDGES ACT DIFFERENTLY?

While much more research is needed in this area to make a stronger and more definitive argument, several studies in recent years point not only to ways that women judges can act differently than their male colleagues, but also how their presence can make a difference in the outcome of specific cases or in the shaping of public policy. An early study of how women on the bench may act differently than their male counterparts showed that in terms of convicting and sentencing, women trial judges generally did not convict and sentence felony defendants differently than men judges. However, the study of 30,000 felony cases during the time period 1971–1979 showed that male judges took a more paternalistic view toward women defendants, and women judges were twice as likely to sentence female defendants to prison than their male colleagues.[47] Since then, other studies have noted that women judges do vote differently on certain issues, and that the presence of a female judge on a panel may influence how other judges view the case, although no definitive relationship between gender and judicial decision making has been shown to exist.[48]

Other studies since then have showed that women judges, regardless of ideology or partisan preference, tend to be stronger supporters of women's rights claims in cases then men judges and that at least one woman serving on a bench (for example, an appeals court that hands down rulings with more than one judge participating) had a strong impact on the outcomes of sex-discrimination cases in favor of women.[49] The appointment of Sandra Day O'Connor in 1981 to the U.S. Supreme Court shifted support for women's rights on the Court, with a smaller impact coming from Ruth Bader Ginsburg's appointment in 1993. However, the two women justices wrote half of the Court's majority opinions in the area of sex discrimination and often served as the Court's "spokespeople" for women's rights issues.[50]

Some feminist scholars have also looked for what is considered a "different" or "feminist" voice in legal decisions emanating from women judges. Little evidence exists to date to show that placing women on the bench has altered modes of legal reasoning throughout the judiciary. Yet, while some argue that more women judges are needed because they bring a different life perspective and empathy to the judicial process, others argue that despite the symbolic nature of having more women judges, a litmus test based on gender for judicial appointments should not exist. According to Judge Diane S. Sykes, U.S. Court of Appeals for the Seventh District, "If the case is being made for the appointment of women judges just because they are women, then I think we are making a mistake about the qualities necessary in a good judge, which of course are not gender-specific. If the case is being made for the appointment of women judges because they subscribe to a gender-based brand of judging, then we are making an even bigger mistake about the nature of the judicial role. To assign gender a kind of qualifying significance risks diminishing the contributions of women judges by emphasizing their gender as if it has something to do with their qualifications for judicial office or has sub-stantive significance in their work."[51]

CONCLUSION

As with other political institutions, women are just starting to make an impact in terms of their representation as judges at all levels of the judicial system. While it may be too early to tell if women judges will dramatically change the processes and outcomes of the judiciary's role in policymaking at both the state and national level, women continue to enter the legal profession in record numbers and will no doubt continue to gain many more judicial positions in the coming years. According to Sandra Day O'Connor, her role and that of her colleague Ruth Bader Ginsburg as the first two women on the Supreme Court was to serve as an important role model for other women aspiring to top leadership positions: "My intuition and my experience persuade me that having women on the bench, and in other positions of prominence, is extremely important. The self-perception of women is informed by such examples, and by the belief of women that they, too, can achieve professional success at the highest levels."[52]

The appointments of O'Connor and Ginsburg, according to Lawrence Baum, reflected "changes in society that made it at least somewhat less difficult for people other than white men to achieve high positions." And as we have seen in recent years, particularly with the confirmation of Sonia Sotomayor and Elena Kagan to the Supreme Court, presidents are now more willing to consider women and members of racial minority groups as judicial nominees. But, according to Baum, "because of the various advantages they enjoy, white men are [still] more likely to enjoy disproportionate representation on the Court for some time."[53] That dominance within the legal profession, however, is not nearly as strong as it once was as women continue to break down barriers to achieve positions of power and leadership within the federal and state judicial branches. With much more work to be done in terms of researching the impact of women judges as they continue to move beyond token status, as well as increasing the number of women nominees to judicial positions, "real changes in the law have been, and will continue to be, the result of the hard work done by women in the American judiciary."[54]

CHAPTER SUMMARY

- For most of the nation's history, women did not have access to the law and the tools that it provided in shaping the political system. The legal disenfranchisement of women in American life lasted throughout the nineteenth and well into the twentieth century. Women faced discrimination in the workplace regarding hours, working conditions, and wages; women lost all legal and property rights on marriage; married women were also denied equal custody rights, the right to keep their wages, and the right to divorce; women were banned from entering into legal contracts and could not file a suit in a court of law; and women were excluded as jurors for decades after they received the right to vote in 1920.
- Only in recent decades have women gained access to the law as equal citizens, as a profession, and as a means to enact political changes. Most barriers for women entering the legal profession did not disappear until the 1970s, with passage of Title IX of the Education Act of 1972, which guaranteed equal access to academic and athletic resources regardless of gender. This dramatically increased the number of women attending law school. By 2014, women represented nearly half (47.7 percent) of all first-year law students in the United States and 34 percent of all attorneys.
- Systemic gender bias within the justice system has long remained a problem for women, both as attorneys and litigants. Subtle discrimination still occurs regarding the demographics of the bench (judges), bar (attorneys), and court personnel; differences in the outcomes for men and women during bail hearings or custody awards; and the general perception of participants based on gender.
- Not until the 1970s did more women become federal judges. Jimmy Carter was the first president to seriously increase the number of women serving in the judiciary. Since then, progress has been slow but steady during the Clinton, Bush, and Obama presidencies.
- Four women—Sandra Day O'Connor, Ruth Bader Ginsburg, Sonya Sotomayor, and Elena Kagan—have served on the U.S. Supreme Court. A fifth woman, Harriet Miers, was nominated to the Supreme Court by President George W. Bush in 2005, but withdrew her nomination.
- Women judges within the federal branch represent important political actors for women's rights. Like other areas of politics, a women's voice within judicial

policymaking has the potential to bring a different perspective to the law. However, recent studies have not shown significant differences between the actions of female and male judges.

- The legal system provides many institutional constraints in the exercise of power for the members of the Supreme Court, including precedent, the parameters of constitutional and statutory law, concern for the integrity of the Court as an institution, and the decision-making process of the nine individuals who sit on the Court.

- In 2016, 5,596 women were serving as state judges (31 percent of the 18,006 positions). The increase in the number of women judges at the state level indicates a change in attitudes among voters in the states that either elect or retain judges through the ballot box.

- Several studies in recent years point not only to ways that women judges can act differently than their male colleagues, but also how their presence can make a difference in the outcome of specific cases or in the shaping of public policy. Women judges, regardless of ideology or partisan preference, tend to be stronger supporters of women's rights claims in cases than men judges, and least one woman serving on a bench (such as an appeals court that hands down rulings with more than one judge participating) can have a strong impact on the outcomes of sex-discrimination cases in favor of women.

STUDY/DISCUSSION QUESTIONS

- What progress have women made in the legal profession since the 1970s? Why has this been so important for women entering judicial positions at both the state and federal level?
- Why have women experienced difficulty in achieving presidential appointment to judicial positions at the federal level?
- How did Sandra Day O'Connor make a difference for women in the legal profession with her service on the U.S. Supreme Court?
- What role have women played within state court systems in recent years?
- How might women judges have an impact on public policies affecting women?

CASE STUDIES

1. **Why have women been more successful moving into the judiciary?**
   Roughly one-third of judicial posts are held by women, compared to about one-fifth of legislative positions and one-tenth of executive positions. In other words, while women have yet to make considerable gains in any branch of government that match their numbers in the broader population, they have enjoyed comparatively more success in the judicial branch. What factors do you think account for this? What norms, expectations, or structural differences make the judiciary more accommodating to women than the other branches?

2. **Do you agree with Sonia Sotomayor?**

As noted previously, a video surfaced during Sonia Sotomayor's confirmation hearing in which she stated, "I would hope that a wise Latina woman with the richness of her experiences would more often than not reach a better conclusion than a white male who hasn't lived that life." Throughout this chapter, we presented evidence that judicial decisions vary little by gender, but some experts disagree, especially when it comes to Supreme Court justices who have more power to put issues on the agenda. Do you agree with Sotomayor that gender and race matter when it comes to reaching better conclusions in court cases? Why or why not?

3. **Are Supreme Court justices more or less powerful than representatives in the other branches?**

Judges are typically thought of as removed from politics because they are experts who are appointed instead of elected, so they are not beholden to campaign contributors or constituent opinion. Also, the job of a judge is to apply an existing set of rules that are established by previous cases and legislative decisions, although there is room for interpretation. How does the political power of a Supreme Court justice compare to the political power of a U.S. senator or a president? What structural or other factors give a Supreme Court justice more power than a senator or president, and what factors limit their political power? What does your analysis tell you about why more women have been able to move into the judiciary compared to the other branches of government?

RESOURCES

- The **National Association of Women Judges** is an organization dedicated to supporting women jurists and promoting equal justice and access to the courts for women.
  http://www.nawj.org
- The **Women's Legal History Biography Project** is a database of articles and papers on pioneering women lawyers in the United States. http://www.law .stanford.edu/library/wlhbp
- The **National Conference of Women's Bar Associations**, an affiliate of the American Bar Association, is an organization representing women lawyers.
  http://www.ncwba.org
- The **Federal Judicial Center** is a research and education agency of the federal courts and includes a biographical database of all former and current federal judges dating back to 1789.
  http://www.fjc.gov

CHAPTER 10

Public Policy: Economic Rights

In 1942, 21-year-old Naomi Parker went to work at a metal press machine at the Alameda Naval Base in Alameda, California. It was the height of World War II, and women across the country had moved into factory work to support the wartime effort. Naomi remembers walking with her father and her 19-year-old sister Ada to the naval base to apply for the job. During her job interview, she was quizzed on the use of different machines and tools, and Ada was asked whether she knew what a differential was. Both young women had an impressive knowledge of tools, and they were hired on the spot. Naomi and Ada were some of the first of more than 300 women who worked in the machine shop at the naval base during the war.

A few months into her work on a lathe machine, a photographer visited the naval base to take some photos for a newspaper story. He snapped a photo of Naomi leaning over the press and captioned it "Well dressed woman worker"; the photo was reprinted in newspapers across the nation. In 1943, J. Howard Miller used Naomi's likeness in a propaganda poster for Westinghouse Electric that was intended to boost moral for factory workers across the country and to attract more women to work in the factories. The likeness of Naomi was featured in a popular poster, wearing the white polka-dot bandana. She was later given the name Rosie the Riveter and became an icon of women's empowerment. After the war, Naomi moved to Palm Springs and worked at the legendary Doll House restaurant that counted Frank Sinatra and other celebrities as regulars. Ada and Naomi are now in their 90s, and they live together in Northern California. Naomi did not discover that she was the face of women's empowerment until 2009. She saved a clipping of the original newspaper article from 1942 that confirmed that she is Rosie the Riveter.

Naomi's experience was typical of the time. Young women went to work in factories in droves during World War II to fill the demand left by men fighting the war. Women were employed in the building of aircraft, ships, weaponry, and vehicles. By the end of the war in 1945, more than 2.2 million women were working in factories, and women constituted 50 percent of the paid workforce. The gains

Rosie the Riveter

This iconic image was part of a government campaign to recruit female workers for the munitions industry during WWII.

SOURCE: SBT4NOW; Flickr

women made were quickly reversed at the end of the war, however, even though 80 percent of women wanted to remain in the jobs they had acquired.[1] But this was not to be. The government worked with private employers to get women back into their homes at war's end. Factories quickly converted to peacetime production and laid off or demoted their female employees. The federal government also stopped funding day care in 1946 to encourage women to return to homemaking.

In the late 1940s, the federal government redirected the propaganda it had used to attract women to factory positions to get them back into the kitchen. From the founding of the nation until the 1940s, most Americans believed that women were "naturally" suited for homemaking, but the workplace experience of World War II proved that women were capable of a variety of roles. The government spent millions on a slick campaign featuring scenes from middle-class suburban life with smiling children and contented wives. The government push to get women back into the private sector was a tough sell because post–World

War II technologies reduced the time required for housekeeping. Washing machines, dryers, self-cleaning ovens, dishwashers, and other advances meant that housekeeping was no longer an all-day task, so middle-class, mostly white women who were able to afford these conveniences had more disposable time than before the war.

The World War II factory work experience profoundly shifted the economic landscape for white, middle-class women. It also shifted the opinion of millions of women that their natural place was working in the home, and once that genie was out of the bottle, it was impossible to lure her back in. Women continued to move into the workforce after the war, mostly in service jobs such as nursing and teaching, because these jobs were deemed socially appropriate for women. This period marked the beginning of women moving in force into paid labor.

There are different ways to measure gains in gender equality in the United States: social, political, and economic. Social advancement refers to the status that women hold in society, a status that intersects with race, class, and sexuality. Political advancement can be seen in the number of women moving into positions of power in governmental institutions, as well as the success of policies aimed at bringing about gender equality. We have explored social and political inequalities in previous chapters in this book, and we now turn our focus to economic measures. Economic equality refers to differences in resources that men and women are able to amass, as well as obstacles to economic success. As with social and political equality, women have seen some improvement in economic equality since the second wave of the women's movement, but inequalities remain.

In this chapter, we examine the economic rights of women and the continuing fight for equity in education and the workplace. We begin with a look at major legislation that has been passed to remedy gender inequality in education. Access to education is the key to higher earnings and economic advancement. Next, we turn to gender inequalities in the workplace. We examine the dearth of women in corporate leadership positions, the wage gap, family leave policy, and sexual harassment and gender harassment. We also consider the causes of the gender wage gap and discuss implicit gender bias in the workplace.

EDUCATIONAL EQUALITIES

Parity in education is important for gender justice because education predicts future earnings, and this is especially true for younger generations. The median annual income for full-time workers ages 25 to 32 with a college degree is $45,500, compared to $28,000 for those with a high school degree.[2] The number of women with college degrees has increased ten-fold since 1940, when 3.8 percent of women completed college.[3] More women have matched men in earning college degrees since the late 1990s, and in 2015, the number of women earning degrees surpassed that of men. According to the U.S. Census, 29.9 percent of men now hold a bachelor's degree compared to 30.2 percent of women.[4] The educational gap is even greater for younger Americans: 37.5 percent of women younger than

35 hold a bachelor's degree compared to 29.5 percent of men under 35. The gender gap is even larger for blacks (12 percent) and Latinas (13 percent).

Experts have provided many reasons for women surpassing men when it comes to earning a college degree. First, due to gender discrimination in the workplace, women need a college degree to escape low-wage labor, while men can typically avoid low-wage jobs with just a high school degree.[5] Another factor that explains the education gender gap is behavior and disciplinary problems in the K–12 years. On average, girls have better school attendance records and higher grades than boys, and boys are far more likely to have a disciplinary record.[6] Cultural expectations of masculine identity encourage defiant and aggressive behavior and simultaneously devalue the educational experience because book learning is framed as "feminine."[7] The current educational achievement gap in higher education advantages women; however, it does not translate into equitable wages. As examined below, the wage gap is even more pronounced for women with college degrees, meaning that even though they now exceed men with regard to the number of college degrees earned, they do not get the same economic return.

The remarkable growth in women's educational attainment is the result of shifting societal norms about women's place in the world and a series of laws intended to make education more gender equitable. Second wave feminists fought tirelessly against great odds and opponents for legal and policy reforms to open doors that most young women today take for granted. The foremost law promoting gender equality in education is Title IX.

Title IX

Title IX of the educational amendments of 1972 outlawed gender discrimination in institutions that receive federal funds, either directly through public schools or indirectly through financial aid. The Civil Rights Act prohibited gender discrimination in the workplace and public spaces, but it did not extend to educational institutions, so Title IX extended similar protections in K–12 schools and colleges and universities. In the year that Title IX passed, 18 percent of women graduating from high school went on to complete a four-year college degree compared to 26 percent of men.[8] As noted previously, that gap has now disappeared, and Title IX played a key role by making educational spaces more gender inclusive.

Title IX exists because of three women. In the 1950s, Edith Green dreamed of being an electrical engineer, but schools would not accept a woman. Patsy Mink wanted to become a doctor, but women were not allowed in the schools where she applied. Bernice Sandler could not get hired as a full-time professor after earning her doctorate because she was a woman.[9] Two decades later, these three women worked together in Congress to champion Title IX legislation. The law was officially sponsored by Representative Patsy Mink (D-HI) and Senator Birch Bayh (D-IN), and it was signed into law by President Richard Nixon with bipartisan support during the height of the women's rights movement.[10]

Bayh's remarks on the Senate floor addressed cultural stereotypes that impede women's education:

> We are all familiar with the stereotype of women as pretty things who go to college to find a husband, go on to graduate school because they want a more interesting husband, and finally marry, have children, and never work again. The desire of many schools not to waste a "man's place" on a woman stems from such stereotyped notions. But the facts absolutely contradict these myths about the "weaker sex" and it is time to change our operating assumptions.[11]

Title IX was originally applied to hiring and employment practices for university employees, but has since been applied to collegiate sports, sexual harassment, and most recently sexual assault/rape.[12] During its 40 years, the impact of Title IX has been dramatic.[13] It has mostly eliminated blatant gender discrimination for students in higher education and has addressed the more subtle forms of discrimination found in differential financial aid packages, housing accommodations, and sexual harassment.[14] Title IX has brought about seismic change in the number of female students, faculty, and administrators on college campuses. In 1970, women earned only 14 percent of PhD degrees, but they now earn nearly 50 percent and comprise nearly 40 percent of the professorate.[15] The number of female college presidents jumped from three percent to 23 percent during this time, and women now outnumber men in the ranks of undergraduate students.[16] Women's participation in Division I sports has risen from 15 percent to 44 percent since the early 1970s.[17]

As discussed in Chapter 12, the Department of Education extended Title IX protections to gendered sexual violence. All students face a higher risk of rape by going to college than not, but female students are far more likely to be assaulted/raped than their male counterparts.[18] The Department of Education has deemed that the elevated likelihood of facing sexual violence for female students creates a gender-inequitable learning environment. The experience of sexual violence in K–12 schools or college is a gender equity issue because survivors typically see a significant decline in their grades and may take time away from school for a time or permanently, all of which affect their career trajectory and earnings potential. Institutional mishandling of sexual violence cases, also known as institutional betrayal, increases the likelihood that a survivor will experience trauma symptoms.[19] This means that institutions can take measures not only to reduce rates of sexual violence, but also to react to survivors in ways that reduce their trauma.

The federal government recently extended Title IX protections to transgender individuals. In 2014 and 2016, the Department of Education issued two nonbinding memos that directed public schools to treat transgender students in ways that are consistent with their gender identity. The 2014 directive specifies that institutions "must treat transgender, or gender non-conforming, consistent with their gender identity in all aspects of the planning, implementation, enrollment, operation, and evaluation of single-sex classes."[20] For example, a transgender girl should be able to use the girl's restroom and participate in girls-only classes and group activities. Transgender students also have the right to be called by pronouns of their choice and to be protected from bullying and harassment. According to a survey conducted by the National Center on Transgender Equality, 82 percent of transgender students feel unsafe at school. Two-thirds (67 percent) have been bullied online, 44 percent have been physically abused, and 59 percent have been denied access to the restroom of their choice.[21] Transgender protections under Title IX are in their infancy and will become further defined in the next decade through lawsuits and federal complaints.

The Women's Educational Equality Act

A second law was passed a few years after Title IX to fund research and programs to address gender discrimination in education. The aim of the Women's Educational Equality Act (WEEA) of 1974 was to address sex-role stereotyping and other gender inequities in primary and secondary schools. The WEEA's mission was mostly accomplished through the funding of grants for gender equity programs and research in schools. The WEEA also established a resource center to share the latest research and information on best practices for gender equity in education, and for the first decade, it was the clearinghouse for research on this subject. Legislators passed WEEA to tackle subtle gender discrimination in education that may not be detected using the Civil Rights Act or Title IX gender provisions. The idea was that discriminatory effects of often invisible gender stereotypes that intersect with other identities may not be actionable through a lawsuit or a federal complaint, but they can be identified and counteracted with research and best practices.

The WEEA never achieved its potential because it was chronically underfunded and understaffed. Since its passage, the White House, under both Republican and Democratic presidents, funded WEEA at a fraction of the amount authorized by Congress. In 1982, President Ronald Reagan changed the implementation of the law by appointing WEEA directors who were openly antifeminist. In response to Reagan actions, Congress rewrote the WEEA legislation to make its mission more explicit. In 2003, President George W. Bush stopped funding the WEEA Resource Center, and in 2010, President Barack Obama stopped funding for WEEA altogether. One directive of the WEEA that never got off the ground was the directive to develop a sustainable Title IX action network at the national, state, and local level to provide incentives and training for Title IX coordinators. Had this network been developed when the WEEA was passed in 1974, the campus sexual violence epidemic might have been addressed decades ago.

Title IX, and to a lesser extent WEEA, has accomplished greater access to education for women and sought to improve the educational environment for all genders. Given the higher risk of sexualized violence against women and transgender individuals in educational settings and high rates of bullying and harassment against LGBTQ students, there is still work to be done to achieve gender equality in education. The gender inequalities, discrimination, and harassment that exist in educational settings also exist in the workplace.

WORKPLACE INEQUALITIES

Women have moved into the workplace in record numbers in the past 50 years and now constitute 47 percent of the paid workforce, but they have yet to achieve parity on wage and leadership measures. The sharp gains of the 1970s and 1980s in corporate leadership have slowed and, in some sectors, even reversed.[22] The number of women in professional positions has steadily increased since the 1970s, with women now occupying 40 percent of all managerial positions in the United States, but progress into the highest echelons of leadership has been slow.[23] Only six percent of the highest managerial positions are held by women, and only four percent of chief executive officers of major companies are female. Women comprise only three percent of the top earners in Fortune 500 companies.[24] According to economist Linda C. Babcock, "I don't think we have come as far as we think we have. We do see some visible women out there at the top of organizations and those with political power, so we just automatically think that everything has changed. But those are really still tokens."[25] A recent survey of senior business executives in the United States and Europe finds that "men are still viewed as 'default leaders' and women as 'atypical leaders.'"[26]

Women have not achieved economic parity with men, as evidenced by the "second shift" of housework that women still perform, the wage gap, family leave policies, and experiences of sexual harassment and other forms of gender-based discrimination in the workplace.

The Second Shift

Women have historically been unduly burdened by the expectation that they manage affairs inside the home, even if they are working part- or full-time outside the home. So even though two-thirds of women work outside the home and women earn more than their husbands in 38 percent of households,[27] women continue to perform a greater share of household chores. According to the Bureau of Labor Statistics, in a typical day, 82 percent of women and 65 percent of men spend some time on household activities such as lawn care, cooking, financial management, and cleaning.[28] Women spend an average of 2.6 hours per day on these activities compared to 2.0 hours for men. Men are half as likely as women to perform cleaning responsibilities, and women do two-thirds of the cooking for the household. This means that even the most financially successful women are typically stuck with what has been called a "second shift" when they get home from work.

The second shift can be traced to the gendering of the public and private domains and the persistent framing of the private sphere as a feminine domain. Liberal feminism, the most popular "brand" of feminism from the second wave, pursued gender equity in business and politics, primarily through new laws, and opened educational and employment doors for American women.[29] The idea that women could and should be able to do anything men do was liberating in tangible ways for millions of American women who chose to work outside the home, but despite their participation in the workforce, women continue to serve as the primary homemakers and caretakers in the private sphere. Marriage and parenting continue to be heavily gendered when it comes to divisions of labor as a result of early socialization. According to psychologist Virginia Valian, "the sexual division of children's play and labor induces both boys and girls to see housework and child care as women's responsibility, a responsibility that, ideally, is performed with love and pleasure."[30] It is therefore not surprising that women who live with a partner/spouse are nine times more likely than men to be primarily responsible for child care and homemaking.[31]

Recent trends in parenting expectations have exacerbated the stress on women who work outside the home and further limited their ability to pursue management opportunities in the workplace. Despite time-saving technological advancements in homemaking, women currently spend more time on housework and child care per week than earlier generations. For example, in 1965, married mothers spent 10.6 hours per week in housekeeping activities, and today, they spend an average of 12.9 hours.[32] These new parental expectations leave women with little time to build professional networks compared to men. Social networking is a more important predictor of advancement in corporations than work performance, so the second shift harms women's upward mobility in the workplace.

PROFILE IN POWER

Esther Peterson

Esther Eggertsen Peterson (1906–1997) was a lifelong advocate for women's rights, worker's rights, and consumer rights. She was one of the most influential leaders of the twentieth century on these issues. Peterson was the fifth of six children born to Danish immigrant parents. She was raised in a Mormon family in Utah. Peterson graduated with a degree in physical education from Brigham Young University and a master's degree in teaching from Columbia University. When she was 12, she witnessed her first labor action when rail-way workers went on strike demanding an

SOURCE: U.S. National Archives and Records Administration

eight-hour workday. Peterson's parents taught her that unions were bad trouble-makers, but she shifted her position on labor activism as a young adult.

As a young adult, she worked as a teacher and a volunteer at the local Young Women's Christian Association (the Y) in Boston. Her first political act was to successfully push for racial integration at the Y after she noted that there were no women of color at her location. Peterson's interest in worker's rights started when most of her students at the Y went on strike. She visited the home of one of her students to learn more about why her classes were so empty and discovered that all of the children in her student's home had to work to pay the bills. Most of the girls in her classes sewed clothing in the garment industry for pittance wages, and they were striking for better pay. Peterson joined the "heartbreakers strike" picket line the next day and became involved with the International Ladies Garment Workers Union. Peterson's next job was with the American Federation of Teachers union. She went on to be the first female lobbyist for the American Federation of Labor–Congress of Industrial Organizations, a federation of labor organizations, and the president of the National Consumers League.

In 1961, President John F. Kennedy appointed Peterson the head of the Women's Bureau in the Department of Labor. She established the President's Commission on the Status of Women to study the status of women in the workplace and private life, and the first report of the Commission sparked a national debate over the lesser value placed on women's work. Peterson was the primary driving force behind passage of the Equal Pay Act in 1963. After Kennedy's death, President Lyndon Johnson appointed Peterson to the new post of special assistant for consumer affairs, and President Jimmy Carter appointed her as the director of the Office of Consumer Affairs. For the next two decades, she established many consumer protections we take for granted today, including "sell dates" on perishable foods, unit pricing in supermarkets so consumers can compare across products, standardization in packing, and nutritional labels. Peterson was awarded the Presidential Medal of Freedom in 1981 by President Ronald Reagan.

The Wage Gap *Purple*

Another barrier to economic gender justice is the wage gap. This gap has inspired nearly a century of activism and policymaking.

History of the Wage Gap

Men have been paid significantly more than women for the same or similar work since the advent of wage labor. Wage labor was rare prior to the Industrial Revolution that started in the 1760s, but when machine production replaced hand production, multiple employees and wage labor became the new norms. Women were paid less than men from the start because men were seen as the family breadwinners and women as working for "pin money"—a small amount of money for nonessential items like clothing or jewelry. According to historian Joyce Burnette, higher male productivity in manual labor jobs also accounted for part of the early wage gap during the Industrial Revolution.[33]

First wave feminists in the United Kingdom and the United States introduced the idea of equal pay in the 1830s. The first strike was organized by members of the Women Power Loom Weavers Association, who went on strike for equal pay in 1832 in textile and clothing factories across London.[34] The following year, members of the Grand National Consolidated Trades Union demanded equal pay in their journal *Pioneer*, arguing that "the low wages of women are not so much the voluntary price she sets upon her labour, as the price which is fixed by the tyrannical influence of male supremacy."[35] This activism was not successful in closing the

↓ radical
 feminists

wage gap. More than 50 years later, female wage workers once again banded to-gether to demand equal pay. In 1888, union delegate Clementina Black proposed the first equal pay resolution to the Trades Union Congress, a federation of trade unions in England and Wales. In response, the Trades Union Congress tried to deny Black entry to their national meeting, but she attended anyway and proposed a motion that garnered only a few votes. Two decades later, Mary Macarthur formed the National Federation of Women Workers to unionize women and strike for equitable wages. The organization raised public awareness about women working in sweatshop conditions, and their lobbying was influential in passing the 1909 Trade Boards Act that set minimum wages in the more difficult trades.

In the United States, the first organized effort to pass equal pay occurred in the late 1860s. A February 1869 letter to the editor of the *New York Times* called for the government to pay its male and female employees the same wages.[36] The letter noted that the 500 women employed by the Department of Treasury earned only half of what their male colleagues earned. These efforts compelled the House of Representatives to pass a bill making it illegal to pay women less than men for the same work in government jobs. The Senate watered down this bill to only include new hires, and it was never enforced in any meaningful way. Still, it sparked a national conversation about equal pay, and in 1883, women workers at the Western Union Telegraph Company halted communications across the nation with a strike for "equal pay for equal work." This strike was not successful in raising wages, but it kept the issue alive in public dialogue. In 1891, the *Washington Post* editorial board declared that "the working world is rapidly coming to apprehend the justice of giving equal remuneration to women who do as much and as good work as men."[37]

The first substantial equal pay law was passed in New York in 1911 and mandated that male and female teachers be paid the same amount. Activism around this issue grew in the twentieth century. In 1918, at the start of World War I, the National War Labor Board deemed that women and men should be paid equally for the same work. The same standard was applied two decades later during World War II. Many male workers and male-dominated unions were supportive of equal pay during World War II because they were concerned they would be paid less when they returned home from the war if female workers were paid lower wages. After the war, the issue of wage equality seemed dead, but the second wave of the women's rights movement changed everything.

Pay Equity Laws
Second wave feminists altered the legal landscape by passing gender equity laws at the national level in the 1960s. The first attempt at national equal pay legislation was introduced by congresswoman Winifred C. Stanley of Buffalo, New York, in 1944. It failed in the House of Representatives, but both the Republicans and the Democrats added equal pay provisions to their platforms in 1952. Several attempts were made to pass legislation in the 1950s, but they failed as well. The first national wage equality law was passed a century after feminist activists first

fought for equal pay. Three major national pieces of legislation have changed the rules of wage inequality in the United States: the Equal Pay Act (1963), the Civil Rights Act (1964), and the Lilly Ledbetter Fair Pay Act (2009) (see Figure 10.1).

In 1963, President John F. Kennedy signed the Equal Pay Act, which made it illegal to pay women and men different wages if they work in the same place and perform similar work. The Equal Pay Act was made possible because of activism from the Department of Labor's Women's Bureau. In 1961, Kennedy appointed consumer and feminist advocate Esther Peterson the assistant secretary of labor and director of the Women's Bureau. Peterson made the Equal Pay Act a high priority and used her contacts as a union lobbyist to orchestrate a campaign urging Congress to pass the bill. The bill was hotly contested in Congress, but it eventually passed with direct pressure from the White House. During the signing ceremony, Kennedy commended those who passed the bill in Congress, but noted that the work was unfinished:

> While much remains to be done to achieve full equality of economic opportunity—for the average woman worker earns only 60 percent of the average wage for men—this legislation is a significant step forward. . . . I am grateful to those Members of Congress who worked so diligently to guide the Equal Pay Act through. It is a first step. It affirms our determination that when women enter the labor force they will find equality in their pay envelopes.

The Equal Pay Act covers all forms of compensation, including wages, bonuses, holiday and vacation pay, and health-care benefits. It also prohibits employers from retaliating against employees who report gender discrimination in the workplace. Wage gaps are allowed if they are based on seniority, productivity, or some other merit-based criteria.

One year later, in 1964, Congress passed the Civil Rights Act, which makes it unlawful to discriminate based on race, color, religion, national origin, or sex in the workplace or facilities that serve the general public. This bill originated with the Kennedy administration, but it was signed into law by President Lyndon B. Johnson after Kennedy's death. With regard to gender in the workplace, the Civil Rights Act went beyond the wage provisions of the Equal Pay Act to also include the terms and conditions of employment, such as gender job segregation or biased hiring, evaluation, and promotion procedures.

Sex discrimination was not initially included in the Civil Rights Act, but Howard W. Smith, the powerful Democratic chairperson of the House Rules Committee and a staunch opponent of racial equality, added it. The National Women's Party had lobbied for the inclusion of sex for years leading up to the Civil Rights Amendment, and their efforts paid off. Smith proposed the amendment in a jocular manner, and his amendment was met with mocking laughter from many male members of Congress. Five congresswomen spoke in favor of the amendment, including Martha Griffiths, who pointed out that "if there had been any necessity to have pointed out that women were a second-class sex, the laughter would have proved it."[38] Historians are divided on whether Smith proposed the amendment in good faith or as a ploy to defeat the larger bill, which he opposed. Either way, the amendment and the larger bill were ultimately approved.

In the year following passage of the Civil Rights Act, one-third of the complaints filed with the regulatory body, the Equal Employment Opportunity Commission (EEOC), involved sex discrimination.[39] The EEOC's slow response to sex discrimination prompted Shirley Chisholm, Betty Friedan, and more than 40 other activists to form the National Organization for Women in 1966 to pressure the government to enforce the sex discrimination clause of the Civil Rights Act. The organization also provided lawyers to women who were interested in filing lawsuits. This strategy overturned state laws that limited the hours women could work, restrictions on the weight women are allowed to lift, prohibitions on night shift work, and exclusion from jobs considered too dangerous for women. Feminist activism pressured the federal government to enforce its laws.

In 2009, President Barack Obama chose the Lilly Ledbetter Act as the first piece of legislation he signed into law. This law amended the Civil Rights Act of 1964 to extend the time a person has to file a complaint of pay discrimination. The Lilly Ledbetter Act was a response to the 2007 Supreme Court decision in *Ledbetter v. Goodyear Tire & Rubber Company* that placed a restrictive time limit on filing a complaint. Ledbetter was a production supervisor at an Alabama Goodyear tire plant for three decades, and by the time she retired in 1998, she was making significantly less than her 15 male counterparts. The Supreme Court ruled that she did not have a case because victims of wage discrimination must file a complaint within 180 days of the date their employer makes the decision to discriminate against them. This meant that Ledbetter would have had to file a complaint shortly after she was hired, in 1978, but she only became aware of the discrimination decades later. Critics assailed this new time limit as being unreasonable in a culture that discourages employees from discussing their wages with one another. In Ledbetter's case, she was told she would be fired if she discussed her salary with fellow employees. Furthermore, with this time limit, employers simply have to hide gender wage discrimination from their employees for six months to legally get away with it.

The Lilly Ledbetter Act made it possible to file a complaint within 180 days of the latest paycheck, but not before lower courts used the Supreme Court's decision to dismiss more than 300 wage discrimination cases. The political debate surrounding the 180-day provision demonstrates that gender wage equality is still a contested issue. The Court's decision was made possible by a conservative shift with the addition of Chief Justice John Roberts in 2005 and Associate Justice Samuel Alito in 2006. In a rare move, Justice Ruth Bader Ginsburg read the dissenting opinion aloud before the Court, a stinging critique of her colleagues who passed the ruling: "In our view, the court does not comprehend, or is indifferent to, the insidious way in which women can be victims of pay discrimination." This rift in the Court over the Ledbetter decision also played out in the 2008 presidential election, with Obama favoring the legislation and prominent Republicans opposing it.

Figure 10.1   Legislation on Wage Inequality

Activists have been pushing for wage equity laws at the state level as well. In 2010, labor organizer Ai-jen Poo worked to pass New York's landmark Domestic Workers Bill of Rights, helping domestic workers, the majority of whom are women of color. This bill of rights granted domestic workers overtime pay, one rest day every week, and recourse for workers who experience racial or sexual harassment. Hawaii passed a similar bill in 2013 and California did so in 2014.

Today, workers who experience gender discrimination can file a federal complaint with the EEOC, a regulatory commission in the executive branch of government that has the power to rule in cases and offer remedies to discrimination victims. Another way to hold public and private institutions accountable for gender discrimination in the workplace is to file a lawsuit through the judicial branch of government. Both tools are used by gender justice advocates to enforce wage and other discrimination laws.

The Current Wage Gap

Even though activists have been fighting for equal wages for nearly a century, the wage gap persists. The overall wage gap is 78 cents, but it varies by race and ethnicity. Asian American women make 90 cents for every dollar a white man makes, followed by white women at 78 cents, African American women at 64 cents, and Latinas at 54 cents. National Equal Pay Day is celebrated in April each year to mark the extra workdays the average woman would have to put in to achieve wage parity with men the previous year. The wage gap narrowed considerably from the 1970s to the 1990s, but little progress has been made since 2001.[40]

The compensation gender gap is even larger than the pay gap. According to White House data, women are less likely to be offered an employee health insurance plan than men, and they are less likely to have a retirement savings plan with their employers. Women with college degrees in higher paying jobs are just as likely as men to have a retirement plan, but men in lower paying jobs are far more likely than women in lower paying jobs to have a retirement plan. Women with retirement plans have significantly lower savings accumulated than men with retirement plans, mostly as a function of the wage gap.

Why do women continue to earn less than men? There is a healthy debate about the causes of the wage gap, but some arguments are better supported by data than others. One popular explanation that is not supported by data is the idea that the wage gap is caused by differences in educational level. Men were more likely than women to graduate from college for most of the twentieth century, but women have matched the number of men's overall degrees since the late 1990s. Women now account for almost half of students enrolled in law school, medical school, and graduate programs in business administration. Differences in overall levels of education no longer exist, and in many fields, they now favor women. This means that educational differences contribute little, if anything, to the gap.

Another popular explanation for the wage gap is the fact that women see a significant decline in wages over time when they have children, but men continue to enjoy pay increases when they become parents. Early research on why this is the case focused on women with children working fewer hours and taking more leave time, but more recent research attributes the childbearing penalty to patterns of workplace discrimination against women.[41] The United States is the only industrialized nation that does not provide paid family leave, and given that most Americans still see women as the default primary caregivers of children, childrearing has a disproportionate impact on women's career potential and earnings.

Another popular explanation for the wage gap is occupational gender segregation, meaning that women are concentrated in certain professions (e.g., teachers, nurses, and librarians), while men are concentrated in other professions (e.g., pharmacists, lawyers, and civil engineers).[42] Occupational segregation does exist, and it does account for some of the wage gap, but it begs the questions of why occupations that attract men are paid more and whether women would choose feminized occupations if given more freedom of choice.

The case of computer science illustrates how implicit gender bias and overt sexism can influence occupational "choice." Many of the people who programmed the first digital computers were women, but the percentage of women in this field declined from a high of 35 percent in 1985 to around 20 percent today.[43] This drop began when personal computers became part of the household and the narrative that computers were for boys emerged. Parents were far more likely to purchase a computer for their sons than for their daughters in the early years of this technology, and narratives showing mostly white and male computer geeks in the late 1980s solidified the cultural narrative that computer science was for men. Today, only 35 percent of degrees in science, technology, engineering, and math (STEM) are received by women, and more than half of women in these careers leave by mid-career because of a "macho" environment that is hostile to women. Cultural norms and expectations reflected and influenced by popular culture limit the workplace options men and women think are appropriate and available to them.

The idea of occupational choice is further complicated by the fact that wages fall when women move into previously male-dominated occupations, regardless of their number of children.[44] According to sociologist Paula England, once women move into a male-dominated occupation, "it just doesn't look like it's as important to the bottom line or requires as much skill. Gender bias sneaks into those decisions."[45] Indeed, researchers at the Council of Economic Advisers find that occupational choice accounts for about 20 percent of the wage gap, but about two-thirds of the gap is not explained by potential experience, age, race, education, industry, or occupation.[46] What does account for the unexplained majority of the wage gap? At a fundamental level, it appears that women's labor is simply valued less than men's labor.

Resume experiments confirm gender bias in evaluating men's and women's labor. A dozen experiments conducted in the past decade show that identical resumes in which only the name differs (by applicant gender) affect evaluations of candidate quality, whether they are hired, and their starting salary. Stark biases against resumes with female names have been found in studies on medical doctors, professors, postdoctoral awardees, general laborers, and musicians. In one study, researchers sent resumes to scientists at an Ivy League university and asked them to rate the applicants. The resumes were identical except for the gender of the applicant, and female applicants were rated significantly lower on competency hierarchy and whether the science professor would be willing to mentor the applicant.[47] The scientists also offered to pay the female applications an average of $26,507 compared to an average of $30,238 for men. Both male and female scientists evaluating the candidates engaged in gender bias, which means that female scientists have internalized the idea that women's labor is worth less than men's labor. It is also notable that when scientists gave harsh evaluations to the applicant, they used ostensibly gender-neutral reasons for their criticism that they did not apply to men at the same rate. This shows that gender bias often comes in forms that are not readily identifiable as such. Resume studies expose gender biases in the workplace that are confirmed by data and experiences in the "real world."

Evidence of the lower status of women's labor can be found in their overrepresentation in low-paying jobs such as child-care provider, fast-food worker, maid, cashier, and home health aide.[48] According to the National Women's Law Center, women make up nearly two-thirds of the 20 million Americans employed in low-wage jobs. Even when education level, age, race, parental status, and marital status are taken into account, women still make up more of the low-wage workforce than men. Nearly half of women in low-wage jobs are women of color, and about 80 percent have at least a high school degree. One in three women in low-wage jobs are mothers, and 40 percent have family incomes below $25,000.[49] Women are concentrated in low-paying jobs because their labor is devalued, as discussed previously. Women require a bachelor's degree to avoid working in low-wage jobs, but men can escape these jobs with just a high school degree. It is also revealing that men in low-wage jobs are paid 13 cents more on average than women, and the gap is even greater for black and Hispanic women. So even in low-paying service jobs, a premium is put on men's labor.

Additional evidence that women's labor is simply valued less than men's is found in the fact that women's education does not yield the same bang for the buck as men's education in terms of earnings. According to White House figures, men and women have similar starting salaries for most occupations requiring professional degrees, but within five years, men's wages start to pass women's wages.[50] According to the American Association of University Women, when major and occupation are accounted for, women still make seven percent less than men on graduating from college, and the gap grows to 12 percent within a decade.[51] Also, the more education a woman acquires, the larger her pay gap. Women with professional degrees are paid an average of 67 cents for every dollar paid to men with professional degrees, and women with master's degrees are paid less on average than men with bachelor's degrees.[52] This means that having more women complete college and earn advanced degrees has not solved the problem of the wage gap. Education does not open the same wage doors for women as it does for men.

Another possible explanation for the wage gap is that women are not as assertive in salary negations as men, but recent research finds that the explanation is not this simple. Overall, women are less likely to negotiate the terms of their first job offer, but even when they do negotiate, they receive less than men. Furthermore, researchers Hannah Riley Bowles, Linda Babcock, and Lei Lai find that women are more likely than men to be penalized for trying to negotiate than men, and women who negotiate are more likely to be viewed as socially incompetent by evaluators.[53] This means that teaching women to "lean in" with salary negotiations can be harmful to their careers because of implicit gender bias and that more women negotiating better salaries will not eliminate the wage gap.

To summarize, the contemporary wage gap is partially caused by caregiving responsibilities, occupational choice, and a lower likelihood of negotiating, all of which derive from cultural gendered expectations. In addition to these factors, the wage gap is also a result of implicit gender bias that causes both men and women to place a lower value on women's labor. Addressing this issue requires altering societal norms and expectations that disadvantage women in the workforce, establishing public policies (e.g., paid family leave) that minimize workplace biases that undercut women, and eradicating implicit gender bias in how we value labor.

PROFILE IN POWER

Ai-jen Poo

Ai-jen Poo is a labor rights activist who has been a force in establishing better working conditions for domestic workers. Her parents emigrated from Taiwan in the early 1970s, and Poo was born in Pittsburgh in 1974. She earned a bachelor's degree in women's studies from Columbia University, where she learned about the power of grass-roots organizing. In April 1995, she was arrested with fellow students during a protest of police brutality that closed down the

SOURCE: Jeremy Bigwood (Institute for Policy Study Flickr)

Manhattan Bridge. She also occupied a building at Columbia University along with about 100 other students to demand more culturally diverse course offerings. Three years later, Columbia's Center for the Study of Race and Ethnicity was created.

Poo first organized on behalf of domestic workers as soon as she graduated from Columbia, and she went on to found Domestic Workers United, an organization in New York that advocates for better working conditions and fair pay for immigrant nannies, housekeepers, and elderly caregivers. In 2010, Domestic Workers United passed the first law in the United States guaranteeing domestic workers basic rights, including overtime pay and legal protections from discrimination and harassment. This Domestic Workers Bill of Rights affected more than 200,000 workers in New York state, and activists across the nation are now using it as a blueprint for legislation in other states.

Today, Poo is the director of the National Domestic Workers Alliance, a coalition of organizations that are working to implement basic rights for domestic workers in every state. After witnessing an increase in domestic workers being employed in home health care, Poo founded Caring Across Generations, a coalition of more than 200 advocacy groups working to reform long-term health-care provisions in the United States to better fit the needs of the elderly, people with disabilities, and caregivers. Poo has received many awards, including the MacArthur "Genius" Award, the Open Society Institute Community Fellowship, and the Woman of Vision Award from the Ms. Foundation. She has been named one of *New York Moves* magazine's "Power Women," one of *Time Magazine*'s 100 most influential people in the United States, and one of *Fortune's* 50 Greatest Leaders.

Family Leave

Women are economically disadvantaged by workplace conditions that fail to accommodate family life since women are still expected to be the primary caretakers of children and other family members in need. Lack of a paid family leave policy means that only financially secure women can take time away from their jobs to fulfill gendered societal expectations of caretaking and that when they come back to the paid workforce, they will face a wage penalty as a result. Although the United States lags with regard to what is seen as a basic right in other countries, political leaders have enacted two major laws to improve the work–life balance in ways that mostly benefit women.

The Pregnancy Discrimination Act of 1978 protects pregnant employees from being fired. This act amended the Civil Rights Act to ban sex discrimination on the basis of pregnancy. It also included a provision for sick leave for women who are recovering from pregnancy or abortion complications and requires employers to cover pregnancy-related health expenses in their employee health-care plans. This law was passed in response to a 1976 Supreme Court decision that pregnancy was not a form of sex discrimination in *General Electric Company v. Gilbert*. In this case, the majority opinion ruled that pregnancy differed from other medical conditions because it was undertaken voluntarily, while the dissenting opinion noted that other voluntary conditions were included in health-care coverage (e.g., vasectomies, attempted suicides, sports injuries). Congress disagreed with the Supreme Court that pregnancy discrimination does not constitute a form of sex discrimination, so they reversed the Court's decision by passing the Pregnancy Discrimination Act two years later. This tug-of-war between two branches of government is typical for advances in gender justice and other culture war issues involving contested rights.

Congress passed a second major act to help new parents navigate their work life. The 1993 Family and Medical Leave Act made it possible for both parents to take time away from work without being fired. It requires larger employers (with 50 or more employees) to provide up to 12 weeks of unpaid leave for emergency medical and family reasons, such as a personal or family illness, military leave, adoption, or pregnancy. The purpose of this bill was to make the balance between work and life easier for employees and to improve child development by allowing mothers and fathers to bond with their children early. When President Bill Clinton signed the Family and Medical Leave Act into law, he was joined on the stage by Vicki Yandle, a receptionist whose employer fired her when she requested a few weeks away from work to care for her teen daughter, Dixie, who had been diagnosed with cancer.

States must uphold federal laws, but states have the constitutional right to extend their application as federal law dictates. With the Family and Medical Leave Act, some states have extended it to apply to smaller employers. For example, in Maine and Maryland, the act is enforced with businesses with 15 or more employees (compared to 50 or more with the federal law). In February 2015, the Department of Labor expanded the definition of "family" under the act to include employees in same-sex marriages or common-law marriages (relationships that are like marriages but without a marriage certificate). The question of precisely how the Family and Medical Leave Act will be applied to these marriages will be worked out through court cases and clarifying directives from the Department of Labor in the coming years.

Sexual Harassment

Another barrier to economic gender justice is the experience of sexual harassment in the workplace. Women have endured sex-based mistreatment in the workplace for most of American history, with little or no recourse. Sexual coercion and violence were commonplace for female slaves held in captive working conditions and "free" domestic workers in the eighteenth and nineteenth centuries. Later, women employed in new clerical and manufacturing positions in the early twentieth century routinely faced verbal, physical, and sometimes sexual assaults from their male bosses. Sexual harassment was a fact of life for women working outside the home for most of the last century, even as greater numbers of women moved into the workforce after the war. Second wave feminist activists changed the workplace landscape by passing laws to protect against workplace discrimination and harassment and through lawsuits and federal complaints with the EEOC to enforce these laws.

The EEOC defines sexual harassment as unwelcome sexual advances, requests for sexual favors, and other verbal or physical harassment of a sexual nature. The legal standards for sexual harassment in the workplace are set by state law and vary from state to state. The harasser can be any person in the workplace—a direct supervisor, an indirect supervisor, a coworker, a client—and men, women, and transgender individuals can file sexual harassment claims. According to a 2016 report from the EEOC, 40 percent of women and about 15 percent of men report behaviors that fit the criteria of workplace sexual harassment.[54] Sexual harassment was deemed unlawful in the 1964 Civil Rights Act because it constitutes sex-based discrimination.

Experiences of sexual harassment vary. According to the EEOC, 51 percent of those who file claims are harassed by their supervisor, and 12 percent involve threats of termination if the worker does not comply with the requests. Industries with the highest rates of sexual harassment include trade, banking, and finance. Sexual harassment in the workplace intersects with gender identity and sexual orientation. Half of all transgender employees report being harassed at work, sometimes involving physical assault and sexual violence, and 60 percent of LGBTQ employees report the same. These high rates of sexual harassment in the workplace have remained constant, despite three decades of employer-mandated training to address this unlawful behavior.

Second wave feminist activists raised public awareness of sexual harassment that led to the enactment of public policy to combat it. Professor Lin Farley from Cornell University popularized the term "sexual harassment" to describe a range of behaviors women face in the workplace. In 1978, she published *Sexual Shake-Down: The Sexual Harassment of Women on the Job*, which detailed shocking experiences of women whose careers and lives had been severely damaged by workplace sexual harassment. In 1979, feminist legal scholar Catharine MacKinnon published the book *Sexual Harassment of Working Women*, which serves as the legal foundation for sexual harassment law. She identified two types of sexual harassment: actions that create a hostile work environment for women and quid pro quo, meaning an employee is offered something (e.g., a promotion) in exchange for a sexual favor.

Sexual harassment law was refined and enforced through many court cases. The first sexual harassment lawsuit, *Barnes v. Train*, was filed in 1974. The plaintiff was fired after rebuffing the advances of her male supervisor, but the Court ruled that this did not rise to the occasion of sexual harassment. Instead, they ruled that it was a case of a supervisor dealing with rejection from an employee he found to be attractive. In the second sexual harassment case, *Williams v. Saxbe* (1976), a court found a supervisor guilty of sexual harassment when he humiliated and eventually fired a female employee who rejected his advances. In 1977, the finding in *Barnes v. Train* was overturned on appeal, a sign that the legal tides were turning for such cases. Starting in 1980, the EEOC began to actively enforce the Civil Rights Act clause that unwanted sexual advances are a type of sexual harassment. Dozens of sexual harassment cases were filed in the following years, but it would take another decade and a high-profile Senate hearing to put sexual harassment back on the public policy agenda.

Sexual harassment was still a relatively unknown phenomenon in 1991 when Anita Hill testified before the U.S. Senate during the confirmation process of

Supreme Court nominee Clarence Thomas. Hill was a law professor who had previously worked under Thomas when he was the head of the EEOC. Hill reported that Thomas had sexually harassed her with discussions of pornographic films (including those with rape and bestiality), women's bodies, and sexual acts after she declined to date him. Hill also told the Senate about an incident in which Thomas pointed at a can of Coke on his desk and asked, "who has put pubic hair on my Coke?" Thomas framed the debate as "a high-tech lynching for uppity Blacks." In other words, Thomas asked the Senate to view these allegations through the lens of race only, instead of Hill's intersectional experience of both race and gender. Thomas was confirmed 52–48, and it was later revealed that four other women were prepared to testify during the Senate hearings with similar allegations, although they were not asked to speak.

The Senate hearing was a loss for advocates against sexual harassment, but it produced two unintended consequences that advanced women's rights. First, the number of sexual harassment claims filed with the EEOC more than doubled within five years after the Hill–Thomas hearings because of heightened awareness of this unlawful behavior. The second unintended consequence of the hearings was to increase women's participation in politics; 1992 was dubbed the "Year of the Woman" because a record number of women ran for and won public office. Political analysts widely attributed this surge in female candidates and voters to public perception that senators would have taken Anita Hill's allegations more seriously if the Senate were not 98 percent male. In October 2010, Thomas's wife and conservative activist Virginia Thomas left a voicemail at Hill's office asking her to apologize for her 1991 testimony against Thomas. Hill publicly responded, "I have no intention of apologizing because I testified truthfully about my experience and I stand by my testimony."[55]

Hundreds of lawsuits and federal investigations have further defined the nuances of sexual harassment law in the United States since the Hill–Thomas hearings. In 2015, the EEOC received more than 6,800 complaints involving sexual or gender harassment, and cases from men are increasing. For example, in *EEOC v. Boh Bros. Constr. Co. LLC* (2015), the EEOC won a jury verdict of $451,000 for Kerry Woods, a construction worker who was routinely harassed by his supervisor for being feminine and not conforming to the gender stereotype of an iron worker. The EEOC is now prioritizing cases of gender harassment against transgender individuals.

In 2012, the EEOC issued a strategic enforcement plan that prioritized the issue of workplace harassment and discrimination based on sexual orientation and gender identity. This strategic plan included specific prohibitions against firing, failing to hire, denying restroom access, harassing, denying a promotion, wage discrimination, or denial of employee benefits based on sexual orientation or gender identity. The EEOC filed its first lawsuits against employers for LGBTQ discrimination in 2016, introducing a new policy area that activists have put on the public agenda. Protections against discrimination based on sex, gender, and sexuality at the state level are far behind the protections offered at the federal level.

Only 19 states currently have laws prohibiting discrimination based on sexuality and gender identity in employment, housing, and public accommodations.

Since 2010, dozens of lawsuits have been filed across the nation by transgender people regarding gender-based workplace discrimination. In 2015, Marlo Kaitlin, a transgender woman, settled her lawsuit against her employer, Wells Fargo. Kaitlin worked at a customer call center, where she was routinely heckled by her colleagues while transitioning, and she was denied access to the restroom of her choice. Kaitlin developed severe depression and contemplated suicide because of the stress from her work environment. That same year, transgender woman Victoria Ramirez settled a lawsuit in Orange County, California, against Barnes and Noble. Ramirez reported that she was repeatedly harassed by her colleagues and told that her appearance was upsetting to customers.

In 2016, Grace Mcallister, a transgender woman, filed a lawsuit against Bear Valley Community Hospital in Big Bear, California, where she worked as an emergency medical technician and emergency room technician. Her harassment started in 2011 when she began transitioning. Mcallister's lawsuit reports that she was bullied and belittled daily by her colleagues and supervisors. Other hospital staff called her "ugly girl" and made fun of her make-up. Administrators also changed her medical insurance policy to avoid covering her gender-confirmation surgery, but state officials ordered the hospital to reinstate Mcallister's previous coverage. She suffered panic attacks and severe depression and did not return to work after an attempted suicide in January 2015 as a result of her work environment. Transgender individuals who face gender harassment in the workplace can now seek legal and other remedies in response because the EEOC has prioritized this form of discrimination.

CONCLUSION

Women have seen significant economic advancement in the past five decades as a result of the second wave of the women's movement, but inequalities remain in educational and workplace settings. In education, women have closed the education gap and are now more likely than men to earn a college degree. However, women and transgender individuals are at a higher risk than male students for sexual violence and gender-based harassment in educational settings. The Department of Education is now focused on reducing rates of sexual violence and gender-based harassment of transgender students to ensure a truly level educational playing field. Another way that gender inequality persists in education is that a college degree does not financially benefit women as much as it benefits men. The gender wage gap is even larger for professional jobs than for jobs that do not require a degree, meaning that women do not receive the same economic return on their college education as men.

Gender bias also exists in the workplace. Women have moved into the paid workforce in record numbers, but they are still mostly missing from top management positions. Women are also paid significantly less than men, especially women of color. The contemporary wage gap can be attributed to gendered living responsibilities, occupational choice, women's lower likelihood of negotiating, implicit gender bias that causes both men and women to place a lower value on women's labor, and sex discrimination. Lack of a paid family leave policy disadvantages women in the workplace in ways that limit their economic advancement. Women also face higher rates of sexual harassment than men in the workplace. Since 2012, the federal government has prioritized gender harassment targeting transgender individuals in the workplace, and a series of lawsuits are helping to define how this protection will be enforced.

CHAPTER SUMMARY

- Economic equality refers to differences in resources that men, women, and transgender people are able to amass, as well as obstacles on the way to economic success. Women have seen some improvement in economic equality since the second wave of the women's movement, but inequalities remain.
- In 2015, women surpassed men in terms of completing a college degree. The remarkable growth in women's educational attainment is the result of shifting societal norms about women's place in the world and a series of laws intended to make education more gender equitable.
- Title IX of the educational amendments of 1972 outlawed gender discrimination in institutions that receive federal funds, either directly through public schools or indirectly through financial aid.
- Title IX was originally applied to hiring and employment practices for university employees, but has since been applied to collegiate sports, sexual harassment, and most recently sexual assault/rape.
- The impact of Title IX has been dramatic. It has increased the number of female students, faculty, and administrators, as well as female athletes.
- In recent years, Title IX protections have been extended to gendered sexual violence on campus as well as transgender harassment and discrimination.
- The Women's Educational Equality Act of 1974 was passed to address sex-role stereotyping and other gender inequities in primary and secondary school through grants for gender equity programs and research in schools. The act was chronically underfunded, and its funding was eliminated in 2010.
- Women have moved into the workplace in record numbers in the past 50 years and now constitute 47 percent of the paid workforce, but they have yet to achieve parity on wage and leadership measures.
- The number of women in professional positions has steadily increased since the 1970s, but few women hold the top management positions, and men are still seen as "default leaders."
- Another barrier to women's economic progress is the second shift, where even the most financially successful women are typically stuck with housework and child-care responsibilities when they get home from paid labor.

- Men have been paid significantly more than women for the same or similar work since the advent of wage labor, and feminist activists have been fighting to change this since the 1830s.
- The first equal pay law was passed in New York in 1911, and the National War Labor Board deemed that women and men should be paid equally for the same work during both world wars.
- In 1963, President Kennedy signed the Equal Pay Act, which made it illegal to pay women and men different wages if they work in the same place and perform similar work. It covers all forms of compensation, including wages, bonuses, holiday and vacation pay, and health-care benefits. It also prohibits employers from retaliating against employees who report gender discrimination in the workplace.
- One year later, in 1964, Congress passed the Civil Rights Act, which made it unlawful to discriminate based on race, color, religion, national origin, or sex in the workplace or in facilities that serve the general public.
- In 2009, President Obama signed the Lilly Ledbetter Act as the first piece of legislation he signed into law in response to a Supreme Court decision that limited the time in which a person can file a claim of wage discrimination.
- Although activists have been fighting for equal wages for nearly a century, Asian American women make 90 centers for every dollar a white man makes, followed by white women at 78 cents, African American women at 64 cents, and Latinas at 54 cents.
- The wage gap is not explained by educational differences, but it is partially accounted for by occupational choice (which is complicated by the fact that societal expectations cause women to "choose" lower-paying professions, and the wages of male-dominated professions decline as more women move into them). Part of the wage gap can be attributed to women negotiating at lower rates than men, although negotiating causes women to be seen as less socially competent.
- The wage gap is partially explained by men and women ascribing less value to women's work. This is evident in resume studies showing that identical candidates are evaluated differently based on gender, as indicated by the applicant's name. It is also evidenced by the concentration of women in low-paying jobs and the fact that the wage gap is even larger for women with college degrees.
- Another bias that explains the gender wage gap is the fact that women see a significant decline in wages over time when they have children, but men continue to enjoy pay increases when they become parents. The United States is the only industrialized nation that does not provide paid family leave that would address this issue.
- The Pregnancy Discrimination Act of 1978 protects pregnant employees from being fired. This act amended the Civil Rights Act to ban sex discrimination on the basis of pregnancy. It also included a provision for sick leave for women who are recovering from pregnancy or abortion complications and requires

employers to cover pregnancy-related health expenses in their employee health-care plans.

- The 1993 Family and Medical Leave Act made it possible for both parents to take time away from work without being fired. It requires larger employers (with 50 or more employees) to provide up to 12 weeks of unpaid leave for emergency medical and family reasons, such as a personal or family illness, military leave, adoption, or pregnancy.

- Another barrier to economic gender justice is the experience of sexual harassment in the workplace. About 40 percent of women and 15 percent of men experience sexual harassment. This behavior is unlawful under the 1964 Civil Rights Act because it constitutes sex-based discrimination.

- Half of all transgender employees report being harassed at work, sometimes involving physical assault and sexual violence, and 60 percent of LGBTQ employees report the same. These high rates of sexual harassment in the workplace have remained constant, despite three decades of employer-mandated training to address this unlawful behavior.

- Feminist legal scholar Catharine MacKinnon published the book *Sexual Harassment of Working Women*, which serves as the legal foundation for sexual harassment law. She identified two types of sexual harassment: actions that create a hostile work environment for women and quid pro quo, meaning an employee is offered something (e.g., a promotion) in exchange for a sexual favor.

- Sexual harassment was still a relatively unknown phenomenon in 1991 when Anita Hill testified before the U.S. Senate during the confirmation process of Supreme Court nominee Clarence Thomas. Thomas was confirmed 52–48, and it was later revealed that four other women were prepared to testify during the Senate hearings with similar allegations, although they were not asked to speak.

- The Hill–Thomas hearings produced two unintended consequences that advanced women's rights: a massive increase in the filing of sexual harassment claims and the "Year of the Woman" in 1992, when a record number of women ran for and won public office.

- In 2012, the EEOC issued a strategic enforcement plan that prioritized the issue of workplace harassment and discrimination based on sexual orientation and gender identity. This strategic plan included specific prohibitions against firing, failing to hire, denying restroom access, harassing, denying a promotion, wage discrimination, or denial of employee benefits based on sexual orientation or gender identity.

- The EEOC filed its first lawsuits against employers for LGBTQ discrimination in 2016, introducing a new policy area that activists have put on the public agenda. Only 19 states currently have laws prohibiting discrimination based on sexuality and gender identity in employment, housing, and public accommodations.

STUDY/DISCUSSION QUESTIONS

- What factors account for the rapid growth in the number of women in higher education since the 1970s?
- What has Title IX accomplished in terms of gender equity in education, and what issues remain?
- What are the causes of the contemporary wage gap?
- What laws have been passed to promote gender equity in the workplace?
- How does sexual harassment differ from gender harassment, and how is the federal government addressing both issues?

CASE STUDIES

1. Should political leaders follow public opinion?

Title IX was initially used to advance women in employment and admissions at colleges and universities. Later, it was used to bring about a more equal playing field for male and female athletes. More recently, Title IX protections have been extended to sexual violence and transgender harassment. This policy evolves as new barriers to gender equity in education are identified and prioritized, but the path has not been smooth or easy. Each new application of Title IX has come with substantial political resistance. On May 13, 2016, President Obama enraged some conservatives when he mandated that transgender students in public schools be able to use the bathroom of their choice. The opposition was quick and fierce. In North Carolina, the governor signed a law that contradicted the White House directive that will work its way through the courts. Critics of Obama's decision accused him of using laws to legislate social policy that most Americans do not agree with. According to a *New York Times*–CBS poll taken shortly after the White House directive, 41 percent of Americans support transgender people using the bathroom of their choice, while 46 percent oppose it and the remainder are unsure. What is the proper role of government in addressing controversial cultural issues? Should our political leaders pass policies that do not have majority public support, or should they be following public opinion? What do your answers to these questions say about how you think democracy should work?

2. Is occupational choice really choice?

Industries tend to be segregated by gender. For example, more men can be found in finance and more women work in K–12 educational institutions. As noted previously, occupational choice is one factor that accounts for the gender wage gap. But do women really choose to go into low-paying jobs? And for professional positions, do women just happen to choose occupations that tend to be lower paying? Studies show that wages decline in male-dominated professions when women enter them, which suggests that the presence of women in occupations is driving wages rather than aspects of the profession. Industry gender segregation and occupational choice must be addressed if we want to eliminate the wage gap. What policy or social change do you think can remedy the fact that women's labor is not valued as highly as men's labor?

3. **Why aren't men taken seriously when they file harassment and discrimination cases?**

Most cases of sexual harassment involve discrimination against women, but in some cases, the harassment is aimed at men. Although victims of sexual harassment can experience severe consequences in their personal and professional lives, it is not viewed as a serious issue by many people. Sexual harassment against men is especially not taken seriously. About 15 percent of men will experience sexual harassment during their working years that comes in the form of unwanted sexual attention, sexual coercion, or being demeaned based on their gender (for example, being teased for taking time away from work when a baby is born). What cultural dynamics cause sexual harassment against men to not be taken as seriously as harassment against women? What double standards and expectations do men and women encounter in the workplace and, beyond that, explain why sexual harassment targeting men is not seen as a real issue?

RESOURCES

- The **National Coalition for Girls and Women in Education** is a coalition of more than 50 groups that are dedicated to improving educational opportunities for girls and women through policy advocacy and research.
http://www.ncwge.org
- The mission of the **American Association of University Women** is to promote equity and education for girls and women by advocating for educational, social, economic, and political issues.
http://www.aauw.org
- The **National Committee on Pay Equity** is a coalition of organizations with the shared goal of achieving pay equity through research and policy advocacy.
http://www.pay-equity.org
- The **National Women's Law Center** advocates for policies and laws that advance the interests of girls and women.
http://nwlc.org
- The **National Center for Transgender Equality** is the leading nonprofit advocacy organization for the interests of transgender people.
http://www.transequality.org

CHAPTER 11

Public Policy: Reproductive Rights

Norma McCorvey (née Nelson) was born in Texas in 1947. Her father left the family when she was a young teen, and she was raised by her mother, who suffered from alcoholism. Having been neglected and sexually abused by a male relative, she frequently acted out and got in trouble with the law. At 16, she met and quickly married an older man, Woody McCorvey, who physically abused her. McCorvey left her husband within a year, shortly after their first child was born. As a single mother and a survivor of rape and domestic abuse, McCorvey became depressed and developed a drinking problem. She lost custody of her first child, and when she became pregnant with a second child a year later, she put that baby up for adoption.

When McCorvey became pregnant for the third time in 1969, she tried to get an abortion. However, the state of Texas only allowed women to obtain abortions in cases of incest or rape. McCorvey was contacted by two young attorneys, Linda Coffee and Sarah Weddington, who filed a lawsuit on her behalf, arguing that she had a fundamental right to obtain an abortion. McCorvey, also known as "Jane Roe," became the plaintiff in the case that would make its way to the U.S. Supreme Court (*Roe v. Wade*) in 1973. This case established abortion as a fundamental right under privacy rights implied in the Constitution, but McCorvey gave birth well before the case was decided. She put her third baby up for adoption.

After *Roe v. Wade*, McCorvey went to work in a Dallas abortion clinic. In 1994, she published her autobiography, *I Am Roe*, in which she identified her long-time lesbian partner, Connie Gonzalez. McCorvey also detailed her conversion to Christianity, her shift to the pro-life position, and her work with the pro-life organization Operation Rescue that organized protests outside of abortion clinics. She expressed regret that she was the test case that gave women abortion rights across the nation. A decade later, McCorvey renounced her lesbianism. For many decades, she was a vocal pro-life advocate. In 2005, she unsuccessfully petitioned the Supreme Court to overturn *Roe v. Wade*. In 2009, she protested outside of President Barack Obama's commencement speech at the University of Notre Dame because of his pro-choice stance on abortion. McCorvey remained committed to overturning *Roe v. Wade*, the case that blazed the trail for what is now seen as a fundamental right for women, until her death in 2017.

There are two primary ways to prevent reproduction: abortion and contraception. McCorvey's experience speaks to the many issues involved in family planning, defined as the ability to control the number of children in a family and the timing of their birth. Despite advances in social, economic, and political gender equality in the past half century, women are still expected to be the primary caretakers of children. This makes family planning a fundamentally gendered issue. Self-determination in family planning varies intersectionally. Women with greater economic resources have more access to family planning tools, which means they have more control over the number and timing of their offspring. Experiences of sexual violence and domestic violence may also diminish a woman's power to plan her family. Additionally, some women subscribe to religious or political beliefs that limit family planning options. We analyze the various types of family planning tools available to women as well as factors that enable women to have more or less freedom in their reproductive decisions.

The more notable contemporary trend in family planning is that more women today are choosing not to have children than ever before. The trend started in the late 2000s, and according to the U.S. Census Bureau, nearly half of women of childbearing age (ages 15–44) today do not have children.[1] As a result of innovative technologies and more flexible roles for women in society, family planning is more of a choice than it has ever been (although this varies by socioeconomic status). For the first time in U.S. history, about half of American women are choosing to have children, and the other half are choosing not to. But the choice is often not simple because family planning is fraught with politics, as explored throughout this chapter. Reproductive rights are highly political because they involve the ability of women and men to choose when and how they will have children, which are fundamentally questions about personal freedom.

We organize this chapter on family planning into two sections: efforts to prevent the birth of children (abortion and contraception) and efforts to have children (in vitro fertilization [IVF] and adoption). In the first part of this chapter, we examine efforts to prevent reproduction, starting with abortion. The battle surrounding abortion has been going for more than half a century, and we examine the arguments and activism on both sides of the debate, as well as laws regulating abortion. Next, we examine the history of contraceptive development and use in the United States and controversies involving birth control, laws and controversies surrounding sex education, and sterilization.

We then examine family planning efforts to have children. We describe the development of IVF technology and laws governing this practice. IVF entails fertilizing an egg with sperm in a laboratory and then implanting the egg in a woman's uterus. Some religions and pro-life activists vocally oppose this procedure. We also examine adoption trends and laws with a specific focus on controversies involving same-sex couples, transracial adoptions, international adoptions, and a gender preference for female babies.

WAYS TO PREVENT REPRODUCTION

In this section, we describe the history, laws, and controversies surrounding abortion and family planning. We include birth control, fertility, sterilization, and adoption in our examination of family planning.

Abortion

As noted in the chapter opening, abortion is a highly controversial public policy issue. In terms of rates of abortion, half of all pregnancies in the United States are unplanned, and of those, four in ten end in abortion.[2] In other words, about one in four pregnancies is terminated each year in the United States. Most abortions (61 percent) are performed on women who already have one or more children.[3] Each year, approximately two percent of women in the United States have an abortion,[4] adding up to 1.1 million abortions annually.[5] Rates of legal abortion immediately rose after *Roe v. Wade*, hit a plateau in the 1980s, and have steadily declined in the decades since.[6] This decline is likely the result of a combination of more reliable contraceptive methods and efforts by pro-life activists to stigmatize abortion, which we discuss below.[7]

Abortion rates vary by age, race, income, and religion. About one in five abortions are performed on women under 18,[8] while women in their 20s account for half of all abortions performed.[9] One in three abortions are performed on women older than 30. White women account for 36 percent of abortions, while African American women account for 30 percent, Latinas account for 25 percent, and women of other ethnicities account for nine percent of abortions.[10] Since abortion became legal in 1973, it has become more concentrated among low-income women of color than among white woman.[11] Four in ten women who receive abortions live well below the poverty line.[12] In terms of religious identification, 37 percent of women who obtain an abortion identify as Protestant, while 28 percent identify as Catholic.[13]

When asked why they had an abortion, 75 percent of women cited concerns about existing responsibilities to other people (e.g., children, elderly parents). Three in four women say they had an abortion because they could not afford a(nother) child. About half say they had an abortion because they were experiencing problems with their partner or husband.[14] In short, the vast majority of women who choose to have an abortion do so out of concern that they will not be able to adequately provide for the child. Most women have no short- or long-term negative mental health effects, and most also report a sense of relief after an abortion because unintended pregnancies are stressful.[15]

The Abortion Debate

People who oppose abortion take the pro-life side of the debate. Members of the pro-life movement believe that life begins at conception, so they view abortion as the taking of a human life. Some pro-lifers also believe that abortion constitutes unjust discrimination against the unborn because it deprives the potential person of a future. People who support a woman's right to an abortion are on the pro-choice side of the debate. The primary pro-choice arguments are that a woman has a right to control her own body and that denying women the right to abortion promotes inequality between the sexes when it comes to self-determination. Each side has articulated its positions through well-organized public education and political lobbying campaigns.

The abortion debate began in the 1960s with a few organized pro-life efforts led by Catholic organizations, but the prominent pro-life movement of today was started by the Evangelical arm of Protestantism in the late 1970s. The pro-life movement has often been characterized as a response to *Roe v. Wade*, but in actuality, it started nearly a decade later when Protestant religious leaders decided they needed to increase their political clout in response to government efforts to desegregate private Christian schools.[16] Prominent reverend Jerry Falwell formed the Moral Majority in 1979 to work with the Republican Party on the school segregation issue and a host of other moral issues, including abortion.[17] This new alliance of Protestant religious leaders and Republican Party leaders was successful in attracting moral voters away from the Democratic Party and in giving religious ideas more of a voice in public policy.[18] A pro-life position has become a requirement for Republican presidential contenders, and during the presidencies of Ronald Reagan and George W. Bush, the pro-life side enjoyed a vocal advocate in the White House.

Over the years, the pro-life movement developed into a well-funded, sophisticated operation that involves national demonstrations, lobbying of state and national officials, mobilizing voters during elections, picketing clinics that provide abortions, "sidewalk counseling" of women going into clinics that provide abortions, and the creation of crisis pregnancy centers that front as abortion clinics to reach and discourage women from having an abortion.[19]

On the pro-choice side, Planned Parenthood is the most prominent pro-choice organization in the United States. In 1955, Planned Parenthood kicked off the national abortion debate when it hosted the conference "Abortion in the United States," which featured experts from across the nation. This conference sparked a national dialogue about the pros and cons of making the procedure legal and put pro-choice activists on the path to legalizing abortion. As religious groups were organizing to move against the legalization of abortion in the 1960s, more pro-choice organizations formed to fight for legalizing them, notably, the National Association for the Repeal of Abortion Laws (NARAL).[20] Abortion activists from the women's rights movement of the 1960s successfully fought to enact *Roe v. Wade*, and since *Roe*, the pro-choice movement has grown in size and membership.[21] Pro-choice organizations continue to engage in legal, legislative, and political battles to keep abortions legal and accessible to women in need. While pro-life advocates "lost" with *Roe* at the federal level, they redirected efforts to the state level, and many of these efforts have come to fruition in the past few years.

In other words, even though abortion was legalized 40 years ago, the abortion debate in America rages on.

Both the pro-life and the pro-choice sides claim that public opinion is on their side, and in different ways, it is. A close examination of public opinion polls shows that a majority of Americans do support abortion rights for women, but with significant restrictions. Sixty percent of Americans support abortion in the first trimester (the first three months), but support drops significantly for abortions in the second (28 percent) and third (14 percent) trimesters.[22] Even during the first trimester, support for abortion is only high in cases of rape and incest or when the mother's health is at risk. One in four Americans support abortion with no restrictions, which means that three-quarters of Americans favor some restrictions on abortion.[23] Looking beyond legality to morality, half of Americans (49 percent) think that having an abortion is morally wrong, 15 percent say it is morally acceptable, and 23 percent do not consider it a moral issue.[24]

Support for abortion varies by religion, education, race, region, income, political party, and gender. Pro-choice Americans are more likely to be female, Democratic, white, have no religious attachments, have a higher level of education, have higher incomes, and live outside the South.[25] By contrast, pro-life Americans are more likely to be people of color, male, Republican, Catholic or Protestant, live in the South, and have lower levels of income and education levels.[26] A majority of women under age 50 identify as pro-choice, while a majority of women 50 and older are pro-life.[27]

When it comes to the *Roe v. Wade* decision, most Americans support *Roe*, but 29 percent want it overturned. Somewhat surprising is the finding that young Americans seem to know little about this landmark abortion rights case. In a 2013 poll, only 44 percent of individuals under 30 accurately identified that *Roe v. Wade* concerned abortion, while one-third inaccurately linked it to another policy area and one-quarter stated that they did not know the content of the case.[28] These findings indicate that the pro-life and pro-choice movements have both failed at informing young people about this important policy issue.

Public support for abortion has been stable for decades, but moderate shifts have occurred in the past two decades. The number of Americans identifying as pro-choice dropped from 56 percent in 1996 to 48 percent in 2013, while the number of pro-life identifiers increased from 33 percent to 45 percent during this same period.[29] In other words, even though more Americans identify as "pro-choice" than as "pro-life," the pro-life label is becoming more popular as the pro-choice position is losing popularity. Furthermore, while the percentage of Americans who support abortion with restrictions has also remained stable—around 50 percent—the percentage of Americans who support abortion with no restrictions dropped from 34 percent in 1993 to 26 percent in 2013. These shifts indicate that while the United States is still a majority pro-choice nation, the pro-life movement has successfully persuaded some Americans in recent decades.

PROFILE IN POWER

Wendy Davis

Wendy Davis is a lawyer and Democratic politician from Fort Worth, Texas, who became a household name in 2013 after a valiant effort to stop Texas from passing a bill that severely restricted women's reproductive rights. This was her first nationally televised fight, but likely not her last. Davis was a poor child from a medium-size Texas city who made it all the way to Harvard Law School. She was born in Rhode Island in 1963, and her family relocated to Texas when she was 11. Her parents divorced soon after, and Davis and her three siblings were supported by her mother, who worked a series of low-paying jobs. Davis started selling newspaper subscriptions and working at a juice stand when she was 14 to help with family expenses. She

SOURCE: Gage Skidmore

worked throughout her high school years and still managed to become a member of the National Honor Society. After working odd jobs for years to take care of her young daughters, Davis went back to school. She graduated from Texas Christian University with a degree in English and then went on to Harvard Law School.

In 1999, Davis was elected to the Fort Worth City Council as a Republican, a position she held for nine years. She was then elected to the Texas Senate, where she served from 2009 to 2015. Davis shot into the national spotlight on June 25, 2013, when she led an 11-hour-long filibuster in the Texas legislature to block Measure 5, a bill that banned abortions after 20 weeks of pregnancy, required that abortion facilities meet the same standards as hospital surgical centers, and required abortion providers to have privileges at a nearby hospital. Davis wore a pair of bright-pink running shoes during the filibuster, which became an iconic symbol of her fight for reproductive rights that went late into the night.

Davis was able to block the bill's passage that session, but it was passed the following month. Measure 5 resulted in the closure of more than half of the 40 abortion clinics in Texas, but on June 27, 2016, the Supreme Court struck down Measure 5, ruling that the regulations are medically unnecessary and pose an unconstitutional threat to women's right to abortions. Davis's filibuster drew national media attention, and she was encouraged to run for governor by prominent Democratic funders in 2014. As a Democrat in a solidly Republican state, Davis lost by a significant margin. But this will likely not be her last political race since she has developed a reputation as a fearless advocate for women's reproductive rights.

Abortion Laws

In ancient times, abortion and the killing of infants (infanticide) were decisions made by family patriarchs with little consideration for the rights of women, fetuses, or infants.[30] Questions of when life begins were posed in public discussions, but abortion and infanticide were not legally or socially sanctioned during this time, and patriarchs used them routinely for population control and to ensure that they had male heirs to inherit property. Abortions have been performed for thousands of years in every society studied.

Abortion was legal when the United States was founded, and state restrictions on abortion are a recent development. Connecticut was the first state to criminalize abortion in 1821, and by 1900, every state had laws limiting abortion.[31] Prior to this wave of laws, abortion was common and acceptable prior to the "quickening" (about four months into a pregnancy), and commercial abortion remedies were widely sold.[32] The American Medical Association (AMA) was instrumental in passing early abortion bans to establish their professional credibility compared to midwives.[33] The AMA's antiabortion campaign played on the nativist and anti-Catholic sentiments of the time from a decline in white Protestant birthrates coupled with a dramatic increase in nonwhite and Catholic immigrants.[34] In other words, white Protestant Americans favored abortion restrictions to increase their numbers in the face of immigration "threats."

Making abortion illegal also served as an important tool for controlling women's sexuality. Women who suffered complications from an illegal abortion were routinely denied medical care until they named the "back-alley" (illegal) abortion provider and the man who got them pregnant. (It is important to keep in mind that birth control was not widely available in the United States until the 1960s.) Many doctors continued to provide abortions, some estimate at the rate of two million a year, twice the number that are performed today.[35] Physicians performed about 90 percent of abortions during the approximately 70 years it was illegal, and back-alley abortions resulted in the deaths of an estimated 5,000 to 10,000 women per year.[36] These deaths disproportionately affected poor women and women of color.[37]

The *Roe v. Wade* decision deemed abortion a fundamental constitutional right in 1973. At the time, 30 states prohibited all abortions, and 20 states had some exceptions (e.g., incest and rape). The justices ruled that a woman's right to privacy is protected under the due process clause of the Fourteenth Amendment, which prevents an arbitrary denial of life, liberty, or property by the government. The *Roe* ruling confirmed that the government has two competing interests to consider with abortion: protecting the mother's health and the "potentiality of human life." Given these competing interests, the Court held that, prior to fetal viability (the ability of the fetus to live outside of the mother),[38] decisions to terminate a pregnancy should be left up to a woman and her physician. The Court also ruled that the state's interest in the health of the fetus and the woman increases over the course of her pregnancy and that states could limit postviability abortions. Forty-one states now have limits on postviable abortions.

Roe also established the trimester (12 weeks) threshold for state interest in the life of the fetus, but this standard was modified in the 1992 Supreme Court case *Planned Parenthood v. Casey*, which replaced the trimester standard with the "fetal viability" standard. Casey also made it easier for states to justify restrictions on a woman's right to abortion. *Casey* established that states could limit abortion rights as long as they do not create an "undue burden" for women, as determined by state authorities. In 2003, Congress enacted a ban on late-term abortions, and the Supreme Court upheld the constitutionality of the law five years later in *Gonzales v. Carhart.*

More than 20 court cases have been decided since *Roe v. Wade*, all of which have upheld a woman's fundamental right to an abortion. However, states have passed many laws limiting access to abortion, including requiring parental permission, banning late-term abortions, and implementing mandatory ultrasounds, mandatory waiting periods, and required "counseling sessions" to discourage women from obtaining abortions. In the four decades since *Roe v. Wade*, states have passed 1,074 laws that restrict abortion. One-third of these laws were passed from 2010 to 2015, making this period the most restrictive since the landmark decision.[39] This means that while pro-choice advocates have established a woman's constitutionally protected right to an abortion, pro-life advocates have recently been able to limit the exercise of these rights by passing restrictions at the state level.

In the past decade, pro-life activists have come up with a new way to limit abortion rights: fetal pain laws. These laws are based on the idea that abortion should be banned as soon as a fetus can feel pain, which has inspired a fierce political debate as to when this happens. A thorough study of 112 articles on fetal pain found an emerging consensus among neurobiologists that fetuses likely cannot feel pain until the third trimester, too late in the pregnancy to legally have an abortion unless the mother's life is in danger.[40] Despite the scientific evidence, legislation to ban abortions earlier in the pregnancy based on fetal pain have twice been proposed in Congress, and legislators in 25 states have considered similar legislation. Since 2010, six states have banned abortion on or after 20 weeks on the basis of fetal pain, despite overwhelming scientific evidence that fetuses do not feel pain until 24 weeks into a pregnancy. The Supreme Court will likely hear cases involving fetal pain restrictions on abortion in the near future since it appears to violate the viability provisions in *Roe v. Wade*.[41]

The practical ability of a woman to obtain an abortion has been curbed at the state level in recent years through a series of state restrictions that stop short of outlawing abortion. For example, there were more than 40 abortion clinics in Texas in 2013 when the state legislature initiated a series of restrictions to curb abortions.[42] Today, there are fewer than 20 clinics in Texas. One restriction was to require abortion providers to have admitting privileges at a hospital within 30 miles of their clinic, which meant that abortion clinics in rural areas had to close their doors. Other measures required clinics to meet hospital-like standards for room size, doorways, and anesthesia that were difficult to comply with. Many of these restrictions were overturned by the Supreme Court in 2016, but not before half of the abortion clinics in the state were forced to close. These closures mostly affected poorer Latina women in rural areas. In other words, efforts to restrict abortion intersectionally affected women based on race and class. While middle-class, white women in cities like Houston and Dallas still have access to multiple abortion providers, women of color in the panhandle and West Texas have limited access to exercising their right to an abortion.

Contraception

Contraception, also known as birth control, comes in many different forms, including devices placed in the uterus (intrauterine devices), hormonal methods (e.g., pills, patches, vaginal rings, and injections), physical barriers (e.g., diaphragms, female and male condoms, and sponges), sterilization (tubal ligations for women and vasectomies for men), and fertility calendar approaches that avoid days of the menstrual cycle when pregnancy is possible. There are also less effective methods for preventing pregnancy, such as spermicides and withdrawal before male ejaculation. According to the Guttmacher Institute, 99 percent of women of childbearing age have used some form of contraception at some point, and 62 percent are currently using birth control.[43] Married women are more likely to use birth control, while poor women and African American women are less likely to use contraception. Although some religions are opposed to birth control use, contraception use is common for women of all religions. Nine in ten Catholic and Protestant women use some form of birth control.

Different forms of birth control are more popular than others. Female sterilization and the pill have been the two most used methods since the early 1980s. Two-thirds of women use a nonpermanent form of birth control, such as the pill, the patch, a vaginal ring, or an intrauterine device. One in four women use sterilization for birth control.[44] Nearly six million women rely on male condoms as their primary form of birth control, and teens and women in their 20s are more likely to use this method.

Many young women and men do not have easy access to information about contraception because religious activists have lobbied successfully for abstinence-only sex education programs, which have been funded by the federal government since 1982. Today, one in three high schools offer abstinence-only sex education.[45] Two decades of research on the subject finds that abstinence-only sex education increases the rate of teenage pregnancy if it is offered without education on birth control and that comprehensive sex education with access to birth control significantly decreases the rate of unwanted pregnancies for teens.

PROFILE IN POWER

Margaret Sanger

Margaret Sanger (1879–1966) is the founder of the modern birth control movement. She was born in Corning, New York, to Irish immigrants who shaped her dedication to women's rights. Her father, Michael, was a stonecutter, atheist, and activist for women's suffrage. Her mother, Anne, experienced 18 pregnancies with 11 live births before dying at the young age of 40. Sanger was the sixth of 11 children, and she spent most of her free time in childhood caring for younger siblings. Later, she attended nursing school at White Plains Hospital before moving to New York City with her husband and their three children.

Sanger worked as a nurse in impoverished neighborhoods on the east side of New York City, where she witnessed working-class immigrant women's struggles with unwanted pregnancies and attempted abortions. In 1911, she wrote two columns on the issue for the *New York Call* about birth control, and the publication received many complaints regarding her frank discussion of sex, which was considered too racy for the time. She had found her calling.

SOURCE: Library of Congress Prints and Photographs division, reproduction number LC-USZ62-29808

Sanger's early activism involved writing and speaking about birth control, a taboo subject in the early twentieth century. In 1914, she was prosecuted under obscenity laws for her book, *Family Limitation*, so she fled to the United Kingdom until it was safe to return to the United States. In 1916, she opened the first American birth control clinic in Brooklyn, soon after which she was arrested for distributing birth control pamphlets. Her trial generated controversy and raised the profile of her efforts, and donations poured in from numerous benefactors, including John D. Rockefeller.

Sanger wanted women to have control over family planning as a way to have more control over their lives, and she also wanted to prevent the back-alley abortions that were common at the time. She believed that contraception would prevent abortions, so she focused her efforts there. In 1921, she started the American Birth Control League, later renamed Planned Parenthood. This nonprofit is now the world's largest nongovernmental provider of women's health care and family planning. Sanger was Planned Parenthood's first president. In the early 1950s, she convinced philanthropist Katharine McCormick to fund the research of biologist Gregory Pincus, who was developing the first birth control pill. After years of research, the pill was ready for public use, and Sanger and other activists successfully lobbied for its approval by the Food and Drug Administration. Sanger's work spanned nearly a century, and she remained the president of Planned Parenthood until she was 80 years old. Without her, this chapter on reproductive rights would tell a different story.

The Pill

Various forms of birth control have been used since antiquity, but effective methods were discovered in the twentieth century, the most notable being the pill. In 1916, feminist writer and nurse Margaret Sanger opened the first birth control clinic in New York City, and a line of women formed outside the clinic to obtain contraception information. Nine days after opening the clinic, Sanger was arrested under obscenity laws. The clinic was closed, but a political movement to give women access to birth control information and supplies began. Sanger founded the American Birth Control League, a network of women with a mission to share information about birth control that was the precursor to Planned Parenthood. Chapters of the American Birth Control League opened across the United States, and its efforts to raise public awareness politicized the topic of birth control and empowered women to demand access to contraceptive methods.

In the 1950s, Sanger worked with endocrinologist Gregory Pincus and heiress Katharine McCormick to create a safe hormonal form of birth control. In 1957, the U.S. Food and Drug Administration (FDA), which regulates medication, approved "the pill," but only for severe menstrual disorders, not as birth control. In the following years, an unusual number of women came forward to report menstrual disorders. The pill was approved for contraceptive use in 1960, and within two years, 1.2 million women were using it for family planning purposes. Six million women were using the pill within five years of its approval by the FDA.

FDA approval of the pill for birth control ignited controversy. In 1968, the Pope formally stated his opposition to the pill, and in 1969, Dr. Barbara Seaman published *The Doctor's Case against the Pill*, which examined the side effects, including heart attacks, weight gain, stroke, and blood clots. In 1970, the Senate held hearings on the safety of the pill, which resulted in more warnings for the medication, and nearly two decades later, the original high-dose pill was taken off the market based on new studies showing that second-generation birth control pills had fewer side effects. The pill used to contain higher levels of estrogen, a hormone that tricks the body into thinking it is already pregnant, but newer pills have far lower levels to prevent blood clots.

Newer birth control does not mean more effective or safer birth control. Fourth-generation birth control pills were developed in the past decade by pharmaceutical companies to maintain their profits as patents on older pills expired. Medical research shows that these fourth-generation contraceptives contain the chemical drospirenone, which is significantly more likely to cause blood clots than previous-generation pills. Multiple studies have found that these pills—Yaz, Yasmin, and Beyaz—have twice the risks of other hormonal contraceptives.[46] Similarly, the Nuvaring, a hormonal form of birth control that is inserted into the vagina, has been found to have a higher risk of blood clots. To date, more than 10,000 plaintiffs have filed lawsuits against the manufacturers of fourth-generation birth control products claiming that consumers were not properly informed about the elevated risk of blood clots from these pills compared to previous-generation pills. To date, pharmaceutical companies have paid hundreds of millions of dollars to settle these claims, and thousands of cases are still pending. What started out at a feminist project to give women more control over their lives has now become big business, where profits are sometimes prioritized over women's health.

Sterilization

Sterilization is another form of birth control that has been embroiled in controversy. For women, sterilization entails a tubal ligation in which the fallopian tubes are severed and tied together to prevent pregnancy. In the first half of the twentieth century, countries across the globe instituted forced sterilization policies, including the United States. In 1907, Indiana passed a state eugenics law that enabled state officials to sterilize women who were poor, had mental health issues, or engaged in criminal behavior. These sterilizations were performed without the consent of the women involved. This law was intended to reduce poverty, mental illness, and criminal behavior, which public officials believed was hereditary. Under this law, sterilization was mandatory for certain women in state custody. The Indiana Supreme Court deemed the law unconstitutional in 1921, but not before more than 2,500 women were sterilized without their consent, most of whom were poor or women of color.

Around the same time, similar laws were passed in 30 other states that allowed women in state custody to be forcibly sterilized if they were feeble-minded, dependent, or otherwise deemed incapable of making family planning decisions. The last of these laws was repealed in the 1970s after tens of thousands of women had been forcibly sterilized. States such as North Carolina set up a eugenics board to review petitions from private and government agencies to sterilize poor, mentally disabled, or unwed women and other people deemed unfit. In 1927, the Supreme Court upheld a state's right to sterilize people who are intellectually disabled "for the protection and health of the state" in *Buck v. Bell*. This ruling has never been expressly overturned. From the 1930s through the 1970s, North Carolina sterilized more than 7,600 women, men, and children.[47] In 2011, the state established the Office for Justice of Sterilization Victims, and in 2013, they set aside $10 million to compensate forced sterilization victims, most of whom were poor, disabled, and black. Two-thirds of coercive sterilization procedures were performed on African American women.

Native American women were also targeted by forced sterilization practices for most of the twentieth century. The Indian Health Service first offered family planning services to Native American families in 1965, and by 1970, one in four Native women of childbearing age were sterilized—many times the rate of other U.S. women. When feminist activists investigated sterilization rates in Native American communities, they discovered many cases in which girls and women were sterilized without their consent when they were hospitalized for other procedures.

U.S. sterilization policies also affected Puerto Rico. When the United States took control of the territory in 1898, it instituted a eugenics board to oversee population control on the island. By 1965, one-third of Puerto Rican women were found to be sterilized—a rate ten times that of women in the United States. This was accomplished using coercive strategies such as visits from health workers and employers encouraging women to get sterilized and misinformation about the procedure. According to a 1968 survey, one-third of Puerto Rican women who were sterilized did not realize that the procedure is difficult to reverse. Local medical doctor Helen Rodriguez Trias worked with other activists to overturn U.S. sterilization laws and practices in Puerto Rico that denied women self-determination in family planning.

Rodriguez Trias went on to advocate for women who were coerced into sterilization while in state custody. For example, one woman in jail discovered she was pregnant, and when she went to the hospital to have an abortion, she was misinformed about sterilization being her only option for birth control. An untold number of women were coerced into sterilization under similar circumstances, even though eugenics boards and state sterilization laws were a thing of the past. Rodriguez Trias formed the Committee to End Sterilization Abuse in 1970, and by 1974, their lobbying efforts produced new sterilization guidelines from the Department of Health and Human Services. These guidelines abolished sterilization of women under the age of 21 and for people without the mental capacity to consent.

Coercive sterilization is not a practice of the distant past. A recent investigation from the Center for Investigative Reporting finds that approximately 150 women were illegally sterilized in the California prison system from 2006 to 2010, and hundreds more were likely victims of the practice in previous years.[48] Prisoner advocates believe that women who were likely to return to prison in the future were coerced into getting sterilized. Federal and state laws are in place that prohibit the use of federal funds for inmate sterilizations, and state funds can only be used when approved by medical officials on a case-by-case basis. The 150 procedures discovered by the Center for Investigative Reporting had not gone through the proper medical channels for approval, and interviews with inmates revealed that the procedures were often performed under pressure from prison medical staff. This contemporary case of coercive sterilization echoes a history in which approximately 20,000 women and men were stripped of their right to family planning throughout the twentieth century.

Plan B

Emergency contraception, also known as Plan B or the morning-after pill, was approved by the FDA in 1999 for prescription use, and in 2013, it was approved for over-the-counter use. Plan B can prevent pregnancy if it is taken within 120 hours of unprotected sex, and rates of effectiveness are much higher the sooner the pill is taken. Since its approval, Plan B has been embroiled in controversy that is fueled by the scientifically inaccurate belief that the pill prevents a fertilized egg from implanting in the uterus, but that is not how Plan B works. Instead, the morning-after pill prevents pregnancy by delaying ovulation, which means the sperm and the egg never meet up. Sperm wait in the fallopian tubes for days after sex, waiting for an egg, and Plan B ensures that an egg will not appear. Despite readily available information on how Plan B works, pro-life advocates insist that it is akin to an abortion. In 2012, a district court judge ruled that the owners of Ralph's Thriftway, a neighborhood grocery store and pharmacy in Washington State, could refuse to sell Plan B because it contradicts the antiabortion position of their Christian faith. This decision was overturned by an appeals court in 2015 that ruled that Washington State can mandate that pharmacies stock and sell Plan B.

Obamacare and Birth Control

Another family planning controversy is whether employers should be mandated to cover birth control in their employee health benefit plan. In 2000, the Equal Employment Opportunity Commission ruled that employers must cover prescription contraception in employee health-care plans, but this mandate was recently challenged during the 2010 passage of the Patient Protection and Affordable Care Act, also known as the ACA or Obamacare. The Catholic Church raised concerns about the contraception provision in the ACA before it was passed, and the Obama administration responded by exempting religious employers, such as churches, from the birth control mandate. Private employers then fought for the same exemption as religious organizations.

In September 2012, the retail craft store Hobby Lobby filed suit against the U.S. government for the right to deny employees Plan B in the store's health-care plan. The Supreme Court found in Hobby Lobby's favor and exempted "closely held corporations" from laws that interfere with the owner's religious beliefs. A closely held corporation is a corporation with only a few shareholders with stock that is occasionally publicly traded. These corporations are basically owned by just a few people. The Hobby Lobby case marks the first time the Supreme Court recognized a for-profit entity's claim to religious beliefs. The decision was based on an interpretation of the Religious Freedom Restoration Act that was passed by Congress in 1993. The Hobby Lobby case allowed other closely held corporations to deny contraceptive coverage to their employees based on the religious beliefs of their owners, including the furniture company Conestoga Wood Specialties, owned by a Mennonite family. To date, more than 80 other companies have decided to deny their employees contraception coverage in their health-care plan.

During the debate over the ACA, popular radio talk show host Rush Limbaugh revealed that some conservatives are motivated to limit contraception coverage as a way of curtailing women's sexuality. On his radio show, Limbaugh called law school student and birth control advocate Sandra Fluke a "slut" and a "prostitute." The previous week, Fluke had testified before the House Democrats on behalf of the importance of mandating employer contraceptive coverage in Obamacare. Limbaugh attempted to undercut Fluke's position with personal attacks about her sex life, indicating that more than just religious beliefs are at stake in the fight over contraception coverage:

> What does it say about the college co-ed Susan Fluke [sic], who goes before a congressional committee and essentially says that she must be paid to have sex, what does that make her? It makes her a slut, right? It makes her a prostitute. She wants to be paid to have sex. She's having so much sex she can't afford the contraception.

For the following two days, Limbaugh made similar comments about Fluke, despite the negative press he drew as a result of the remarks. Limbaugh also stated that Fluke is "having so much sex, it's amazing she can still walk." He followed up with the suggestion that female students at Georgetown should use aspirin between their knees as birth control, a not-so-subtle suggestion that they should be closing their legs and abstaining from sex altogether. Limbaugh's comments are best understood within the context of many religious conservatives that women should refrain from sexual activity before marriage. Many religious groups reject premarital sex on moral grounds and feel that teaching children or teenagers about contraception implies that premarital sex is permissible.

WAYS TO ENCOURAGE REPRODUCTION

Family planning also includes the decision to have children, and for some people, this is only possible through fertility treatment or adoption. In this section, we provide an overview of the history, policies, and controversies of efforts to have children when conventional methods are not available.

Fertility Treatment

Fertility treatment, also known as IVF, is a public policy issue that has drawn debate in the United States. IVF involves removing an egg from a woman's ovary, fertilizing it with sperm in a laboratory, and then implanting the fertilized egg into a woman's uterus. People who use IVF can use various combinations of eggs, sperm, and donors. For example, single women can use a sperm donor to fertilize her eggs, gay couples can use egg donors and a "rented" womb, or infertile heterosexual couples can use egg or sperm donors (depending on the source of the infertility). Women are also able to freeze "young" eggs for implantation later in life. This relatively new reproductive technology allows tens of thousands of people who otherwise could not reproduce to have children.

In 1977, Drs. Robert G. Edwards and Patrick Steptoe completed the first successful IVF treatment. Nine months later, Louise, the first "test tube" baby, was born in the United Kingdom. A second test tube baby, Durga, was born in India just 67 days after Louise using the unique method developed by Dr. Subhash Mukhopadhyay. In 1981, Elizabeth, the first test tube baby in the United States, was born. Since its inception, IVF technology has advanced and is now widely available to people who have the economic means to pay for the expensive procedure.

According to the Society for Assisted Reproductive Technology, more women in the United States are carrying IVF babies to term than ever before, and about 12 percent of women of childbearing age have used infertility services.[49] In 2014, clinics performed approximately 165,000 IVF procedures that resulted in just over 60,000 babies. Approximately 48 percent of IVF cycles are successful for women 35 and younger, a success rate that rapidly diminishes as women age. Thirty percent of IVF cycles are effective between the ages of 36 and 40, while only 20 percent are effective after the age of 40. The growing trend of using IVF to reproduce is linked to the fact that couples are having babies later in life. In 1980, the average age for a first-time mother was 22, and today it is 26. IVF is a public policy issue that is fraught with controversy over whether it promotes abortion, as well as moral concerns about sex selection and genetic testing.

Pro-life advocates are concerned that IVF is a risky procedure that promotes abortion. This argument is laid out in the 2011 documentary film *Eggsploitation*, which follows several young women who work as egg donors for IVF. These young women encounter medical issues, including adverse reactions to fertility drugs and infertility. While pro-life activists are concerned about IVF egg donors, their larger concern is that multiple embryos are discarded in the process of implantation. Also, IVF commonly produces multiple embryos, which result in selective abortions after implantation to ensure the health of the mother and the remaining embryos. In other words, IVF increases rates of abortion in the eyes of pro-life activists.

Another point of controversy is that IVF embryos can be screened for genetic disorders and the sex of the fetus. These tests allow parents to discard embryos based on disorders, such as Down's syndrome or multiple sclerosis. The ability to select the sex of the baby is another controversial aspect of IVF. Sex selection has been banned in 36 countries, including the United Kingdom, Canada, China, and India, but it is a legal practice in the United States. Restrictions on IVF in some countries have produced "fertility tourism," where people with economic resources travel to other countries for IVF treatment that allows them to run genetic tests and choose the sex of their child. IVF in general and the ability to test for disorders and sex more specifically raise ethical questions about when life begins and whether humans should be "playing God." No consensus exists in science, philosophy, or religion about when an embryo should be considered a person. Many pro-life advocates believe that life begins at the moment of conception, while most scientists place personhood at viability outside the womb. The fundamental questions in the debate about IVF look similar to the questions raised in the abortion debate.

A last point of controversy regarding IVF involves the cost and who has access to this family planning method. One round of IVF treatment costs anywhere from $15,000 to $25,000, and multiple cycles of IVF are often required. The average cost of a birth from IVF in the United States is $41,000.[50] The high cost of IVF means this procedure is generally out of reach for most Americans. The IVF industry has faced strong criticism in recent years from academics and medical practitioners who worry that the industry places profits above the personal health of the mother and public health more broadly. For example, in 2008, Nadya Suleman birthed eight babies after a California physician implanted 12 embryos in her uterus. This case made international headlines and ignited a debate about doctors endangering the health of potential mothers to make more profit, and the doctor who performed the procedure lost his medical license. Critics also accuse the industry of overstating how common infertility is in the United States to get couples to consider IVF as an early option rather than a last resort.

IVF inherently involves power dynamics because of its high price tag and the ability to "rent" the wombs of women, who are often of lower socioeconomic status. When the U.S. economy crashed in 2008, fertility clinics saw a significant surge in women willing to donate their eggs and use their wombs for reproduction as a way to pay their bills. An egg donor is generally compensated between $5,000 and $10,000 for the intensive six- to eight-week process of cultivating her eggs, while surrogate mothers are compensated in the range of $20,000 to $40,000 for their nine months of work.

The power dynamics inherent in IVF and surrogacy were laid bare during the 2015 earthquake in Nepal when the international press reported that 26 new-born surrogate babies were evacuated to Israel. Headlines such as "Israel Evacuates Surrogate Babies from Nepal but Leaves Mothers Behind" raised awareness of the issues of class privilege involved in surrogacy.[51] Laws in Israel make it virtually impossible for gay couples and single parents to use surrogacy, so they travel to other countries to bear children. Most Asian and European countries ban commercial surrogacy, and it is prohibitively expensive in the United States and Canada, but Nepalese agencies offer surrogacy at a cheap rate with few restrictions. After the devastating earthquake that killed more than 8,000 people, the Israeli government scrambled to evacuate the surrogate babies but offered no evacuation assistance to the surrogate mothers. Mostly white Israeli men of means flying to Nepal to collect mostly white surrogate babies from the rented wombs of women of color after a major natural disaster starkly exposed the privileges involved in IVF and surrogacy.

IVF Laws

IVF is a loosely regulated policy issue. Health centers are mandated to screen embryos for infectious diseases, but federal and state governments do not regulate how many babies can be derived from one egg donor, what genetic tests can or must be performed on embryos, the minimum age of a donor, or how many embryos can be implanted at a single time. Politicians are reluctant to regulate the IVF industry because it involves embryos, and for pro-life activists, that brings up the divisive culture war issue of abortion.

Nondiscrimination laws have been applied to IVF that require doctors to provide IVF treatment to same-sex individuals and couples. In 2009, the California Supreme Court unanimously decided that medical providers could not deny IVF treatments based on the sexuality of the parents. In *North Coast Women's Care Medical Group v. Superior Court*, lesbian Guadalupe Benitez sued the medical group after a doctor denied her IVF treatment based on the doctor's religious objection to her homosexuality. Many interest groups weighed in on the issue, and in 2009, the American Society for Reproductive Medicine issued a report that children are not disadvantaged or harmed when they are raised by unmarried parents, homosexual parents, or single parents. This group recommended that IVF be available to parents, regardless of their marital status or sexuality. Benitez's right to IVF was affirmed by the court, but conservative activists are still working to pass laws that curb IVF options for same-sex couples. In 2009, conservative activists in Tennessee proposed two laws that would have barred unmarried couples (and by definition, same-sex couples) from using IVF, but these bills were not passed into law. Similar laws are proposed at the state level each year.

U.S. laws do not regulate the anonymity of sperm or egg donors. In many countries, including the United Kingdom, donor-conceived babies have a right to medical information that includes the identity of their biological parents. In the United States, there is no such right, and donors often assume that their identity will be kept private. However, new websites have cropped up, such as the Donor Sibling Registry, that connect donor-conceived offspring with others who share their DNA. These websites allow people born from IVF procedures to circumvent the anonymity of sperm banks to locate biological siblings and parents. Social media and other online communication technologies mean that donors cannot assume their contributions will remain anonymous.

ADOPTION

Adoption is another form of family planning that is governed by a series of international, federal, and state laws. Adoption is placing a minor under 18 years of age with a parent or parents who are other than the child's biological parents. Approximately 135,000 children are adopted in the United States each year, and more than two million people in the United States are adoptees.[52] Adoptions can take place through a private agency, a state agency, or an independent arrangement. Adoption in the United States has changed significantly in the past few decades in terms of closed versus open adoptions, an emphasis on keeping biological families intact versus an emphasis on what is best for the child, same-sex couples being allowed to adopt, greater acceptance of adoption across races, and growth in the number of international adoptions.

Adopted children have led several reforms since adoption became legal in the United States, the most significant being the move toward open adoptions, where children know the identity of their birth parents. Adoptee Jean Paton, the author of the 1954 book *The Adopted Break Silence*, is the founder of the movement to reunite adoptees with their biological parents, and Florence Fisher founded the Adoptees Liberation Movement Association in 1972 to fight for adoptee rights. These activists have filed lawsuits and lobbied for laws to gain access to birth certificates and set up registries to connect adoptees to biological parents. By the mid-1980s, more than 500 organizations had formed to fight for adoptee rights. Nearly 30 states and Washington, DC, have laws allowing open adoption agreements, and activists are pushing for similar laws in the remaining states. As of 2013, more than 85 percent of adoptions in the United States are semiopen or fully open adoptions in which adoptees have the option of contacting their biological parents.

Perhaps the most significant change in adoption policy in recent decades is a shift in emphasis from keeping biological families together to a greater focus on the health and safety of the child. In 1980, Congress passed the Adoption and Child Welfare Act, which made it a priority to keep children with their biological parent(s). Nearly two decades later, in 1997, President Bill Clinton signed the Adoption and Safe Families Act into law to rectify issues created by the earlier law. The act shifted the emphasis to the health and safety of the child rather than on keeping biological families intact. This later law recognized that sometimes the best place for a child is with a family they were not born into. Within a few years of its passage, the Adoption and Safe Families Act doubled the number of children adopted from the foster care system. The idea of the Adoption and Safe Families Act originated in an article written by First Lady Hillary Clinton, and she played a key role in brokering its passage through Congress.

Same-Sex Adoption

Another adoption trend is the rapid growth in the number of adoptions by same-sex couples. Adoption by homosexual couples has been legal in many states for decades, and in June 2015, it became legal in every state. The rate of same-sex couple adoption has tripled since the 1990s, and today, more than 16,000 couples are raising more than 20,000 adopted children in the United States.[53] LGBTQ parents are raising an estimated four percent of all adopted children in the United States. LGBTQ adoption issues were debated in the 1980s after IVF procedures allowed lesbian couples to produce biological offspring from one partner. Critics were concerned that adopted children in same-sex households would not be as well adjusted as children in opposite-sex households, but two decades of research find that same-sex parents raise children who are just as likely to be well adjusted as those raised by heterosexual parents.[54]

Transracial Adoption

Transracial adoptions have also become more socially acceptable in recent decades. Today, about one in four adoptions is transracial, meaning that the child is of a different race than the adoptive parent(s). The most common arrangement is white parents adopting a baby or child of color. The practice of adopting a child of a different race has been legal in the United States since 1948, but it has always been controversial. When transracial adoption first became legal, most Americans believed that adopted children should be placed with someone of the same race. After the civil rights movement, Americans became more accepting of cross-racial adoption. Also, rates of transracial adoption rapidly increased after new contraceptive technology decreased the number of white infants available for adoption.

People who support transracial adoption argue that it is important because there are more minority children up for adoption (40 percent of children up for adoption are white, while 41 percent are black and 15 percent are Latino).[55] Critics of transracial adoptions express concern about a long history of removing children from families of color in the United States. During slavery and post-slavery, black children were commonly removed from their parents to regulate and oppress them. Critics are also concerned that white parents may not be able to adequately prepare children of color for the racism they will face and that children in these arrangements grow up feeling like outsiders in white social circles.

International Adoptions

Another trend in family planning in recent decades is an increase in international adoptions. At the height of the transracial adoption debate in the 1970s that discourages some white families from adopting children of color, some parents turned to international adoption, a trend that accelerated from the 1970s through the 1990s. Americans have adopted more than 200,000 children from overseas in the past decade, most of whom come from Asian countries, with China being the most popular country for U.S. adoptions. Adoptions that cross national lines are regulated by the Protection of Children and Co-Operation in Respect of Intercountry Adoption. This international treaty protects all parties from exploitation during the adoption process. The Child Citizen Act of 2000 allows more foreign-born adoptees to become automatic citizens when they enter the United States. In 2014, Congress passed the Preventing Sex Trafficking and Strengthening Families Act to prevent the use of overseas adoption to traffic children.

Gender Preference

Adoption is a family planning issue, one that involves questions of race, sexual orientation, and international relationships. It is also an issue involving gender and power. Women are the primary drivers in the adoption process since U.S. culture still expects women to be the primary caretakers of children, and they have a strong preference for adopting female babies. Between 70 and 90 percent of people seeking to adopt have a preference for a girl, whether they are adopting domestically or internationally.[56] It is difficult to know why this preference exists since adoptions are private affairs, but researchers speculate that it is due to perceptions that girls are easier to raise than boys. It may also be because women are the primary decision makers in the process, and they want to raise a child who shares their gender. Steven Landsburg offers a different explanation. He argues that biological parents prefer sons because society gives them higher value, so adoptive parents assume that boy adoptees must have something seriously wrong with them, while girls may be put up for adoption simply because they are girls. Whatever the reason, boys are less likely to have the opportunity for a stable home than girls because of gender stereotypes that work against them in the adoption process.[57]

CONCLUSION

In this chapter, we explored different facets of family planning. The first part of the chapter was dedicated to ways of preventing reproduction through abortion and family planning. We analyzed the contentious abortion battle that has been waged for more than half a century. Pro-choice advocates have established a woman's constitutional right to have an abortion, but in recent years, pro-life advocates have passed a series of laws at the state level that limit abortion rights. We also looked at the history and controversies surrounding contraception in the United States, including the higher risks of fourth-generation hormonal birth control, forced sterilization that has disproportionately targeted poor women and women of color, and the path for legalizing emergency contraception. We also examined the controversy surrounding the Obamacare mandate that requires employers to offer contraception coverage in their employee health plans. Activists have successfully challenged this mandate, which indicates that the debate surrounding access to contraception is still active. The fight over access to contraceptives is also seen in the ongoing debate about whether high schools should provide comprehensive sex education.

In the second part of this chapter, we examined family planning efforts aimed at having children. We looked at IVF and abortion as types of family planning. IVF treatment has inspired a debate about when life begins that is similar to the abortion debate. Many pro-life advocates believe that life begins at conception, so they argue that IVF treatments that discard embryos are akin to abortion. We also analyzed adoption trends in the United States, including a growing number of open adoptions, same-sex couples, transracial adoptions, and international adoptions, as well as the policy shift from an emphasis on keeping biological families together to an emphasis on what is in the child's best interest.

CHAPTER SUMMARY

- In *Roe v. Wade* (1973), the Supreme Court ruled that women have a constitutionally protected right to an abortion.
- Half of all pregnancies in the United States are unplanned, and of those, four in ten end in abortion. In other words, about one in four pregnancies is terminated each year in the United States.
- In the four decades since *Roe v. Wade*, states have passed 1,074 laws that restrict abortion. One-third of these laws were passed from 2010 to 2015, making this period the most restrictive since this landmark decision.
- Contraception, also known as birth control, comes in many different forms, including devices placed in the uterus (intrauterine devices), hormonal methods, physical barriers, sterilization, and fertility calendar approaches.
- Virtually all women of childbearing age (99 percent) have used some form of contraception at some point, and 62 percent are currently using birth control.
- The most popular form of contraception is the pill, approved for birth control use by the FDA in 1960.
- Medical research shows that the most recent generation of contraceptives is significantly more likely to cause blood clots than previous-generation pills.
- For most of the twentieth century, states had eugenics laws that allowed officials to sterilize women who were poor, had mental health issues, or engaged in criminal behavior without their permission. Tens of thousands of women were sterilized, and poor women of color were disproportionately sterilized.
- A recent investigation found that inmates in the California prison system faced coercive sterilization as late as 2010.

- Emergency contraception, also known as Plan B or the morning-after pill, was approved by the FDA in 1999 for prescription use, and in 2013 it was approved for over-the-counter use.
- The Obama administration recently exempted religious employers, such as churches, from providing birth control in their employee health plans. In 2012, the Supreme Court ruled that this birth control exemption also applied to closely held corporations.
- The first IVF treatment took place in 1977, and today, about 12 percent of women of childbearing age have used some infertility services.
- Pro-life activists opposed IVF due to concerns that embryos are discarded and fetuses are aborted in the IVF process.
- Approximately 135,000 children are adopted in the United States each year, and more than two million people in the United States are adoptees.
- Recent trends in adoption include an increase in same-sex adoptions, transracial adoptions, and international adoptions.
- Women make the majority of adoption decisions, and they tend to have a strong preference for adopting female children.

STUDY/DISCUSSION QUESTIONS

- What are the most popular forms of family planning? Why are these methods more popular than others?
- What did the Supreme Court decide in *Roe v. Wade*, and how has this decision been challenged by pro-life advocates in recent years?
- When and why did forced sterilization come about, and who was disproportionally affected by this practice?
- Why are pro-life activists opposed to IVF? Analyze the core issue driving opposition to both abortion and IVF.
- What trends are happening in terms of adoption in the United States?

CASE STUDIES

1. **Why are more women choosing to not have children?**
   For the first time in U.S. history, nearly half of women of childbearing age are choosing to not have children. Why do you think this is happening? What factors contribute to family planning decisions, and how have these factors changed in the past decade in ways that explain the new popularity of choosing not to opt into motherhood?

2. **What difference does sexual education make?**
   One-third of high schools in the United States offer abstinence-only sex education programs. Reflect on your sex education experience. What did you learn that was helpful in empowering you in making family planning decisions?

What else would have been helpful to learn? Using this knowledge, analyze why abstinence-only sex education programs are less effective than other sex education programs when it comes to preventing unwanted and teen pregnancies.

3. **What impact does greater family planning freedom have for women?**
In the past half century, family planning has come a long way. Women now have access to the pill, emergency contraception, abortion, and IVF. How have these new options changed women's lives? What restrictions remain in terms of full freedom for family planning?

RESOURCES

- **Advocates for Youth** is an organization that advocates for comprehensive sexual education to create sexual health equity for all youth.
  http://www.advocatesforyouth.org
- **The National Family Planning & Reproductive Health Association** provides culturally sensitive family planning and reproductive health services.
  http://www.nationalfamilyplanning.org
- **Planned Parenthood** is a nonprofit organization that provides health care, sex education, and advocacy for reproductive health.
  http://www.plannedparenthood.org
- **The Guttmacher Institute** provides the most comprehensive research on family planning and reproduction in the United States.
  http://www.guttmacher.org
- **The Center for Reproductive Rights** uses legal means to advance reproductive freedoms in the United States.
  http://www.reproductiverights.org

CHAPTER 12

Public Policy: Gendered Violence

In 2011, Harvard Law School student Kamilah Willingham filed a complaint with the university and the Cambridge police alleging that fellow student Brandon Winston had sexually assaulted her and raped her friend in the same evening. Willingham furnished the police and campus authorizes with damning text messages from Brandon, in which he admits to the crimes. He texted Willingham that he had fondled her and "put a finger briefly in the v" of her friend while both women were passed out on a bed. A grand jury indicted Winston on sexual assault charges, and he was found guilty of "misdemeanor touching of a nonsexual nature" for fondling Willingham's friend's breasts. Harvard hired an outside attorney to investigate, who found that Winston was responsible for sexual assault and recommended Winston be expelled. Willingham was relieved that the man who had sexually violated her and her friend would no longer be on campus. Winston appealed the expulsion, and his appeal was initially rejected. However, a group of Harvard Law faculty then stepped in and overturned the finding, allowing him back on campus.

Willingham filed a Title IX complaint with the Department of Education (ED) against Harvard, claiming that her right to a fair and equitable education was violated by the university's handling of the case. In 2014, the ED found in Willingham's favor and concluded that Harvard often gave more rights to accused offenders than to victims, such as overturning Winston's expulsion and not informing Willingham: "As such, [Willingham] was not provided an adequate, reliable and impartial investigation of that sexual assault complaint."

The decision to let Winston back on campus was criticized in the national press and the documentary *The Hunting Ground*. Nineteen Harvard Law professors—many of whom were involved in overturning Winston's expulsion—wrote a public letter in the *New York Times* proclaiming Winston's innocence based on rape myth logic that the two women got themselves drunk and that the assaults did not involve force (ignoring the fact that incapacitation is the basis for rape). The "Harvard 19" letter also suggested that Winston was being unfairly targeted because of a long history of black men being falsely accused of rape in the United States, disregarding the fact that Willingham is a black woman and black women have historically faced high rates of sexual violence. Willingham shot back with a letter of her own, condemning the Harvard faculty for their attempt to discredit her:

> If you believe that people should not refrain from undressing and probing the bodies of unconscious peers, you have no business teaching law. The notion is insulting to the man you defend, as well as anyone who prefers not to be fingered while they're asleep. . . . You are not helping Black men by defending the actions of one who had to hold a barely conscious woman up so that he could put his tongue in her mouth. You are not helping women by asserting that they deserve to be assaulted if they become intoxicated. You are not helping to foster a safe environment for current or future Harvard Law students by institutionally betraying a former student who is a survivor.

Willingham graduated and went on to practice public interest law in California. She wrote the language for a law that overturned the time limit (ten years) for prosecuting sexual assault in California, and she stood on stage with 49 other campus survivors and held Lady Gaga's hand at the 2016 Academy Awards, where Lady Gaga performed "Till It Happens to You," a song she cowrote for *The Hunting Ground*.

Kamilah Willingham, Harvard Law School graduate.
She filed a Title IX complaint against Harvard for its mishandling of a sexual assault case.
SOURCE: Courtesy of Kamilah Willingham

Willingham's story illustrates many of the typical experiences of rape survivors on college campuses—convoluted, biased adjudication processes, lengthy legal battles with light sanctions, and institutional betrayal. College students face a higher risk of being raped than their non-college-bound peers, which makes going to college a risk factor for rape. Although schools have known of this crisis for decades, they took little action until late 2011. To date, no school has determined how to effectively reduce the rate of rape on its campus, and few schools are willing to make the drastic changes necessary to discourage the crime. One sticking point is sanctions, or the fact that even when rapists are found responsible ("guilty"), they receive light punishments. A year-long study by the Center for Public Integrity found that schools permanently expelled only ten percent to 25 percent of respondents found responsible for sexual assault.[1] In the vast majority of cases, students found responsible for sexual assault either stay on campus or are allowed to return after a suspension. Given that approximately half of respondents are found "responsible," only five percent to 12 percent of all formal complaints of sexual assault on college campuses result in an expulsion. Campus inaction is a public issue because rape often derails survivor's educational plans and achievements, which they have a right to receive equitably under Title IX.

Since 2013, the new Campus Anti-Rape Movement (CARM) has raised awareness of the epidemic of sexual violence on college campuses, a long history of schools hiding the problem, institutional betrayal when survivors come forward and report a sexual assault, and retaliation against survivor activists who blow the whistle on campus rape. Sexual violence is one of two policy issues we examine in this chapter about gendered violence, meaning violence that disproportionately affects women. We examine two specific policy areas, sexual violence and domestic violence, in turn.

SEXUAL VIOLENCE

Sexual violence against women is a global epidemic. According to the World Health Organization,[2] one in three women will experience sexual violence at some point in their life. Sexual violence comes in different forms: sexual battery (nonconsensual touching of a sexual nature outside of clothing), sexual assault (nonconsensual touching of a sexual nature underneath clothing), and rape (nonconsensual penetration of any orifice). This is a gender justice issue since women and transgender individuals are far more likely than men to face sexual violence. It is an issue of individual rights, in this case, the right to be free from violence. It is a public health issue because it disproportionately affects more than half the population and costs billions of dollars in hospital and mental health costs and lost wages. In this section, we examine the sexual violence crisis in the United States and the history of activism to address this issue. We examine experiences of sexual violence from an intersectional perspective, who perpetrates sexual violence, rape myths, the effects of sexual violence on survivors, and the history of anti–sexual violence efforts with a focus on the new CARM.

Rates of Sexual Violence in the United States

Many people in the United States will experience sexual violence at some point in their life, and people who are socially marginalized (e.g., poor people; women; people of color; LGBTQ individuals; disabled individuals) are at a greater risk for sexual violence. According to the National Intimate Partner and Sexual Violence Survey, one in five women (18 percent) experience an attempted or completed rape in their lifetime in the United States, and nearly half (49 percent) experience sexual violence other than rape.[3] Approximately 293,000 people over the age of 12 are raped each year, 91 percent of whom are women. One in thirty-three men (three percent) will face attempted or completed rape, and 20 percent experience some other form of sexual violence. A staggering 64 percent of transgender people will experience sexual violence in their lifetime.[4] Women and transgender individuals experience far higher rates of sexual violence than men because of their marginalized status in society. Societal acceptance of women's sexual objectification is dehumanizing, which is a contributing factor to the high rates of violence perpetrated against them. Transgender individuals are marginalized by homophobia, which makes them a target for hate crimes, which sometimes take the form of sexual violence.

Experiences of rape and other forms of sexual violence vary by race, according to the National Intimate Partner and Sexual Violence Survey. About one in ten Asian American women (seven percent) experience rape in their lifetime, while one in seven Latinas (14 percent), one in five white (18 percent) and black women (19 percent), one in four mixed-race women (24 percent), and one in three Native American women (34 percent) experience rape. It is important to note that two-thirds of perpetrators against Native women are non-Native. The dual marginalization of women and people of color intersects to produce higher rates of sexual violence against women of color, especially Native women and women of mixed race.

Rates of sexual violence also vary by sexuality. According to the National Intimate Partner and Sexual Violence Survey, nearly half of bisexual women (46 percent) have been raped compared to 17 percent of heterosexual women and 13 percent of lesbian women. Gay men also face much higher rates of sexual violence than heterosexual men. Nearly half of bisexual men (47 percent) and 40 percent of gay men experience some form of sexual violence compared to 21 percent of heterosexual men. These high rates of sexual violence can be attributed to higher rates of marginalization, stigmatization, and poverty in the LGBTQ community, as well as hate crimes that involve sexual assault.

People with mental or physical differences suffer sexual violence at much higher rates than others. Women with disabilities are twice as likely to be raped as other women, and almost 80 percent have faced some form of sexual violence.[5] Men with disabilities are ten times more likely to experience sexual violence than other men. One in three men with disabilities experience rape or sexual assault compared to about three percent of other men. People with disabilities face higher rates of violence because perpetrators see them as "easy targets" who are less able to defend themselves.

One population of men also faces a high rate of sexual violence: men in prison. Nearly 1,400 people in prison are raped each day in the United States.[6] According to the Department of Justice, 216,000 male inmates are raped each year in the U.S. prison system. Commonly used statistics on rape and sexual assault rarely, if ever, include incarcerated individuals, and the crisis of prison rape receives little attention in media coverage or public discussions of the issue because prisoners are socially marginalized in society. Prison rape is the punch line of popular films and office water-cooler jokes, and some people see prisoners as deserving of rape as part of the prison experience.

Predators of Sexual Violence

Nearly all perpetrators (98 percent) are men, which does not mean that all or most men are perpetrators. Approximately six percent of men rape at least one person in their lifetime. The typical rapist is a 31-year-old white man who commits an average of six rapes over the course of his lifetime.[7] One in three rapists (36 percent) will rape only once, but nearly two-thirds of men who rape are repeat offenders. Rape is a crime that is motivated by gender dynamics within the broader culture. Research on rapists finds that they exhibit high levels of hypermasculinity. They also exhibit anger toward women, a need to dominate women, and a general lack of empathy. About half of rapists were victims of sexual violence when they were children.

Rape is rarely perpetrated by strangers. According to the Department of Justice, 82 percent of rapes are perpetrated by someone the victim knows. Nearly half (47 percent) are someone the victim considers a friend, and one in four (25 percent) are someone with whom the victim is intimate. One-third of rapes happen during the day, while two-thirds happen at night. Sixty percent of rapes and sexual assaults take place in the victim's home, at a family member's home, or a friend's house.

The most common tool rapists use to perpetrate this crime is alcohol. In 61 percent of rapes, perpetrators targeted victims who were incapacitated by alcohol, while 23 percent used force and 16 percent used both incapacitation and force. Approximately one in ten rapes involve the use of a weapon, such as a gun (three percent) or a knife (six percent). Only seven percent of rapists target strangers, while more than 90 percent target acquaintances and friends. Stephanie McWhorter and her colleagues interviewed admitted rapists and found that all who used force did so with acquaintances and friends, while all who targeted strangers used incapacitation by drugs or alcohol.[8] In other words, the scenario of a rapist hiding in the bushes who jumps out and uses force on a stranger is by and large a myth. Additionally, rape is most often a premeditated crime that the rapist plans beforehand, not a "crime of passion," where he or she loses control in the moment. Alcohol does not turn people into rapists; it makes rapists more likely to rape.

Table 12.1 Common Rape Myths in the United States

Rape Myth 1: Most rapes are perpetrated by strangers.

Fact: Only seven percent of rapes are perpetrated by strangers.[9]

Rape Myth 2: Rapists are individuals who act on impulse.

Fact: Approximately 70 percent of rapes are premeditated and planned.[10]

Rape Myth 3: Most rapes involve the use of weapons.

Fact: 90 percent of rapes do not involve the use of a weapon.[11]

Rape Myth 4: False rape reports are common.

Fact: Between two percent and eight percent of rape claims are false reports, the same false reporting rate as with other crimes.[12]

Rape Myth 5: A woman cannot be raped by her husband.

Fact: As of 1993, marital rape became a crime in all 50 states.[13]

Rape Myth 6: People who are drunk or high cannot be held responsible for rape.

Fact: Being under the influence of substances cannot be used as the basis for excusing any crime. For example, drunk drivers cannot be excused because they were drunk.

Rape Myths

Most Americans comprehend rape through popular societal rape myths that are not supported by data. These rape myths have the general effect of discouraging survivors from coming forward to seek justice and services. For some of the more common myths held in the United States, see Table 12.1.

The prevalence of rape myths and general inaction from law enforcement discourage survivors from coming forward to report this crime. Only one-third of rapes (32 percent) are ever reported to the police. Sexual assault has the lowest conviction rate of any violent crime. Because of widely held rape myths, it is difficult to obtain a "guilty" conviction from a jury, so only two percent of rapists will ever see a day in prison.[14] In the rare instances when a rapist is convicted, he or she will spend an average of 11 months behind bars. For comparison, someone who has been charged with robbery is 30 percent more likely to receive a guilty verdict than a rapist, and in the sentencing phase, a convicted robber is 50 percent more likely to receive jail time than a convicted rapist. In other words, the bias against taking rape seriously as a crime exists at all stages of the criminal justice process.

Survivors are also discouraged from reporting because they face stigma resulting from unconscious, deep-seated biases that assume they "asked for it" or could/should have done something to prevent their violation. They may lose support from family members and friends who blame the survivor for what happened, because rape is the only crime where the victim is treated like a perpetrator. Part of the problem is the cultural belief that men are entitled to women's bodies, that men have a "right" to have sex with women. This makes it difficult for some to believe that a crime has occurred, especially if the victim knows the perpetrator, which is most often the case.

Survivors of color, men, and LGBTQ individuals have greater barriers when it comes to reporting sexual violence. Coming forward as a survivor is never easy, but it is especially difficult for those who do not fit the media stereotype of a young, white, heterosexual woman. Regardless of their sexuality, male survivors who are public about suffering assault/rape run the risk of being seen as weak, violable, and feminized. Male survivors of all races and sexualities are less likely to report a sexual assault/rape than are female survivors.

Rape as a Public Health Issue

In addition to the gender justice issues involved in rape, sexual violence is a public health issue. Compared to other crimes, rape has the highest victim crime cost, estimated to be $127 billion annually in the United States.[15] Researchers estimate that each rape costs the survivor $151,000 in medical care, mental health support, and lost wages; this figure is $210,012 for people who are raped as children. About 60 percent of adult rape survivors miss work because of the crime. The vast majority of survivors develop some degree of post-traumatic stress disorder after being raped, and they are far more likely to experience physical problems such as headaches, asthma, chronic sleep problems, irritable bowel syndrome, and diabetes. Survivors are four times more likely to contemplate suicide. If survivors cannot afford the cost of their trauma from rape, taxpayers foot the bill.

Anti-Rape Activism in the United States

The United States has experienced four peaks of activism against sexual violence: during the post–Civil War Reconstruction Era, leading up to the civil rights movement, during the second wave of the feminist movement, and the new CARM.

Activism during Reconstruction

According to author Gillian Greensite, the early history of the "rape crisis movement in the United States is also a history of the struggle of African American women against racism and sexism."[16] During slavery, white slave owners routinely raped female slaves, and an estimated three-fourths of black Americans in the United States today are descendants of at least one white ancestor. During the Civil War, despite President Abraham Lincoln's prohibition against it, women of all races were raped throughout the South, and black women were especially vulnerable to this crime. Historian Crystal Feimster writes that the rape of white women by Northern soldiers sent the message that "Southern men were unable to protect their mothers, wives and daughters," while the rape of black slaves sent the message that they could not protect their property.[17] The systemic rape of African American women continued after the Civil War, especially in the South. Once slavery was outlawed, white men reestablished racial control over black men through lynching and over black women through rape. Between 1882 and 1946, approximately 5,000 African Americans (mostly men) were lynched, and countless women were raped to maintain social control over blacks. The Reconstruction Era from 1865 to 1877 was particularly violent because the Ku Klux Klan and other terror organizations raped black women and burned black homes and churches with regularity to maintain the racial order.

Black women organized in response to sexual violence during this era. The earliest organized anti-rape efforts can be traced back to 1866 when a group of black women testified before Congress about a white mob that perpetrated gang rapes during the Memphis Riot. The riot was a class conflict between poor whites and a group of black soldiers that lasted three days, during which white policemen and civilians rampaged through black neighborhoods, injuring more than 100 African Americans, killing 46 people, and raping at least five black women. Seventeen-year-old Lucy Smith testified that seven white men, including two police officers, demanded dinner before raping her and her elderly, crippled friend, Frances Smith. Both women testified before Congress, along with several other black women, but in the end, none of the perpetrators was punished. In the 1870s, under the leadership of Ida B. Wells, Anna Julia Cooper, and Fannie Barrier Williams, activists organized to combat these heinous crimes. The formation of the Black Women's Club in the 1890s was the first antiviolence organization in the United States, and it laid the groundwork for activism against violence of all forms during the first half of the twentieth century.

Around the same time that black women were organizing, Sarah Winnemucca of the Northern Paiute tribe was waging a one-woman war against the routine rape of Native American women by white men. According to historian Rose Stremlau, the rape of First Tribes women at the hands of non-Native men was part of the conquest of the American West. Winnemucca documented widespread sexual violence in her 1883 biography and traveled the country to raise awareness of routine violence perpetrated against Native women. She lobbied military leaders, the Interior Department, and President Rutherford B. Hayes to provide state protection against sexual violence on reservations. Winnemucca also raised public awareness through lectures and press interviews.

PROFILE IN POWER

Ida B. Wells-Barnett

Ida Bell Wells-Barnett (1862–1931) was a journalist, antilynching activist, women's rights activist, and suffragette. She is best known for her investigative journalism in the 1890s that exposed lynching as a tool to control recently freed slaves, but she was also one of the most influential women's rights activist of her time. Wells-Barnett was born into slavery in Holy Springs, Mississippi, a few months before President Abraham Lincoln issued the Emancipation Proclamation that (on paper) freed slaves in the South. Her father was a master carpenter and an activist on race issues after the Civil War, and her mother cared for their eight children. Wells-Barnett was their firstborn. As former slaves, her parents knew the importance of education as a source of power

SOURCE: Mary Garrity, restored by Adam Cuerden

for whites. They encouraged her to attend the local university at the age of 16, but she was expelled after a confrontation with the college president. That same year, her parents and infant brother died during the yellow fever epidemic. Officials tried to split up the family, but Ida went to work as a teacher to keep her remaining siblings together.

As a teacher in a racially segregated school system, Wells-Barnett was paid only $30 a month compared to white teachers, who earned $80 a month. This experience of discrimination further politicized her, as did an experience of racism in 1884 when she was removed from a train after refusing to move from the Ladies' Car to the Jim Crow car. She sued the railroad company and won, but the finding was overturned by an appeals court. She wrote about her experience for the newspaper *The Living Way* under the pen name Lola, and her thoughtful analysis earned her a reputation. In 1889, she became the editor of the antisegregation newspaper *Free Speech and Headlight*, where she uncovered the fact that lynching was being used for the social control of black men.

In 1909, Wells-Barnett cofounded the National Association for the Advancement of Colored People, and she used her position to shine a spotlight on sexual violence as a tool of social control for recently freed black women. She cofounded the Alpha Suffrage Club and was an active leader in the movement for women's suffrage. Wells-Barnett marched in the famous 1913 march for universal voting rights in Washington, DC, and worked tirelessly for women's suffrage until passage of the Nineteenth Amendment in 1920. She was also one of the first women to hyphenate her last name instead of assuming her husband's name. In 1930, Wells-Barnett ran for a seat in the Illinois State Legislature, making her the first black woman in the nation to run for public office. She ran as an independent and lost the election, and a year later, she passed away. In 1990, the U.S. Postal Service issued a stamp in her honor.

Pre–Civil Rights Activism

African American women led the efforts against sexual violence in the twentieth century. A decade before longtime activist Rosa Parks refused to sit at the back of a city bus, she was a leading anti-rape activist. In 1944, Parks formed the Committee for Equal Justice to fight sexual violence against women. She and other activists were galvanized by the experience of Recy Taylor, a 24-year-old mother who was raped by six white men with guns and knives as she was walking home from church. The rapists first threatened to shoot Taylor's mother. A few days after this gang rape, the National Association for the Advancement of Colored People branch office in Montgomery, Alabama, dispatched their best investigator, Rosa Parks. In response to the rape, Parks formed the Committee for Equal Justice; the committee eventually became the Montgomery Improvement Association, which organized the Montgomery bus boycott a decade later. Its early mission, however, was to raise awareness and prevent the routine sexual violence perpetrated against black women. Activists also fought back when 15-year-old Flossie Hardman was raped by her boss, the owner of a grocery store. When he was found "not guilty" after five minutes of jury deliberation, African American shoppers put him out of business with a boycott. In the book *At the Dark End of the Street: Black Women, Rape, and Resistance*, historian Danielle McGuire notes that early anti-rape efforts were pivotal in launching the civil rights movement of the 1960s.

Second Wave Activism

White feminists joined anti-rape efforts in force in the 1960s, and this new coalitional movement raised national public awareness of sexual violence through consciousness-raising efforts and speak-outs that revealed rape as a common experience for women. They established a network of rape crisis centers across the United States, and the Feminist Alliance Against Rape formed in 1974 to coordinate activism. In 1975, Susan Brownmiller published her now classic book *Against Our Will*, acknowledging the systemic role of rape in maintaining social orders:

> That *some* men rape provides a sufficient threat to keep all women in a constant state of intimidation, forever conscious of the knowledge that the biological tool must be held in awe, for it may turn to weapon with sudden swiftness born of harmful intent. . . . Rather than society's aberrants or "spoilers of purity," men who commit rape have served in effect as front-line masculine shock troops, terrorist guerrillas in the longest sustained battle the world has ever known.[18]

African American anti-rape activists had arrived at this conclusion a century earlier, but in a sophisticated way that took into consideration the intersectional nature of rape as a tool of both racial and gendered power.

Consciousness-raising groups and speak-outs sprang up across the United States in the 1970s. In the decades that followed, activists successfully lobbied for laws making it illegal to rape one's spouse and rape shield laws that prevent consideration of the survivor's previous sexual behavior. Anti-rape activists also implemented more equitable legal definitions of "rape" and better enforcement of rape laws, and they vastly expanded governmental support for rape prevention.

Early Campus Activism

Anti-rape efforts on college campuses began in earnest in the 1970s as an increasing number of women started attending colleges and universities. Campus activists collaborated with community rape crisis centers to provide advocacy, support services, and self-defense workshops. Student activists fought for the first campus rape crisis center at the University of Maryland in 1972, a rape crisis center and a women's studies program at the University of Pennsylvania in 1973, and campus-wide rape prevention programs throughout the University of California system in 1976.

Researchers were first aware of the campus rape problem in the 1950s. The first study, titled "Male Sex Aggression on a University Campus," was published by sociologists Clifford Kirkpatrick and Eugene Kanin in 1957, but it took another two decades for the crisis to receive widespread public attention when Mary Koss published "Date Rape: A Campus Epidemic" in *Ms. Magazine* in 1982. Her three-year study of more than 7,000 students at 35 schools showed not only that assault/rape is common on campus, but also that most of these crimes are committed by an acquaintance or friend.

Koss' work made "date rape" part of the national dialogue in the late 1980s, but by the early 1990s, it had inspired a "tremendous backlash" over its prevalence and whether date rape constituted "real rape" from men's rights organizations and political conservatives. Katie Roiphe's *The Morning After: Fear, Feminism, and Sex* dismisses Koss' data based on a misunderstanding of basic statistics and the idea that women are partially to blame for being raped because of their drug and alcohol intake. Roiphe also painted anti-rape activists as hysterical and unattractive. This 1990s debate about college date rape may seem humorous now in light of numerous studies confirming Koss' data and more recent enlightened rejection of victim-blaming rhetoric, but at the time, it effectively dampened public outrage and action surrounding the issue.

Four decades of campus activism have produced a variety of programs aimed at raising awareness and preventing sexual violence. Many campuses host Take Back the Night, a public open-mic event where survivors share their experiences. This event was created in 1975 in Philadelphia after the rape and murder of microbiologist Susan Alexander Speeth. Some campuses also host a sexual assault awareness week, often with the Clothesline Project, where survivors display t-shirts with messages to share their stories. Many schools across the nation organize performances of *The Vagina Monologues* in February to raise awareness and money for local intimate partner violence (IPV) and rape crisis centers. Since 1999, some campuses have celebrated Denim Day USA, where students wear jeans to protest an Italian judge's ruling that a woman wearing tight jeans was not raped because she must have helped her rapist remove her jeans. Much of the campus activism of the past 40 years has focused on raising awareness and service provision.

The New Campus Anti-Rape Movement

The story of the new CARM that emerged in 2011 is the story of survivor activists filing Title IX complaints until the ED responded. In 2006, Laura Dunn, a student at the University of Wisconsin, filed a Title IX complaint against the school for failing to conduct a timely investigation of her rape at the hands of two rowing crewmates. The college took nine months to decide that they would not investigate the case because there were no eyewitnesses, and the ED determined that the university's nine-month deliberation and failure to investigate were "reasonable." In 2009, Wagatwe Wanjuki filed a Title IX complaint against Tufts University for the failed handling of her report of an abusive relationship involving sexual assault. The ED declined to investigate her case, citing a technicality in terms of timing. In 2010, attorney Wendy Murphy filed new Title IX complaints against Harvard, Princeton, and the University of Virginia for troubling patterns in their handling of sexual assault/rape cases.

The first case to make national headlines was filed by Alexandra Brodsky and Hannah Zeavin against Yale University in March 2011. This complaint, filed on behalf of 15 current and former students, detailed many troubling instances of a sexually hostile environment. For example, fraternity members gathered outside a frosh dorm yelling, "No means yes, and yes means anal" and "My name is Jack, I'm a necrophiliac, I fuck dead women and fill them with my semen!"; a fraternity shouting "dick, dick, dick!" in front of the Yale Women's Center; a 2007 petition signed by 150 medical students alleging groping, verbal abuse, and rape; and an email ranking 53 first-year female students by "how many beers it would take to have sex with them." The ED promptly opened an investigation into Yale's handling of assault/rape, and the school entered a resolution agreement, the outcome of which was deemed insufficient two years later by the campus activists who filed the complaint. A month after activists filed the Yale complaint, the ED issued the Dear Colleague Letter detailing new guidelines strengthening the Title IX application to sexual assault/rape issues.

The new CARM is more effective than previous waves because of social media tools that allow survivors to hold schools accountable. This important activist tool was simply not available prior to the mid-2000s when Facebook (2004) and Twitter (2006) went online. Wanjuki was a social media pioneer in the anti-rape movement when she starting chronicling her sexual assault and the school's betrayal in 2009 on her blog "Raped at Tufts University." Tucker Reed at the University of Southern California followed Wanjuki's model with her blog, "Covered in Band-Aids," which chronicled her assault and the adjudication process. Grace Brown started the "Project Unbreakable" Tumblr to document rapists' statements to survivors. In 2012, Mount Holyoke College senior Ali Safran began the "Surviving in Numbers" Tumblr for survivors to post their experiences.

New online technologies have also helped survivor activists connect and organize. When a survivor comes forward, they are connected to a network of information from campus activists across the country. They can be instantly connected to informational resources and templates that have been used on other campuses, and the anti-rape network provides ample coaching and other forms of support through Skype conversations, text messages, and myriad other communication tools. Online networking has also enabled survivors to network in ways that help them cope with post-traumatic stress disorder and other symptoms of trauma. Campus activists have developed an informal counseling network where they share their fears and anxieties and assist one another in obtaining professional counseling when needed. Twenty years ago, campus activists had to rely on national media outlets to learn about activism at other schools, and telephone conversations were the primary means of communication.

Young people have often been at the forefront of major social movements that have "transformed human history," including the civil rights movement, the environmental justice movement, the movement for LGBTQ rights, different feminist movements, antiwar movements, immigrant rights movements, and others. The CARM flies in the face of stereotypes of young people as politically inactive or "slactivists." This movement has taught us once again that young people can be innovative, effective agents of change, even with issues on which others have been working for decades. Campus activists use a sophisticated arrangement of formal political and legal tactics (lobbying, filing lawsuits, filing federal complaints, passing new laws, etc.) in tandem with unconventional political tactics (sit-ins, demonstrations, protests, online shaming campaigns, online petitions, etc.). Young people are more likely to engage in unconventional political participation than older generations, and the tactics of the new CARM reflect this.

PROFILE IN POWER

Wagatwe Wanjuki

SOURCE: courtesy of Wagatwe Wanjuki

Wagatwe Wanjuki is one of the leading activists in the new Campus Anti-Rape Movement. In 2009, she chronicled Tuft University's response to her experience of sexual violence on campus in her blog, "Raped at Tufts University." The blog detailed the many times she was assaulted by a fellow Tufts student with whom she was in a relationship. When Wanjuki reported it to campus officials, they initially responded to her complaint, but then mysteriously dropped it. Later, campus officials informed her that they were not legally obligated to take any action in her case. Wanjuki's response was to organize. She worked with other students at Tufts and the national organization Students Active for Ending Rape to pressure Tufts to improve their sexual violence policy and procedures. Wanjuki also collaborated with other activists to organize a protest, write op-eds in the student newspaper, and host a community forum to raise awareness of the problems with Tuft's policy. These efforts paid off when Tufts adopted a series of new policies in response to student activism.

Trauma from the sexual violence and institutional betrayal took its toll on Wanjuki, and in the spring of 2009, she was dismissed from Tufts University for poor academic performance. She appealed the decision, but her appeal was decided by her assailant's academic advisor, who rejected it. Wanjuki took some time away from school, but then enrolled in a community college and transferred to Rutgers University, where she completed her bachelor's degree in sociology in 2014. That same year, students at Tufts University nominated Wanjuki for an honorary degree. The university did not award her one.

In May 2014, Wanjuki ignited a national conversation with her hashtag #SurvivorPrivilege. She tweeted the hashtag in response to an opinion piece by conservative writer George Will in the *Washington Post* in which he suggested that campus rape survivors were lying about their experiences to get attention. In the op-ed, Will dismissed reputable statistics on campus rape and then stated that being a survivor is a "coveted status that confers privilege." Wanjuki responded with a tweet: "Where's my survivor privilege? Was expelled & have $10,000s of private student loans used to attend school that didn't care I was raped. #SurvivorPrivilege" Within hours, the #SurvivorPrivilege hashtag was trending as survivors and allies across the nation used it to share their stories. Many tweeted about their personal experiences of sexual violence and institutional betrayal that were anything but "privileged."

Wanjuki went on to create the popular Tumblr blog *Fuck Yeah, Feminists!* and she is a contributor to Know Your IX, an online resource clearinghouse for campus sexual violence. Wanjuki also cofounded ED Act NOW, a group that lobbies the Department of Education to speed up the processing of federal Title IX complaints. She continues to advocate for survivors and women of color through her writing, lectures, and media appearances.

Sexual Violence Policy

The sustained efforts of anti-rape activists during the second wave of the women's rights movement culminated in passage of the Violence Against Women Act (VAWA) in 1994, the first national law requiring law enforcement to treat gendered violence as a crime rather than a private family matter. This law was the first to establish sexual violence as a national public policy issue. VAWA also established the Office of Violence Against Women within the Department of Justice to guide states in policies and practice to reduce sexual and other forms of violence against women. Senator Joe Biden (D-DE) led the charge to pass VAWA, and the law was reauthorized in 2000, 2005, and again in 2013 over stiff opposition from congressional Republicans regarding extended protections for Native American, gay, lesbian, and transgendered victims.[19]

Campus activists have three primary laws at their disposable to hold campuses accountable: the Clery Act, Title IX, and the Campus Sexual Assault Violence Elimination (SaVE) Act. The Jeanne Clery Disclosure of Campus Security Policy and Campus Crime Statistics Act of 1990, referred to as the Clery Act,[20] applies to public and private colleges and universities that receive funds from the federal government, such as financial aid. Virtually every school of the 7,500 institutions of higher education in the United States receives some sort of federal funding, whether it is public or private. The Clery Act requires campuses to maintain and report information about ten different types of crime that occur on and near campus: criminal homicide, sex offenses, robbery, aggravated assault, burglary, motor vehicle theft, arson, domestic violence, dating violence, and stalking. Schools are required to maintain a daily crime log and publish an annual crime report on October 1 of each year that reports the crimes that occurred during the previous calendar year. Colleges are also required to issue alerts for crimes that are an ongoing threat to the safety of the campus.

Although the Clery Act has been law since 1990, only one-third of schools are in full compliance with federal law.[21] Four-year colleges and historically black institutions are doing a better job of reporting sexual crimes, but most institutions have a long way to go in terms of achieving promising practices. A 2009 report by the Center for Public Integrity found vast underreporting of sexual assault data because of confusion about reporting requirements, failure to gather data, and institutional exploitation of loopholes such as the counselor and clergy exemption.[22] Three-quarters of two- and four-year institutions report zero sexual assaults in their annual security report.[23] The Clery Act allows the ED to impose civil penalties against schools for up to $35,000 per infraction and suspends federal funds from institutions that are not in compliance, but this provision has only recently been used to punish schools.[24]

The second major body of law that campus anti-rape activists have used is the Title IX educational amendment of 1972. Title IX exists because of three women. In the 1950s, Edith Green dreamed of being an electrical engineer, but no school would accept a woman. Patsy Mink wanted to become a doctor, but women were not accepted at the 20 schools to which she applied. Bernice Sandler could not get hired for a full-time professorship after earning her doctorate because she was a woman.[25] These three women worked together in Congress in the early 1970s to champion Title IX legislation prohibiting discrimination on the basis of sex in educational programs that receive federal financial assistance. The law was officially sponsored by Representative Patsy Mink (D-HI) and Senator Birch Bayh (D-IN), and it was signed into law by President Richard Nixon with bipartisan support.[26] Title IX was originally enacted to address hiring and employment practices for university employees, but has since been best known for increasing the number of women in collegiate sports.[27]

During its 40 years, the impact of Title IX has been dramatic.[28] It has mostly eliminated blatant gender discrimination for students in higher education and has somewhat addressed the more subtle forms of discrimination found in differential financial aid packages, housing accommodations, and sexual harassment. Title IX has brought about seismic change in the number of female students, faculty, and administrators. In 1970, women earned only 14 percent of PhDs; they now earn nearly 50 percent of PhDs and comprise nearly 40 percent of the professorate. The number of female college presidents jumped from three percent to 23 percent during this same time, and women now outnumber men in the ranks of undergraduate students. Women's participation in Division I sports rose from 15 percent to 44 percent.[29] But subtle, powerful gender barriers still exist on college campuses, where all students face a higher risk of rape by going to college than not, but female students are far more likely to be assaulted/raped than their male counterparts.[30] Title IX is now being applied to sexual violence to ensure that male and female students have an equitable learning experience.

The third law that governs rape at colleges and universities is the Campus SaVE Act of 2013, by far the most comprehensive law to prevent campus assault/rape.[31] The Campus SaVE Act was included in the reauthorized VAWA that went into effect in 2014. Campus SaVE is actually a major overhaul of the Clery Act, and its provisions are enforced by the Clery division of the ED. Beyond assault/rape, Campus SaVE requires schools to do a better job of addressing IPV, stalking, and dating violence.[32] Campus SaVE goes further than any existing laws by explicitly holding schools responsible for the *prevention* of sexual violence . Schools are now required to hold prevention programming for all incoming students and new employees that includes a clear definition of consent, the process for reporting, risk reduction advice, and bystander intervention training. Schools are also responsible for providing ongoing student and employee training and information on how to recognize abusive behavior.[33] According to attorney S. Daniel Carter, who was instrumental in writing the original Clery Act and the Campus SaVE Act, "Much of what was in the old law [Clery Act] focused on treating the symptoms. The Campus SaVE Act will focus on inoculating against the disease."[34]

The Campus SaVE Act also mandates standard procedures for processing complaints of assault/rape, including letting students and employees know of their right to report to local authorities in writing; their right to receive legal advocacy and mental health services; their right to request (and receive) a change in living, academic, transportation, and working situations; honoring restraining orders on campus; disclosing sanctions for assault/rape; and detailed information about the investigation and adjudication process. The Campus SaVE Act mandates greater transparency about policies and procedures and encourages colleges and universities to undertake research on best practices for preventing and handling assault/rape.

INTIMATE PARTNER VIOLENCE

Domestic violence, also known as IPV, is a global epidemic first identified by the United Nations as a serious international concern at the 1985 Nairobi World Conference. Since that time, many studies have demonstrated that the lives of girls and women are marked by violence across the globe. IPV includes physical violence, emotional abuse, financial abuse, sexual violence, and stalking. The 2013 World Health Organization report on violence against women estimates that one in three women experience lifetime IPV.[35] Someone is beaten or assaulted every nine seconds in the United States.[36] Each year, more than ten million men, women, and transgender individuals are the victims of physical abuse by an intimate partner. On a typical day in the United States, more than 20,000 people call IPV hotlines. IPV is a major public policy and public health issue given that it constitutes 15 percent of all violent crime in the United States.

In recent years, authorities and political leaders have begun to take stalking more seriously. Stalking is the repeated harassment of another person, whether in person, over the phone, or online. In the United States, one in seven women and one in 18 men experience stalking from an intimate partner to the point where they felt that the stalker would harm or kill them or someone close to them. To date, 19 million women and five million men in the United States have been stalked at some point.

IPV is a gendered policy issue since women and transgender individuals are significantly more likely to experience domestic violence than men. Women constitute 85 percent of IPV victims, while men make up 14 percent. Over the course of their lifetime, one in three women and one in seven men will experience physical abuse by an intimate partner. Women between the ages of 18 and 24 are at the highest risk of violence from an intimate partner. Approximately 45 percent of women in physically abusive relationships are also raped or sexually assaulted by their abuser.

Pregnant women are also a higher risk of IPV than are women who are not pregnant. The World Health Organization finds that the rate of IPV for pregnant women that involves specifically kicking or punching them in the abdomen to hurt the baby ranges from one percent to 15 percent. Researchers have yet to identify why abuse increases during pregnancy, but studies find that abuse rates are higher if the pregnancy is unplanned or unwanted.

The experience of IPV varies intersectionally. LGBTQ individuals face alarming rates of IPV. According to the National Intimate Partner and Sexual Violence Survey, 61 percent of bisexual women experience physical violence, rape, or stalking from intimate partners compared to 44 percent of lesbians and 35 percent of heterosexual women. Nearly four in ten bisexual men (37 percent) experience the same, followed by 26 percent of gay men and 29 percent of heterosexual women. LGBTQ individuals have less access to domestic violence prevention resources and support because of the myth that domestic violence is not a problem with same-sex partners.

IPV experiences also vary by race. Multiracial women are the most likely to experience IPV (54 percent), while approximately one in four black women (44 percent) and Native American women (43.7 percent) are victims of IPV. These rates are 30 percent to 50 percent higher than the rates of IPV suffered by Asian American, Latina, and white women. Rates of IPV are also high for Native American (45 percent), black (39 percent), and multiracial men (39 percent). These rates are twice as high as the rate of IPV experienced by Latino and white men. Racial differences in IPV cannot be explained by a single factor, but poverty has been linked to IPV, and marginalized groups are at a greater risk for poverty and related factors such as substance abuse and unemployment. In other words, systemic racism that prevents marginalized groups from the same opportunities and outcomes as other groups leads to poverty, which is in turn linked to IPV.

Disability is another identity on which experiences of IPV vary widely. Both men and women with disabilities are at a greater risk of IPV, but this is especially true for women. Women with mental or physical disabilities are 40 percent more likely than other women to experience IPV, and their abuse typically lasts longer and is more intense. Women with disabilities are most often abused by someone they know, but they also face abuse from health-care providers, both of whom can withhold medicine, basic assistance (e.g., bathing, food), and assistive devices (e.g., wheelchairs and braces). Abusers prey on the vulnerability of people with limited mobility and cognitive faculties.

Types of Abuse

IPV comes in five major forms: (1) physical abuse, (2) sexual violence, (3) psychological abuse, (4) emotional abuse, and (5) financial abuse. Physical abuse ranges in severity from grabbing to punching to stabbing or shooting. Other forms of physical abuse include withholding medical assistance or forcing the victim to consume drugs or alcohol to control them. Sexual violence ranges from sexual battery to rape, as discussed previously. Perpetrators use psychological abuse to control their victim through intimidation and fear. Examples of this type of abuse include threatening to harm children or pets, harming property or pets, and stalking. It is also common for abusers to isolate victims from their family and friends so they do not have a support network to help them out of the situation. Perpetrators also use emotional abuse, such as belittling their victim, name-calling, "silent treatment," and constant criticism. This robs the victim of a sense of self-worth, which makes the victim feel like they deserve the abuse. Financial abuse is also used to control victims by maintaining control of the victim's income, forbidding employment, harassing the victim at their job, and requiring justification for every penny spent. IPV perpetrators typically combine most or all of these tools of domestic abuse.

Many people question why IPV survivors do not just leave the abuse situation. There are many factors that explain this. First, abusers make it difficult to leave the relationship. They often threaten more serious violence should the victim leave, and a woman is 70 times more likely to be murdered within a few weeks of leaving a relationship than she is if she stays and endures the abuse. Additionally, 98 percent of abusers manipulate the money supply to their victim, leaving them with no resources to leave the household, which is why IPV is one of the leading causes of homelessness (when the victim leaves the abusive situation). Another reason some victims stay in an abusive relationship is the cycle of abuse that includes a "honeymoon period," during which time the abuser is loving and kind and promises he or she will not abuse again. Once that period has passed, the abuser continues the cycle.

Homicide

Some acts of IPV end in homicide. Each day in the United States, three women are killed by their intimate partners. To put this into perspective, the number of U.S. troops killed in Afghanistan from 2001 to 2012 was 6,488, and the number of American women killed by intimate partners during that time was nearly double, at 11,766. One in five acts of IPV involve a weapon, and the presence of a gun in an IPV situation increases the risk of homicide by 500 percent. IPV is the leading cause of female homicide during pregnancy. Nearly three in four murder–suicides (72 percent) in the United States involve an abuser killing their intimate partner, and 94 percent of the victims are women. Beyond the intimate partner, one in five murder victims of IPV were friends, family members, neighbors, bystanders, and law enforcement officers on the scene. IPV calls are the second most dangerous calls (after burglary) to which police officers respond. Intimate partner homicide rates are also intersectional. A transgender person of color is two and a half times more likely to be a victim of partner violence than a non-LGBTQ person of color. In 2013, 21 LGBTQ individuals were murdered by their intimate partner.

Perpetrators

One in four people (25 percent) in the United States admit to having perpetrated some form of domestic violence. Multiple studies find that women are more likely to perpetrate IPV than men (28 percent compared to 22 percent, respectively), but the level of violence and injury differs significantly. Women are far more likely than men to engage in stalking behavior, and studies that take into account the level of fear and injury experienced by victims find that male-perpetrated abuse is much more likely to cause high levels of fear, injury, and serious injury than abuse perpetrated by women. This difference in the level of violence enacted accounts for a gap in arrest rates for male and female perpetrators, where more than three in four of those arrested are men. Most people arrested for IPV offenses have a previous criminal history of both violent and nonviolent offenses. One factor that determines perpetration of IPV for both men and women is whether they were exposed to domestic violence in their home while growing up. Children who witness abuse are much more likely to abuse an intimate partner later in life.

Effects of Intimate Partner Violence

Health-care workers, such as doctors and nurses, are on the front line for identifying IPV because they see injured victims. In addition to obvious physical injuries that result from violence, victims typically suffer from other medical problems because of prolonged exposure to stress from the violence, including nutritional deficiency, irritable bowel syndrome, chronic pain, miscarriages, stillbirth, cardiovascular disease, and cancer. IPV victims are also more vulnerable to contracting sexually transmitted infections and HIV because of their weakened immune system. Most victims of IPV also suffer a host of mental health issues, such as post-traumatic stress disorder, anxiety, higher rates of depression, and suicidal behavior. IPV victims are also at a much higher risk of having addiction issues with alcohol and drugs. IPV is a public health issue that costs the American public $8.3 billion per year in law enforcement as well as medical, mental health, and other support services. The annual burden on taxpayers is enormous, even though only one in three IPV survivors seek medical care for their injuries. IPV also impacts the private sector. IPV is the cause of eight million days of lost work per year, and as many as 60 percent of victims lose their job as a result of issues stemming from IPV.

Intimate Partner Violence Activism in the United States

Domestic violence has a long history of being socially and politically acceptable. The Law of Chastisement in eighth-century Rome allowed men to physically punish their wives and children, and except for a few historical moments of resistance (e.g., the Puritans who forbade wife abuse in colonial Massachusetts), IPV has been perpetrated by men for most of recorded human history. Activism to end domestic violence in the United States began in the 1970s. Prior to that time, family violence was not considered a problem in the legal system or medical field, and it was tacitly condoned in broader society. A 1968 Harris Poll found that one in five Americans found it acceptable to slap one's spouse. A husband beating his wife was considered a private matter, not a public concern. This distinction was in fact exploited by perpetrators whose lawyers routinely transferred their cases from criminal courts to family courts with civil procedures so their clients would receive more lenient sentences. In other words, perpetrators received a fraction of the sentence for beating their wives compared to what they would receive if they beat a complete stranger. In New York in 1966, physical violence was added as grounds for divorce, but only if the abuser had engaged in a "sufficient" number of beatings. The second wave of the women's rights movement changed laws and cultural norms.

In just one decade, feminist activism in what was first known as the battered women's movement shifted IPV from a neglected private concern to a significant public concern. Within a decade, the movement mostly achieved its goals of raising awareness of the issue, establishing support services for victims, and changing laws to reduce or eliminate IPV. Activists organized using the motto "we will not be beaten" to expose the problem. They opened the first battered women's shelter in 1973 in St. Paul, Minnesota, and two more shelters—Rosie's Place in Boston and the Atlanta Union Mission in Atlanta—opened their doors the following year. Activists went on to open nearly 200 shelters and abuse hotlines in many major cities in the first few years of the battered women's movement. Early shelters were often established in makeshift places, such as homes and donated spaces. Activists also overturned laws and practices denying welfare to women who left their husbands because the state considered their husband's income. They also created laws enabling IPV victims to bring criminal charges against their abusers, which were technically in place already under existing criminal codes, but were not enforced in family situations.

At the 1977 National Women's Conference in Houston, activists added the issue of domestic violence as a policy of concern, and they identified obstacles that prevented women from leaving abusive relationships and seeking help. This was the first time the issue was addressed at a national gathering of feminists. After the conference, activists established support groups for IPV victims that sprang up in cities across the United States. Activists also turned their attention to legislation at the state and federal level to increase program funding and pass laws criminalizing domestic violence. In 1977, IPV victim Francine Hughes was acquitted for murdering her husband on the grounds of "temporary insanity." Hughes had suffered severe physical abuse since 1963, but provided evidence that social workers and law enforcement did not assist her. Hughes divorced her husband, but he refused to move out and continued his cycle of abuse. Hughes became the face of domestic violence through a widely read book about her experience and the film *The Burning Bed: The True Story of an Abused Wife*.

Social justice activist Kip Tiernan opened Rosie's Place in Boston after discovering that homeless women dressed up like men to get into male-only shelters. Rosie's House became a model for many other shelters that were opened in the first years of the movement. Susan Schechter, also a prominent activist in the movement, started the first program in the country that addressed child abuse in families facing IPV. She later became a professor of social work at the University of Iowa, where she researched the links among IPV, child abuse, poverty, and substance abuse. Early on, the movement was mostly led by white women, and in the mid-1980s, women of color pressed for better representation of the concerns of marginalized women. Numerous accounts from women of color encountering racial and cultural bias from service providers sparked lively discussions in the movement and led to reforms of service provision to better serve women of color. The struggle to best serve all victims of IPV who have a diversity of needs continues.

Intimate Partner Violence Policy

In the 1970s, activists raised public awareness and established an infrastructure to serve victims of IPV, and in the 1980s, they passed hundreds of laws requiring the state to take the crime seriously. In 1984, anti-IPV activists lobbied for the Family Violence Prevention Services Act authorizing the Department of Health and Human Services to provide grants to states to open domestic violence shelters and related assistance programs for victims. By the end of the decade, 48 states had passed laws against domestic violence, and state funding to address IPV went from $200,000 to $5.5 million. The systemic reforms that activists put into place in the 1980s were significantly expanded in the 1990s. In 1992, the U.S. Surgeon General published a report showing that the leading cause of injury to women aged 15 to 44 was domestic abuse, and that same year, the American Medical Association issued guidelines that doctors should screen for signs of IPV. In 1993, the United Nations officially recognized domestic violence as a human rights issue and issued a Declaration on the Elimination of Violence Against Women encouraging all countries to address the issue.

As with sexual violence, the most significant piece of legislation in the fight against domestic violence is the VAWA, which was passed in 1994. WAVA was the first federal law to recognize IPV as a crime and to provide federal resources to address the problem. VAWA also allocated $1.6 billion in funds to investigate and prosecute violence against women. It established mandatory sentences for those convicted of domestic violence since criminal courts typically imposed light sentences for the crime and made it possible for IPV victims to sue prosecutors who choose not to prosecute their abusers.

Today, there are more than 1,900 programs to address IPV in the United States and substantial yearly funding for intervention and research. Support services have evolved significantly since they were first offered in the 1970s. For example, shelters now do a better job of providing psychological and other support for children whose parents have been abused. Nearly 50 percent of people in domestic violence shelters are children, and 80 percent of the women in domestic violence shelters bring at least one child with them. Domestic violence shelters today also provide more personal and professional development for victims than in the past. Today's shelter model promotes the idea that the best method to support IPV victims is to work on ways they can gain confidence and financial independence.

CONCLUSION

Many women in the United States will experience sexual violence and domestic violence at some point in their life, and people who are marginalized face a greater risk of these types of violence. With regard to sexual violence, nearly all perpetrators are men, most rapists are repeat rapists, and most are known to the victim. Many Americans believe in rape myths, for example, that most rapes are perpetrated by strangers, that rapists act on impulse, that many rapes involve the use of weapons, that false rape reporting is common, that a woman cannot be raped by her husband, and that perpetrators who are high or drunk cannot be held responsible for raping. These myths, in addition to stigmatization and victim blaming, discourage survivors of rape and sexual assault from reporting rape. Sexual violence is a public health issue with the highest victim crime cost of any violent crime. College students face a higher risk of sexual violence than their non-college-bound peers, and after more than a century of antiviolence activism and five decades of activism on college campuses, the new CARM has put the issues on the national policy agenda. CARM activists have passed new legislation and enforced existing laws by filing federal Title IX complaints.

Domestic violence or IPV is a global epidemic, and LGBTQ individuals, people with disabilities, and women are at greater risk. Black and Native American women are especially vulnerable to IPV. This abuse comes in many different forms, and it is difficult for IPV victims to leave abusive situations because of abuser threats and manipulation. Women face an elevated risk of violence if they leave. Three women are murdered each day in the United States by a husband or boyfriend. IPV is a public health issue because abuse causes physical injuries, medical problems as a result of long-term exposure to stress, and mental health issues. Activism against domestic violence in the United States started in the 1970s, and in 1994, Congress passed the VAWA. This is the most significant piece of legislation in the fight against domestic violence.

CHAPTER SUMMARY

- Many people in the United States will experience sexual battery, sexual assault, or rape at some point in their life, and people who are marginalized (e.g., poor people, women, people of color, LGBTQ individuals, transgender people, disabled individuals) are at a greater risk for sexual violence.
- Nearly all perpetrators of sexual violence are men, and most rapists are repeat rapists. The vast majority of rapes are perpetrated by someone the victim knows.

- Alcohol is the most common weapon used in perpetrating rape. Only about ten percent of rapes involve a gun or a knife.
- Many Americans believe in rape myths, such as the myths that most rapes are perpetrated by strangers, that rapists act on impulse (most rapes are premeditated), that most rapes involve the use of weapons, that false rape reporting is common, that a woman cannot be raped by her husband, and that perpetrators who are high or drunk cannot be held responsible for raping.
- Rape myths, stigmatization, and victim blaming discourage survivors of rape and sexual assault from reporting this crime. Only one in three survivors report this crime to law enforcement, and on college campuses, approximately ten percent of survivors report their rape to campus authorities.
- Overall reporting rates are low, and survivors who do not fit the media stereotype of a young, heterosexual white woman are even less likely to report rape or sexual assault to authorities. LGBTQ survivors, people of color, and male survivors are the least likely to report sexual violence to authorities.
- Sexual violence is a public health issue with the highest victim crime cost of any violent crime. Most survivors suffer physical issues, post-traumatic stress disorder, and other mental health issues.
- College students face a higher risk of being raped than their non-college-bound peers, which makes going to college a risk factor for sexual violence.
- The United States has experienced four peaks of activism against sexual violence: during the post–Civil War Reconstruction Era, leading up to the civil rights movement, during the second wave of the feminist movement, and the new CARM.
- The new CARM that emerged in 2011 has been more effective than previous efforts because it has used social media to raise public consciousness. Survivors are also using group lawsuits and new laws to force colleges and universities to do a better job of responding to sexual violence on campus.
- The primary laws used by anti-rape activists are the VAWA, the Clery Act, Title IX, and the Campus SaVE Act.
- Domestic violence, also known as IPV, is a global epidemic, with one in three women and one in seven men in the United States experiencing it during their lifetime. Rates for LGBTQ individuals are about twice as high. Black and Native American women also experience much higher rates of IPV than other women. People with disabilities also face a substantially higher risk of IPV.
- There are five major forms of IPV: (1) physical abuse, (2) sexual violence, (3) psychological abuse, (4) emotional abuse, and (5) financial abuse.
- It is difficult for IPV victims to leave abusive situations because the abuser threatens violence, manipulates their finances so they have no resources to leave, and promises that they will never abuse again, also known as the "honeymoon period" in the cycle of violence.
- Three women are killed by intimate partners per day in the United States, and the vast majority of murder–suicides are attributed to IPV.

- One in four people admit to perpetrating domestic violence. Women are slightly more likely than men to commit IPV, but male abuse is much more likely to cause high levels of fear and serious injuries. Male perpetrators constitute the vast majority of domestic violence arrests.
- Victims of IPV commonly suffer physical injuries and other medical problems as a result of long-term exposure to stress, including heart disease and cancer. Victims of IPV also commonly suffer many mental health issues.
- IPV costs the American public $8.3 billion per year in law enforcement, medical, mental health, and other support services.
- Activism to end domestic violence in the United States started in the 1970s. Prior to that time, family violence was not considered a problem in legal or medical fields, and it was tacitly condoned in society.
- Activists opened the first battered women's shelter in 1973 and nearly 200 additional shelters opened within a matter of years. Today, there are 1,900 shelters and similar programs in the United States serving victims of IPV.
- In the 1970s, activists raised public awareness and established an infrastructure to serve victims of IPV, and in the 1980s, they passed hundreds of laws requiring the state to take the crime seriously. In 1994, activists passed the VAWA, the most significant piece of legislation in the fight against domestic violence in the United States.

STUDY/DISCUSSION QUESTIONS

- How do rates of sexual violence vary by gender, race, sexuality, and ability?
- What are some common rape myths?
- Why is the new CARM more effective than previous efforts to address campus rape?
- How do rates of domestic violence vary by gender, race, sexuality, and ability?
- What factors make it difficult for domestic violence victims to leave their abusers?

CASE STUDIES

1. **Why have colleges and universities waited so long to address sexual violence on campus?**

   As noted in this chapter, the first study on campus violence was released in 1957, and the public became aware of the epidemic in the 1980s as a result of Mary Koss's groundbreaking data on campus rape. The Clery Act was passed in 1990, which required schools to follow certain rules of fairness in adjudicating cases of sexual violence. When the new CARM exposed the issue that campus officials have known about for half a century, many feigned ignorance of the problem, while others insisted that their institutions were doing a decent job of handling cases of sexual violence. Hundreds of campus survivor stories attest to the fact that campuses are still not handling sexual violence in a just and equitable fashion. What factors do you think account for the slow response from campus administrators to the campus rape crisis?

2. **Where do rape myths come from?**
Many Americans buy into myths about rape that stem from an underlying assumption that many men and women hold that heterosexual men are entitled to women's bodies. Rape myths have been around for centuries and seem to be passed down from generation to generation. How are rape myths perpetuated? What role do parents, teachers, entertainment media, religion, political leaders, and other societal institutions and leaders have in perpetuating rape myths? Identify specific examples of how institutions and leaders reinforce and perpetuate rape myths.

3. **What sexual violence resources exist on your campus?**
Do some research to find out more about your campus sexual assault policy. Is it easy to locate? Are the definitions of sexual violence clear? Is the process for reporting accessible and easy to follow? Once you have evaluated your school's policy, ask your fellow students what they know about the policy. Would they know where to go if they experienced sexual violence?

4. **Why do people believe it is easy for IPV victims to leave their abusers?**
A common question for domestic violence victims is "why don't they just leave?" Why do you think so many people hold victims responsible for not leaving the situation when the barriers to leaving are so high?

5. **Why are rates of sexual violence and domestic violence still so high?**
Awareness of epidemic levels of sexual violence and domestic violence started in the 1960s (although activism surrounding both issues started much earlier). Epidemic rates of both types of violence have persisted, even though the public is more aware of these issues, national and state laws have been passed to address them, and activists have developed networks of support services for rape survivors and IPV victims. Why haven't these reforms been more effective? What reforms are needed to reduce or eliminate sexual violence and domestic violence in the United States?

RESOURCES

- The **National Sexual Violence Resource Center** provides leadership in preventing and responding to sexual violence through collaboration, sharing and creating resources, and promoting research.
http://www.nsvrc.org/organizations
- The **Rape, Abuse & Incest National Network** is the largest anti–sexual violence organization in the United States. It operates the National Sexual Assault Hotline and carries out programs to prevent sexual violence, help victims, and ensure that rapists are brought to justice.
http://www.rainn.org

- **Know Your IX** is a survivor- and youth-led organization that aims to empower students to end sexual and dating violence in their schools.
  http://knowyourix.org
- The **National Coalition Against Domestic Violence** aims to change society to have zero tolerance for domestic violence through public policy, increasing understanding of the impact of domestic violence, and providing programs and education that drive that change.
  http://www.ncadv.org
- **Black Women's Blueprint** works to place black women and girls' lives as well as their particular struggles squarely within the context of the larger racial justice concerns of black communities, including a focus on sexual violence and domestic violence.
  http://www.blackwomensblueprint.org

Notes

Chapter 1

1. For example, see Sheila Ellison, *If Women Ruled the World: How to Create the World We Want to Live In* (Novato, CA: New World Library, 2004); Shelly Rachanow, *If Women Ran the World, Sh*t Would Get Done: Celebrating All the Wonderful, Amazing, Stupendous, Inspiring, Butt-kicking Things Women Do* (Newburyport, MA: Conari Press, 2006); and Shelly Rachanow, *What Would You Do If You Ran the World? Everyday Ideas from Women Who Want to Make the World a Better Place* (Newburyport, MA: Conari Press, 2009).
2. See Harold D. Lasswell, *Who Gets What, When, How* (New York: McGraw–Hill, 1936).
3. Barbara Kellerman, "You've Come a Long Way, Baby—And You've Got Miles to Go," in *The Difference "Difference" Makes: Women and Leadership*, ed. Deborah L. Rhode (Stanford, CA: Stanford University Press, 2003), 54.
4. Deborah L. Rhode and Barbara Kellerman, "Women and Leadership: The State of Play," in *Women & Leadership: The State of Play and Strategies for Change*, ed. Barbara Kellerman and Deborah L. Rhode (New York: Wiley, 2007), 1–2.
5. Deborah L. Rhode, "Introduction," in *The Difference "Difference" Makes: Women and Leadership*, ed. Deborah L. Rhode (Stanford, CA: Stanford University Press, 2003), 6.
6. Susan C. Bourque, "Political Leadership for Women: Redefining Power and Reassessing the Political," in *Women on Power: Leadership Redefined*, ed. Sue J. M. Freeman, Susan C. Bourque, and Christine M. Shelton (Boston: Northeastern University Press, 2001), 86–89.
7. Virginia Sapiro, *Women in American Society: An Introduction to Women's Studies*, 5th ed. (Boston: McGraw–Hill, 2003), 7–10.
8. Susan J. Carroll and Linda M. G. Zerilli, "Feminist Challenges to Political Science," in *Political Science: The State of the Discipline II*, ed. Ada W. Finifter (Washington, DC: American Political Science Association, 1993), 55–72.
9. Bourque, "Political Leadership," 106.

Chapter 2

1. Mission statement of the ERA Coalition, http://www.eracoalition.org/mission.php.
2. Steven Zeitchik, "Oscars 2015: Patricia Arquette Stirs Controversy with Equal-Pay Remarks," *Los Angeles Times*, February 23, 2015, http://www.latimes.com/entertainment/

movies/moviesnow/la-et-mn-oscars-patricia-arquette-speech-equal-pay-20150223
-story.html.

3. Anne N. Costain, "Paving the Way: The Work of the Women's Movement," in *Antici-pating Madam President*, ed. Robert P. Watson and Ann Gordon (Boulder, CO: Lynne Rienner, 2003), 31.

4. See Dorothy Sue Cobble, Linda Gordon, and Astrid Henry, *Feminism Unfinished: A Short, Surprising History of American Women's Movements* (New York: Liveright, 2015), xviii.

5. Sandra F. VanBurkleo, *"Belonging to the World:" Women's Rights and American Constitu-tional Culture* (New York: Oxford University Press, 2001), 46–47. Linda Kerber coined the phrase "republican motherhood" in *Women of the Republic* (Chapel Hill: University of North Carolina Press, 1997).

6. Quoted in Phyllis Lee Levin, *Abigail Adams: A Biography* (New York: St. Martin's Press, 1987).

7. Lee Epstein and Thomas G. Walker, *Constitutional Law for a Changing America: A Short Course*, 4th ed. (Washington, DC: CQ Press, 2009), 6.

8. Jean V. Matthews, *Women's Struggle for Equality: The First Phase 1828–1876.* (Chicago: Ivan R. Dee, 1997), 5.

9. Robin Morgan, ed., Introduction to *Sisterhood Is Forever: The Women's Anthology for a New Millennium* (New York: Washington Square Press, 2003), xxxiii–xxxiv.

10. Sojourner Truth, "Ain't I a Women?," delivered at the 1851 Women's Convention in Akron, Ohio, full transcript available at Feminist.com, http://www.feminist.com/resources/artspeech/genwom/sojour.htm.

11. Anne Firor Scott and Andrew MacKay Scott, *One Half the People: The Fight for Woman Suffrage* (Urbana: University of Illinois Press, 1982), 12.

12. For example, see Alana S. Jeydel, *Political Women: The Women's Movement, Political Institutions, the Battle for Women's Suffrage and the ERA* (New York: Routledge, 2004), 46–48.

13. Scott and Scott, *One Half the People*, 25–27.

14. Annelise Orleck, *Rethinking American Women's Activism* (New York: Routledge, 2015), 20–21.

15. Judith E. Harper, "Biography of Susan B. Anthony and Elizabeth Cady Stanton," *PBS*, http://www.pbs.org/stantonanthony/resources/index.html.

16. Bruce Miroff, *Icons of Democracy: American Leaders as Heroes, Aristocrats, Dissenters, & Democrats* (Lawrence: University Press of Kansas, 2000), 125.

17. Ibid., 125–26.

18. Lois W. Banner, "Elizabeth Cady Stanton," in *The Oxford Companion to United States History*, ed. Paul S. Boyer (New York: Oxford University Press, 2001), 742.

19. Ellen C. DuBois, "Susan B. Anthony," in *The Oxford Companion to United States History*, ed. Paul S. Boyer (New York: Oxford University Press, 2001), 38–39.

20. David M. O'Brien, *Constitutional Law and Politics, Volume Two: Civil Rights and Civil Liberties*, 7th ed. (New York: W. W. Norton, 2008), 1517.

21. Jane J. Mansbridge, *Why We Lost the ERA* (Chicago: University of Chicago Press, 1986), 1–7.

22. Cobble, Gordon, and Henry, *Feminism Unfinished*, 23.

23. Sara M. Evans, *Tidal Wave: How Women Changed America at Century's End* (New York: Free Press, 2003), 18–19.

24. Orleck, *Rethinking American Women's Activism*, 85.

25. See Betty Friedan, *It Changed My Life: Writings on the Women's Movement* (New York: Random House, 1978).

26. "HerStory: 1971-Present," *Ms. Magazine*, http://www.msmagazine.com/about.asp.

27. Melissa Denes, "Feminism? It's Hardly Begun," *The Guardian*, January 17, 2005, http://www.guardian.co.uk/g2/story/0,3604,1391841,00.html.

28. Ruth Rosen, *The World Split Open: How the Modern Women's Movement Changed America* (New York: Penguin Books, 2000), 35.

29. Cobble, Gordon, and Henry, *Feminism Unfinished*, 69–70.

30. Astrid Henry, *Not My Mother's Sister* (Bloomington: Indiana University Press, 2004), 16–17.

31. Ibid.

32. Evans, *Tidal Wave*, 230–32.

33. Henry, *Not My Mother's Sister*, 7.

34. For example, see Barbara Findlen, ed., *Listen Up: Voices from the Next Feminist Generation* (Seattle: Seal Press, 1995); and Rebecca Walker, ed., *To Be Real: Telling the Truth and Changing the Face of Feminism* (New York: Anchor Books, 1995).

35. Debra Michaels, "Stealth Feminists: The Thirtysomething Revolution," in *Sisterhood Is Forever: The Women's Anthology for a New Millennium*, ed. Robin Morgan (New York: Washington Square Press, 2003), 139.

36. Jennifer Baumgardner and Amy Richards, *Manifesta: Young Women, Feminism, and the Future* (New York: Farrar, Straus and Giroux, 2000), 17.

37. Jennifer Baumgardner, "Is There a Fourth Wave? Does It Matter?," excerpt from *F'em: Goo, Gaga and Some Thoughts on Balls* (Berkeley: Seal Press, 2011), http://www.feminist.com/resources/artspeech/genwom/baumgardner2011.html.

38. Stephanie Rosenbloom, "Evolution of a Feminist Daughter," *New York Times*, March 18, 2007, http://www.nytimes.com/2007/03/18/fashion/18walker.html?pagewanted=1&_r=3.

39. Rebecca Walker, "The Power of Palin," *Huffington Post*, September 22, 2008, http://www.huffingtonpost.com/rebecca-walker/the-power-of-palin_b_128377.html.

40. Costain, "Paving the Way," 36.

41. Orleck, *Rethinking American Women's Activism*, 200.

42. Ronnee Schreiber, *Righting Feminism: Conservative Women and American Politics* (New York: Oxford University Press, 2008), 4.

43. Cobble, Gordon, and Henry, *Feminism Unfinished*, 152.

44. Ednie Kaeh Garrison, "U.S. Feminism—Grrrl Style! Youth (Sub)Cultures and the Technologies of the Third Wave," in *No Permanent Waves: Recasting Histories of U.S. Feminism*, ed. Nancy Hewitt (New Brunswick, NJ: Rutgers University Press, 2010), 382.

45. Cobble, Gordon, and Henry, *Feminism Unfinished*, 171.

46. Baumgardner, "Is There a Fourth Wave?"

47. Evans, *Tidal Wave*, 2–3.

48. Barbara Arneil, *Politics & Feminism* (Oxford: Wiley–Blackwell, 1999), 3–4.

49. Evangelina Holvino, "Women and Power: New Perspectives on Old Challenges," in *Women & Leadership: The State of Play and Strategies for Change*, ed. Barbara Kellerman and Deborah L. Rhode (New York: Wiley, 2007), 363–64.

Chapter 3

1. We owe a debt of gratitude to Rosemary Tong, who wrote the classic book *Feminist Thought* that first laid out all of the different branches of feminism. We rely on her descriptions of second wave feminisms in this chapter. See Rosemary Tong, *Feminist Thought: A More Comprehensive Introduction* (Boulder, CO: Westview Press, 1988).

2. See Betty Friedan, *The Feminine Mystique* (New York: W. W. Norton, 1963).

3. See Tong, *Feminist Thought*.

4. See Anne Koedt, *The Myth of the Vaginal Orgasm* (Somerville, NJ: New England Free Press, 1970).

5. See Kate Millet, *Sexual Politics* (New York: Doubleday, 1970).

6. See Catharine Mackinnon and Andrea Dworkin, *In Harm's Way: The Pornography Civil Rights Hearing* (Cambridge, MA: Harvard University Press, 1997).

7. Robin Morgan, *Going Too Far: The Personal Choice of a Feminist* (New York: Vintage Books, 1978), 169.

8. See Tong, *Feminist Thought.*

9. See Zillah Eisenstein, *Capitalist Patriarchy and the Case for Socialist Feminism* (New York: Monthly Review Press, 1978).

10. See Sigmund Freud, *Three Essays on the Theory of Sexuality*, 1905.

11. See Juliet Mitchell and Jacqueline Rose, *Feminine Sexuality: Jacques Lacan and the école freudienne* (New York: W. W. Norton, 1983).

12. See Mary Daly, *Gyn/Ecology: The Metaethics of Radical Feminism* (Boston: Beacon Press, 1978).

13. See Chandra Talpade Mohanty, "Under Western Eyes: Feminist Scholarship and Colonial Discourses," *boundary 2* 12, no. 3 (1984): 333–58.

14. See Audre Lord, *Cables to Rage* (London: Paul Breman, 1970).

15. See Cherríe Moraga, *Loving in the War Years: Lo que nunca paso por sus labios* (Boston: South End Press, 1983).

16. See Cherríe Moraga and Gloria Anzaldúa, *This Bridge Called My Back: Writings by Radical Women of Color* (New York: Kitchen Table Press, 1983).

17. The Combahee River Collective, "A Black Feminist Statement," in *The Second Wave: A Reader in Feminist Theory*, ed. Linda Nicholson (New York: Routledge, 1997), 63–70.

18. Kimberlé Crenshaw, "Mapping the Margins: Intersectionality, Identity Politics, and Voice Against Women of Color," *Stanford Law Review* 43, no. 6 (1991): 1241–99.

19. The White House, *Gender Gap Pay: Recent Trends and Explanations*, Council on Economic Advisers Issue Brief, April 2015, https://obamawhitehouse.archives.gov/sites/default/files/docs/equal_pay_issue_brief_final.pdf.

20. See Judith Butler, *Gender Trouble: Feminism and the Subversion of Identity* (New York: Routledge, 1990).

21. See Rebecca Walker, ed., *To Be Real: Telling the Truth and Changing the Face of Feminism* (New York: Anchor Books, 1995).

22. Jennifer Baumgardner and Amy Richards, *Manifesta: Young Women, Feminism, and the Future* (New York: Farrar, Straus and Giroux, 2000), 102.

23. As quoted in Nadine Monem, *Riot Grrrl: Revolution Girl Style Now!* (London: Black Dog, 2007), 238.

24. As quoted in Rhonda Hammer, *Antifeminism and Family Terrorism: A Critical Feminist Perspective* (New York: Rowman & Littlefield, 2001).

25. As quoted in "Robertson Letter Attacks Feminists," *New York Times*, August 26, 1992, http://www.nytimes.com/1992/08/26/us/robertson-letter-attacks-feminists.html.

26. See Shira Tarrant, *Men and Feminism* (Berkeley: Seal Press, 2009).

Chapter 4

1. As quoted in Ashley Iasimone, "Lady Gaga Urges Sony to Drop Dr. Luke: 'Do What Is Right, Not What Is Better for Business,'" *Billboard Magazine*, February 27, 2016, http://www.billboard.com/articles/news/6890506/lady-gaga-sony-free-kesha-dr-luke.

2. See Shanto Iyengar, *Is Anyone Responsible? How Television Frames Political Issues* (Chicago: University of Chicago Press, 1984); and Shanto Iyengar and Donald R. Kinder, *News That Matters: Television and American Opinion* (Chicago: University of Chicago Press, 2010).

3. See the Henry J. Kaiser Foundation, *Daily Media Use among Children and Teens up Dramatically from Five Years Ago*, January 20, 2010, http://kff.org/disparities-policy/press -release/daily-media-use-among-children-and-teens-up-dramatically-from-five-years-ago/.

4. See the Pew Research Center, *Teens, Social Media, and Privacy*, May 21, 2013, http:// www.pewinternet.org/2013/05/21/teens-social-media-and-privacy/.

5. See Arielle Sumits, "The History and Future of Internet Traffic," *Cisco Blogs*, August 28, 2015, http://blogs.cisco.com/sp/the-history-and-future-of-internet-traffic.

6. See Joanna Stern, "Cellphone Users Check Phone 150Xs a Day and Other Fun Inter- net Facts," *ABC News*, May 29, 2013, http://abcnews.go.com/blogs/technology/2013/05/ cellphone-users-check-phones-150xday-and-other-internet-fun-facts/.

7. See Art Swift, "Americans Say Social Media Have Little Sway on Their Purchases," *Gallup*, June 23, 2014, http://www.gallup.com/poll/171785/americans-say-social-media-little -effect-buying-decisions.aspx.

8. As quoted in Jennifer Posner, *Reality Bites Back: The Troubling Truth about Guilty Pleasure TV* (New York: Seal Press, 2010), 30.

9. See Stacy L. Smith and Marc Choueiti, "Gender Disparity On-Screen and Behind the Camera in Family Films," Geena Davis Institute on Gender in Media, 2010, http:// seejane.org/wp-content/uploads/key-findings-gender-disparity-family-films-2013.pdf.

10. See Smith and Choueiti, *Gender Disparity*.

11. See Stacy L. Smith et al., "Gender Roles and Occupations: A Look at Character Attri- butes and Job-Related Aspirations in Film and Television," Geena Davis Institute on Gender and Media, 2012, http://seejane.org/wp-content/uploads/key-findings-gender -roles-2013.pdf.

12. See Martha M. Lauzen, "Women and the Big Picture: Behind-the-Scenes Employment on the Top 700 Films of 2014," Center for Women in Film and Media, 2014, http:// womenintvfilm.sdsu.edu/files/2014_Women_and_the_Big_Picture_Report.pdf.

13. See the Representation Project, "The Issue," 2017, http://therepresentationproject.org/ film/miss-representation/the-issue/.

14. See Jean Kilbourne, "Beauty . . . and the Beast of Advertising," Center for Media Literacy, 2010, http://www.medialit.org/reading-room/beautyand-beast-advertising.

15. See Louise Story, "Anywhere the Eye Can See, It's Likely to See an Ad," *New York Times*, January 15, 2007, http://www.nytimes.com/2007/01/15/business/media/15everywhere.html.

16. As quoted in Story, "Anywhere the Eye Can See."

17. As quoted in Sarah K. Murnen et al., "Thin, Sexy Women and Strong, Muscular Men: Grade-School Children's Responses to Objectified Images of Women and Men," *Sex Roles: A Journal of Research* 49, no. 9/10 (2003): 427–37.

18. See Christine R. Starr and Gail Ferguson, "Sexy Dolls, Sexy Grade-Schoolers? Media & Maternal Influences on Young Girls' Self-Sexualization," *Sex Roles* 67, No. 7–8 (2012): 463–76.

19. See Gigi Durham, *The Lolita Effect: The Sexualization of Young Girls and What We Can Do about It* (New York: Overlook, 2008).

20. See Barbara L. Fredrickson and Tomi-Ann Roberts, "Objectification Theory: Toward Understanding Women's Lived Experiences and Mental Health Risks," *Psychology of Women Quarterly* 21, no. 2 (1997): 173–206.

21. See Barbara L. Fredrickson and Tomi-Ann Roberts, "Objectification Theory: Toward Understanding Women's Lived Experiences and Mental Health Risks," *Psychology of Women Quarterly* 2 (1997): 173–206. See also Jennifer J. Muehlenkamp and Renee Saris-Baglama, "Self-Objectification and Its Psychological Outcomes for College Women," *Psychology of Women Quarterly* 26, no. 4 (2002): 371–79.

22. See Bonnie Moradi and Yu-Ping Huang, "Objectification Theory and Psychology of Women: A Decade of Advances and Future Directions," *Psychology of Women Quarterly* 32, no. 4 (2008): 377–98.

23. See Susan T. Fiske, "From Dehumanization and Objectification, to Rehumanization: Neuroimaging Studies on the Building Blocks of Empathy," *Annals of the New York Academy of Science* 1167 (June 2013): 31–34.

24. See Nathan A. Heflick and Jamie L. Goldenberg, "Objectifying Sarah Palin: Evidence That Objectification Causes Women to Be Perceived as Less Competent and Less Fully Human," *Journal of Experimental Social Psychology* 45, no. 3 (2009): 598–601.

25. See the National Association for the Education of Young Children, "Violence in the Lives of Children," 1993, https://www.naeyc.org/files/naeyc/file/positions/PSVIOL98.PDF.

26. See Meghan Casserly, "Are Men the Latest Victims of Media Missrepresentation?," *Forbes*, November 4, 2012, http://www.forbes.com/sites/meghancasserly/2012/11/14/are-men-the-latest-victims-of-media-misrepresentation/#6beabac35825.

27. See Jackson Katz, "Men, Masculinity, and Media: Some Introductory Notes," WCW Research Report, Spring 1999, https://www.biscmi.org/wp-content/uploads/2015/01/Men_Masculinities_and_Media.pdf.

28. For a summary on how masculinity harms men, see James Hamblin, "Toxic Masculinity and Murder," *The Atlantic*, June 16, 2016, http://www.theatlantic.com/health/archive/2016/06/toxic-masculinity-and-mass-murder/486983/.

29. See Craig A. Anderson et al., "Violent Video Game Effects on Aggression, Empathy, and Prosocial Behavior in Eastern and Western Countries: A Meta-Analytic Review," *Psychological Bulletin* 136, no. 2 (2010): 151–73.

30. See GLAAD, "Where We Are on TV Report," 2015, http://www.glaad.org/files/GLAAD-2015-WWAT.pdf.

31. Ibid.

32. See Smith et al., *Gender Roles*.

33. As quoted in Pippa Norris and Ronald Inglehart, "Women and Democracy: Cultural Obstacles to Equal Representation," *Journal of Democracy* 12, no. 3 (2001): 126–40.

34. See Meredith Conroy, *Media, Masculinity, and the American Presidency* (New York: Palgrave, 2015).

35. See Caroline Heldman, Susan J. Carroll, and Stephanie Olson, "'She Brought Only a Skirt': Print Media Coverage of Elizabeth Dole's Bid for the Republican Nomination," *Political Communication* 22, no. 3 (2005): 315–35. Also see Regina Lawrence and Melody Rose, *Hillary Clinton's Race for the White House: Gender Politics and Media on the Campaign Trail* (Boulder, CO: Lynne Rienner, 2009).

36. Dianne G. Bystrom et al., *Gender and Candidate Communication: Videostyle. Webstyle. Newstyle* (New York: Routledge, 2004).

37. Gina Serignere Woodall and Kim L. Fridkin, "Shaping Women's Chances: Stereotypes and the Media," in *Rethinking Madam President: Are We Ready for a Woman in the White House?*, ed. Lox Cox Han and Caroline Heldman (Boulder, CO: Lynne Rienner, 2007).

38. See Bystrom et al., *Gender and Candidate Communication.*
39. See Katie Heimer, "Hillary Clinton and the Media: From Intelligent and Fair to Appallingly Sexist and Pointless," March 28, 2007, http://www.reclaimthemedia.org/media_literacy_bias/hillary_clinton_and_the_media_%3D5069.html.
40. See Lawrence and Rose, *Hillary Clinton's Race.*
41. See Erika Falk, *Women for President: Media Bias in Nine Campaigns,* 2nd ed. (Champaign: University of Illinois Press, 2010).
42. See Woodall and Fridkin, "Shaping Women's Chances."
43. See Iyengar and Kinder, *News That Matters.*
44. See Jennifer L. Lawless and Richard L. Fox, "Men Rule: The Continued Under-Representation of Women in Politics" (Washington, DC: Women & Politics Institute, American University, 2012).
45. See the Women's Media Center, "WMC Divided 2015: The Media Gender Gap," http://www.womensmediacenter.com/pages/2015-wmc-divided-media-gender-gap.
46. As quoted in Lorraine Code, *What Can She Know? Feminist Theory and the Construction of Knowledge* (Ithaca, NY: Cornell University Press, 1991), 9.
47. See Lauzen, *Women and the Big Picture.*
48. See Working Mother, "Chore Wars: A New Working Mother Report Reveals Not Much Has Changed at Home," April 17, 2015, http://www.workingmother.com/content/chore-wars-new-working-mother-%20report-reveals-not-much-has-changed-home.
49. As quoted in Lisa Belkin, "The Feminine Critique," *New York Times,* November 1, 2007, http://www.nytimes.com/2007/11/01/fashion/01WORK.html.
50. See the American Press Institute, "How American Get Their News," March 17, 2014, https://www.americanpressinstitute.org/publications/reports/survey-research/how-americans-get-news/.

Chapter 5

1. Alicia Garza, "A Herstory of the #BlackLivesMatter Movement by Alicia Garza," *Feminist Wire,* October 7, 2014, http://www.thefeministwire.com/2014/10/blacklivesmatter-2/.
2. Gender-nonconforming individuals may have approaches to politics that are distinct from men and women, but to date, their political participation has not been measured by researchers. This limits our discussion to the sex/gender binary of male/female in this chapter.
3. Jennifer L. Lawless and Richard L. Fox, "Girls Just Wanna Not Run: The Gender Gap in Young American's Political Ambition," American University School of Public Affairs, March 2013, https://www.american.edu/spa/wpi/upload/Girls-Just-Wanna-Not-Run_Policy-Report.pdf.
4. Kim L. Fridkin and Patrick J. Kennedy, "How the Gender of U.S. Senators Influences People's Understanding and Engagement in Politics," *Journal of Politics* 76, no. 4 (2014): 1017–31.
5. Economic and Social Research Council, "The Global Gender Gap Report 2014," http://reports.weforum.org/global-gender-gap-report-2014/.
6. James C. Garand, Emily Guynan, and Monique Fournet, "The Gender Gap in Political Knowledge: Men and Women in National and State Politics," paper presented at the 2004 Southern Political Science Association Conference, http://citation.allacademic.com/meta/p_mla_apa_research_citation/0/6/7/9/9/p67995_index.html

7. Women's Media Center, "WMC Divided 2015: The Media Gender Gap," http://www .womensmediacenter.com/pages/2015-wmc-divided-media-gender-gap.

8. Michael X. Delli Carpini and Scott Keeter, "Gender and Political Knowledge," in *Gender and American Politics*, ed. Sue Tolleson-Rinehart and Jyl J. Josephson (Armonk, NY: M. E. Sharpe, 2000), 21–52.

9. Rodney E. Hero and Caroline Tolbert, "Minority Voices and Citizen Attitudes about Government Responsiveness in the American States: Do Social and Institutional Context Matter?," *British Journal of Political Science* 34, no. 1 (2004):109–21.

10. Victoria M. Hurst, "The Impact of Self-Objectification on Political Efficacy: Does Self-image Affect Feelings of Political Adequacy?," Honors Program Theses, 2014, http:// scholarworks.uni.edu/cgi/viewcontent.cgi?article=1114&context=hpt.

11. Lawless and Fox, "Girls Just Wanna Not Run."

12. Ibid.

13. Jennifer L. Lawless and Richard L. Fox, "Men Rule: The Continued Under-Representation of Women in U.S. Politics," Women and Politics Institute, American University, January 2012, https://www.american.edu/spa/wpi/upload/2012-Men-Rule-Report-web.pdf.

14. Ibid.

15. Sophie von Stumm, Tomas Chamorro-Premuzic, and Adrian Furnham, "Decomposing Self-estimates of Intelligence: Structure and Sex Differences across 12 Nations," *British Journal of Psychology* 100, no. 2 (2009): 429–42.

16. Center for American Women and Politics, "The Gender Gap: Attitudes on Policy Issues," CAWP Election Watch, 2012, http://www.cawp.rutgers.edu/sites/default/files/resources/ gg_issuesattitudes-2012.pdf.

17. The Pew Research Center, "The Gender Gap: Three Decades Old, as Wide as Ever," March 29, 2012, http://www.people-press.org/2012/03/29/the-gender-gap-three-decades -old-as-wide-as-ever/.

18. Ibid.

19. Pamela Johnston Conover, "Feminists and the Gender Gap," *The Journal of Politics* 50, no. 4 (1988): 985–1010.

20. The Pew Research Center, "A Deep Dive into Party Affiliation," April 7, 2015, http:// www.people-press.org/2015/04/07/a-deep-dive-into-party-affiliation/.

21. Sidney Verba, Kay Lehman Schlozman, and Henry Brady, *Voice and Equality: Civic Volunteerism in American Politics* (Cambridge, MA: Harvard University Press, 1995).

22. Steven J. Rosenstone and John Mark Hansen, *Mobilization, Participation, and Democracy in America* (New York: Pearson, 1993).

23. Martha Ackelsberg, "Broadening the Study of Women's Participation," in *Women and American Politics: New Questions, New Directions*, ed. Susan J. Carroll (New York: Oxford University Press, 2003).

24. See Nancy Burns, Kay Lehman Schlozman, and Sidney Verba, *The Private Roots of Public Action: Gender, Equality, and Political Participation* (Cambridge, MA: Harvard University Press, 2001).

25. Tim Mak, "Democrats Pay Black Staffers 30 Percent Less," *The Daily Beast*, August 11, 2014, http://www.thedailybeast.com/articles/2014/08/11/washington-s-race-pay-gap.html.

26. Zephyr Teachout and Kelly Nuxoll, "Presidential Campaigns Staffs Dominated by Men: Giuliani the Worst Offender," *The Huffington Post*, May 25, 2011, http://www .huffingtonpost.com/zephyr-teachout-and-kelly-nuxoll/presidential-campaign -sta_b_69698.html.

27. Pew Research Center, "When Discussing Politics, Family Plays Larger Role for Women Than Men," August 5, 2015, http://www.pewresearch.org/fact-tank/2015/08/05/when-discussing-politics-family-plays-larger-role-for-women-than-for-men/.

28. William McQuillan and Danielle Ivory, "Gender Gap Tops $1 Million for CEO Pay at Lobbying Groups," *Bloomberg News*, March 28, 2012, http://www.bloomberg.com/news/articles/2012-03-28/gender-gap-tops-1-million-for-ceo-pay-at-lobbying-groups-1-.

29. Pippa Norris, *Democratic Phoenix: Reinventing Political Activism* (Cambridge: Cambridge University Press, 2002).

30. Robert D. Putnam, *Bowling Alone: The Collapse and Revival of American Community* (New York: Simon & Schuster, 2001).

31. Pippa Norris, *Democratic Phoenix: Reinventing Political Activism* (New York: Cambridge University Press, 2002).

32. Rebecca Deen and Beth Anne Shelton, "Bake Sales for a Better America: The Role of School Volunteers in Civic Life," in *The International Journal of Interdisciplinary Social Sciences* 6, no. 7 (2012): 25–38.

33. See Carol Hardy-Fanta, *Latina Politics, Latino Politics: Gender, Culture, and Political Participation in Boston* (Philadelphia: Temple University Press, 1993).

34. Rupert Neate, "SeaWorld Sees Profits Plunge 84 percent as Customers Desert Controversial Park." *The Guardian*, August 6, 2015, available at http://www.theguardian.com/us-news/2015/aug/06/seaworld-profits-plunge-customers?CMP=share_btn_fb.

35. Melissa Cronin, "Landmark Resolution: San Francisco Recognizes the Rights of Whales and Dolphins," TheDodo.com, October 22, 2014, https://www.thedodo.com/san-francisco-cetacean-rights-777140486.html.

36. Manuel Castells, *Networks of Outrage and Hope: Social Movements in the Internet Age* (Cambridge, UK: Polity Press, 2012).

Chapter 6

1. Sue Thomas, "Introduction," in *Women and Elective Office: Past, Present, and Future*, 3rd ed., ed. Sue Thomas and Clyde Wilcox (New York: Oxford University Press, 2014), 1–2.

2. Deborah Jordan Brooks, *He Runs, She Runs: Why Gender Stereotypes Do Not Harm Women Candidates* (Princeton, NJ: Princeton University Press, 2013), 143.

3. Susan C. Bourque, "Political Leadership for Women: Redefining Power and Reassessing the Political," in *Women on Power: Leadership Redefined*, ed. Sue J. M. Freeman, Susan C. Bourque, and Christine M. Shelton (Boston: Northeastern University Press, 2001), 86–89.

4. Nancy E. McGlen et al., *Women, Politics, and American Society*, 4th ed. (New York: Longman, 2002), 90–102.

5. R. Darcy, Susan Welch, and Janet Clark, *Women, Elections, and Representation* (Lincoln: University of Nebraska Press, 1994), 15–18.

6. Frank C. Thames and Margaret S. Williams, *Contagious Representation: Women's Political Representation in Democracies around the World* (New York: New York University Press, 2013), 127–28.

7. Ibid., 130–32.

8. "Women in National Parliaments," Inter-Parliamentary Union, May 14, 2016, http://www.ipu.org/wmn-e/classif.htm.

9. Susan J. Carroll and Richard L. Fox, "Introduction: Gender and Electoral Politics in the Twenty First Century," in *Gender and Elections: Shaping the Future of American Politics*,

3rd ed., ed. Susan J. Carroll and Richard L. Fox (New York: Cambridge University Press, 2014), 1–8.

10. Ruth B. Mandel, "A Question about Women and the Leadership Option," in *The Difference "Difference" Makes: Women and Leadership*, ed. Deborah L. Rhode (Stanford, CA: Stanford University Press, 2003), 72.

11. Darcy, Welch, and Clark, *Women, Elections, and Representation*, 27–28.

12. Susan J. Carroll, *Women as Candidates in American Politics*, 2nd ed. (Bloomington: Indiana University Press, 1994), 42–44.

13. Darcy, Welch, and Clark, *Women, Elections, and Representation*, 175–76.

14. Kira Sanbonmatsu, "Candidate Recruitment and Women's Election to the State Legislatures," report prepared for the Center for American Women and Politics, Eagleton Institute of Politics, Rutgers, State University of New Jersey, September 2003.

15. Carroll, *Women as Candidates*, 91.

16. Georgia Duerst-Lahti, "The Bottleneck: Women Becoming Candidates," *Women and Elective Office: Past, Present, and Future*, ed. Sue Thomas and Clyde Wilcox (New York: Oxford University Press, 1998), 15.

17. Laurel Elder, "Why Women Don't Run: Explaining Women's Underrepresentation in America's Political Institutions," *Women & Politics* 26, no. 2 (2004): 27–56.

18. Richard L. Fox and Jennifer L. Lawless, "Entering the Arena? Gender and the Decision to Run for Office," *American Journal of Political Science* 48, no. 2 (April 2004): 264–80.

19. See Richard L. Fox, "The Future of Women's Political Leadership: Gender and the Decision to Run for Elective Office," in *Women & Leadership: The State of Play and Strategies for Change*, ed. Barbara Kellerman and Deborah L. Rhode (New York: Wiley, 2007), 251–70.

20. "Reelection Rates over the Years, 1964-2016," Center for Responsive Politics, http://www.opensecrets.org/bigpicture/reelect.php.

21. Carroll, *Women as Candidates*, 119.

22. Richard A. Seltzer, Jody Newman, and Melissa Voorhees Leighton, *Sex as a Political Variable: Women as Candidates and Voters in U.S. Elections* (Boulder, CO: Lynne Rienner, 1997), 7.

23. Heather L. Ondercin and Susan Welch, "Women Candidates for Congress," in *Women and Elective Office: Past, Present, and Future*, 2nd ed., ed. Sue Thomas and Clyde Wilcox (New York: Oxford University Press, 2005), 60–80.

24. Jennifer L. Lawless and Kathryn Pearson, "The Primary Reason for Women's Underrepresentation? Reevaluating the Conventional Wisdom," *The Journal of Politics* 70, no. 1 (January 2008): 67–82.

25. Sue Thomas, "Introduction," in *Women and Elective Office: Past, Present, and Future*, ed. Sue Thomas and Clyde Wilcox (New York: Oxford University Press, 1998), 6–8.

26. Barbara Burrell, "Campaign Finance: Women's Experience in the Modern Era," in *Women and Elective Office: Past, Present, and Future*, 2nd ed., ed. Sue Thomas and Clyde Wilcox (New York: Oxford University Press, 2005), 26–40.

27. Barbara Burrell, "Campaign Finance: Women's Experience in the Modern Era," in *Women and Elective Office: Past, Present, and Future*, ed. Sue Thomas and Clyde Wilcox (New York: Oxford University Press, 1998), 26–40.

28. "Incumbent Advantage," Center for Responsive Politics, http://www.opensecrets.org/overview/incumbs.php?cycle=2014.

29. Victoria Farrar-Myers and Brent D. Boyea, "Campaign Finance: A Barrier to Reaching the White House?," in *Women and Executive Office: Pathways and Performance*, ed. Melody Rose (Boulder, CO: Lynne Rienner, 2013), 224–26.

30. Michael H. Crespin and Janna L. Deitz, "If You Can't Join 'Em, Beat 'Em: The Gender Gap in Individual Donations to Congressional Candidates," *Political Research Quarterly* 63, no. 3 (2010): 581–93.

31. Peter L. Francia, "Early Fundraising by Nonincumbent Female Congressional Candidates: The Importance of Women's PACs," *Women & Politics* 23, no. 1/2 (2001): 7–20.

32. Ailsa Chang, "From Humble Beginnings, A Powerhouse Fundraising Class Emerges," NPR, May 6, 2014, http://www.npr.org/2014/05/06/310134589/from-humble-beginnings -a-powerhouse-fundraising-class-emerges.

33. Barbara C. Burrell, "Money and Women's Candidacies for Public Office," in *Women and American Politics: New Questions, New Directions*, ed. Susan J. Carroll (New York: Oxford University Press, 2003), 82.

34. Victoria A. Farrar-Myers, "A War Chest Full of Susan B. Anthony Dollars: Fund-raising Issues for Female Presidential Candidates," in *Anticipating Madam President*, ed. Robert P. Watson and Ann Gordon (Boulder, CO: Lynne Rienner, 2003), 92.

35. "Geraldine Anne Ferraro," *infoplease*, available at http://www.infoplease.com/ce6/people/ A0818528.html.

36. "Geraldine Ferraro: Women of the Hall," *National Women's Hall of Fame*, http://www .greatwomen.org/women.php?action=viewone&id=61.

37. Geraldine A. Ferraro and Linda Francke, *Ferraro: My Story* (New York: Bantam Books, 1985), 174–80.

38. Ibid., 179–80.

39. "Convention Notebook: During Drafty Delay in a Garage, Protocol Rules It's Ladies First," *Los Angeles Times*, July 20, 1984, A7.

40. Jane Perlez, "'Gerry, Gerry,' the Convention Chants," *New York Times*, July 20, 1984, A1.

41. Bernard Weinraub, "Mississippi Farm Topic: Does She Bake Muffins?," *New York Times*, August 2, 1984, 16.

42. Braden, *Women Politicians*, 134.

43. Jim Farber, "Geraldine Ferraro Lets Her Emotions Do the Talking," *Daily Breeze*, March 7, 2008.

44. Julia Baird, "From Seneca Falls to . . . Sarah Palin?," *Newsweek*, September 13, 2008, http://www.juliabaird.me/from-seneca-falls-to-%e2%80%a6-sarah-palin/.

45. Douglas Martin, "Geraldine A. Ferraro, 1935–2011: She Ended the Men's Club of National Politics," *New York Times*, March 26, 2011, http://www.nytimes.com/2011/03/27/ us/politics/27geraldine-ferraro.html?pagewanted=all&_r=0.

46. Patricia Rice, "Women out of the Myths and into Focus," in *Women and the News*, ed. Laurily Keir Epstein (New York: Hastings House, 1978), 45–49.

47. See Gaye Tuchman, *Hearth and Home: Images of Women in the News Media* (New York: Oxford University Press, 1978), 7–8; and David L. Paletz, *The Media in American Politics: Contents and Consequences*, 2nd ed. (New York: Longman, 2002), 135–39.

48. Leonie Huddy and Nayda Terkildsen, "Gender Stereotypes and the Perception of Male and Female Candidates," *American Journal of Political Science* 37, no. 1 (February 1993): 119–47.

49. Kim Fridkin Kahn, *The Political Consequences of Being a Woman* (New York: Columbia University Press, 1996), 134–36.

50. Marie C. Wilson, *Closing the Leadership Gap: Why Women Can and Must Help Run the World* (New York: Penguin, 2004), 37–38.

51. Martha E. Kropf and John A. Boiney, "The Electoral Glass Ceiling? Gender, Viability, and the News in U.S. Senate Campaigns," *Women & Politics* 23, no. 1/2 (2001): 79–101.

52. Dianne G. Bystrom et al., *Gender and Candidate Communication: VideoStyle, WebStyle, NewsStyle* (New York: Routledge, 2004), 21.

53. Maria Braden, *Women Politicians and the Media* (Lexington: University Press of Kentucky, 1996), 1–4.

54. Ibid., 6–7.

55. Diane J. Heith, "The Lipstick Watch: Media Coverage, Gender, and Presidential Campaigns," in *Anticipating Madam President*, ed. Robert P. Watson and Ann Gordon (Boulder, CO: Lynne Rienner, 2003), 124–26.

56. For example, see Paletz, *The Media in American Politics*, 135–39; Kahn, *Political Consequences*, 134–36; Kropf and Boiney, "The Electoral Glass Ceiling"; Bystrom et al., *Gender and Candidate Communication*, 21; and Caroline Heldman, Susan J. Carroll, and Stephanie Olson, "'She Brought Only a Skirt:' Print Media Coverage of Elizabeth Dole's Bid for the Republican Nomination," *Political Communication* 22, no. 3 (2005): 315–35.

57. Georgia Duerst-Lahti, "Presidential Elections: Gendered Space and the Case of 2012," in *Gender and Elections: Shaping the Future of American Politics*, 3rd ed., ed. Susan J. Carroll and Richard L. Fox (New York: Cambridge University Press, 2014).

58. Dianne Bystrom, "Advertising, Websites, and Media Coverage: Gender and Communication along the Campaign Trail," in *Gender and Elections: Shaping the Future of American Politics*, 3rd ed., eds. Susan J. Carroll and Richard L. Fox (New York: Cambridge University Press, 2014), 262.

59. Ibid., 264.

60. Danny Hayes, Jennifer L. Lawless, and Gail Baitinger, "Who Cares What They Wear? Media, Gender, and the Influence of Candidate Appearance," *Social Science Quarterly* 95, no. 5 (December 2014): 1194–212.

61. Kathleen Dolan and Timothy Lynch, "It Takes a Survey: Understanding Gender Stereotypes, Abstract Attitudes, and Voting for Women Candidates," *American Politics Research* 42, no. 4 (2014): 656–76.

62. Kathleen Dolan, "Gender Stereotypes, Candidate Evaluations, and Voting for Women Candidates: What Really Matters," *Political Research Quarterly* 67, no. 1 (March 2014): 96–107.

63. Elizabeth Adell Cook, "Voter Reaction to Women Candidates," in *Women and Elective Office: Past, Present, and Future*, ed. Sue Thomas and Clyde Wilcox (New York: Oxford University Press, 1998), 69–71.

64. Timothy R. Lynch and Kathleen Dolan, "Voter Attitudes, Behaviors, and Women Candidates," in *Women and Elective Office: Past, Present, and Future*, 3rd ed., ed. Sue Thomas and Clyde Wilcox (New York: Oxford University Press, 2014), 65.

65. Brooks, *He Runs, She Runs*, 130–31.

66. Ibid., 169.

67. Ibid., 174.

68. Dolan, "Gender Stereotypes," 105.

Chapter 7

1. "Women in the U.S. Congress 2016," Center for American Women and Politics, Eagleton Institute of Politics, Rutgers, State University of New Jersey, http://www.cawp.rutgers.edu/women-us-congress-2016.

2. Ibid.; see also Marie C. Wilson, *Closing the Leadership Gap: Why Women Can and Must Help Run the World* (New York: Penguin, 2004), 4.

3. Cindy Simon Rosenthal, *When Women Lead: Integrative Leadership in State Legislatures* (New York: Oxford University Press, 1998), 7.

4. Ibid., 162.

5. Ibid., 21–22.

6. Ibid., 160.

7. Cindy Simon Rosenthal, "Women Leading Legislatures: Getting There and Getting Things Done," in *Women and Elective Office: Past, Present, & Future*, 2nd ed., ed. Sue Thomas and Clyde Wilcox (New York: Oxford University Press, 2005), 197–212.

8. For example, see Alana Jeydel and Andrew Taylor, "Are Women Legislators Less Effective? Evidence from the U.S. House in the 103rd–105th Congress," *Political Research Quarterly* 56 (2003): 19–27; Kathleen Bratton and Kerry L Haynie, "Agenda Setting and Legislative Success in State Legislatures: The Effects of Gender and Race," *Journal of Politics* 61 (1999): 658–79; and Sarah Anzia and Christopher R. Berry, "The Jackie (and Jill) Robinson Effect: Why Do Congresswomen Outperform Congressmen?," *American Journal of Political Science* 55 (2011): 478–93.

9. Craig Volden, Alan E. Wiseman, and Dana E. Wittmer, "When Are Women More Effective Lawmakers Than Men?," *American Journal of Political Science* 57 (2013): 326–41.

10. Kathryn Pearson and Logan Dancey, "Elevating Women's Voices in Congress: Speech Participation in the House of Representatives," *Political Research Quarterly* 64 (2011): 910–23.

11. Chris Suellentrop, "The Leader the House Democrats Deserve," *Slate*, November 13, 2002, http://www.slate.com/articles/news_and_politics/assessment/2002/11/nancy_pelosi.html.

12. Sheryl Gay Stolberg, "A Nation at War: The House Minority Leader; With Democrats Divided on War, Pelosi Faces Leadership Test," *New York Times*, March 31, 2003, B13.

13. Pat Schroeder, "Running for Our Lives: Electoral Politics," in *Sisterhood Is Forever: The Women's Anthology for a New Millennium*, ed. Robin Morgan (New York: Washington Square Press, 2003), 28–31.

14. Ibid., 33.

15. Barbara Mikulski, quoted in Catherine Whitney et al., *Nine and Counting: The Women of the Senate* (New York: William Morrow, 2000), 117–18.

16. Barbara Boxer, quoted in Whitney et al., *Nine and Counting*, 47–48.

17. Sue Thomas, *How Women Legislate* (New York: Oxford University Press, 1994), 153.

18. "Women of Color in Elective Office 2016," Center for American Women and Politics, Eagleton Institute of Politics, Rutgers, State University of New Jersey, http://www.cawp .rutgers.edu/women-color-elective-office-2016.

19. Tracy L. Osborn, *How Women Represent Women: Political Parties, Gender, and Representation in the State Legislatures* (New York: Oxford University Press, 2012), 19–20.

20. Thomas, *How Women Legislate*, 100.

21. Amy Caiazza, "Does Women's Representation in Elected Office Lead to Women-Friendly Policy? Analysis of State-Level Data," *Women & Politics* 26 (2004): 35–70.

22. Kim L. Fridkin and Patrick J. Kenney, "How the Gender of U.S. Senators Influences People's Understanding and Engagement in Politics," *The Journal of Politics* 76 (October 2014): 1017–31.

23. Susan J. Carroll, "Representing Women: Congresswomen's Perceptions of Their Representational Roles," in *Women Transforming Congress*, ed. Cindy Simon Rosenthal (Norman: University of Oklahoma Press, 2002), 66.

24. Ibid.

25. John D. Griffin, Brian Newman, and Christina Wolbrecht, "A Gender Gap in Policy Representation in the U.S. Congress?," *Legislative Studies Quarterly*, 37 (February 2012): 35–65.

26. Brian Frederick, "A Longitudinal Test of the Gender Turnover Model among U.S. House and Senate Members," *The Social Science Journal* 52 (2015): 102–11.

27. Tracy Osborn, "Women State Legislators and Representation: The Role of Political Parties and Institutions," *State and Local Government Review* 46 (2014): 146–55.

28. Michele L. Swers and Carin Larson, "Women in Congress: Do They Act as Advocates for Women's Issues?," in *Women and Elective Office: Past, Present, & Future*, 2nd ed., ed. Sue Thomas and Clyde Wilcox (New York: Oxford University Press, 2005), 110–28.

29. Whitney et al., *Nine and Counting*, 125–27.

30. Sheryl Gay Stolberg, "More Women Than Ever in Congress, but with Less Power Than Before," *New York Times*, February 2, 2015, http://www.nytimes.com/2015/02/03/us/politics/republican-takeover-of-senate-pushes-women-out-of-powerful-committee-posts.html?_r=0.

31. Michele L. Swers, *Women in the Club: Gender and Policy Making in the Senate* (Chicago: University of Chicago Press, 2013), 231–32.

32. Olympia Snowe, quoted in Whitney et al., *Nine and Counting*, 129–30.

33. Whitney et al., *Nine and Counting*, 3.

34. Zornitsa Keremidchieva, "Legislative Reform, the Congressional Caucus for Women's Issues, and the Crisis of Women's Political Representation," *Women & Language* 35 (Spring 2012): 13–38.

35. Cynthia A. Hall, "The Congressional Caucus for Women's Issues at 25: Challenges and Opportunities," in *The American Woman 2003–2004: Daughters of a Revolution-Young Women Today*, ed. Cynthia B. Costello, Vanessa R. Wight, and Anne J. Stone (New York: Palgrave Macmillan, 2003), 348.

36. Sahil Kapur, "The 5 GOP Senators Most Likely to Work with Democrats," *Talking Points Memo*, November 13, 2012, http://talkingpointsmemo.com/dc/the-5-gop-senators-most-likely-to-work-with-democrats.

37. Swers, *Women in the Club*, 231–32.

38. Ibid.

39. Ibid.

40. Michele L. Swers, "Representing Women's Interests in a Polarized Congress," in *Women and Elective Office: Past, Present, and Future*, 3rd ed., ed. Sue Thomas and Clyde Wilcox (New York: Oxford University Press, 2014), 178–79.

41. Rosenthal, *When Women Lead*, 161.

42. John M. Carey, Richard G. Niemi, and Lynda W. Powell, "Are Women Legislators Different?," in *Women and Elective Office: Past, Present, & Future*, ed. Sue Thomas and Clyde Wilcox (New York: Oxford University Press, 1998), 100–101.

43. Michael J. Epstein, Richard G. Niemi, and Lynda W. Powell, "Do Women and Men State Legislators Differ?," in *Women and Elective Office: Past, Present, & Future*, 2nd ed., ed. Sue Thomas and Clyde Wilcox (New York: Oxford University Press, 2005), 94–109.

44. Susan J. Carroll, "Representing Women: Women State Legislators as Agents of Policy-Related Change," in *The Impact of Women in Public Office*, ed. Susan J. Carroll (Bloomington: Indiana University Press, 2001), 17–18.

45. Carey, Niemi, and Powell, "Are Women Legislators Different?," 101.

46. Sue Thomas and Susan Welch, "The Impact of Women in State Legislatures: Numerical and Organizational Strength," in *The Impact of Women in Public Office*, ed. Susan J. Carroll (Bloomington: Indiana University Press, 2001), 178.

47. Lynne E. Ford and Kathleen Dolan, "Women State Legislators: Three Decades of Gains in Representation and Diversity," in *Women in Politics: Outsiders or Insiders?*, 3rd ed., ed. Lois Duke Whitaker (Upper Saddle River, NJ: Prentice Hall, 1999), 205.

48. Ibid., 216.

49. Rosenthal, *When Women Lead*, 13–14.

50. "Women in State Legislatures 2017," Center for American Women and Politics, Eagleton Institute of Politics, Rutgers, State University of New Jersey, http://www.cawp.rutgers.edu/women-state-legislature-2017.

51. See "Women in State Legislatures 2017."

52. See "Women in State Legislative Leadership 2017," Center for American Women and Politics, Eagleton Institute of Politics, Rutgers, State University of New Jersey, http://cawp.rutgers.edu/sites/default/files/resources/stleg-leadership-2017.pdf.

53. Susan J. Carroll, "Women in State Government: Historical Overview and Current Trends," in *The Book of the States*, ed. Council of State Governments, http://cawp.rutgers.edu/sites/default/files/resources/womeninstategov_overviewandtrends.pdf.

54. Marcia Lynn Whicker and Malcolm Jewell, "The Feminization of Leadership in State Legislatures," in *Women and Elective Office: Past, Present, & Future*, ed. Sue Thomas and Clyde Wilcox (New York: Oxford University Press, 1998), 174.

55. Cindy Simon Rosenthal, "Getting Things Done: Women Committee Chairpersons in State Legislatures," in *Women and Elective Office: Past, Present, & Future*, ed. Sue Thomas and Clyde Wilcox (New York: Oxford University Press, 1998), 186.

56. Thomas, *How Women Legislate*, 147.

57. Carroll, "Women in State Government: Historical Overview and Current Trends."

58. Rosenthal, *Women Transforming Congress*, 11.

Chapter 8

1. Charlotte Hays, "Advice Given to Hillary: De-Emphasize the 'First' Talk," *Independent Women's Forum*, May 24, 2016, http://iwf.org/blog/2800304/Advice-Given-to-Hillary:-De-emphasize-the-%22First%22-Talk.

2. Lori Cox Han, *In It to Win: Electing Madam President* (New York: Bloomsbury, 2015), 185.

3. Georgia Duerst-Lahti, "Reconceiving Theories of Power: Consequences of Masculinism in the Executive Branch," in *The Other Elites: Women, Politics, and Power in the Executive Branch*, ed. MaryAnne Borrelli and Janet M. Martin (Boulder, CO: Lynne Rienner, 1997), 12.

4. Marie C. Wilson, *Closing the Leadership Gap: Why Women Can and Must Help Run the World* (New York: Penguin, 2004), 8.

5. For example, see Sally Helgesen, *The Female Advantage: Women's Ways of Leadership* (New York: Doubleday, 1990); and Candy Deemer and Nancy Fredericks, *Dancing on the Glass Ceiling* (Chicago: Contemporary Books, 2003).

6. Helgesen, *The Female Advantage*, 3.

7. Esther Wachs Book, *Why the Best Man for the Job Is a Woman: The Unique Female Qualities of Leadership* (New York: HarperCollins, 2000), 15–16.

8. Ibid., 2–5.

9. Ibid., 8–14.

10. Alice H. Eagly and Mary C. Johannesen-Schmidt, "The Leadership Styles of Women and Men," *Journal of Social Sciences* 57, no. 4 (2001): 781–97.

11. The remaining companies included PepsiCo, Lockheed Martin, Oracle, Mondelez International, General Dynamics, the TJX Companies, Duke Energy, Xerox Corporation, Guardian Life Insurance Company of America, Ross Stores, Sempra Energy, CST Brands, Avon Products, Inc., Reynolds American, Campbell's Soup, Graybar Electric, Ingredion, Advanced Micro Devices, and CH2M Hill.

12. Wilson, *Closing the Leadership Gap*, 53.

13. Linda Tischler, "Where Are the Women?" *Fast Company*, February 2004, 52.

14. Rosalind Chait Barnett, "Women, Leadership, and the Natural Order," in *Women & Leadership: The State of Play and Strategies for Change*, ed. Barbara Kellerman and Deborah L. Rhode (New York: Wiley, 2007), 154–56.

15. Ibid., 156–58.

16. Sheryl Sandberg, *Lean In* (New York: Alfred A. Knopf, 2014), 7–10.

17. Debora L. Spar, *Wonder Women: Sex, Power, and the Quest for Perfection* (New York: Farrar, Straus and Giroux, 2013), 231–33.

18. Anne-Marie Slaughter, "Why Women Still Can't Have It All," *The Atlantic*, July/August 2012, http://www.theatlantic.com/magazine/archive/2012/07/why-women-still-cant-have-it-all/309020/.

19. Hanna Rosin, *The End of Men: And the Rise of Women* (New York: Riverhead, 2012).

20. For a discussion of these issues, see Lori Cox Han and Caroline Heldman, eds., *Rethinking Madam President: Are We Ready for a Woman in the White House?* (Boulder, CO: Lynne Rienner, 2007).

21. Han, *In It to Win*, 183.

22. Duerst-Lahti, "Reconceiving Theories," 18.

23. M. Margaret Conway, David W. Ahern, and Gertrude A. Steuernagel, *Women and Political Participation: Cultural Change in the Political Arena* (Washington, DC: CQ Press, 1997), 100.

24. Alexander DeConde, *Presidential Machismo: Executive Authority, Military Intervention, and Foreign Relations* (Boston: Northeastern University Press, 2000), 5.

25. Thomas E. Cronin and Michael A. Genovese, *The Paradoxes of the American Presidency* (New York: Oxford University Press, 1998), 105.

26. Fred I. Greenstein, "George W. Bush and the Ghosts of Presidents Past," *PS: Political Science and Politics* XXXIV, no. 1 (March 2001): 77–80.

27. Lori Cox Han, "Presidential Leadership: Governance from a Woman's Perspective," in *Anticipating Madam President*, ed. Robert P. Watson and Ann Gordon (Boulder, CO: Lynne Rienner, 2003), 171.

28. The election of Barack Obama in 2008 broke a significant barrier in terms of race, but what effect his election will have on electing future candidates of color to the White House remains to be seen. In terms of religion, John F. Kennedy, a Catholic, remains the only non-Protestant to hold the office of the presidency, and Joseph Lieberman remains the only Jewish candidate nominated for president or vice president after his nomination as Al Gore's running mate in 2000.

29. Stephen J. Wayne, *The Road to the White House 2012* (Boston: Wadsworth, 2012), 200–201.

30. Conway, Ahern, and Steuernagel, 112.

31. See Barbara Kellerman and Deborah L. Rhode, eds., *Women & Leadership: The State of Play and Strategies for Change* (New York: Wiley, 2007), 7. See also Kathleen Hall Jamieson, *Beyond the Double Bind: Women and Leadership* (New York: Oxford University Press, 1995).

32. Wilson, *Closing the Leadership Gap*, 36.

33. Diane J. Heith, "The Lipstick Watch: Media Coverage, Gender, and Presidential Campaigns," in *Anticipating Madam President*, ed. Robert P. Watson and Ann Gordon (Boulder, CO: Lynne Rienner, 2003), 123–24.

34. Jennifer L. Lawless, "Women, War, and Winning Elections: Gender Stereotyping in the Post-September 11th Era," *Political Research Quarterly* 57, no. 3 (September 2004): 479–90.

35. Matthew J. Streb et al., "Social Desirability Effects and Support for a Female American President," *Public Opinion Quarterly* 72, no. 1 (2008): 76–89. This study found that roughly 26 percent of polling respondents are "angry or upset" about the prospect of electing a woman president, with this level of dissatisfaction constant across various demographic groups.

36. See Kate Kenski and Erika Falk, "Of What Is This Glass Ceiling Made? A Study of Attitudes about Women and the Oval Office," *Women & Politics* 26, no. 2 (2004): 57–80.

37. For a discussion on trends in news coverage of presidential campaigns, see Stephen J. Farnsworth and S. Robert Lichter, *The Nightly News Nightmare: Media Coverage of U.S. Presidential Elections, 1988–2008*, 3rd ed. (Lanham, MD: Rowman & Littlefield, 2011); and Larry J. Sabato, *Feeding Frenzy: Attack Journalism and American Politics* (Baltimore: Lanahan, 2000).

38. Cronin and Genovese, *The Paradoxes*, 31.

39. See Richard L. Fox and Jennifer L. Lawless, "Entering the Arena? Gender and the Decision to Run for Office," *American Journal of Political Science* 48, no. 2 (April 2004): 264–80.

40. Lilly J. Goren, "Fact or Fiction: The Reality of Race and Gender in Reaching the White House," in *Women and the White House: Gender, Popular Culture, and Presidential Politics*, ed. Justin S. Vaughn and Lilly J. Goren (Lexington: University Press of Kentucky, 2013), 103.

41. Kristina Horn Sheeler and Karrin Vasby Anderson, *Woman President: Confronting Postfeminist Political Culture* (College Station: Texas A&M University Press, 2013), 86.

42. See Wilson, *Closing the Leadership Gap*.

43. Eleanor Clift and Tom Brazaitis, *Madam President: Shattering the Last Glass Ceiling* (New York: Scribner, 2000), 28.

44. Alexandra Marks, "The Quest of Carol Moseley Braun," *The Christian Science Monitor*, November 19, 2003, http://www.csmonitor.com/2003/1120/p01s04-uspo.html.

45. Democrat Shirley Chisholm won a nonbinding "beauty contest" primary in New Jersey in 1972 that awarded no delegates.

46. Michigan and Florida were "beauty contests" with no delegates awarded, and Texas included both a primary (which Clinton won) and a caucus (which Obama won). In addition, although Clinton's popular vote victory in New Hampshire was seen as a major comeback after losing the Iowa caucuses, she and Obama earned an equal number of delegates in the state. Similarly, while Clinton won the popular vote in Nevada, Obama won more delegates (by one).

47. An estimate, according to RealClearPolitics.com, since Iowa, Nevada, Maine, and Washington did not release official vote totals.

48. Natalie Villacorta, "Michele Bachmann: U.S. Not Ready for Female President," *Politico*, February 20, 2014, http://www.politico.com/story/2014/02/michele-bachmann-female-president-103731.html.

49. Janet M. Martin, *The Presidency and Women: Promise, Performance & Illusion* (College Station: Texas A&M University Press, 2003), 6–7.

50. MaryAnne Borrelli, *The President's Cabinet: Gender, Power, and Representation* (Boulder, CO: Lynne Rienner, 2002), 214.

51. James D. King and James W. Riddlesperger Jr., "Diversity and Presidential Cabinet Appointments," *Social Science Quarterly* 96, no. 1 (March 2015): 93–103.

52. Kathryn Dunn Tenpas, "Women on the White House Staff: A Longitudinal Analysis, 1939–1994," in *The Other Elites: Women, Politics, and Power in the Executive Branch*, ed. MaryAnne Borrelli and Janet M. Martin (Boulder, CO: Lynne Rienner, 1997), 91.

53. Ibid., 92–93.

54. James Mann, *Rise of the Vulcans: The History of Bush's War Cabinet* (New York: Viking Press, 2004), 315.

55. Ibid., 99–101.

56. Anne Marie O'Connor, "Hughes Answers the Call; Advisor Who Resigned to Spend More Time with Her Family Is Rejoining the Bush Team," *Los Angeles Times*, April 12, 2004, E1.

57. Robert P. Watson, *The President's Wives: Reassessing the Office of First Lady* (Boulder, CO: Lynne Rienner, 2000), 72.

58. Ibid., 112–13.

59. MaryAnne Borrelli, *The Politics of the President's Wife* (College Station: Texas A&M University Press, 2011), 1.

60. See Hillary Rodham Clinton, *Living History* (New York: Simon & Schuster, 2003).

61. Valerie R. O'Regan and Stephen J. Stambough, "Female Governors and Gubernatorial Candidates," in *Women and Elective Office: Past, Present, and Future*, 3rd ed., ed. Sue Thomas and Clyde Wilcox (New York: Oxford University Press, 2014), 145.

62. Brenda DeVore Marshall and Molly A. Mayhead, "The Changing Face of the Governorship," in *Navigating Boundaries: The Rhetoric of Women Governors*, ed. Brenda DeVore Marshall and Molly A. Mayhead (Westport, CT: Praeger, 2000), 14.

63. See Sara J. Wier, "Women Governors in the 21st Century: Re-Examining the Pathways to the Presidency," in *Women in Politics: Outsiders or Insiders?*, 4th ed., ed. Lois Duke Whitaker (Upper Saddle River, NJ: Prentice Hall, 2006), 226–37.

64. Jay Barth and Margaret R. Ferguson, "Gender and Gubernatorial Personality," *Women & Politics* 24, no. 1 (2002): 63–82.

65. "Women in Statewide Elected Executive Office 2016," Center for American Women and Politics, Eagleton Institute of Politics, Rutgers, State University of New Jersey, http://www.cawp.rutgers.edu/women-statewide-elective-executive-office-2016.

66. "History of Women Governors," Center for American Women and Politics, Eagleton Institute of Politics, Rutgers, State University of New Jersey, http://www.cawp.rutgers.edu/history-women-governors.

67. Sara J. Wier, "Women Governors in the 21st Century: Re-Examining the Pathways to the Presidency," in *Women in Politics: Outsiders or Insiders?*, ed. Lois Duke Whitaker (Upper Saddle River, NJ: Prentice Hall, 2006), 226–37.

68. Richard Herrera and Karen Shafer, "Women in the Governor's Mansion: How Party and Gender Affect Policy Agendas," in *Women and Executive Office: Pathways and Performance*, ed. Melody Rose (Boulder, CO: Lynne Rienner, 2013), 113.

69. Sue Tolleson-Rinehart, "Do Women Leaders Make a Difference?" in *The Impact of Women in Public Office*, ed. Susan J. Carroll (Bloomington: Indiana University Press, 2001), 149–65.

70. Lonna Rae Atkeson and Timothy B. Krebs, "Press Coverage of Mayoral Candidates: The Role of Gender in News Reporting and Campaign Issue Speech," *Political Research Quarterly* 61, no. 2 (June 2008): 239–52.

71. Duerst-Lahti, "Reconceiving Theories," 25.

Chapter 9

1. "Sandra Day O'Connor," Oyez, https://www.oyez.org/justices/sandra_day_oconnor.

2. Joan Biskupic, "Ginsburg 'Lonely' without O'Connor," *USA Today*, December 5, 2007, http://www.usatoday.com/news/washington/2007-01-25-ginsburg-court_x.htm.

3. Susan Gluck Mezey, *In Pursuit of Equality: Women, Public Policy, and the Federal Courts* (New York: St. Martin's Press, 1992), 8.

4. Ibid., 10–17; see also David M. O'Brien, *Constitutional Law and Politics, Volume Two: Civil Rights and Civil Liberties*, 7th ed. (New York: W. W. Norton, 2008), 1514–16.

5. Catharine A. MacKinnon, "Women and Law: The Power to Change," in *Sisterhood Is Forever: The Women's Anthology for a New Millennium*, ed. Robin Morgan (New York: Washington Square Press, 2003), 447.

6. See Jill Norgren, "Ladies of Legend: The First Generation of American Women Attorneys," *Journal of Supreme Court History* 35, no. 1 (March 2010): 71–90.

7. Ibid., 87.

8. "A Current Glance at Women in the Law 2014," Commission on Women in the Profession, American Bar Association, July 2014, http://www.americanbar.org/content/dam/aba/marketing/women/current_glance_statistics_july2014.authcheckdam.pdf.

9. Jacob H. Herring, "Can They Do It? Can Law Firms, Corporate Counsel Departments, and Governmental Agencies Create a Level Playing Field for Women Attorneys?," in *The Difference "Difference" Makes: Women and Leadership*, ed. Deboarh L. Rhode (Stanford, CA: Stanford University Press, 2003), 76.

10. Deborah L. Rhode, "The Unfinished Agenda: Women and the Legal Profession," ABA Commission on Women in the Profession, 2001, 5.

11. "A Current Glance at Women in the Law 2014."

12. Rhode, "The Unfinished Agenda," 6.

13. Ibid., 7.

14. Ibid., 20.

15. Ibid., 20–22.

16. See Barbara Palmer, "Women in the American Judiciary: Their Influence and Impact," *Women & Politics* 23, no. 3 (2001): 91–101.

17. Richard L. Pacelle Jr., "A President's Legacy: Gender and Appointment to the Federal Courts," in *The Other Elites: Women, Politics, and Power in the Executive Branch*, ed. MaryAnne Borrelli and Janet M. Martin (Boulder, CO: Lynne Rienner, 1997), 154.

18. Elaine Martin, "U.S. Women Federal Court Judges Appointed by President Carter," *Feminist Legal Studies* 17 (2009): 43–59.

19. Rhode, "The Unfinished Agenda," 26.

20. Elaine Martin, "Bias or Counterbalance?: Women Judges Making a Difference," in *Women in Politics: Outsiders or Insiders?*, 4th ed., ed. Lois Duke Whitaker (Upper Saddle River, NJ: Prentice Hall, 2006), 255–56.

21. Lawrence Baum, *The Supreme Court*, 9th ed. (Washington, DC: CQ Press, 2007), 35–47.

22. Ibid., 54–57.

23. David M. O'Brien, *Storm Center: The Supreme Court in American Politics*, 8th ed. (New York: W. W. Norton, 2008), 34–55.
24. Mark Silverstein, *Judicious Choices: The Politics of Supreme Court Confirmations*, 2nd ed. (New York: W. W. Norton, 2007), 6.
25. See Baum, *The Supreme Court*, 38–40, and Silverstein, *Judicious Choices*, 213–17.
26. Barack Obama, "The President's Remarks on Justice Souter," May 1, 2009, https://www.whitehouse.gov/blog/2009/05/01/presidents-remarks-justice-souter.
27. Irin Camron and Shana Knizhnik, *Notorious RBG: The Life and Times of Ruth Bader Ginsburg* (New York: Dey Street Books, 2015).
28. Baum, *The Supreme Court*, 34.
29. Henry J. Abraham, *Justices, Presidents, and Senators: A History of the U.S. Supreme Court Appointments from Washington to Clinton* (Lanham, MD: Rowman & Littlefield, 1999), 318.
30. Baum, *The Supreme Court*, 135.
31. Abraham, *Justices, Presidents*, 322.
32. Anita F. Hill, "What Difference Will Women Judges Make?," in *Women & Leadership: The State of Play and Strategies for Change*, ed. Barbara Kellerman and Deborah L. Rhode (New York: Wiley, 2007), 183.
33. Kevin Lyles, *The Gatekeepers: Federal District Courts in the Political Process* (Westport, CT: Praeger, 1997), 262–23.
34. Pacelle, "A President's Legacy," 149.
35. Sandra Day O'Connor, *The Majesty of the Law: Reflections of a Supreme Court Justice* (New York: Random House, 2003), 195.
36. Sue Thomas, *How Women Legislate* (New York: Oxford University Press, 1994), 18–20.
37. "2016 U.S. State Court Women Judges," National Association of Women Judges, https://www.nawj.org/statistics/2016-us-state-court-women-judges.
38. Barbara A. Curran and Clara N. Carson, *The Lawyer Statistical Report: The U.S. Legal Profession in the 1990s* (Chicago: American Bar Foundation, 1994).
39. "Statistics: 2016 Representation of United States State Court Women Judges."
40. Janet M. Martin, *The Presidency and Women: Promise, Performance & Illusion* (College Station: Texas A&M University Press, 2003), 283–84.
41. Greg Goelzhauser, "Diversifying State Supreme Courts," *Law & Society Review* 45, no. 3 (2011): 761–81.
42. Charles S. Bullock III et al., "'Your Honor' Is a Female: A Multistage Electoral Analysis of Women's Successes at Securing State Trial Court Judgeships," *Social Science Quarterly* 95, no. 5 (December 2014): 1322–45.
43. Sophia A. Hall, "In the Pursuit of Justice: Reflections on Changes in the Judicial Role after Three Decades as a State Court Judge," *Judges Journal* 48, no. 1 (Winter 2009): 5–9.
44. Romonda D. Belcher, "The Importance of Women and the Judiciary," *The Journal of Gender, Race & Justice* 17 (2014): 421–26.
45. "Rose Elizabeth Bird," California Supreme Court Historical Society, http://www.cschs.org/history/california-supreme-court-justices/rose-elizabeth-bird/.
46. "The Death Penalty," http://www.rosebirdprocon.org/.
47. John Gruhl, Cassis Spohn, and Susan Welch, "Women as Policymakers: The Case of Trial Judges," *American Journal of Political Science* 25, no. 2 (May 1981): 308–22.
48. For example, see Lisa Baldez, Lee Epstein, and Andrew D. Martin, "Does the Constitution Need an Equal Rights Amendment?," *Journal of Legal Studies* 35 (January 2006):

243–83; and Christina L. Boyd, Lee Epstein, and Andrew D. Martin, "Untangling the Causal Effect of Sex on Judging," *American Journal of Political Science* 54, no. 2 (2010): 389–411.

49. For example, see Sue Davis, Susan Haire, and Donald Songer, "Voting Behavior and Gender on the U.S. Courts of Appeal," *Judicature* 77 (1993): 129–33; and Gerard Gryski, Eleanor Main, and William Dixon, "Models of State High Court Decision Making in Sex Discrimination Cases," *Journal of Politics* 48 (1986): 143–55.

50. Barbara Palmer, "Justice Ruth Bader Ginsburg and the Supreme Court's Reaction to Its Second Female Member," *Women & Politics* 24, no. 1 (2008): 1–23.

51. Diane S. Sykes, "Gender and Judging," *Marquette Law Review* 94 (2001): 1381–90.

52. O'Connor, *The Majesty of the Law*, 189.

53. Baum, *The Supreme Court*, 58.

54. Barbara Palmer, "Women in the American Judiciary: Their Influence and Impact," *Women & Politics* 23, no. 3 (2008): 2001.

Chapter 10

1. Department of Labor, Women's Bureau, "Women Workers in Ten War Production Areas and Their Postwar Employment Plans," Bulletin 209, 1946, Washington: U.S. Government Printing Office, in *America's Working Women*, ed. Rosalyn Baxandall, Linda Gordon, and Susan Reverby (New York: Vintage Books, 1976), 310–12.

2. Pew Research Center, "6 Key Findings about Going to College," FactTank, February 11, 2014, http://www.pewresearch.org/fact-tank/2014/02/11/6-key-findings-about-going-to-college/.

3. Kurt Bauman and Camille Ryan, "Women Now at the Head of the Class, Lead Men in College Attainment," U.S. Census Bureau, October 7, 2014, https://www.census.gov/newsroom/blogs/random-samplings/2015/10/women-now-at-the-head-of-the-class-lead-men-in-college-attainment.html.

4. See Bauman and Ryan, "Women Now."

5. Claudia Goldin, Lawrence F. Katz, and Ilyana Kuziemko, 2006, "The Homecoming of American College Women: The Reversal of the Gender Gap in College," *Journal of Economic Perspectives* 20 (2006): 133–56.

6. See Brian A. Jacob, "Where the Boys Aren't: Non-Cognitive Skills, Returns to School, and the Gender Gap in Higher Education," National Bureau of Economic Research, Working Paper No. 8964, May 2002, http://www.nber.org/papers/w8964.

7. See Kathleen Palmer Cleveland, *Teaching Boys Who Struggle in School: Strategies That Turn Underachievers into Successful Learners* (Alexandria, VA: Association for Supervision & Curriculum Development, 2011).

8. See Bauman and Ryan, "Women Now."

9. Feminist Majority Foundation, "The Triumphs of Title IX," *Ms. Magazine*, 2009, http://www.feminist.org/education/TriumphsOfTitleIX.pdf.

10. Ibid.

11. As quoted in 118th Congressional Record, 1972, 5804.

12. National Center for Education Statistics, "Fast Facts: Title IX," Institute of Education Sciences, 2014, http://nces.ed.gov/fastfacts/display.asp?id=93.

13. Caryn Mctighe Musil, "Scaling the Ivory Towers: Title IX Has Launched Women into the Studies, Professions, and Administrative Jobs of Their Dreams," *Ms. Magazine*, 2009, http://www.feminist.org/education/TriumphsOfTitleIX.pdf.

14. Ibid.

15. Ibid.

16. Ibid.

17. Jennifer Hahn, "Schoolgirl Dreams," *Ms. Magazine*, Fall 2007, http://www.feminist.org/education/TriumphsOfTitleIX.pdf.

18. Robin Hattersley Gray, "Sexual Assault Statistics," *Campus Safety Magazine*, 2012, http://www.crisisconnectioninc.org/sexualassault/college_campuses_and_rape.htm.

19. See Carly Parnitzke Smith and Jennifer J. Freyd, "Dangerous Safe Havens: Institutional Betrayal Exacerbates Sexual Trauma," *Journal of Traumatic Stress* 26 (February 2013): 119–24.

20. U.S. Department of Education, "Questions and Answers on Title IX and Single-Sex Elementary and Secondary Classes and Extracurricular Activities," December 1, 2014, http://www2.ed.gov/about/offices/list/ocr/docs/faqs-title-ix-single-sex-201412.pdf.

21. Jaime M. Grant and Lisa Mottet, *Injustice at Every Turn: A Report of the National Transgender Discrimination Survey*, National Center for Transgender Equality, 2015, http://www.thetaskforce.org/static_html/downloads/reports/reports/ntds_full.pdf.

22. Alice H. Eagly and Linda L. Carli, "Women and the Labyrinth of Leadership," *Harvard Business Review* 85, 9 (2007): 63.

23. Ibid.

24. Michelle Conlin and Wendy Zellner, "The Glass Ceiling: The CEO Still Wears Wingtips," *Business Week*, November 22, 1999.

25. Nancy Hatch Woodward, "Women in the Workplace: Still Fighting Stereotypes (Part One)," *HR Wire*, 11 (20), October 15, 2007, http://www.nancyhatchwoodward.com/womeninworkplace1.html.

26. Susan Nierenberg and Serena Fong, "Damned or Doomed—Catalyst Study on Gender Stereotyping at Work Uncovers Double-Bind Dilemmas for Women," *Catalyst, Inc.*, 2007, http://www.catalyst.org.

27. See Mona Chalabi, "How Many Women Earn More Than Their Husbands?," *FiveThirtyEight*, February 5, 2015, http://fivethirtyeight.com/datalab/how-many-women-earn-more-than-their-husbands/.

28. U.S. Bureau of Labor Statistics, *Women in the Labor Force: A Databook*, March 2011, https://www.bls.gov/cps/wlf-databook-2011.pdf.

29. Rosemary Tong, *Feminist Thought: A More Comprehensive Introduction* (Boulder, CO: Westview Press, 1988), 15.

30. Virginia Valian, *Why So Slow? The Advancement of Women* (Cambridge, MA: MIT Press, 1998), 33.

31. Richard Fox, "Gender, Political Ambition, and the Decision Not to Run for Office," Center for American Woman and Politics, Eagleton Institute of Politics, Rutgers University, 2001, 10.

32. Eagly and Carli, "Women and the Labyrinth," 68.

33. See Joyce Burnette, *Gender, Work, and Wages in Industrial Revolution Britain* (Cambridge: Cambridge University Press, 2008).

34. Mary Davis, "An Historical Introduction to the Campaign for Equal Pay," Union History Information, 2016, http://www.unionhistory.info/equalpay/roaddisplay.php?irn=820.

35. *Pioneer*, April 5, 1834, quoted in *Political Women 1800–1850*, ed. Ruth Frow and Edmund Frow (Winchester, MA: Pluto Press, 1989).

36. See "Women as Government Clerks," *New York Times*, February 1869, http://query.nytimes.com/mem/archive-free/pdf?res=9C07E7D91E3AEF34BC4052DFB4668382679FDE.

37. As quoted in the Women's Law Center, "An Equal Pay History—The Fight Continues . . ." June 10, 2013, https://nwlc.org/blog/equal-pay-history-fight-continues/.

38. Jo Freeman, "How 'Sex' Got into Title VII: Persistent Opportunism as a Maker of Public Policy," *Law and Inequality: A Journal of Theory and Practice* 9, no. 2 (1991): 163–84.

39. As quoted in Freeman, "How 'Sex' Got into Title VII."

40. See White House, "Gender Gap Pay: Recent Trends and Explanations," Council on Economic Advisers Issue Brief, April 2015, https://www.whitehouse.gov/sites/default/files/docs/equal_pay_issue_brief_final.pdf.

41. Claire Cain Miller, "As Women Take over Male-Dominated Field, the Pay Drops," *New York Times*, March 18, 2016, http://www.nytimes.com/2016/03/20/upshot/as-women-take-over-a-male-dominated-field-the-pay-drops.html?_r=0.

42. See Ariane Hegewisch and Heidi Hartmann, "Occupational Segregation and the Gender Wage Gap: A Job Half Done," Institute for Women's Policy Research, 2014, https://iwpr.org/publications/occupational-segregation-and-the-gender-wage-gap-a-job-half-done/.

43. National Public Radio, "When Women Stopped Coding," Planet Money, October 21, 2014, http://www.npr.org/sections/money/2014/10/21/357629765/when-women-stopped-coding.

44. See Claire Cain Miller, "As Women Take Over."

45. Ibid.

46. See White House, "Gender Gap Pay."

47. See Corinne A. Moss-Racusin et al., "Science Faculty's Subtle Gender Bias Favors Male Students," *Proceedings of the National Academy of Sciences of the United States of America* 109, no. 41 (2012): 16474–79.

48. National Women's Law Center, "Underpaid & Overloaded: Women in Low-Wage Jobs," 2014, http://www.nwlc.org/sites/default/files/pdfs/final_nwlc_lowwagereport2014.pdf.

49. Ibid.

50. See White House, "Gender Gap Pay."

51. American Association of University Women, "The Simple Truth about the Gender Pay Gap," 2014, http://www.aauw.org/files/2014/03/The-Simple-Truth.pdf.

52. U.S. Bureau of Labor Statistics, "Women in the Labor Force."

53. Hannah Riley Bowles, Linda Babcock, and Lei Lai, "Social Incentives for Gender Differences in the Propensity to Initiate Negotiations: Sometimes It Does Hurt to Ask," *Organizational Behavior and Human Decision Processes* 103 (2007): 84–103.

54. U.S. Equal Employment Opportunity Commission, "Select Task Force on the Study of Harassment in the Workplace," June 2016, https://www.eeoc.gov/eeoc/task_force/harassment/report.cfm.

55. As quoted in Jess Bravin, "Justice's Wife Seeks Apology from His Accuser," *Wall Street Journal*, October 20, 2010, http://www.wsj.com/articles/SB10001424052702304510704575562993761893962

Chapter 11

1. See the U.S. Census Bureau, 2010, "Fertility," http://www.census.gov/hhes/fertility/data/cps/historical.html.

2. Lawrence B. Finer and Mia R. Zolna, "Shifts in Intended and Unintended Pregnancies in the United States, 2001–2008," *American Journal of Public Health* 104, no. S1 (2013): 43–48.

3. Rachel K. Jones, Lawrence B. Finer, and Susheela Singh, *Characteristics of U.S. Abortion Patients, 2008* (New York: Guttmacher Institute, 2010).

4. Rachel K. Jones and Jenna Jerman, "Abortion Incidence and Service Availability in the United States, 2011," *Perspectives on Sexual and Reproductive Health* 46, no. 1 (2014): 1–12.

5. See Guttmacher Institute, 2014. "Induced Abortions in the United States," https://www.guttmacher.org/fact-sheet/induced-abortion-united-states.

6. See Jones and Jerman, "Abortion Incidence."

7. Erik Eckholm, "Abortions Declining in the U.S., Study Finds," *New York Times*, February 2, 2014, http://www.nytimes.com/2014/02/03/us/abortions-declining-in-us-study-finds.html.

8. See Guttmacher Institute, "Induced Abortions."

9. See Jones, Finer, and Singh, "Characteristics."

10. Ibid.

11. Sarah Kliff, "CHARTS: How *Roe v. Wade* Changed Abortion Rights," *Washington Post*, January 22, 2013, http://www.washingtonpost.com/blogs/wonkblog/wp/2013/01/22/charts-how-roe-v-wade-changed-abortion-rights/.

12. See Jones, Finer, and Singh, "Characteristics."

13. Ibid.

14. Ibid.

15. Academy of Medical Royal Colleges, "Induced Abortion and Mental Health: A Systematic Review of the Mental Health Outcomes of Induced Abortion, Including Their Prevalence and Associated Factors," National Collaborating Center for Mental Health, December 2011, http://www.nccmh.org.uk/reports/ABORTION_REPORT_WEB percent20FINAL.pdf.

16. Jonathan Dudley, "The Not-So-Lofty Origins of the Evangelical Pro-life Movement," *Religion Dispatches,* February 4, 2013, http://www.religiondispatches.org/archive/sexandgender/6801/the_not_so_lofty_origins_of_the_evangelical_pro_life_movement_/.

17. See Dudley, "The Not-So-Lofty Origins."

18. See Steve Bruce, *Conservative Protestant Politics* (New York: Oxford University Press, 1998).

19. Fred Barnes, "Hidden Persuaders: The Unheralded Gains of the Pro-life Movement," *The Weekly Standard*, November 7, 2011, http://www.weeklystandard.com/articles/hidden-persuaders_604174.html?page=1.

20. See Susan Staggenborg, *The Pro-Choice Movement: Organization and Activism in the Abortion Conflict* (New York: Oxford University Press, 1994).

21. Suzanne Staggenborg, "The Survival of the Pro-Choice Movement," *Journal of Policy History* 7, no. 1 (January 1995): 160–76.

22. David Leonhardt, "In Public Opinion about Abortion, Few Absolutes," *New York Times*, July 17, 2013, http://fivethirtyeight.blogs.nytimes.com/2013/07/17/in-public-opinion-on-abortion-few-absolutes/?_php=true&_type=blogs&_r=0. These statistics are based on Gallup polls that were fielded in 2013.

23. Ibid.

24. Pew Research, "Abortion Viewed in Moral Terms: Fewer See Stem Cell Research and IVF as Moral Issues," August 15, 2013, http://www.pewforum.org/2013/08/15/abortion-viewed-in-moral-terms/.

25. Lydia Saad, "In U.S., Nonreligious, Postgrads Are Highly 'Pro-choice,'" Gallup, May 29, 2012, http://www.gallup.com/poll/154946/non-christians-postgrads-highly-pro-choice.aspx.

26. Ibid.

27. Ibid.

28. See Kliff, "CHARTS."

29. See Leonharft, "In Public Opinion."

30. Carla Spivak, "To 'Bring down the Flowers': The Cultural Context of Abortion Law in Early Modern England," *William and Mary Journal of Women and the Law* 14, no. 1 (2007): 107–51.

31. See George Cole, *Abortion and Protection of the Human Fetus: Legal Problems in a Cross-Cultural Perspective* (New York: Springer, 1987).

32. Katha Pollitt, "Abortion in American History," *The Atlantic*, May 1997, http://www .theatlantic.com/past/docs/issues/97may/abortion.htm.

33. See Leslie Reagan, *When Abortion Was a Crime: Women, Medicine, and Law in the United States, 1867–1973* (Berkeley: University of California Press, 1997).

34. Ibid.

35. Ibid.; see also Guttmacher Institute, *Induced Abortion*.

36. See Edwin M. Gold, Jacob Jacobziner, and Freida G. Nelson, *Therapeutic Abortions in New York City: A Twenty-Year Review, in New York Dept. of Health, Bureau of Records and Statistics* (New York: New York City Department of Health, 1963).

37. See Reagan, *When Abortion*.

38. There is no set standard for fetal viability since it varies by organ development and technology. *Roe v. Wade* (1973) placed fetal viability at seven months (28 weeks), but viability could happen sooner than that. According to Tyson et al., "Intensive Care for Extreme Prematurity— Moving beyond Gestational Age," *New England Journal of Medicine* 358, no. 16 (April 2008): 1672–81, fetuses at 24 weeks have a 50 percent chance of surviving on their own.

39. See Guttmacher Institute, "Last Five Years Account for More Than One-Quarter of All Abortion Restrictions Enacted Since Roe," January 13, 2016, https://www.guttmacher .org/article/2016/01/last-five-years-account-more-one-quarter-all-abortion-restrictions -enacted-roe.

40. See Susan J. Lee et al., "Fetal Pain: A Systematic Multidisciplinary Review of the Evidence," *The Journal of the American Medical Association* 294, no. 8 (2005): 947–54.

41. Julie Rovner, "State Laws Limiting Abortion May Face Challenges on 20-Week Limit," National Public Radio, July 22, 2013, http://www.npr.org/blogs/health/2013/07/19/ 203729609/state-laws-limiting-abortion-may-face-challenges-on-20-week-limit.

42. See Alexa Ura et al., "Texas Abortion Clinics Have Closed since 2013," June 28, 2016, https://www.texastribune.org/2016/06/28/texas-abortion-clinics-have-closed-hb2 -passed-2013/.

43. See Guttmacher Institute, "Contraception Use in the United States," October 2015, https://www.guttmacher.org/fact-sheet/contraceptive-use-united-states.

44. Ibid.

45. See Kaiser Family Foundation, Harvard University, National Public Radio, *Sex Education in America* (Menlo Park, CA: Kaiser Foundation, 2004).

46. See the Office of Women's Health, "Birth Control Guide"(Silver Spring, MD: U.S. Food and Drug Administration, 2012).

47. See Kathryn Krase, "History of Forced Sterilization and Current U.S. Abuses," *Our Bodies Our Selves*, October 1, 2014, http://www.ourbodiesourselves.org/health-info/forced -sterilization/.

48. See Corey G. Johnson, "Female Inmates Sterilized in California Prisons without Approval," *The Center for Investigative Reporting*, July 7, 2013, http://cironline.org/ reports/female-inmates-sterilized-california-prisons-without-approval-4917.

49. Society for Assisted Reproductive Technology, *National Summary Report for 2014*, https://www.sartcorsonline.com/rptCSR_PublicMultYear.aspx?ClinicPKID=0.

50. See Georgina M. Chambers et al., "The Economic Impact of Assisted Reproductive Technology: A Review of Selected Developed Countries," *Fertility and Sterility* 91, no. 6 (June 2009): 2281–94.

51. Debra Kamin, "Israel Evacuates Surrogate Babies from Nepal but Leaves Mothers Behind," *Time Magazine*, April 28, 2015, http://time.com/3838319/israel-nepal-surrogates/.

52. Children's Bureau, *How Many Children Were Adopted in 2007 and 2008?*, September 2011, https://www.childwelfare.gov/pubPDFs/adopted0708.pdf#Page=26&view=Fit.

53. See Paul McCaffrey, *Families: Traditional and New Structures* (Ipswich, MA: Salem Press, 2013).

54. See Ellen C. Perrin and Benjamin S. Siegel, "Promoting the Well-Being of Children Whose Parents Are Gay or Lesbian," American Academy of Pediatrics, March 2013, http://pediatrics.aappublications.org/content/early/2013/03/18/peds.2013-0377.

55. See the Centers for Disease Control and Prevention, "National Survey of Adoptive Parents," National Center for Health Statistics, 2007, http://www.cdc.gov/nchs/slaits/nsap.htm.

56. John Gravois, "Bringing Up Babes: Why Do Adoptive Parents Prefer Girls?," Slate.com, January 16, 2004, http://www.slate.com/articles/news_and_politics/hey_wait_a_minute/2004/01/bringing_up_babes.html.

57. Steven E. Landsburg, "Maybe Parents Don't Like Boys Better," *Slate*, October 14, 2003, http://www.slate.com/articles/arts/everyday_economics/2003/10/maybe_parents_dont_like_boys_better.html.

Chapter 12

1. Kristen Lombardi, "A Lack of Consequences for Sexual Assault," Center for Public Integrity, February 24, 2010, http://www.publicintegrity.org/2010/02/24/4360/lack-consequences-sexual-assault.

2. World Health Organization, "Violence against Women: Factsheet," January 2016, http://www.who.int/mediacentre/factsheets/fs239/en/.

3. See Matthew J. Breiding et al., "Prevalence and Characteristics of Sexual Violence, Stalking, and Intimate Partner Violence Victimization—National Intimate Partner and Sexual Violence Survey, United States, 2011," Centers for Disease Control and Prevention, 2014, http://www.cdc.gov/mmwr/preview/mmwrhtml/ss6308a1.htm?s_cid=ss6308a1_e.

4. See Jaime M. Grant and Lisa Mottet, "Injustice at Every Turn: A Report of the National Transgender Discrimination Survey," National Center for Transgender Equality, 2015, http://www.thetaskforce.org/static_html/downloads/reports/reports/ntds_full.pdf.

5. See Leigh Ann Davis, "People with Intellectual Disabilities and Sexual Violence," ARC, 2011, http://www.thearc.org/document.doc?id=3657.

6. National Institute of Justice, "Prison Rape," Office of Justice Programs, 2014, http://www.nij.gov/topics/corrections/institutional/prison-rape/pages/welcome.aspx.

7. See David Lisak and Paul Miller, "Repeat Rape and Multiple Offending among Undetected Rapists," *Violence and Victims* 17, no. 1 (2004): 73–84.

8. Stephanie K. McWhorter et al., "Reports of Rape Perpetration by Newly Enlisted Male Navy Personnel," *Violence and Victims* 24, no. 2 (2009): 209–24.

9. RAINN, "Statistics," The Rape, Abuse & Incest National Network, 2016, https://rainn.org/statistics.

10. See New South Wales Department of Health Sexual Assault Education, "Adult Sexual Assault Information and Education Package," 1988; and Menachem Amir, *Patterns of Forcible Rape* (Chicago: University of Chicago Press, 1971).

11. RAINN, "Statistics."

12. Michelle Ye Hee Lee, "The Truth about a Viral Graphic on Rape Statistics," *Washington Post*, December 9, 2014, https://www.washingtonpost.com/news/fact-checker/wp/2014/12/09/the-truth-about-a-viral-graphic-on-rape-statistics/.

13. Jennifer A. Bennice and Patricia A. Resnick, "Marital Rape: History, Research, and Practice," *Trauma, Violence, & Abuse* 4, no. 3 (2003): 228–46.

14. RAINN, "Statistics."

15. American College of Emergency Physicians, "Evaluation and Management of the Sexually Assaulted or Sexually Abused Patient," 1999, http://www.nhcadsv.org/uploads/evaluationManagementSAPatient.pdf.

16. Gillian Greensite, "History of the Rape Crisis Movement," California Coalition against Sexual Assault, November 1, 2009, http://www.calcasa.org/2009/11/history-of-the-rape-crisis-movement/.

17. Crystal N. Feimster, "Rape and Justice in the Civil War," *New York Times*, April 25, 2013, http://opinionator.blogs.nytimes.com/2013/04/25/rape-and-justice-in-the-civil-war/?_php=true&_type=blogs&_r=0.

18. Susan Brownmiller, *Against Our Will: Men, Women, and Rape* (New York: Simon & Schuster, 1975), 208–9.

19. Ashley Parker, "House Renews Violence against Women Measure," *New York Times*, February 28, 2013, http://www.nytimes.com/2013/03/01/us/politics/congress-passes-reauthorization-of-violence-against-women-act.html?pagewanted=all.

20. Clery Center for Security on Campus, "Summary of the Jeanne Clery Act," 2014, http://clerycenter.org/summary-jeanne-clery-act.

21. National Institute of Justice, "Sexual Assault on Campuses: What Colleges and Universities Are Doing about It," 2005, https://www.ncjrs.gov/pdffiles1/nij/205521.pdf.

22. Center for Public Integrity, "Campus Sexual Assault Statistics Don't Add Up," December 2, 2009, http://www.publicintegrity.org/2009/12/02/9045/campus-sexual-assault-statistics-don-t-add.

23. Ibid.

24. Campus Safety, "Clery Act Fine Increases to 35K Per Violation," *Campus Safety Magazine*, 2012, http://www.campussafetymagazine.com/Channel/University-Security/News/2012/10/02/Clery-Act-Fines-Increased-to-35-000-Per-Violation.aspx.

25. Feminist Majority Foundation, "The Triumphs of Title IX," Fall 2007, http://www.feminist.org/education/TriumphsOfTitleIX.pdf.

26. Ibid.

27. National Center for Education Statistics, "Fast Facts: Title IX," Institute of Education Sciences, 2014, http://nces.ed.gov/fastfacts/display.asp?id=93.

28. Caryn Mctighe Musil, "Scaling the Ivory Towers: Title IX Has Launched Women into the Studies, Professions, and Administrative Jobs of Their Dreams," *Ms. Magazine*, 2009, http://www.feminist.org/education/TriumphsOfTitleIX.pdf.

29. Jennifer Hahn, "Schoolgirl Dreams," *Ms. Magazine*, 2009, 47, http://www.feminist.org/education/TriumphsOfTitleIX.pdf.

30. Robin Gray Hattersley, "Sexual Assault Statistics," *Campus Safety Magazine*, 2012, http://www.crisisconnectioninc.org/sexualassault/college_campuses_and_rape.htm.

31. Clery Center for Security on Campus, "The Campus Sexual Violence Elimination (SaVE) Act," 2014, http://clerycenter.org/policy-resources/the-clery-act/.

32. The American Council on Education, "New Campus Obligations under Violence against Women Act," March 20, 2013, http://www.acenet.edu/news-room/Pages/MEMO-New-Campus-Sexual-Assault-Policies-and-Procedures-Under-Violence-Against-Women-Act.aspx.

33. Clery Center, "The Campus Sexual Violence Elimination (SaVE) Act."

34. Quoted in Carroll, "New Campus Regulations."

35. On June 20, 2013, the World Health Organization, the London School of Hygiene & Topical Medicine, and the South African Medical Research Council released a global report that documented the first global and regional prevalence estimates of violence against women, http://www.who.int/reproductivehealth/publications/violence/9789241564625/en/index.html.

36. See the National Coalition Against Sexual Violence (NCADV), "National Statistics," 2016, http://www.ncadv.org/learn/statistics.

Selected Bibliography

Abraham, Henry J. *Justices, Presidents, and Senators: A History of the U.S. Supreme Court Appointments from Washington to Clinton*. Lanham, MD: Rowman & Littlefield, 1999.

Anderson, Craig A., Akiko Shibuya, Nobuko Ihori Ochanomizu, Edward L. Swing, Brad J. Bushman, Akira Sakamoto, Hannah R. Rothstein, and Muniba Saleem. "Violent Video Game Effects on Aggression, Empathy, and Prosocial Behavior in Eastern and Western Countries: A Meta-Analytic Review." *Psychological Bulletin* 136, no. 2 (2010): 151–73.

Anzia, Sarah, and Christopher R. Berry. "The Jackie (and Jill) Robinson Effect: Why Do Congresswomen Outperform Congressmen?" *American Journal of Political Science* 55 (2011): 478–93.

Arneil, Barbara. *Politics & Feminism*. Oxford: Wiley–Blackwell, 1999.

Atkeson, Lonna Rae, and Timothy B. Krebs. "Press Coverage of Mayoral Candidates: The Role of Gender in News Reporting and Campaign Issue Speech." *Political Research Quarterly* 61, no. 2 (June 2008): 239–52.

Baldez, Lisa, Lee Epstein, and Andrew D. Martin. "Does the Constitution Need an Equal Rights Amendment?" *Journal of Legal Studies* 35 (January 2006): 243–83.

Barth, Jay, and Margaret R. Ferguson. "Gender and Gubernatorial Personality." *Women & Politics* 24, no. 1 (2002): 63–82.

Baum, Lawrence. *The Supreme Court*, 9th ed. Washington, DC: CQ Press, 2007.

Baumgardner, Jennifer. *F'em: Goo Goo, Gaga and Some Thoughts on Balls*. Berkeley: Seal Press, 2011.

Baumgardner, Jennifer, and Amy Richards. *Manifesta: Young Women, Feminism, and the Future*. New York: Farrar, Straus and Giroux, 2000.

Baxandall, Rosalyn, Linda Gordon, and Susan Reverby, eds. *America's Working Women*. New York: Vintage Books, 1976.

Belcher, Romonda D. "The Importance of Women and the Judiciary." *The Journal of Gender, Race & Justice* 17 (2014): 421–26.

Book, Esther Wachs. *Why the Best Man for the Job Is a Woman: The Unique Female Qualities of Leadership*. New York: HarperCollins, 2000.

Borrelli, MaryAnne. *The Politics of the President's Wife.* College Station: Texas A&M University Press, 2011.

_____. *The President's Cabinet: Gender, Power, and Representation.* Boulder, CO: Lynne Rienner, 2002.

Borrelli, MaryAnne, and Janet M. Martin, eds. *The Other Elites: Women, Politics, and Power in the Executive Branch.* Boulder, CO: Lynne Rienner, 1997.

Boyd, Christina L., Lee Epstein, and Andrew D. Martin. "Untangling the Causal Effect of Sex on Judging." *American Journal of Political Science* 54, no. 2 (2010): 389–411.

Braden, Maria. *Women Politicians and the Media.* Lexington: University Press of Kentucky, 1996.

Bratton, Kathleen, and Kerry L. Haynie. "Agenda Setting and Legislative Success in State Legislatures: The Effects of Gender and Race." *Journal of Politics* 61 (1999): 658–79.

Brooks, Deborah Jordan. *He Runs, She Runs: Why Gender Stereotypes Do Not Harm Women Candidates.* Princeton, NJ: Princeton University Press, 2013.

Brownmiller, Susan. *Against Our Will: Men, Women, and Rape.* New York: Simon & Schuster, 1975.

Bruce, Steve. *Conservative Protestant Politics.* New York: Oxford University Press, 1998.

Bullock, Charles S., III, Susan A. MacManus, Karen Padgett Owen, Corttney C. Penberthy, Ralph O. Reid, and Brian McPhee. "'Your Honor' Is a Female: A Multistage Electoral Analysis of Women's Successes at Securing State Trial Court Judgeships." *Social Science Quarterly* 95, no. 5 (December 2014): 1322–45.

Burnette, Joyce. *Gender, Work, and Wages in Industrial Revolution Britain.* Cambridge: Cambridge University Press, 2008.

Butler, Judith. *Gender Trouble: Feminism and the Subversion of Identity.* New York: Routledge, 1990.

Bystrom, Dianne G., Mary Christine Banwart, Lynda Lee Kaid, and Terry A. Robertson. *Gender and Candidate Communication: VideoStyle, WebStyle, NewsStyle.* New York: Routledge, 2004.

Caiazza, Amy. "Does Women's Representation in Elected Office Lead to Women-Friendly Policy? Analysis of State-Level Data." *Women & Politics* 26, no. 1 (2004): 35–65.

Camron, Irin, and Shana Knizhnik. *Notorious RBG: The Life and Times of Ruth Bader Ginsburg.* New York: Dey Street Books, 2015.

Carroll, Susan J., ed. *The Impact of Women in Public Office.* Bloomington: Indiana University Press, 2001.

_____, ed. *Women and American Politics: New Questions, New Directions.* New York: Oxford University Press, 2003.

_____. *Women as Candidates in American Politics,* 2nd ed. Bloomington: Indiana University Press, 1994.

Carroll, Susan J., and Richard L. Fox. *Gender and Elections: Shaping the Future of American Politics,* 3rd ed. New York: Cambridge University Press, 2014.

Carroll, Susan J., and Linda M. G. Zerilli. "Feminist Challenges to Political Science." In *Political Science: The State of the Discipline II,* edited by Ada W. Finifter, 55–72. Washington, DC: American Political Science Association, 1993.

Castells, Manuel. *Networks of Outrage and Hope: Social Movements in the Internet Age.* Cambridge, UK: Polity Press, 2012.

Chambers, Georgina M., Elizabeth A. Sullivan, Osamu Ishihara, Michael G. Chapman, and G. David Adamson. "The Economic Impact of Assisted Reproductive Technology:

A Review of Selected Developed Countries." *Fertility and Sterility* 91, no. 6 (June 2009): 2281–94.

Cleveland, Kathleen Palmer. *Teaching Boys Who Struggle in School: Strategies That Turn Underachievers into Successful Learners.* Alexandria, VA: Association for Supervision & Curriculum Development, 2011.

Clift, Eleanor, and Tom Brazaitis. *Madam President: Shattering the Last Glass Ceiling.* New York: Scribner, 2000.

Clinton, Hillary Rodham. *Living History.* New York: Simon & Schuster, 2003.

Cobble, Dorothy Sue, Linda Gordon, and Astrid Henry. *Feminism Unfinished: A Short, Surprising History of American Women's Movements.* New York: Liveright, 2015.

Code, Lorraine. *What Can She Know? Feminist Theory and the Construction of Knowledge.* Ithaca, NY: Cornell University Press, 1991.

Cole, George. *Abortion and Protection of the Human Fetus: Legal Problems in a Cross-Cultural Perspective.* New York: Springer, 1987.

Conover, Pamela Johnston. "Feminists and the Gender Gap." *The Journal of Politics* 50, no. 4 (1988): 985–1010.

Conroy, Meredith. *Media, Masculinity, and the American Presidency.* New York: Palgrave, 2015.

Conway, M. Margaret, David W. Ahern, and Gertrude A. Steuernagel. *Women and Political Participation: Cultural Change in the Political Arena.* Washington, DC: CQ Press, 1997.

Costello, Cynthia B., Vanessa R. Wight, and Anne J. Stone, eds. *The American Woman 2003–2004: Daughters of a Revolution—Young Women Today.* New York: Palgrave Macmillan, 2003.

Crenshaw, Kimberle. "Mapping the Margins: Intersectionality, Identity Politics, and Voice against Women of Color." *Stanford Law Review* 43, no. 6 (1991): 1241–99.

Crespin, Michael H., and Janna L. Deitz, "If You Can't Join 'Em, Beat 'Em: The Gender Gap in Individual Donations to Congressional Candidates." *Political Research Quarterly* 63, no. 3 (2010): 581–93.

Cronin, Thomas E., and Michael A. Genovese. *The Paradoxes of the American Presidency.* New York: Oxford University Press, 1998.

Curran, Barbara A., and Clara N. Carson. *The Lawyer Statistical Report: The U.S. Legal Profession in the 1990s.* Chicago: American Bar Foundation, 1994.

Daly, Mary. *Gyn/Ecology: The Metaethics of Radical Feminism.* Boston: Beacon Press, 1978.

Darcy, R., Susan Welch, and Janet Clark. *Women, Elections, and Representation.* Lincoln: University of Nebraska Press, 1994.

Davis, Sue, Susan Haire, and Donald Songer. "Voting Behavior and Gender on the U.S. Courts of Appeal." *Judicature* 77 (1993): 129–33.

DeConde, Alexander. *Presidential Machismo: Executive Authority, Military Intervention, and Foreign Relations.* Boston: Northeastern University Press, 2000.

Deemer, Candy, and Nancy Fredericks. *Dancing on the Glass Ceiling.* Chicago: Contemporary Books, 2003.

Dolan, Kathleen. "Gender Stereotypes, Candidate Evaluations, and Voting for Women Candidates: What Really Matters." *Political Research Quarterly* 67, no. 1 (March 2014): 96–107.

Dolan, Kathleen, and Timothy Lynch. "It Takes a Survey: Understanding Gender Stereotypes, Abstract Attitudes, and Voting for Women Candidates." *American Politics Research* 42, no. 4 (2014): 656–76.

Durham, Gigi. *The Lolita Effect: The Sexualization of Young Girls and What We Can Do about It*. New York: Overlook, 2008.

Eagly, Alice H., and Linda L. Carli. "Women and the Labyrinth of Leadership." *Harvard Business Review* 85, no. 9 (2007): 63.

Eagly, Alice H., and Mary C. Johannesen-Schmidt. "The Leadership Styles of Women and Men." *Journal of Social Sciences* 57, no. 4 (2001): 781–97.

Eisenstein, Zillah. *Capitalist Patriarchy and the Case for Socialist Feminism*. New York: Monthly Review Press, 1978.

Elder, Laurel. "Why Women Don't Run: Explaining Women's Underrepresentation in America's Political Institutions." *Women & Politics* 26, no. 2 (2004): 27–56.

Ellison, Sheila. *If Women Ruled the World: How to Create the World We Want to Live In*. Novato, CA: New World Library, 2004.

Epstein, Laurily Keir, ed. *Women and the News*. New York: Hastings House, 1978.

Epstein, Lee, and Thomas G. Walker. *Constitutional Law for a Changing America: A Short Course*, 4th ed. Washington, DC: CQ Press, 2009.

Evans, Sara M. *Tidal Wave: How Women Changed America at Century's End*. New York: Free Press, 2003.

Farnsworth, Stephen J., and S. Robert Lichter. *The Nightly News Nightmare: Media Coverage of U.S. Presidential Elections, 1988–2008*, 3rd ed. Lanham, MD: Rowman & Littlefield, 2011.

Ferraro, Geraldine A., and Linda Francke. *Ferraro: My Story*. New York: Bantam Books, 1985.

Findlen, Barbara, ed. *Listen Up: Voices from the Next Feminist Generation*. Seattle: Seal Press, 1995.

Finer, Lawrence B., and Mia R. Zolna. "Shifts in Intended and Unintended Pregnancies in the United States, 2001–2008." *American Journal of Public Health* 104, no. S1 (2013): 43–48.

Fiske, Susan T. "From Dehumanization and Objectification, to Rehumanization: Neuroimaging Studies on the Building Blocks of Empathy." *Annals of the New York Academy of Science* 1167 (June 2013): 31–34.

Fox, Richard L., and Jennifer L. Lawless. "Entering the Arena? Gender and the Decision to Run for Office." *American Journal of Political Science* 48, no. 2 (April 2004): 264–80.

Francia, Peter L. "Early Fundraising by Nonincumbent Female Congressional Candidates: The Importance of Women's PACs." *Women & Politics* 23, no. 1/2 (2001): 7–20.

Frederick, Brian. "A Longitudinal Test of the Gender Turnover Model among U.S. House and Senate Members." *The Social Science Journal* 52 (2015): 102–11.

Fredrickson, Barbara L., and Tomi-Ann Roberts. "Objectification Theory: Toward Understanding Women's Lived Experiences and Mental Health Risks." *Psychology of Women Quarterly* 21, no. 2 (1997): 173–206.

Freeman, Jo. "How 'Sex' Got into Title VII: Persistent Opportunism as a Maker of Public Policy." *Law and Inequality: A Journal of Theory and Practice* 9, no. 2 (1991): 163–84.

Freeman, Sue J. M., Susan C. Bourque, and Christine M. Shelton, eds. *Women on Power: Leadership Redefined*. Boston: Northeastern University Press, 2001.

Fridkin, Kim L., and Patrick J. Kennedy. "How the Gender of U.S. Senators Influences People's Understanding and Engagement in Politics." *Journal of Politics* 76, no. 4 (2014): 1017–31.

Friedan, Betty. *The Feminine Mystique*. New York: W. W. Norton, 1963.

———. *It Changed My Life: Writings on the Women's Movement*. New York: Random House, 1978.

Frow, Ruth, and Edmund Frow, eds. *Political Women 1800–1850*. Winchester, MA: Pluto Press, 1989.

Goelzhauser, Greg. "Diversifying State Supreme Courts." *Law & Society Review* 45, no. 3 (2011): 761–81.

Goldin, Claudia, Lawrence F. Katz, and Ilyana Kuziemko. "The Homecoming of American College Women: The Reversal of the Gender Gap in College." *Journal of Economic Perspectives* 20 (2006): 133–56.

Greenstein, Fred I. "George W. Bush and the Ghosts of Presidents Past." *PS: Political Science and Politics* XXXIV, no. 1 (March 2001): 77–80.

Griffin, John D., Brian Newman, and Christina Wolbrecht. "A Gender Gap in Policy Representation in the U.S. Congress?" *Legislative Studies Quarterly* 37 (February 2012): 35–65.

Gruhl, John, Cassis Spohn, and Susan Welch. "Women as Policymakers: The Case of Trial Judges." *American Journal of Political Science* 25, no. 2 (May 1981): 308–22.

Gryski, Gerard, Eleanor Main, and William Dixon. "Models of State High Court Decision Making in Sex Discrimination Cases." *Journal of Politics* 48 (1986): 143–55.

Hall, Sophia A. "In the Pursuit of Justice: Reflections on Changes in the Judicial Role after Three Decades as a State Court Judge." *Judges Journal* 48, no. 1 (Winter 2009): 5–9.

Hammer, Rhonda. *Antifeminism and Family Terrorism: A Critical Feminist Perspective*. New York: Rowman & Littlefield, 2001.

Han, Lori Cox. *In It to Win: Electing Madam President*. New York: Bloomsbury, 2015.

Han, Lori Cox, and Caroline Heldman, eds. *Rethinking Madam President: Are We Ready for a Woman in the White House?* Boulder, CO: Lynne Rienner, 2007.

Handelsman, Jo. "Science Faculty's Subtle Gender Bias Favors Male Students." *Proceedings of the National Academy of Sciences of the United States of America* 109, no. 41 (2012): 16474–79.

Hayes, Danny, Jennifer L. Lawless, and Gail Baitinger. "Who Cares What They Wear? Media, Gender, and the Influence of Candidate Appearance." *Social Science Quarterly* 95, no. 5 (December 2014): 1194–212.

Heflick, Nathan A., and Jamie L. Goldenberg. "Objectifying Sarah Palin: Evidence That Objectification Causes Women to Be Perceived as Less Competent and Less Fully Human." *Journal of Experimental Social Psychology* 45, no. 3 (2009): 598–601.

Heldman, Caroline, Susan J. Carroll, and Stephanie Olson. "'She Brought Only a Skirt': Print Media Coverage of Elizabeth Dole's Bid for the Republican Nomination." *Political Communication* 22 (2005): 315–35.

Helgesen, Sally. *The Female Advantage: Women's Ways of Leadership*. New York: Doubleday, 1990.

Henry, Astrid. *Not My Mother's Sister*. Bloomington: Indiana University Press, 2004.

Hero, Rodney E., and Caroline Tolbert. "Minority Voices and Citizen Attitudes about Government Responsiveness in the American States: Do Social and Institutional Context Matter?" *British Journal of Political Science* 34, no. 1 (2004): 109–21.

Hewitt, Nancy, ed. *No Permanent Waves: Recasting Histories of U.S. Feminism*. New Brunswick, NJ: Rutgers University Press, 2010.

Huddy, Leonie, and Nayda Terkildsen. "Gender Stereotypes and the Perception of Male and Female Candidates." *American Journal of Political Science* 37 (1993): 119–47.

Iyengar, Shanto. *Is Anyone Responsible? How Television Frames Political Issues*. Chicago: University of Chicago Press, 1984.

Iyengar, Shanto, and Donald R. Kinder. *News That Matters: Television and American Opinion*. Chicago: University of Chicago Press, 2010.

Jamieson, Kathleen Hall. *Beyond the Double Bind: Women and Leadership*. New York: Oxford University Press, 1995.

Jeydel, Alana S. *Political Women: The Women's Movement, Political Institutions, the Battle for Women's Suffrage and the ERA*. New York: Routledge, 2004.

Jeydel, Alana, and Andrew Taylor. "Are Women Legislators Less Effective? Evidence from the U.S. House in the 103rd–105th Congress." *Political Research Quarterly* 56 (2003): 19–27.

Kahn, Kim Fridkin. *The Political Consequences of Being a Woman*. New York: Columbia University Press, 1996.

Kellerman, Barbara, and Deborah L. Rhode, eds. *Women & Leadership: The State of Play and Strategies for Change*. New York: Wiley, 2007.

Kenski, Kate, and Erika Falk. "Of What Is This Glass Ceiling Made? A Study of Attitudes about Women and the Oval Office." *Women & Politics* 26, no. 2 (2004): 57–80.

Kerber, Linda. *Women of the Republic*. Chapel Hill: University of North Carolina Press, 1997.

Keremidchieva, Zornitsa. "Legislative Reform, the Congressional Caucus for Women's Issues, and the Crisis of Women's Political Representation." *Women & Language* 35 (Spring 2012): 13–38.

King, James D., and James W. Riddlesperger Jr. "Diversity and Presidential Cabinet Appointments." *Social Science Quarterly* 96, no. 1 (March 2015): 93–103.

Koedt, Ann. *The Myth of the Vaginal Orgasm*. Somerville, NJ: New England Free Press, 1970.

Kropf, Martha E., and John A. Boiney. "The Electoral Glass Ceiling? Gender, Viability, and the News in U.S. Senate Campaigns." *Women & Politics* 23, no. 1/2 (2001): 79–101.

Lawless, Jennifer L. "Women, War, and Winning Elections: Gender Stereotyping in the Post-September 11th Era." *Political Research Quarterly* 57, no. 3 (September 2004): 479–90.

Lawless, Jennifer L., and Richard L. Fox. "Men Rule: The Continued Under-Representation of Women in U.S. Politics." Washington, DC: Women and Politics Institute, American University, 2012.

Lawless, Jennifer L., and Kathryn Pearson. "The Primary Reason for Women's Under-representation? Reevaluating the Conventional Wisdom." *The Journal of Politics* 70, no. 1 (January 2008): 67–82.

Levin, Phyllis Lee. *Abigail Adams: A Biography*. New York: St. Martin's Press, 1987.

Lisak, David, and Paul Miller. "Repeat Rape and Multiple Offending among Undetected Rapists." *Violence and Victims* 17, no. 1 (2004): 73–84.

Lord, Audre. *Cables to Rage*. London: Paul Breman, 1970.

Lyles, Kevin. *The Gatekeepers: Federal District Courts in the Political Process*. Westport, CT: Praeger, 1997.

Mackinnon, Catherine, and Andrea Dworkin. *In Harm's Way: The Pornography Civil Rights Hearing*. Cambridge, MA: Harvard University Press, 1997.

Mann, James. *Rise of the Vulcans: The History of Bush's War Cabinet*. New York: Viking Press, 2004.

Mansbridge, Jane J. *Why We Lost the ERA*. Chicago: University of Chicago Press, 1986.

Marshall, Brenda DeVore, and Molly A. Mayhead, eds. *Navigating Boundaries: The Rhetoric of Women Governors*. Westport, CT: Praeger, 2000.

Martin, Elaine. "U.S. Women Federal Court Judges Appointed by President Carter." *Feminist Legal Studies* 17 (2009): 43–59.

Martin, Janet M. *The Presidency and Women: Promise, Performance & Illusion*. College Station: Texas A&M University Press, 2003.

Matthews, Jean V. *Women's Struggle for Equality: The First Phase 1828–1876*. Chicago: Ivan R. Dee, 1997.

McCaffrey, Paul. *Families: Traditional and New Structures*. Ipswich, MA: Salem Press, 2013.

McGlen, Nancy E., Karen O'Connor, Laura van Assendelft, and Wendy Gunther-Canada. *Women, Politics, and American Society*, 4th ed. New York: Longman, 2002.

McWhorter, Stephanie K., Valerie Stander, Lex L. Merrill, Cynthia J. Thomsen, and Joel S. Miller. "Reports of Rape Perpetration by Newly Enlisted Male Navy Personnel." *Violence and Victims* 24, no. 2 (2009): 209–24.

Mezey, Susan Gluck. *Elusive Equality: Women's Rights, Public Policy, and the Law*. Boulder, CO: Lynne Rienner, 2003.

Millet, Kate. *Sexual Politics*. New York: Doubleday, 1970.

Miroff, Bruce. *Icons of Democracy: American Leaders as Heroes, Aristocrats, Dissenters, & Democrats*. Lawrence: University Press of Kansas, 2000.

Mitchell, Juliet, and Jacqueline Rose. *Feminine Sexuality: Jacques Lacan and the école freudienne*. New York: W. W. Norton, 1983.

Monem, Nadine. *Riot Grrrl: Revolution Girl Style Now!* London: Black Dog, 2007.

Moraga, Cherríe. *Loving in the War Years: Lo que nunca pasó por sus labios*. Boston: South End Press, 1983.

Moraga, Cherríe, and Gloria Anzaldúa. *This Bridge Called My Back: Writings by Radical Women of Color*. New York: Kitchen Table Press, 1983.

Morgan, Robin. *Going Too Far: The Personal Choice of a Feminist*. New York: Vintage Books, 1978.

———, ed. *Sisterhood Is Forever: The Women's Anthology for a New Millennium*. New York: Washington Square Press, 2003.

Moss-Racusin, Corinne A., John F. Dovidio, Victoria L. Brescoll, Mark J. Graham, and Jo Handelsman. "Science Faculty's Subtle Gender Biases Favor Male Students." *PNAS* 109, no. 41 (2012): 16474-16479.

Murnen, Sarah K., Linda Smolak, J. Andrew Mills, and Lindsey Good. "Thin, Sexy Women and Strong, Muscular Men: Grade-School Children's Responses to Objectified Images of Women and Men." *Sex Roles: A Journal of Research* 49, no. 9/10 (2003): 427–37.

Nicholson, Linda, ed. *The Second Wave: A Reader in Feminist Theory*. New York: Routledge, 1997.

Norgren, Jill. "Ladies of Legend: The First Generation of American Women Attorneys." *Journal of Supreme Court History* 35, no. 1 (March 2010): 71–90.

Norris, Pippa. *Democratic Phoenix: Reinventing Political Activism*. Cambridge: Cambridge University Press, 2002.

Norris, Pippa, and Ronald Inglehart. "Women and Democracy: Cultural Obstacles to Equal Representation." *Journal of Democracy* 12, no. 3 (2001): 126–40.

O'Brien, David M. *Constitutional Law and Politics, Volume Two: Civil Rights and Civil Liberties*, 7th ed. New York: W. W. Norton, 2008.

———. *Storm Center: The Supreme Court in American Politics*, 8th ed. New York: W.W. Norton, 2008.

O'Connor, Sandra Day. *The Majesty of the Law: Reflections of a Supreme Court Justice*. New York: Random House, 2003.

Orleck, Annelise. *Rethinking American Women's Activism*. New York: Routledge, 2015.

Osborn, Tracy L. *How Women Represent Women: Political Parties, Gender, and Representation in the State Legislatures*. New York: Oxford University Press, 2012.

_____. "Women State Legislators and Representation: The Role of Political Parties and Institutions." *State and Local Government Review* 46 (2014): 146–55.

Paletz, David L. *The Media in American Politics: Contents and Consequences*, 2nd ed. New York: Longman, 2002.

Palmer, Barbara. "Justice Ruth Bader Ginsburg and the Supreme Court's Reaction to Its Second Female Member." *Women & Politics* 24, no. 1 (2002): 1–23.

_____. "Women in the American Judiciary: Their Influence and Impact." *Women & Politics* 23, no. 3 (2001): 91–101.

Pearson, Kathryn, and Logan Dancey. "Elevating Women's Voices in Congress: Speech Participation in the House of Representatives." *Political Research Quarterly* 64 (2011): 910–23.

Posner, Jennifer. *Reality Bites Back: The Troubling Truth about Guilty Pleasure TV*. New York: Seal Press, 2010.

Putnam, Robert D. *Bowling Alone: The Collapse and Revival of American Community*. New York: Simon & Schuster, 2001.

Rachanow, Shelly. *If Women Ran the World, Sh*t Would Get Done: Celebrating All the Wonderful, Amazing, Stupendous, Inspiring, Butt-kicking Things Women Do*. Newburyport, MA: Conari Press, 2006.

_____. *What Would You Do If You Ran the World? Everyday Ideas from Women Who Want to Make the World a Better Place*. Newburyport, MA: Conari Press, 2009.

Reagan, Leslie. *When Abortion Was a Crime: Women, Medicine, and Law in the United States, 1867–1973*. Berkeley: University of California Press, 1997.

Rhode, Deborah L., ed. *The Difference "Difference" Makes: Women and Leadership*. Stanford, CA: Stanford University Press, 2003.

_____. *The Unfinished Agenda: Women and the Legal Profession*. Chicago: ABA Commission on Women in the Profession, 2001.

Riley Bowles, Hannah, Linda Babcock, and Lei Lai. "Social Incentives for Gender Differences in the Propensity to Initiate Negotiations: Sometimes It Does Hurt to Ask." *Organizational Behavior and Human Decision Processes* 103 (2007): 84–103.

Rose, Melody, ed. *Women and Executive Office: Pathways and Performance*. Boulder, CO: Lynne Rienner, 2013.

Rosen, Ruth. *The World Split Open: How the Modern Women's Movement Changed America*. New York: Penguin Books, 2000.

Rosenstone, Steven J., and John Mark Hansen. *Mobilization, Participation, and Democracy in America*. New York: Pearson, 1993.

Rosenthal, Cindy Simon. *When Women Lead: Integrative Leadership in State Legislatures*. New York: Oxford University Press, 1998.

_____, ed. *Women Transforming Congress*. Norman: University of Oklahoma Press, 2002.

Rosin, Hanna. *The End of Men: And the Rise of Women*. New York: Riverhead, 2012.

Sabato, Larry J. *Feeding Frenzy: Attack Journalism and American Politics*. Baltimore: Lanahan, 2000.

Sanbonmatsu, Kira. "Candidate Recruitment and Women's Election to the State Legislatures." Report prepared for the Center for American Women and Politics, Eagleton Institute of Politics, Rutgers, State University of New Jersey, September 2003.

Sandberg, Sheryl. *Lean In*. New York: Alfred A. Knopf, 2014.

Sapiro, Virginia. *Women in American Society: An Introduction to Women's Studies*, 5th ed. Boston: McGraw-Hill, 2003.

Schreiber, Ronnee. *Righting Feminism: Conservative Women and American Politics.* New York: Oxford University Press, 2008.

Scott, Anne Firor, and Andrew MacKay Scott. *One Half the People: The Fight for Woman Suffrage.* Urbana: University of Illinois Press, 1982.

Seltzer, Richard A., Jody Newman, and Melissa Voorhees Leighton. *Sex as a Political Variable: Women as Candidates & Voters in U.S. Elections.* Boulder, CO: Lynne Rienner, 1997.

Sheeler, Kristina Horn, and Karrin Vasby Anderson. *Woman President: Confronting Post-feminist Political Culture.* College Station: Texas A&M University Press, 2013.

Silverstein, Mark. *Judicious Choices: The Politics of Supreme Court Confirmations,* 2nd ed. New York: W.W. Norton, 2007.

Smith, Carly Parnitzke, and Jennifer J. Freyd. "Dangerous Safe Havens: Institutional Betrayal Exacerbates Sexual Trauma." *Journal of Traumatic Stress* 26 (February 2013): 119–24.

Spar, Debora L. *Wonder Women: Sex, Power, and the Quest for Perfection.* New York: Farrar, Straus and Giroux, 2013.

Spivak, Carla. "To 'Bring Down the Flowers': The Cultural Context of Abortion Law in Early Modern England." *William and Mary Journal of Women and the Law* 14, no. 1 (2007): 107–51.

Staggenborg, Susan. *The Pro-Choice Movement: Organization and Activism in the Abortion Conflict.* New York: Oxford University Press, 1994.

———. "The Survival of the Pro-Choice Movement." *Journal of Policy History* 7, no. 1 (January 1995): 160–76.

Starr, Christine R., and Gail Ferguson. "Sexy Dolls, Sexy Grade-Schoolers? Media & Maternal Influences on Young Girls' Self-Sexualization." *Sex Roles* 67, no. 7–8 (2012): 463–76.

Streb, Matthew J., Barbara Burrell, Brian Frederick, and Michael A. Genovese. "Social Desirability Effects and Support for a Female American President." *Public Opinion Quarterly* 72, no. 1 (2008): 76–89.

Swers, Michele L. *Women in the Club: Gender and Policy Making in the Senate.* Chicago: University of Chicago Press, 2013.

Sykes, Diane S. "Gender and Judging." *Marquette Law Review* 94 (2001): 1381–90.

Talpade Mohanty, Chandra. "Under Western Eyes: Feminist Scholarship and Colonial Discourses," *boundary 2* 12, no. 3 (1984): 333–58.

Tarrant, Shira. *Men and Feminism.* Berkeley: Seal Press, 2009.

Thames, Frank C., and Margaret S. Williams. *Contagious Representation: Women's Political Representation in Democracies around the World.* New York: New York University Press, 2013.

Thomas, Sue. *How Women Legislate.* New York: Oxford University Press, 1994.

Thomas, Sue, and Clyde Wilcox, eds. *Women and Elective Office: Past, Present, & Future.* New York: Oxford University Press, 1998.

———. *Women and Elective Office: Past, Present, & Future,* 2nd ed. New York: Oxford University Press, 2005.

———. *Women and Elective Office: Past, Present, and Future,* 3rd ed. New York: Oxford University Press, 2014.

Tolleson-Rinehart, Sue, and Jyl J. Josephson, eds. *Gender and American Politics.* Armonk, NY: M. E. Sharpe, 2000.

Tong, Rosemary. *Feminist Thought: A More Comprehensive Introduction.* Boulder, CO: Westview Press, 1988.

Tuchman, Gaye. *Hearth and Home: Images of Women in the News Media*. New York: Oxford University Press, 1978.

Valian, Virginia. *Why So Slow? The Advancement of Women*. Cambridge, MA: MIT Press, 1998.

VanBurkleo, Sandra F. *"Belonging to the World:" Women's Rights and American Constitutional Culture*. New York: Oxford University Press, 2001.

Vaughn, Justin S., and Lilly J. Goren, eds. *Women and the White House: Gender, Popular Culture, and Presidential Politics*. Lexington: University Press of Kentucky, 2013.

Verba, Sidney, Kay Lehman Schlozman, and Henry Brady. *Voice and Equality: Civic Volunteerism in American Politics*. Cambridge, MA: Harvard University Press, 1995.

Volden, Craig, Alan E. Wiseman, and Dana E. Wittmer. "When Are Women More Effective Lawmakers Than Men?" *American Journal of Political Science* 57 (2013): 326–41.

von Stumm, Sophie, Tomas Chamorro-Premuzic, and Adrian Furnham. "Decomposing Self-estimates of Intelligence: Structure and Sex Differences across 12 Nations." *British Journal of Psychology* 100, no. 2 (2009): 429–42.

Walker, Rebecca, ed. *To Be Real: Telling the Truth and Changing the Face of Feminism*. New York: Anchor Books, 1995.

Watson, Robert P. *The Presidents' Wives: Reassessing the Office of First Lady*. Boulder, CO: Lynne Rienner, 2000.

Watson, Robert P., and Ann Gordon, eds. *Anticipating Madam President*. Boulder, CO: Lynne Rienner, 2003.

Wayne, Stephen J. *The Road to the White House 2012*. Boston: Wadsworth, 2012.

Whitaker, Lois Duke, ed. *Women in Politics: Outsiders or Insiders?*, 3rd ed. Upper Saddle River, NJ: Prentice Hall, 1999.

———. *Women in Politics: Outsiders or Insiders?*, 4th ed. Upper Saddle River, NJ: Prentice Hall, 2006.

Whitney, Catherine, Barbara Mikulski, Kay Bailey Hutchinson, Dianne Feinstein, Barbara Boxer, Patty Murray, Olympia Snowe, Susan Collins, Mary Landrieu, and Blanche L. Lincoln. *Nine and Counting: The Women of the Senate*. New York: William Morrow, 2000.

Wilson, Marie C. *Closing the Leadership Gap: Why Women Can and Must Help Run the World*. New York: Penguin, 2004.

INDEX

Italicized page references indicate photo; followed by "*t*" indicate table; followed by "*f*" indicate figure.

Printed in the USA/Agawam, MA
November 5, 2018

687385.014